SOUL EATER

13

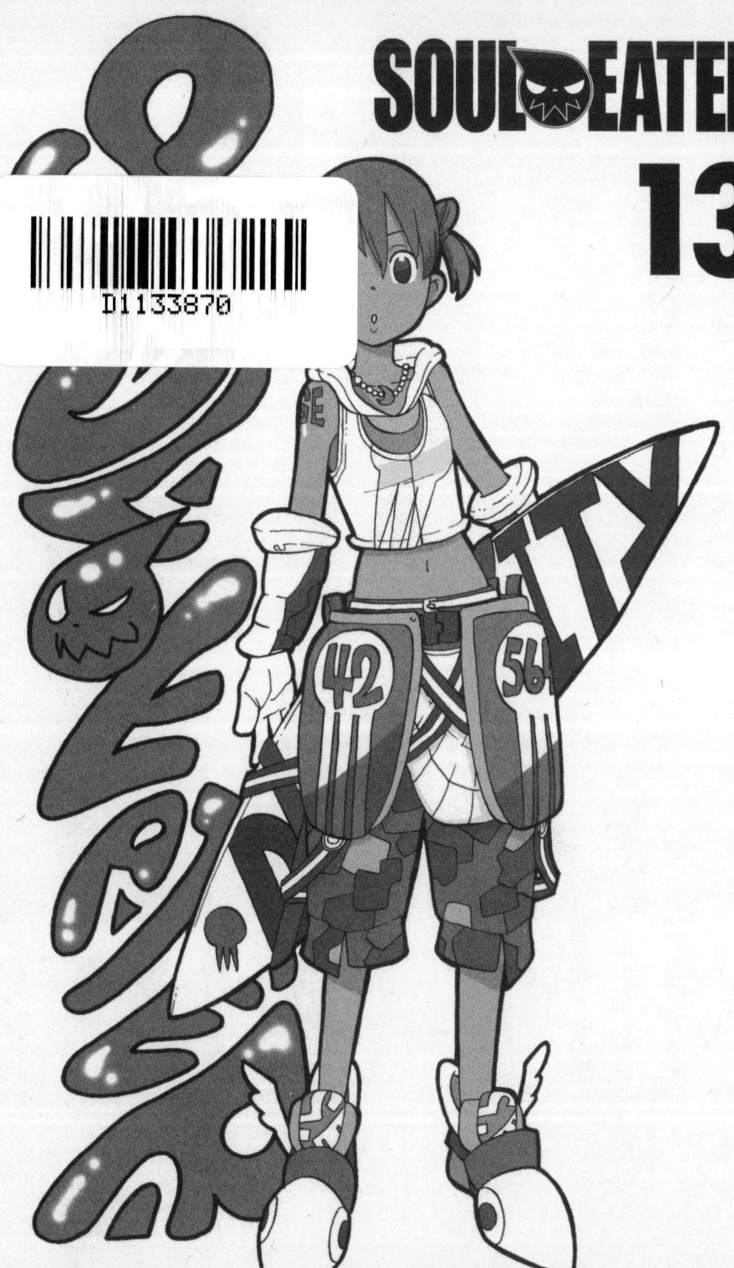

ATSUSHI OHKUBO

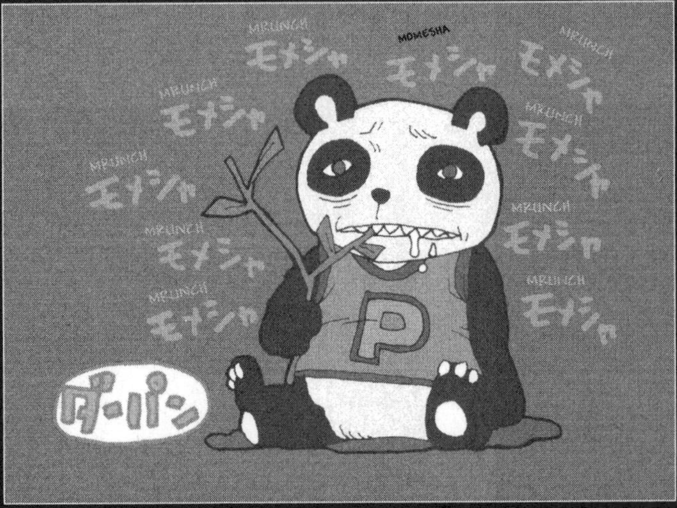
MOMESHA
モメシャ
MRUNCH
モメシャ
MRUNCH
モメシャ
MRUNCH
モメシャ
MRUNCH
モメシャ
MRUNCH
モメシャ
MRUNCH
モメシャ
MRUNCH
モメシャ
MRUNCH
モメシャ
ダーパン

LABEL: PANDA

SOUL EATER

vol. 13

by ATSUSHI OHKUBO

IN THE NAME OF "SOUL"

SOUL EATER 13

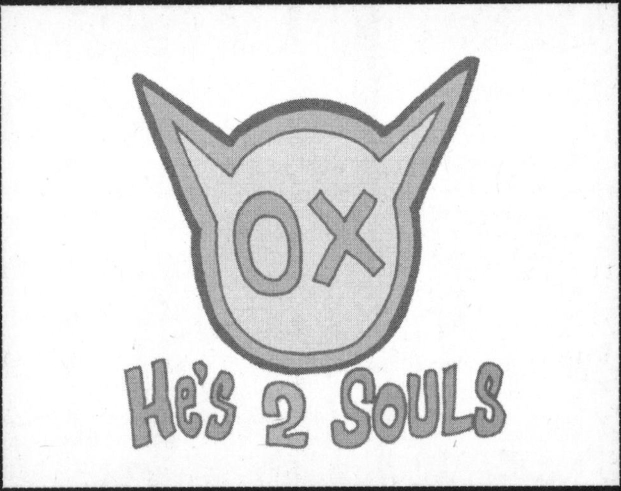
OX
He's 2 SOULS

CONTENTS

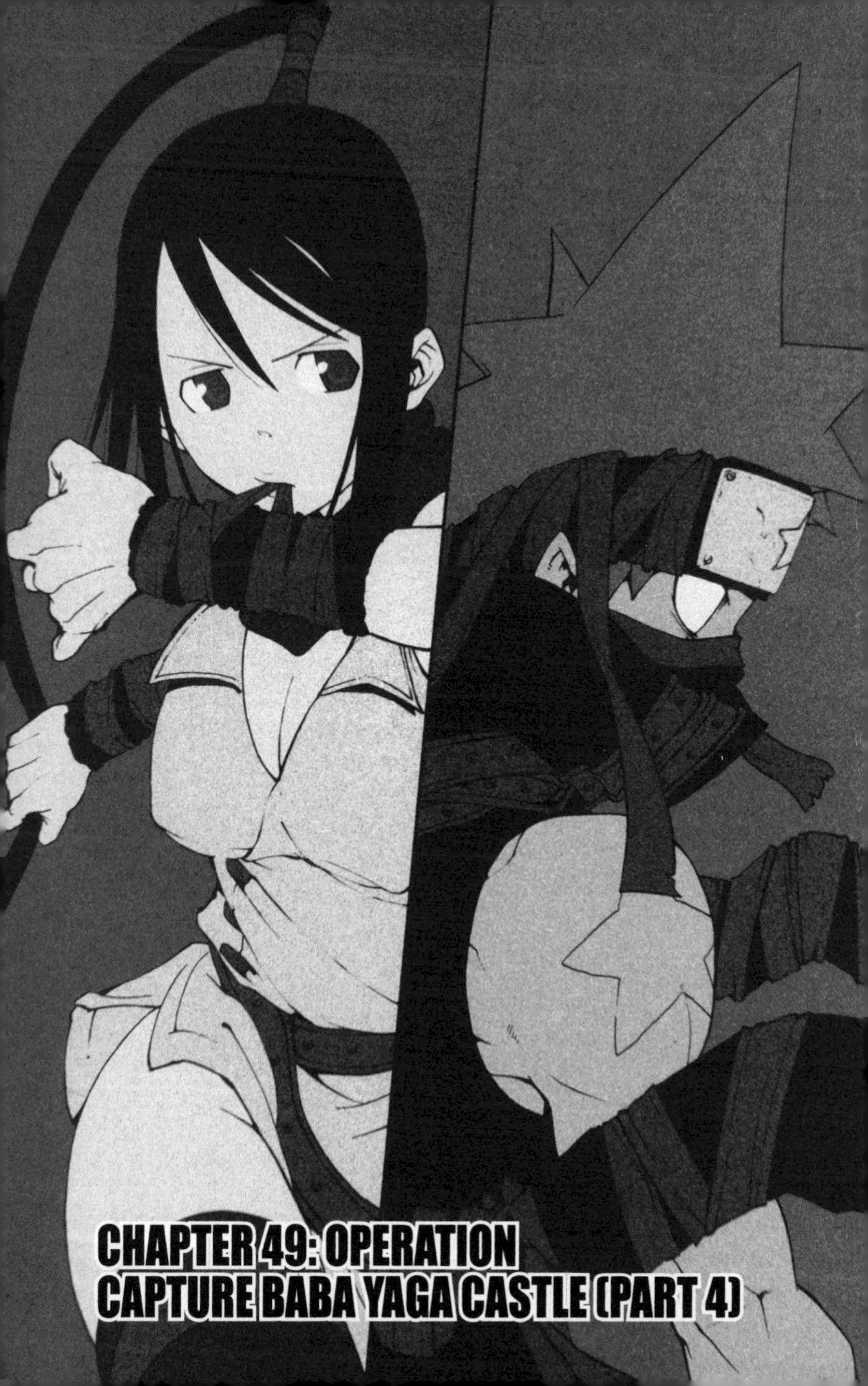

CHAPTER 49: OPERATION CAPTURE BABA YAGA CASTLE (PART 4)

SOUL EATER

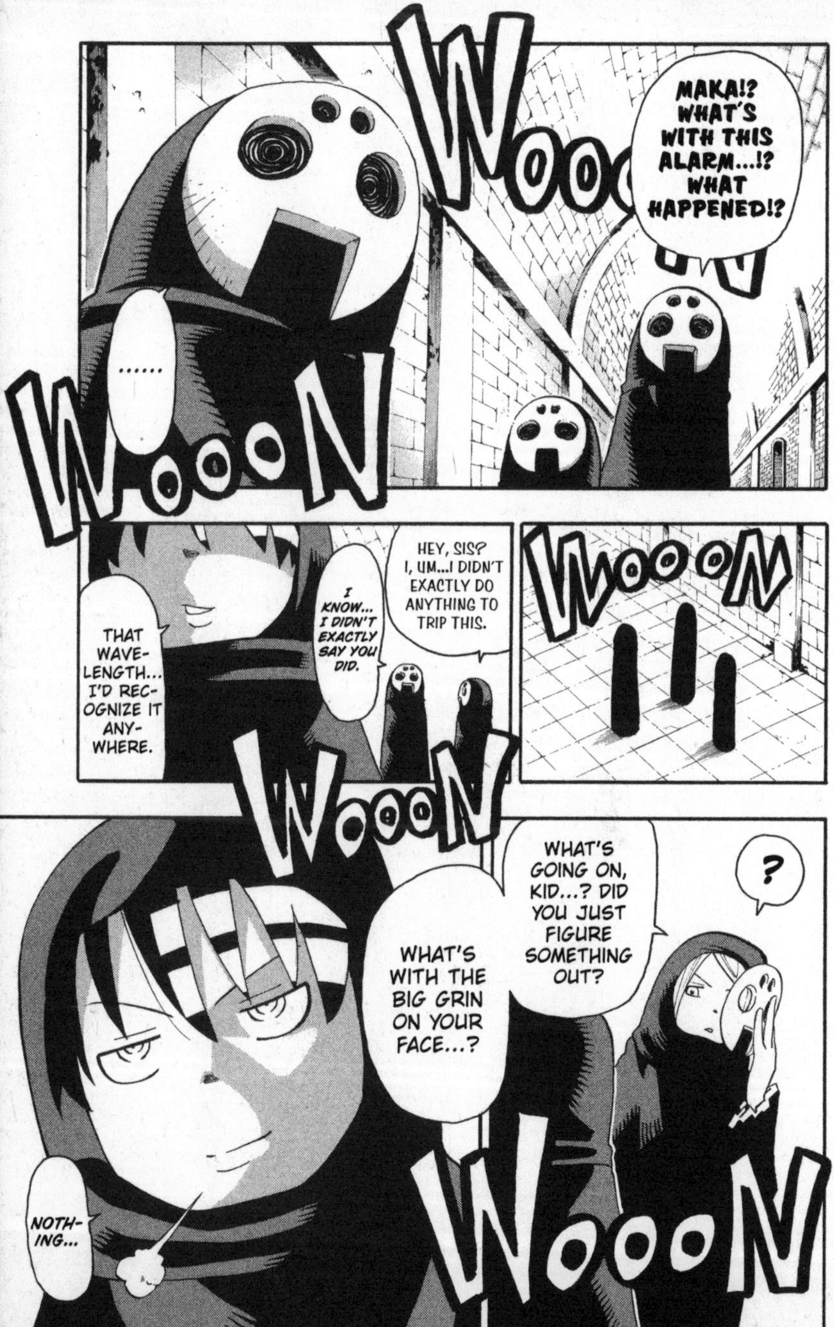
WOOON
MAKA!? WHAT'S WITH THIS ALARM...!? WHAT HAPPENED!?
......
WOOON
WOOON
HEY, SIS? I, UM...I DIDN'T EXACTLY DO ANYTHING TO TRIP THIS.
I KNOW... I DIDN'T EXACTLY SAY YOU DID.
THAT WAVE-LENGTH... I'D REC-OGNIZE IT ANY-WHERE.
WOOON
?
WHAT'S GOING ON, KID...? DID YOU JUST FIGURE SOMETHING OUT?
WHAT'S WITH THE BIG GRIN ON YOUR FACE...?
WOOON
NOTH-ING...

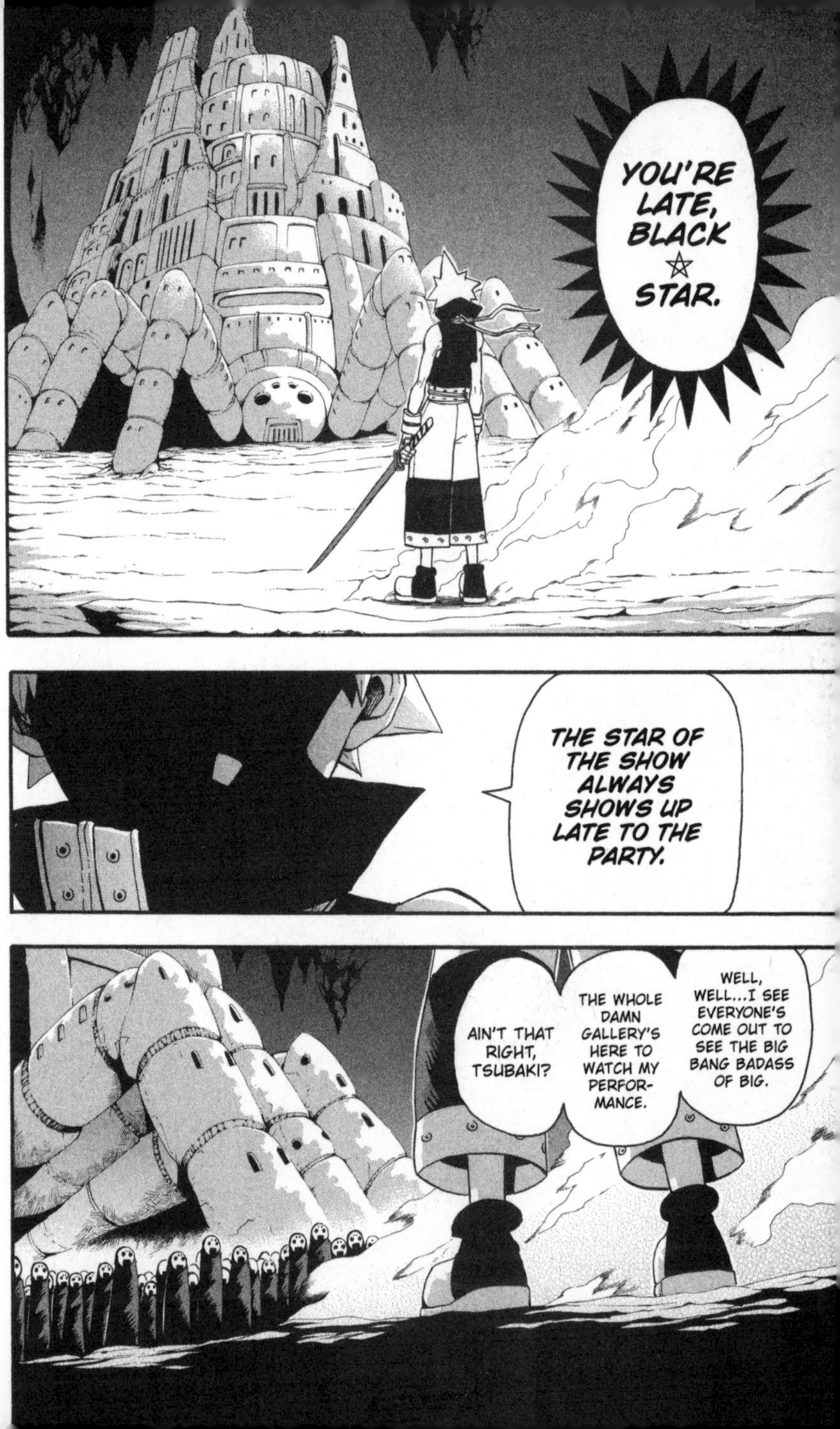
YOU'RE LATE, BLACK☆STAR.
THE STAR OF THE SHOW ALWAYS SHOWS UP LATE TO THE PARTY.
WELL, WELL...I SEE EVERYONE'S COME OUT TO SEE THE BIG BANG BADASS OF BIG.
THE WHOLE DAMN GALLERY'S HERE TO WATCH MY PERFOR-MANCE.
AIN'T THAT RIGHT, TSUBAKI?

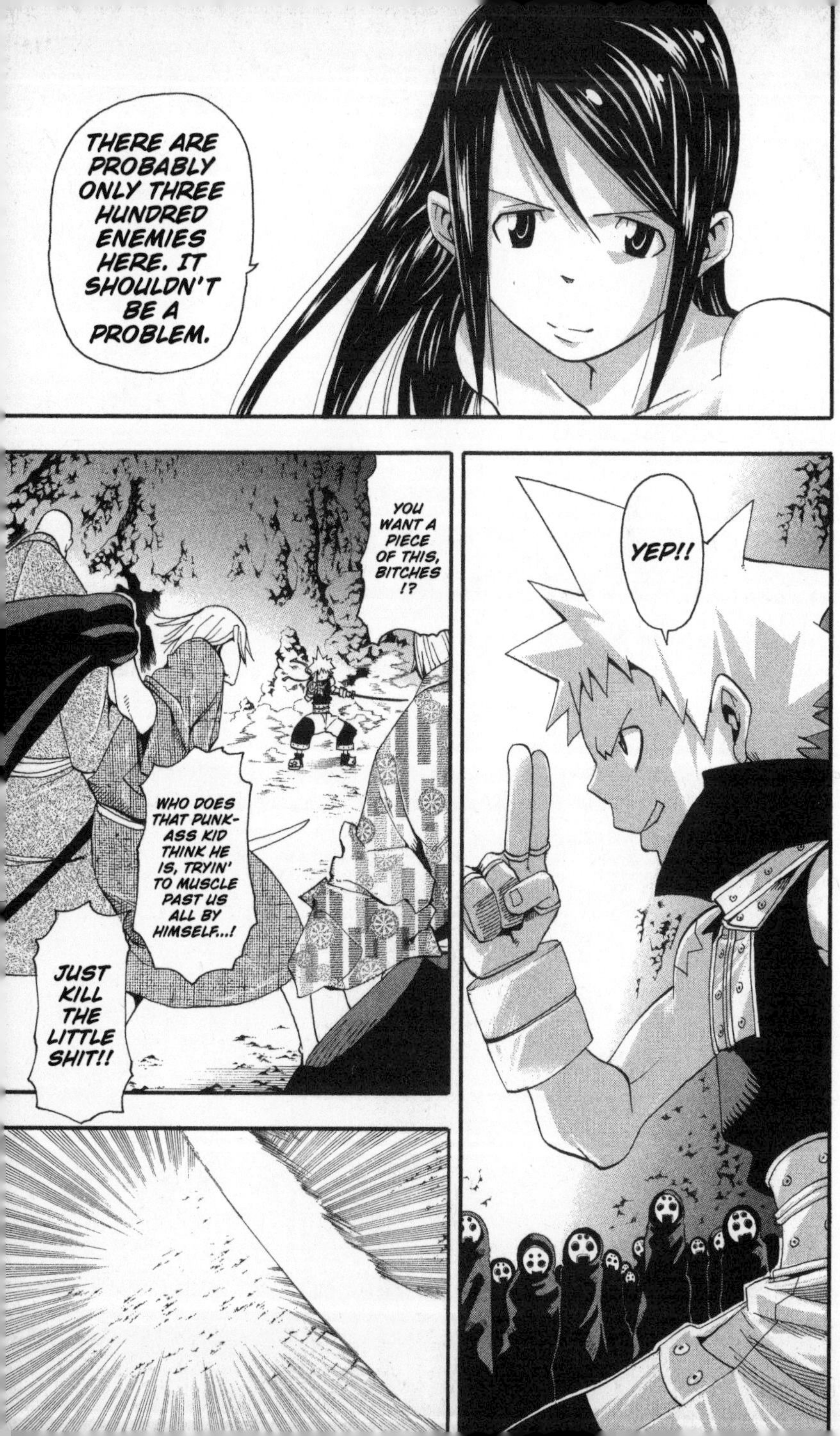
THERE ARE PROBABLY ONLY THREE HUNDRED ENEMIES HERE. IT SHOULDN'T BE A PROBLEM.
YEP!!
YOU WANT A PIECE OF THIS, BITCHES!?
WHO DOES THAT PUNK-ASS KID THINK HE IS, TRYIN' TO MUSCLE PAST US ALL BY HIMSELF...!
JUST KILL THE LITTLE SHIT!!

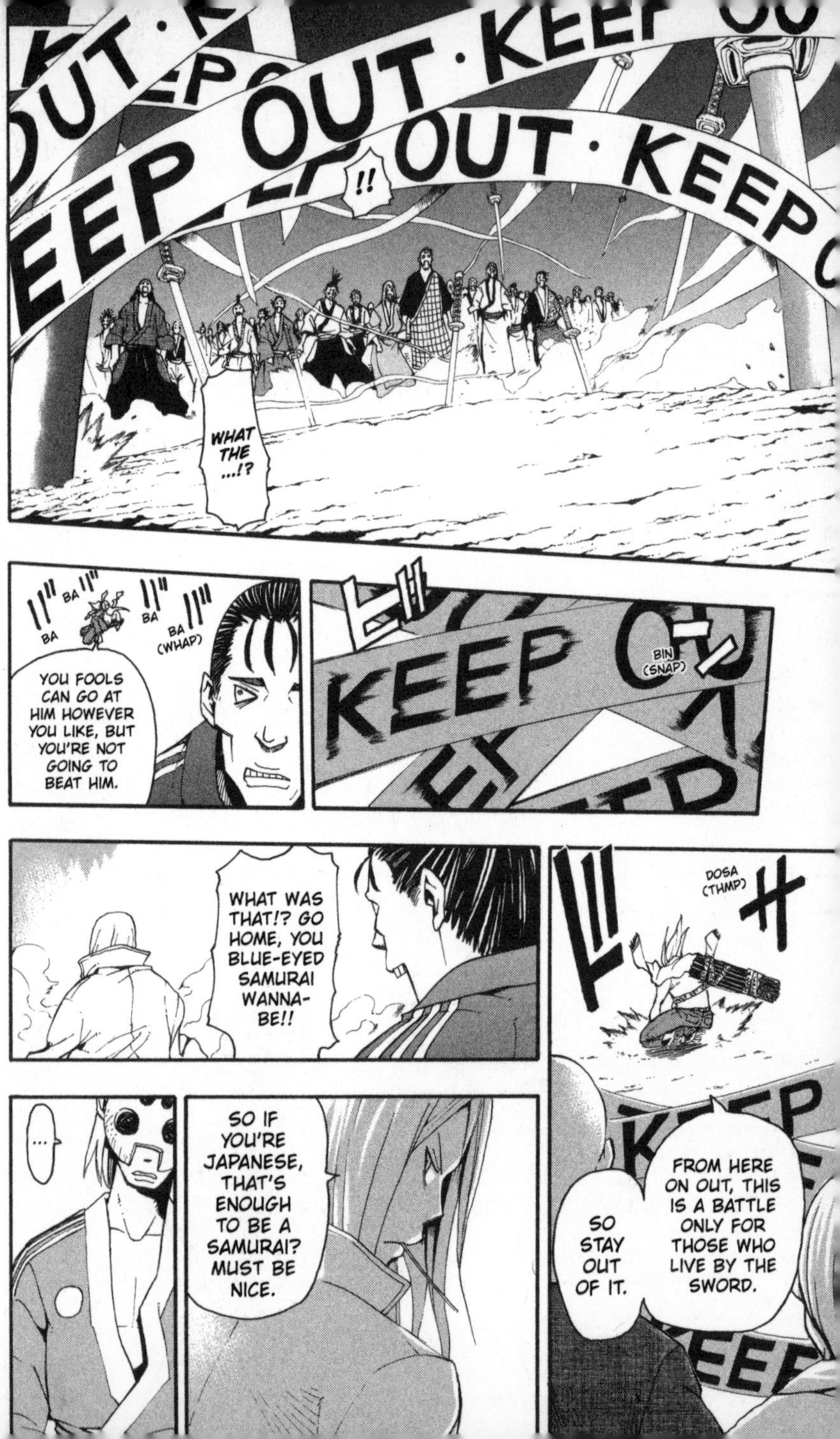
KEEP OUT · KEEP OUT · KEEP
!!
WHAT THE ...!?
BIN (SNAP)
BA BA BA BA (WHAP)
YOU FOOLS CAN GO AT HIM HOWEVER YOU LIKE, BUT YOU'RE NOT GOING TO BEAT HIM.
DOSA (THMP)
FROM HERE ON OUT, THIS IS A BATTLE ONLY FOR THOSE WHO LIVE BY THE SWORD.
SO STAY OUT OF IT.
WHAT WAS THAT!? GO HOME, YOU BLUE-EYED SAMURAI WANNA-BE!!
SO IF YOU'RE JAPANESE, THAT'S ENOUGH TO BE A SAMURAI? MUST BE NICE.
...

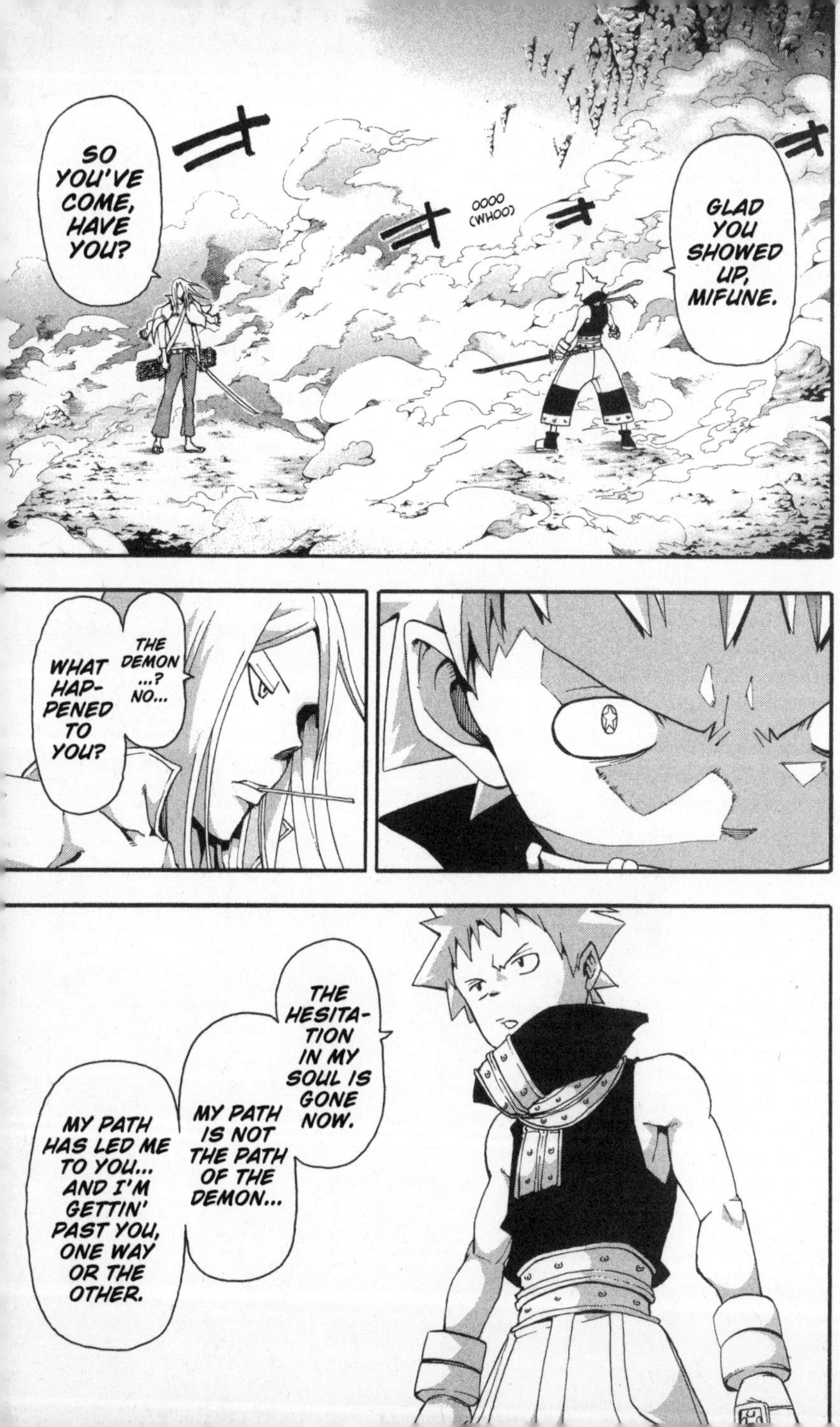
GLAD YOU SHOWED UP, MIFUNE.
OOOO (WHOO)
SO YOU'VE COME, HAVE YOU?
THE DEMON ...? NO...
WHAT HAP-PENED TO YOU?
THE HESITA-TION IN MY SOUL IS GONE NOW.
MY PATH IS NOT THE PATH OF THE DEMON...
MY PATH HAS LED ME TO YOU... AND I'M GETTIN' PAST YOU, ONE WAY OR THE OTHER.

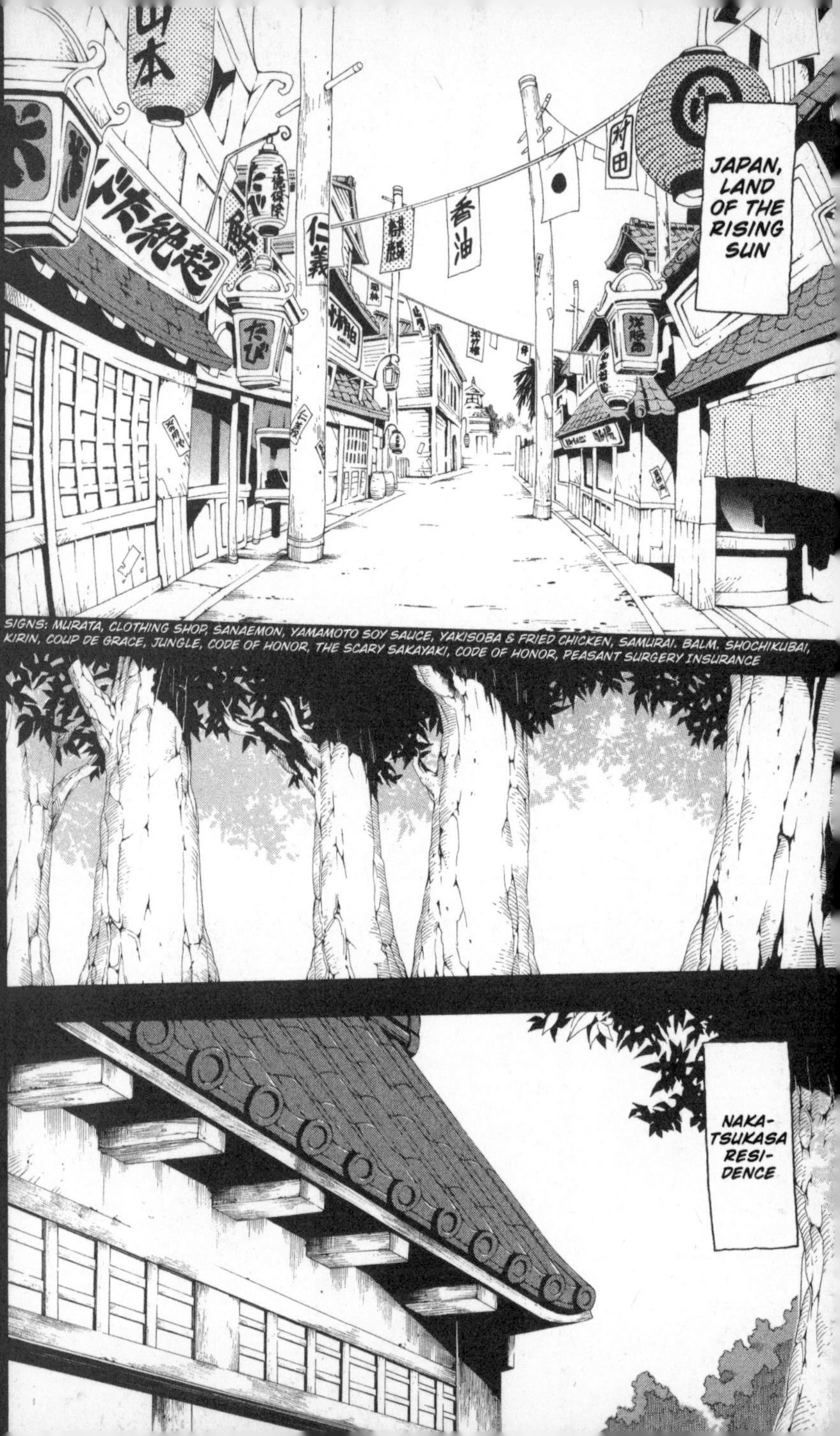
JAPAN, LAND OF THE RISING SUN
SIGNS: MURATA, CLOTHING SHOP, SANAEMON, YAMAMOTO SOY SAUCE, YAKISOBA & FRIED CHICKEN, SAMURAI. BALM. SHOCHIKUBAI, KIRIN, COUP DE GRACE, JUNGLE, CODE OF HONOR, THE SCARY SAKAYAKI, CODE OF HONOR, PEASANT SURGERY INSURANCE
NAKA-TSUKASA RESI-DENCE

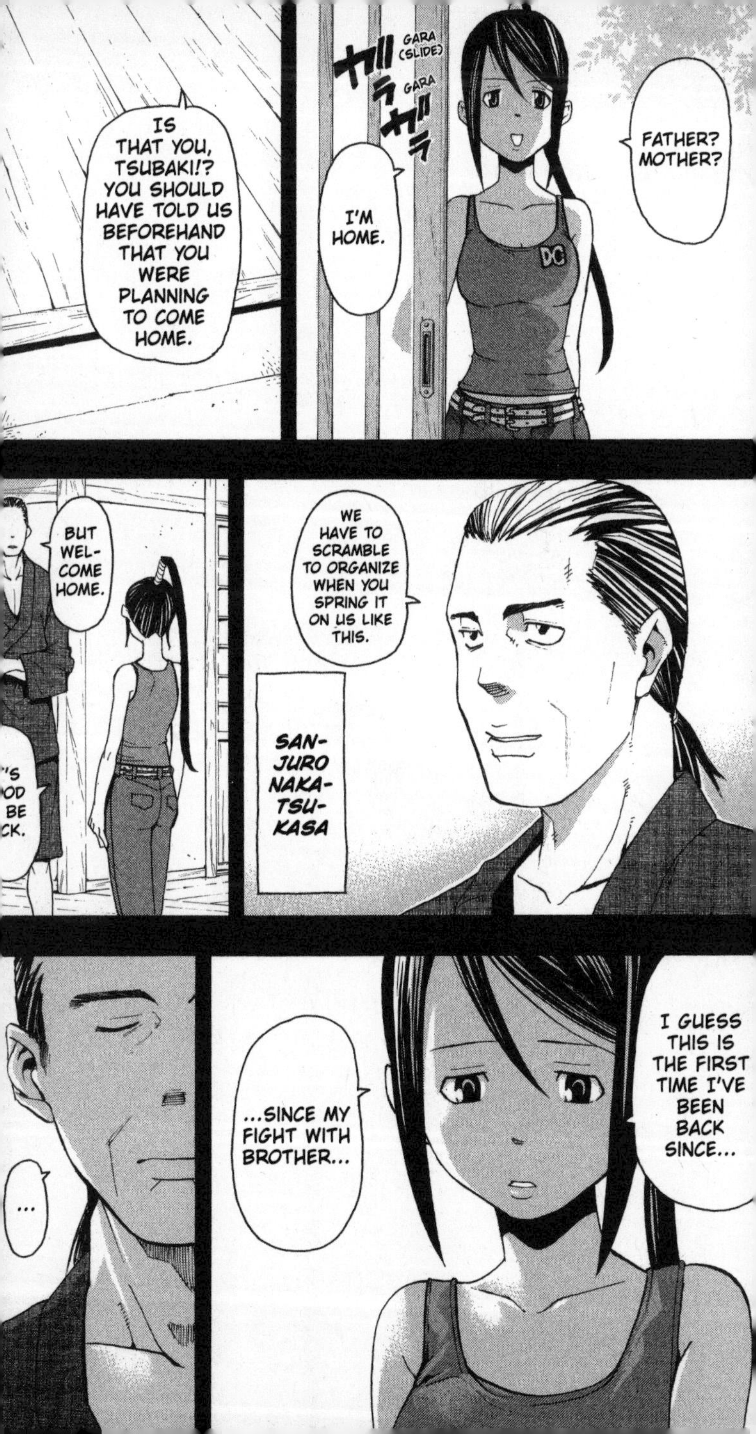
FATHER? MOTHER?
GARA (SLIDE)
GARA
I'M HOME.
IS THAT YOU, TSUBAKI!? YOU SHOULD HAVE TOLD US BEFOREHAND THAT YOU WERE PLANNING TO COME HOME.
WE HAVE TO SCRAMBLE TO ORGANIZE WHEN YOU SPRING IT ON US LIKE THIS.
SAN-JURO NAKA-TSU-KASA
BUT WEL-COME HOME.
I GUESS THIS IS THE FIRST TIME I'VE BEEN BACK SINCE...
...SINCE MY FIGHT WITH BROTHER...
...

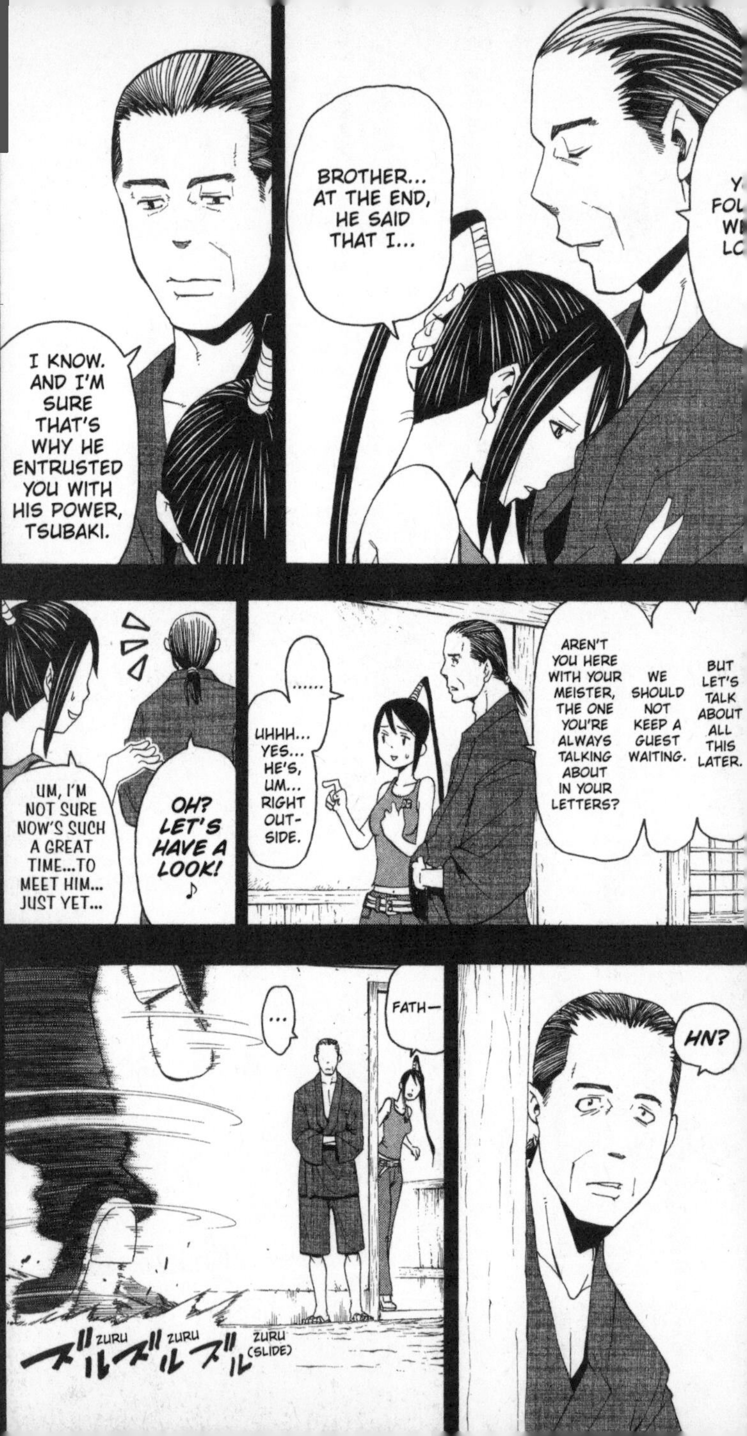
BROTHER... AT THE END, HE SAID THAT I...
I KNOW. AND I'M SURE THAT'S WHY HE ENTRUSTED YOU WITH HIS POWER, TSUBAKI.
BUT LET'S TALK ABOUT ALL THIS LATER.
WE SHOULD NOT KEEP A GUEST WAITING.
AREN'T YOU HERE WITH YOUR MEISTER, THE ONE YOU'RE ALWAYS TALKING ABOUT IN YOUR LETTERS?
......
UHHH... YES... HE'S, UM... RIGHT OUT-SIDE.
OH? LET'S HAVE A LOOK! ♪
UM, I'M NOT SURE NOW'S SUCH A GREAT TIME...TO MEET HIM... JUST YET...
HN?
FATH—
...
ZURU ZURU ZURU (SLIDE)

... | I'M JUST SHIFTIN' THE LOCATION OF THE EARTH'S AXIS SO IT'LL HAVE ME AT THE CENTER. | IT'S 'COS I'M GONNA BE STAYIN' HERE FOR A WHILE. | WHAT'S THE MATTER WITH THIS BOY? WHY IS HE SPINNING IN CIRCLES? | TSUBAKI...?

KURU (TWIRL)
KURU くる
KURU くる
KURU くる
KURU くる
KURU くる
KURU くる
KURU くる
KURU くる
KURU くる
KURU くる
KURU くる
KURU くる
KURU くる
KURU

WHOOOA!

HOLD ON JUST A SEC. | UMMM... WELL...

BWA-HA-HA-HA! SO YOU'RE SPINNING TO SHIFT THE EARTH'S AXIS, HUH? | HE'S BEEN DOING THIS EVER SINCE. I RECENTLY TAUGHT HIM WHAT THE EARTH'S AXIS IS. | ... | YEAH... I GUESS THAT ABOUT DOES IT. HUFF... HUFF...

I'M SO EMBARRASSED... | JUST DON'T GIMME ANY NASTY LOOKS WHEN I KEEP GOIN' BACK FOR SECONDS, 'KAY? | WELL, COME ON THEN, BLACK☆STAR. GO ON IN THE HOUSE AND HAVE YOURSELF SOME TEA AND SNACKS. | GASHI (TOUSLE) | YOU HEARD RIGHT!! | I CAN SEE EVERYTHING WE HEARD ABOUT YOU IS TRUE— YOU REALLY ARE BIG STUFF!

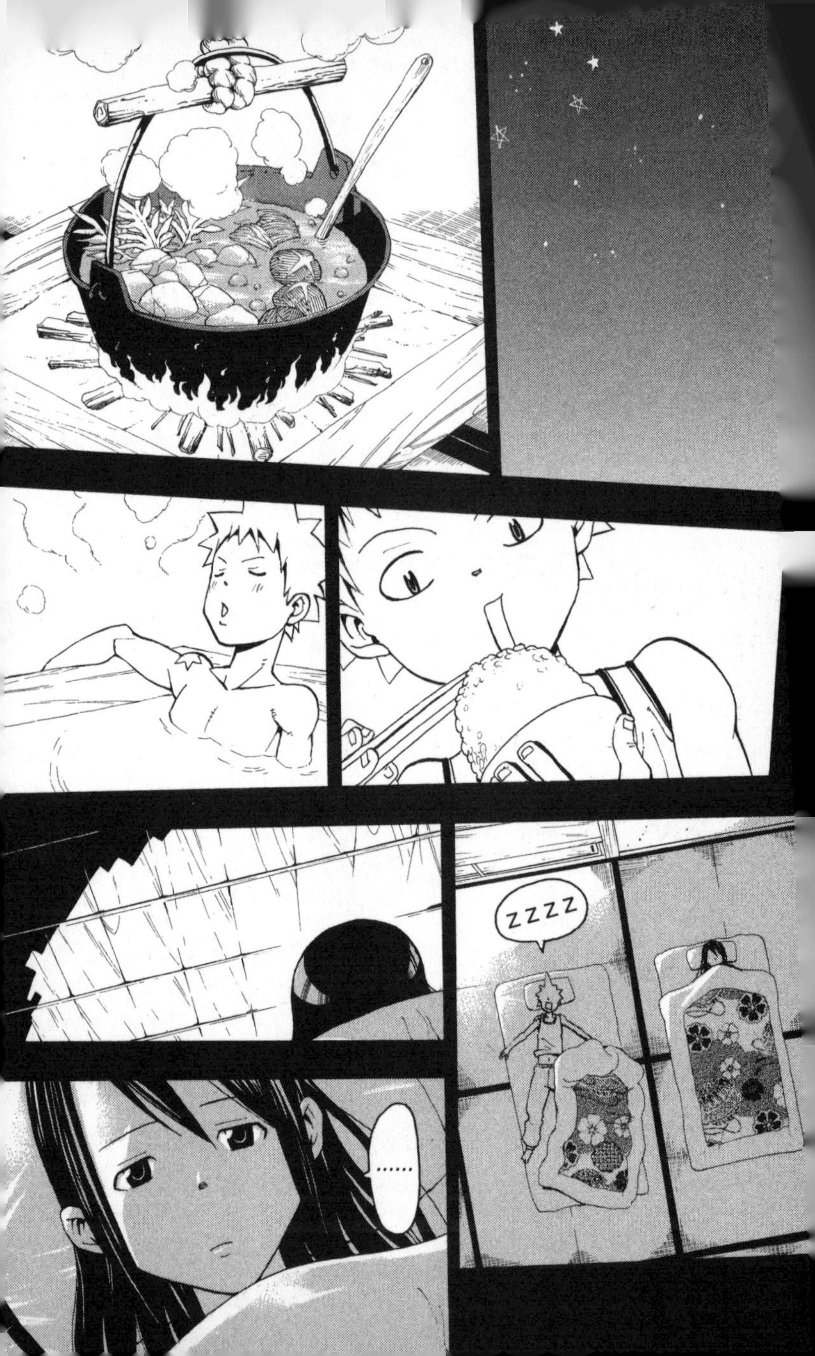
ZZZZ
......

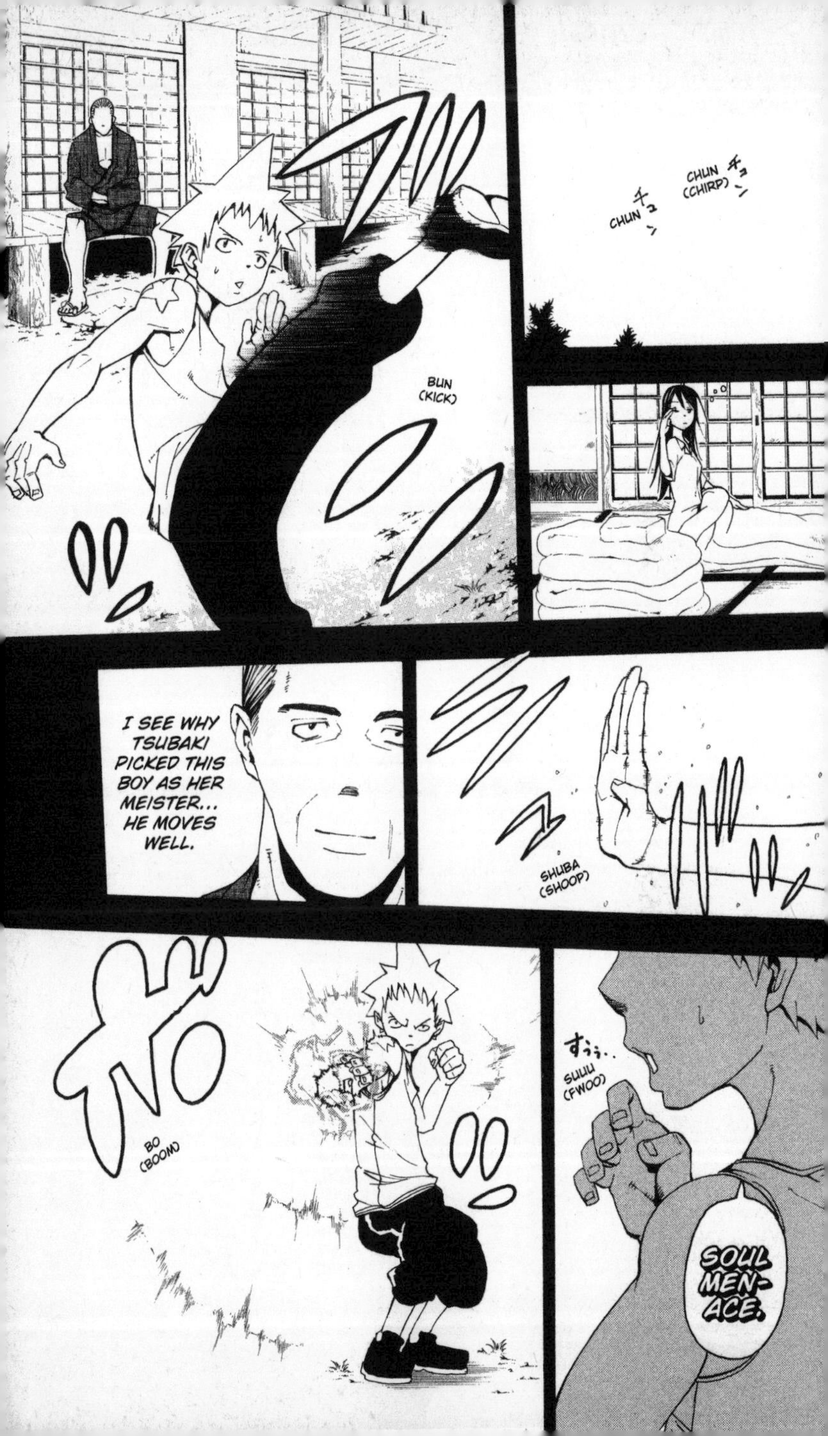

CHUN (CHIRP)
チュン
CHUN
チュン
BUN (KICK)
SHUBA (SHOOP)
I SEE WHY TSUBAKI PICKED THIS BOY AS HER MEISTER... HE MOVES WELL.
すぅぅ..
SUUU (FWOO)
SOUL MEN-ACE.
BO (BOOM)

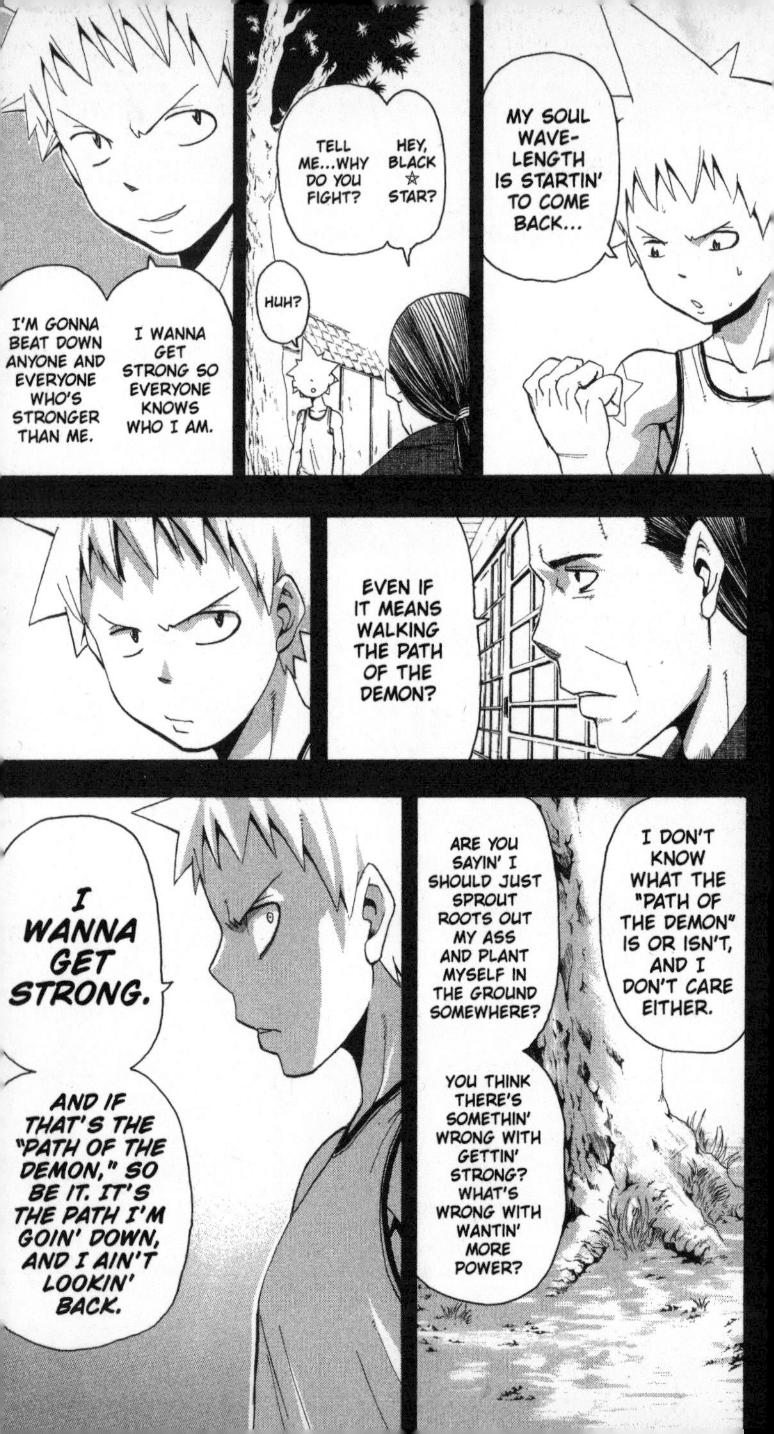
MY SOUL WAVE-LENGTH IS STARTIN' TO COME BACK...
HEY, BLACK ☆ STAR?
TELL ME...WHY DO YOU FIGHT?
HUH?
I WANNA GET STRONG SO EVERYONE KNOWS WHO I AM.
I'M GONNA BEAT DOWN ANYONE AND EVERYONE WHO'S STRONGER THAN ME.
EVEN IF IT MEANS WALKING THE PATH OF THE DEMON?
I DON'T KNOW WHAT THE "PATH OF THE DEMON" IS OR ISN'T, AND I DON'T CARE EITHER.
ARE YOU SAYIN' I SHOULD JUST SPROUT ROOTS OUT MY ASS AND PLANT MYSELF IN THE GROUND SOMEWHERE?
YOU THINK THERE'S SOMETHIN' WRONG WITH GETTIN' STRONG? WHAT'S WRONG WITH WANTIN' MORE POWER?
I WANNA GET STRONG.
AND IF THAT'S THE "PATH OF THE DEMON," SO BE IT. IT'S THE PATH I'M GOIN' DOWN, AND I AIN'T LOOKIN' BACK.

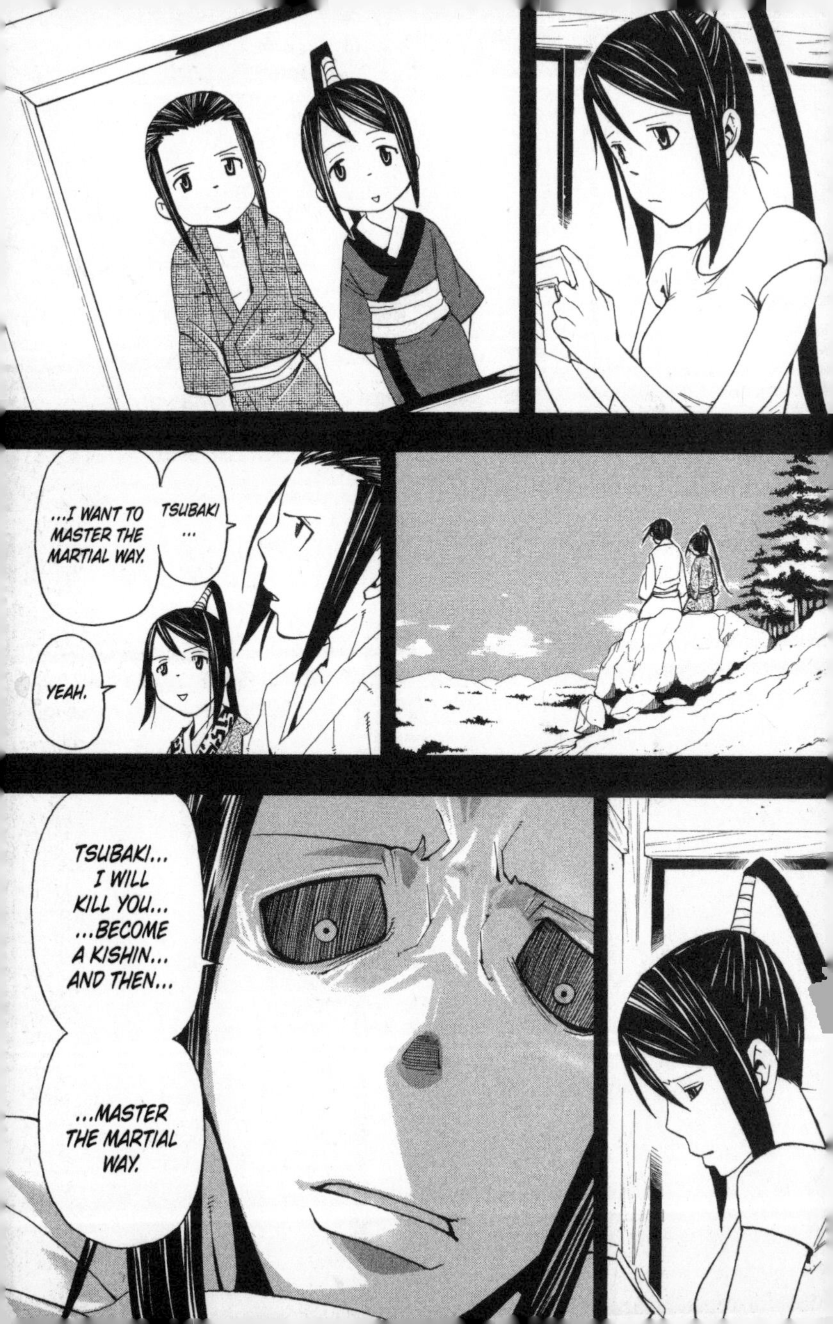
TSUBAKI ...
...I WANT TO MASTER THE MARTIAL WAY.
YEAH.
TSUBAKI... I WILL KILL YOU... ...BECOME A KISHIN... AND THEN...
...MASTER THE MARTIAL WAY.

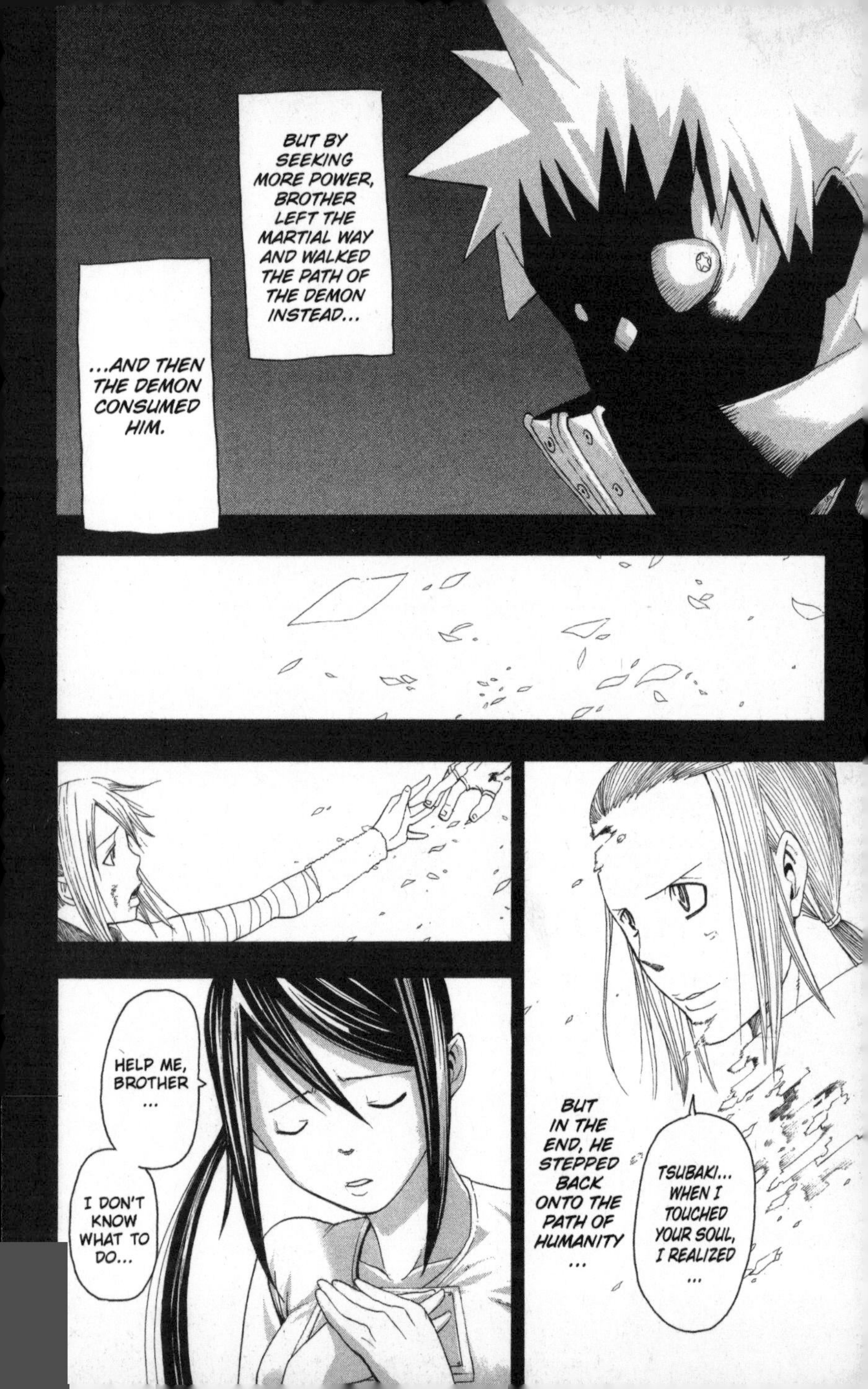
BUT BY SEEKING MORE POWER, BROTHER LEFT THE MARTIAL WAY AND WALKED THE PATH OF THE DEMON INSTEAD...
...AND THEN THE DEMON CONSUMED HIM.
BUT IN THE END, HE STEPPED BACK ONTO THE PATH OF HUMANITY...
TSUBAKI... WHEN I TOUCHED YOUR SOUL, I REALIZED...
HELP ME, BROTHER...
I DON'T KNOW WHAT TO DO...

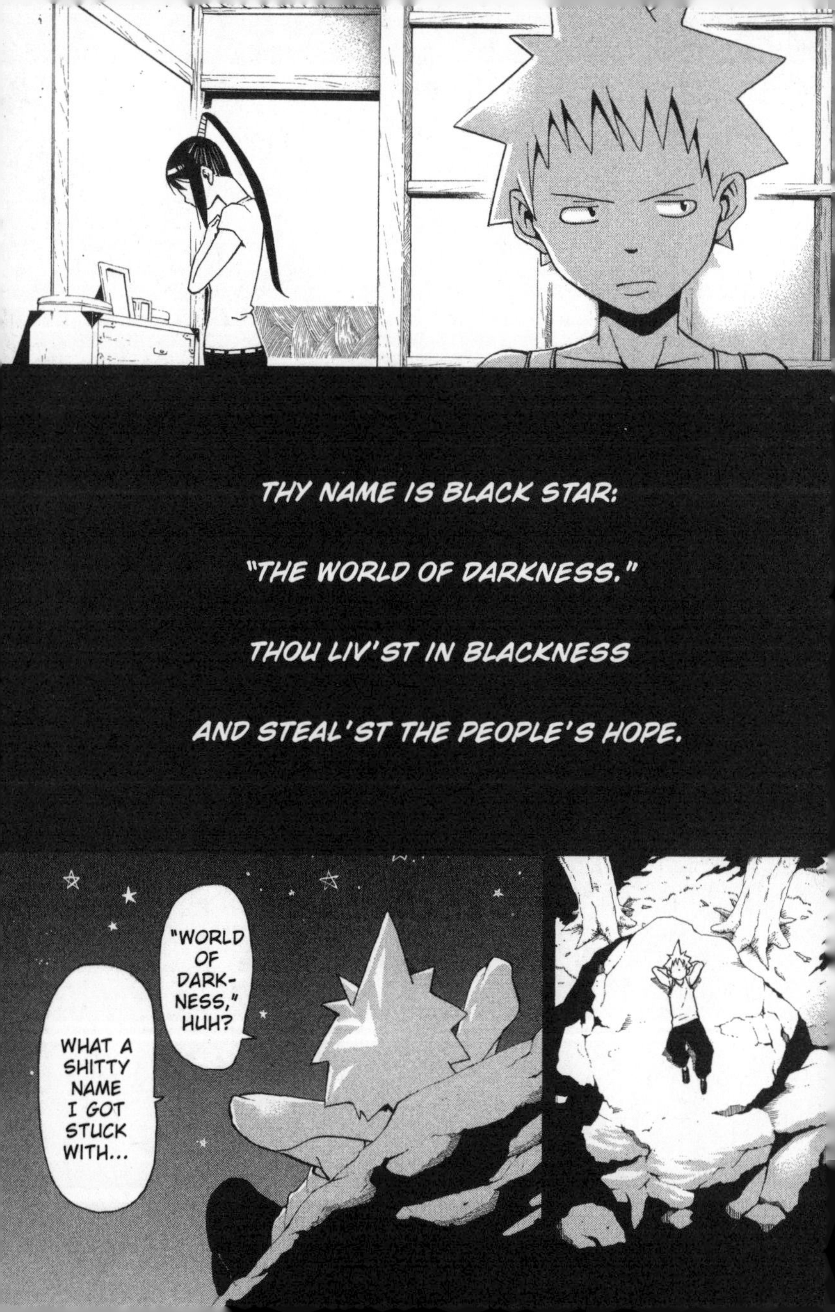
THY NAME IS BLACK STAR:
"THE WORLD OF DARKNESS."
THOU LIV'ST IN BLACKNESS
AND STEAL'ST THE PEOPLE'S HOPE.
"WORLD OF DARKNESS," HUH?
WHAT A SHITTY NAME I GOT STUCK WITH...

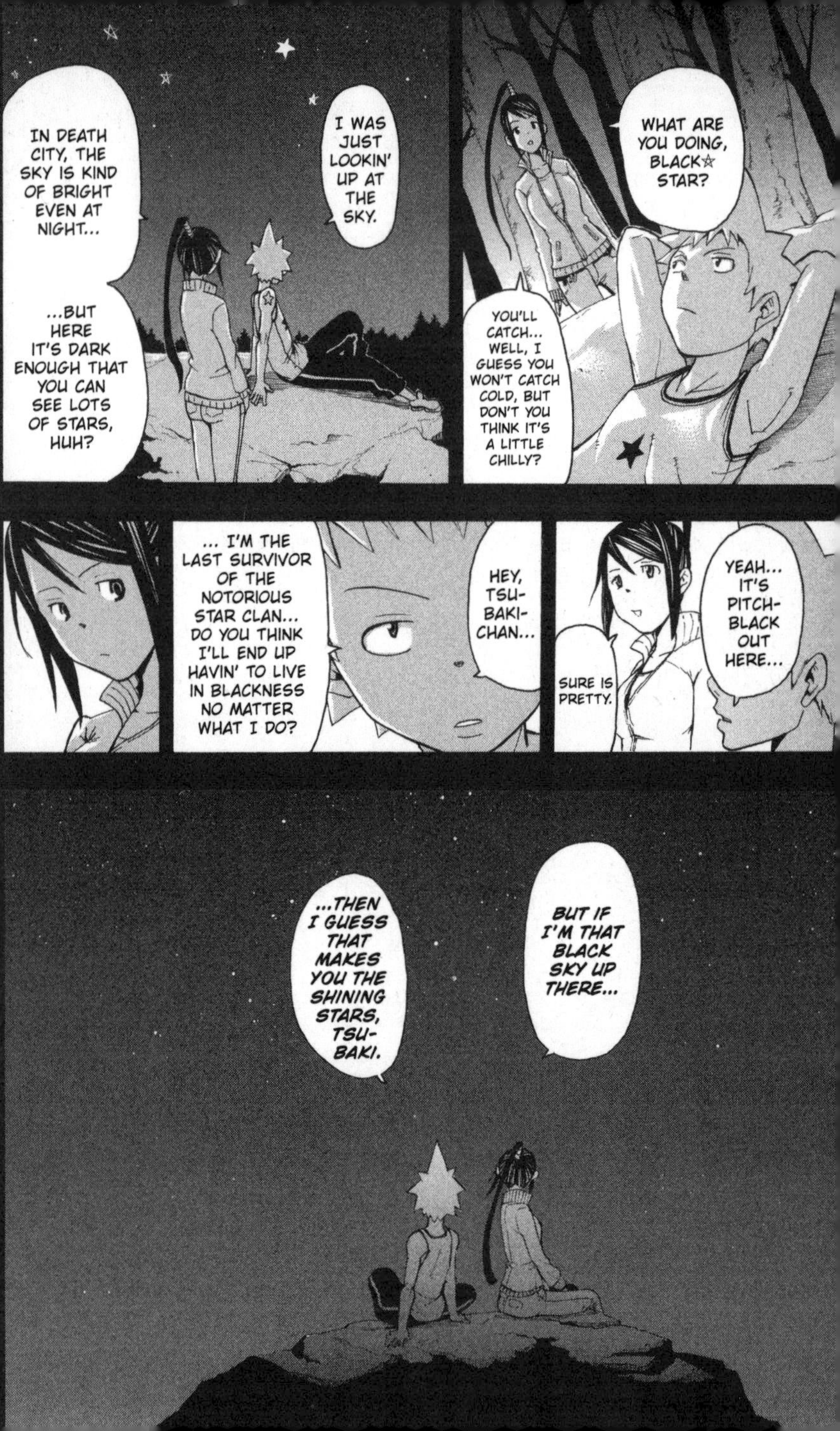
WHAT ARE YOU DOING, BLACK☆STAR?
YOU'LL CATCH... WELL, I GUESS YOU WON'T CATCH COLD, BUT DON'T YOU THINK IT'S A LITTLE CHILLY?
I WAS JUST LOOKIN' UP AT THE SKY.
IN DEATH CITY, THE SKY IS KIND OF BRIGHT EVEN AT NIGHT...
...BUT HERE IT'S DARK ENOUGH THAT YOU CAN SEE LOTS OF STARS, HUH?
YEAH... IT'S PITCH-BLACK OUT HERE...
SURE IS PRETTY.
HEY, TSU-BAKI-CHAN...
... I'M THE LAST SURVIVOR OF THE NOTORIOUS STAR CLAN... DO YOU THINK I'LL END UP HAVIN' TO LIVE IN BLACKNESS NO MATTER WHAT I DO?
BUT IF I'M THAT BLACK SKY UP THERE...
...THEN I GUESS THAT MAKES YOU THE SHINING STARS, TSU-BAKI.

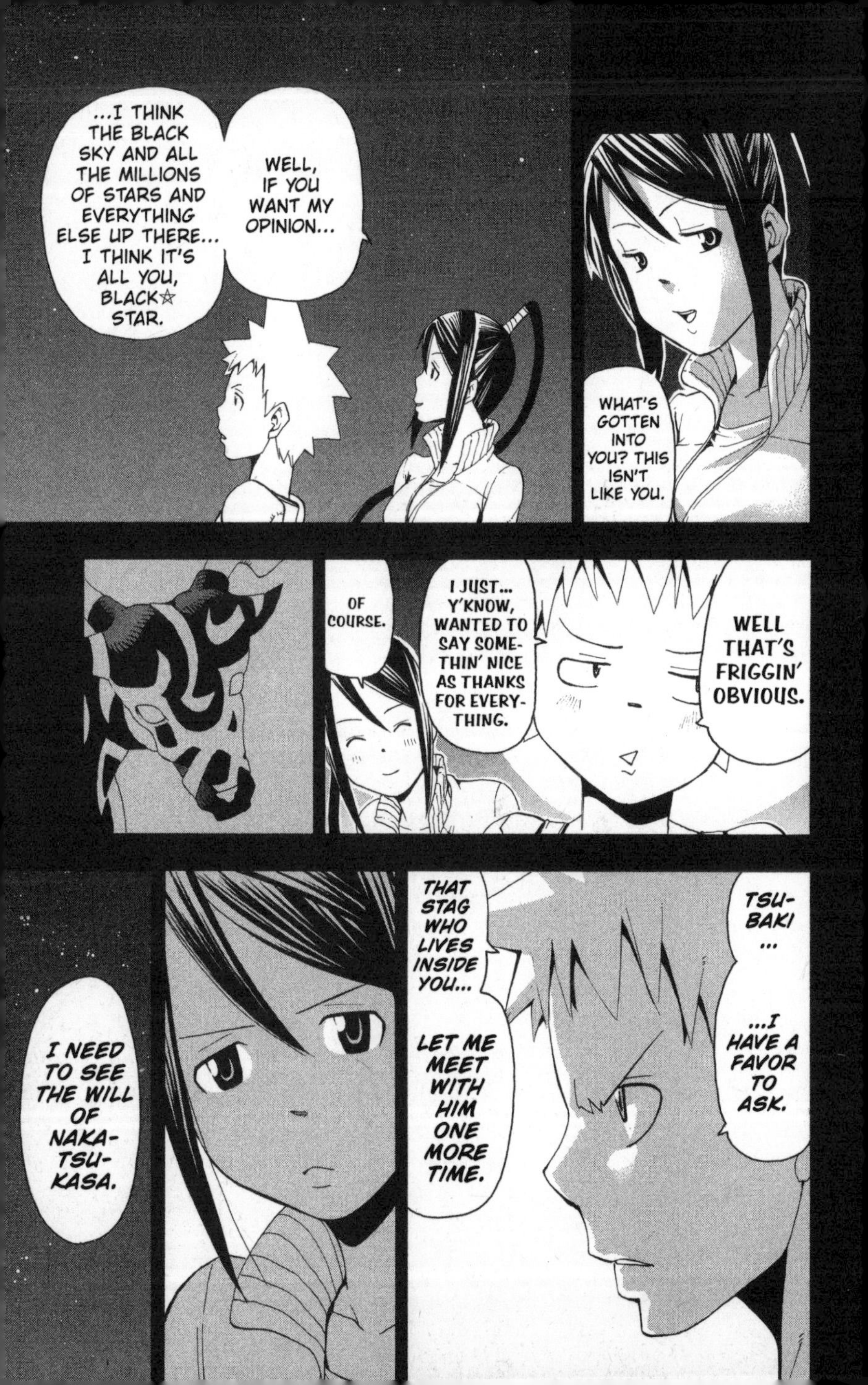
WHAT'S GOTTEN INTO YOU? THIS ISN'T LIKE YOU.
WELL, IF YOU WANT MY OPINION...
...I THINK THE BLACK SKY AND ALL THE MILLIONS OF STARS AND EVERYTHING ELSE UP THERE... I THINK IT'S ALL YOU, BLACK☆STAR.
WELL THAT'S FRIGGIN' OBVIOUS.
I JUST... Y'KNOW, WANTED TO SAY SOME-THIN' NICE AS THANKS FOR EVERY-THING.
OF COURSE.
TSU-BAKI...
...I HAVE A FAVOR TO ASK.
THAT STAG WHO LIVES INSIDE YOU...
LET ME MEET WITH HIM ONE MORE TIME.
I NEED TO SEE THE WILL OF NAKA-TSU-KASA.

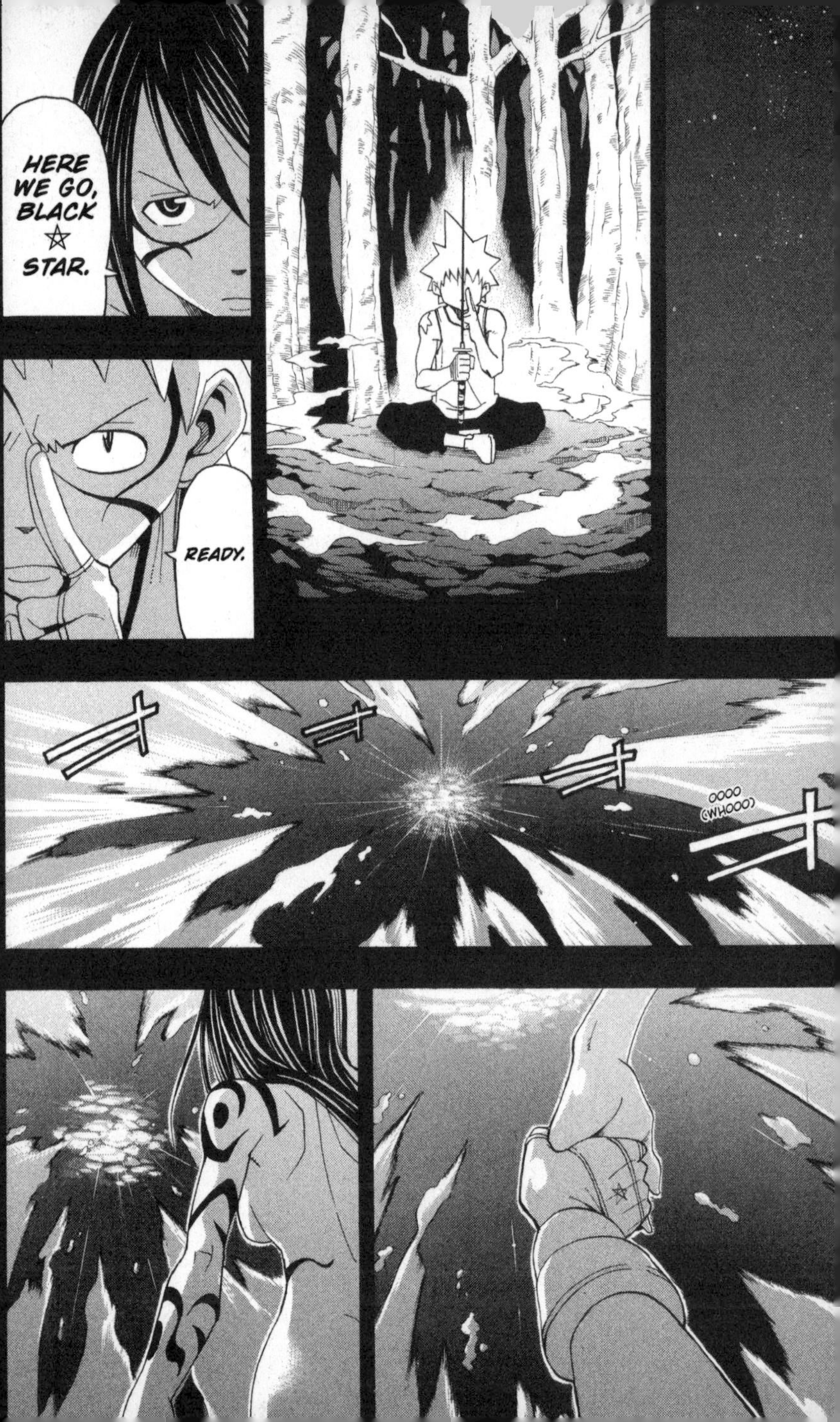
HERE WE GO, BLACK ☆ STAR.
READY.
OOOO (WHOOO)

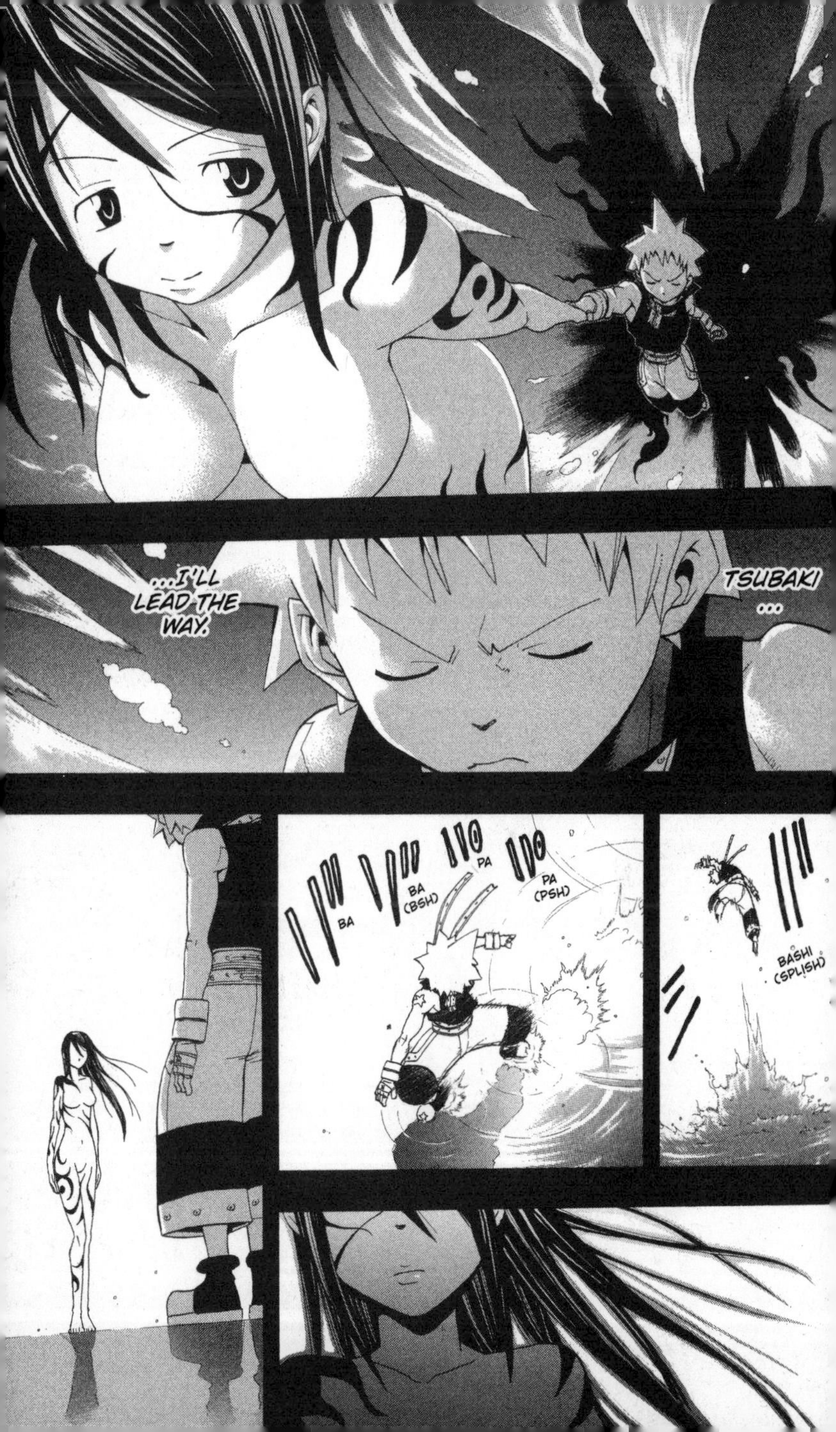
TSUBAKI ...
...I'LL LEAD THE WAY.
BASHI (SPLISH)
PA (PSH)
PA
BA (BSH)
BA

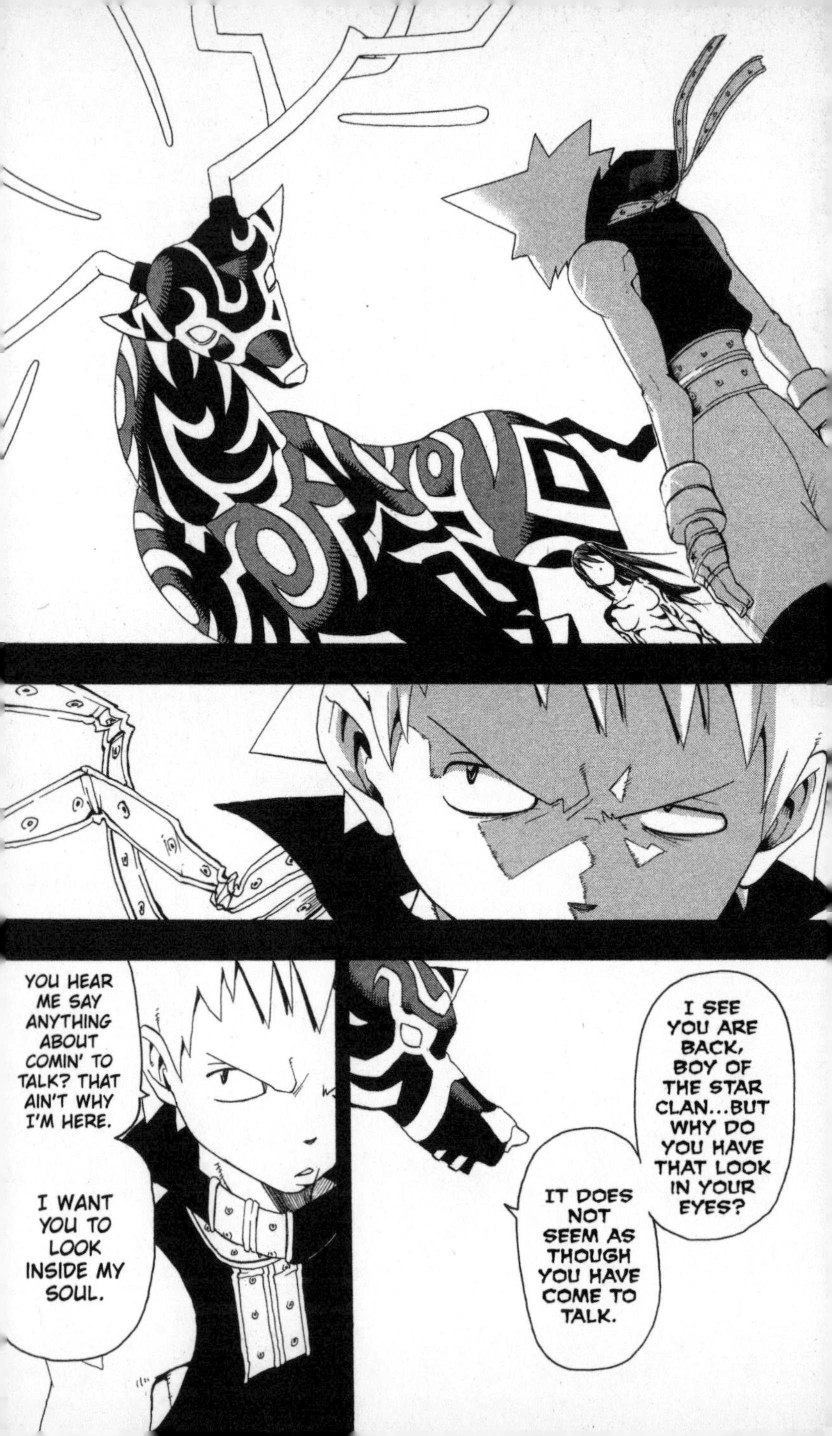
I SEE YOU ARE BACK, BOY OF THE STAR CLAN...BUT WHY DO YOU HAVE THAT LOOK IN YOUR EYES?
IT DOES NOT SEEM AS THOUGH YOU HAVE COME TO TALK.
YOU HEAR ME SAY ANYTHING ABOUT COMIN' TO TALK? THAT AIN'T WHY I'M HERE.
I WANT YOU TO LOOK INSIDE MY SOUL.

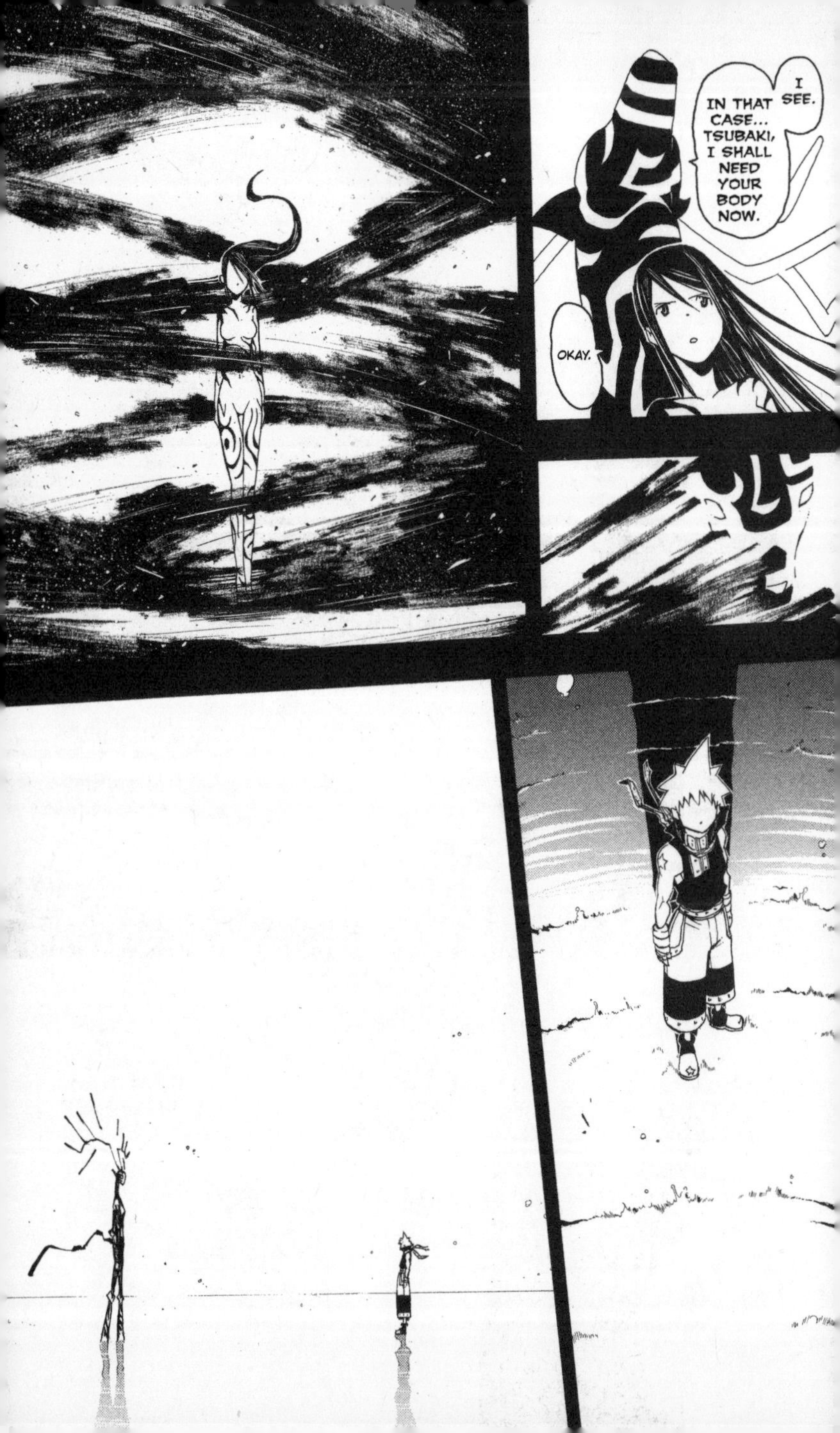
I SEE.
IN THAT CASE... TSUBAKI, I SHALL NEED YOUR BODY NOW.
OKAY.

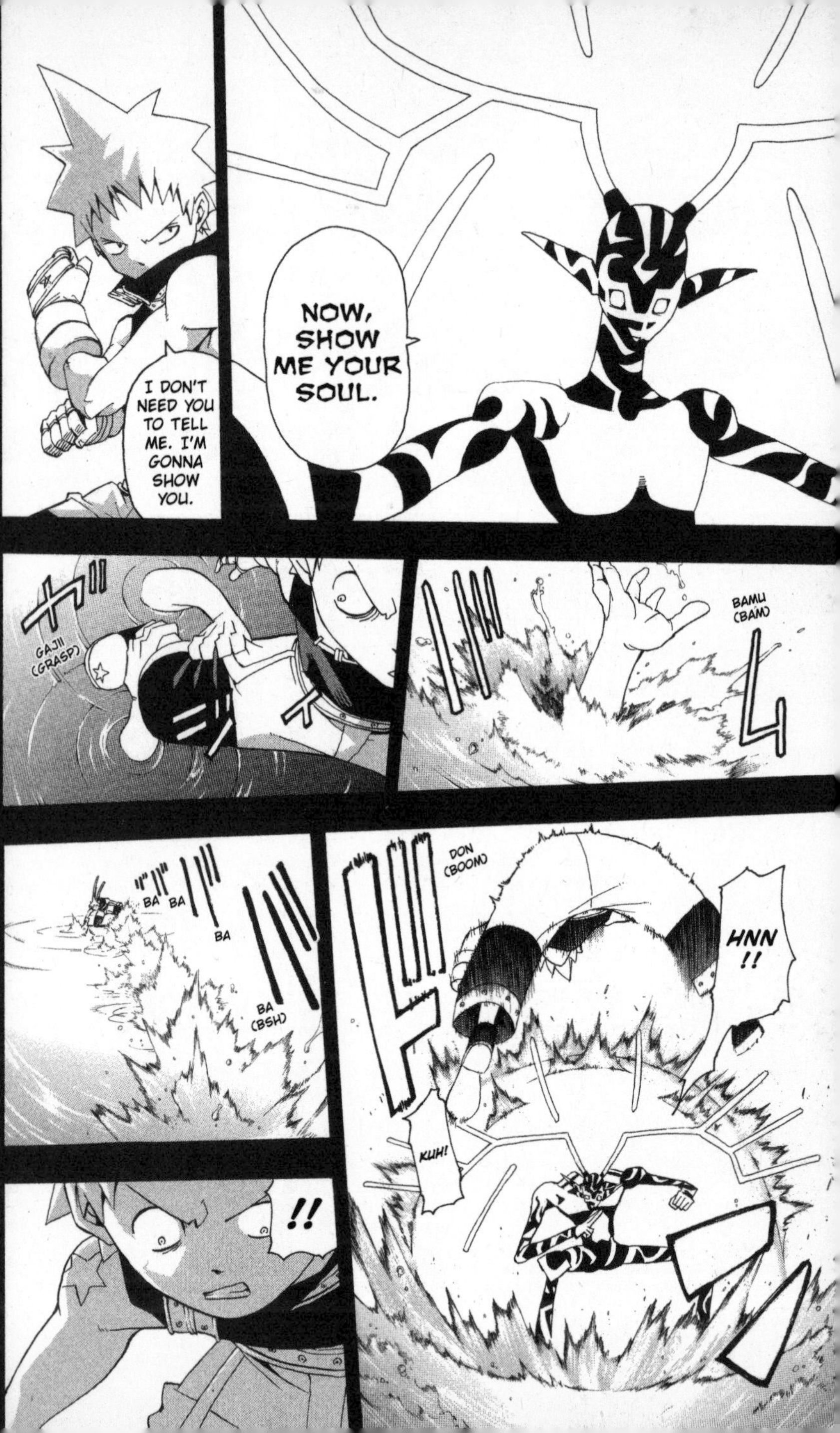
NOW, SHOW ME YOUR SOUL.
I DON'T NEED YOU TO TELL ME. I'M GONNA SHOW YOU.
BAMU (BAM)
GAJII (GRASP)
DON (BOOM)
HNN !!
KUH!
BA
BA
BA
BA (BSH)
!!

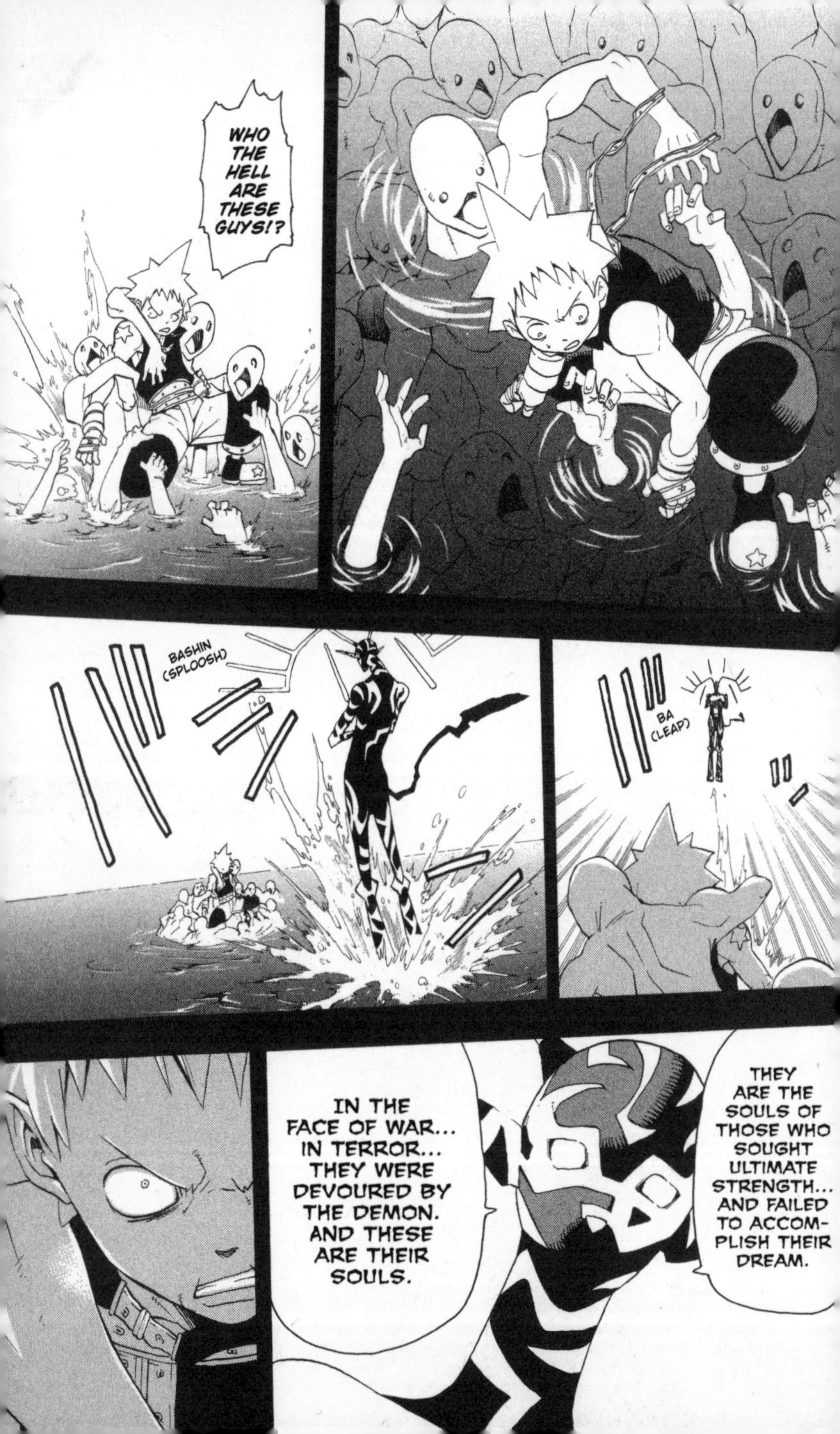
WHO THE HELL ARE THESE GUYS!?
BA (LEAP)
BASHIN (SPLOOSH)
THEY ARE THE SOULS OF THOSE WHO SOUGHT ULTIMATE STRENGTH... AND FAILED TO ACCOMPLISH THEIR DREAM.
IN THE FACE OF WAR... IN TERROR... THEY WERE DEVOURED BY THE DEMON. AND THESE ARE THEIR SOULS.

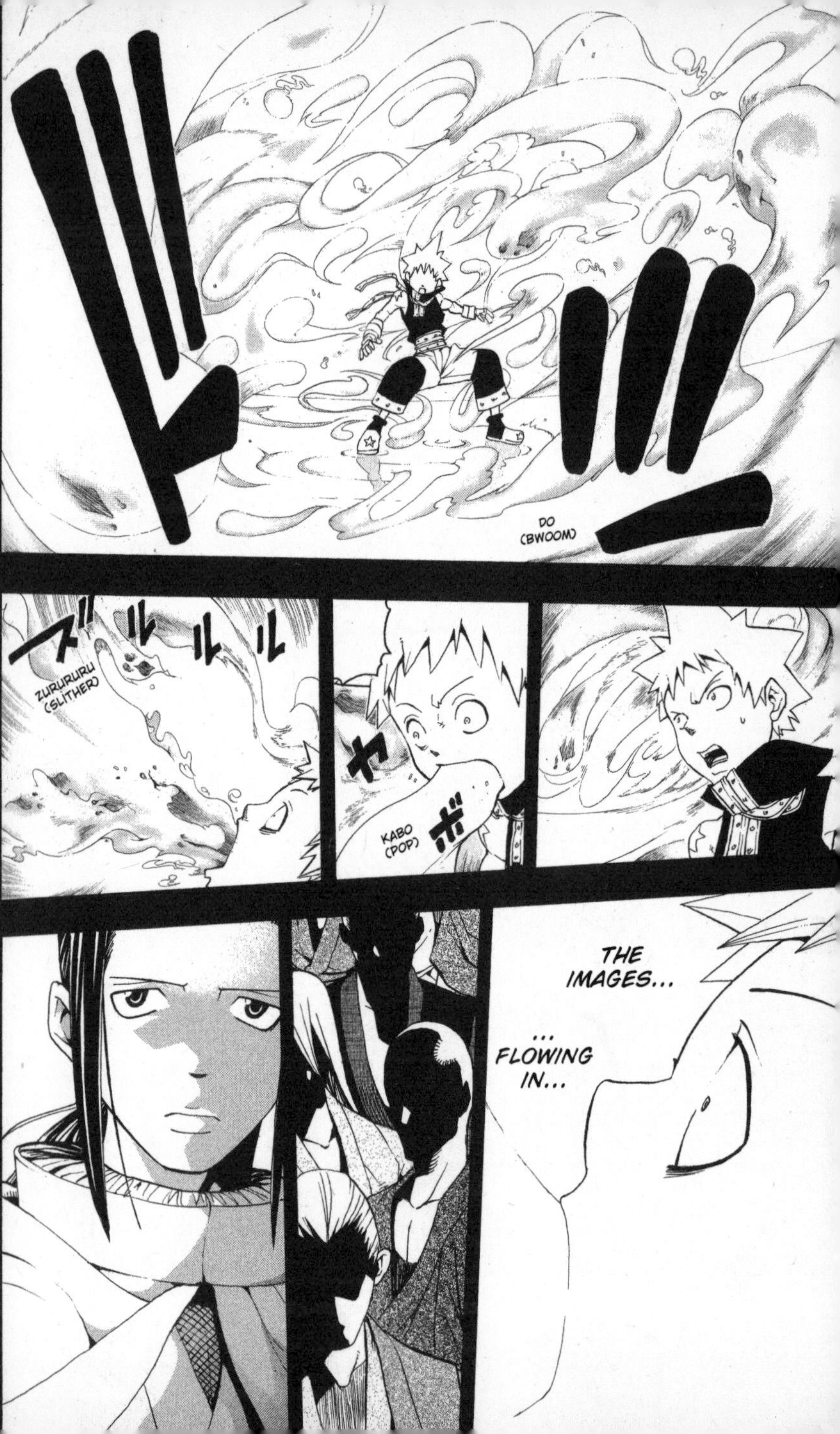
DO
(BWOOM)
KABO
(POP)
ZURURURU
(SLITHER)
THE IMAGES...
... FLOWING IN...

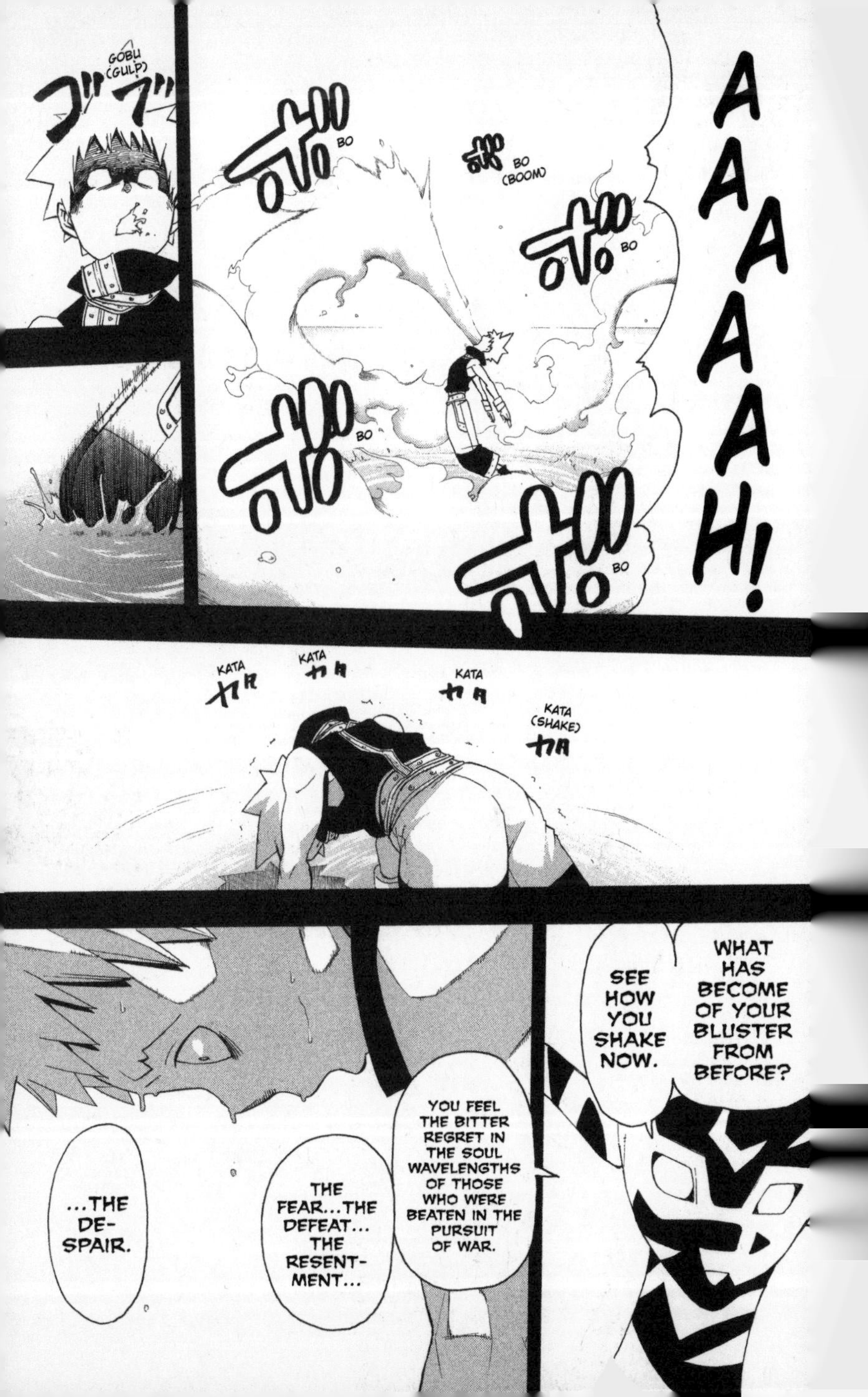
AAAAAAH!
BO
BO (BOOM)
BO
BO
BO
GOBU (GULP)
KATA
KATA
KATA
KATA (SHAKE)
WHAT HAS BECOME OF YOUR BLUSTER FROM BEFORE?
SEE HOW YOU SHAKE NOW.
YOU FEEL THE BITTER REGRET IN THE SOUL WAVELENGTHS OF THOSE WHO WERE BEATEN IN THE PURSUIT OF WAR.
THE FEAR...THE DEFEAT... THE RESENT-MENT...
...THE DE-SPAIR.

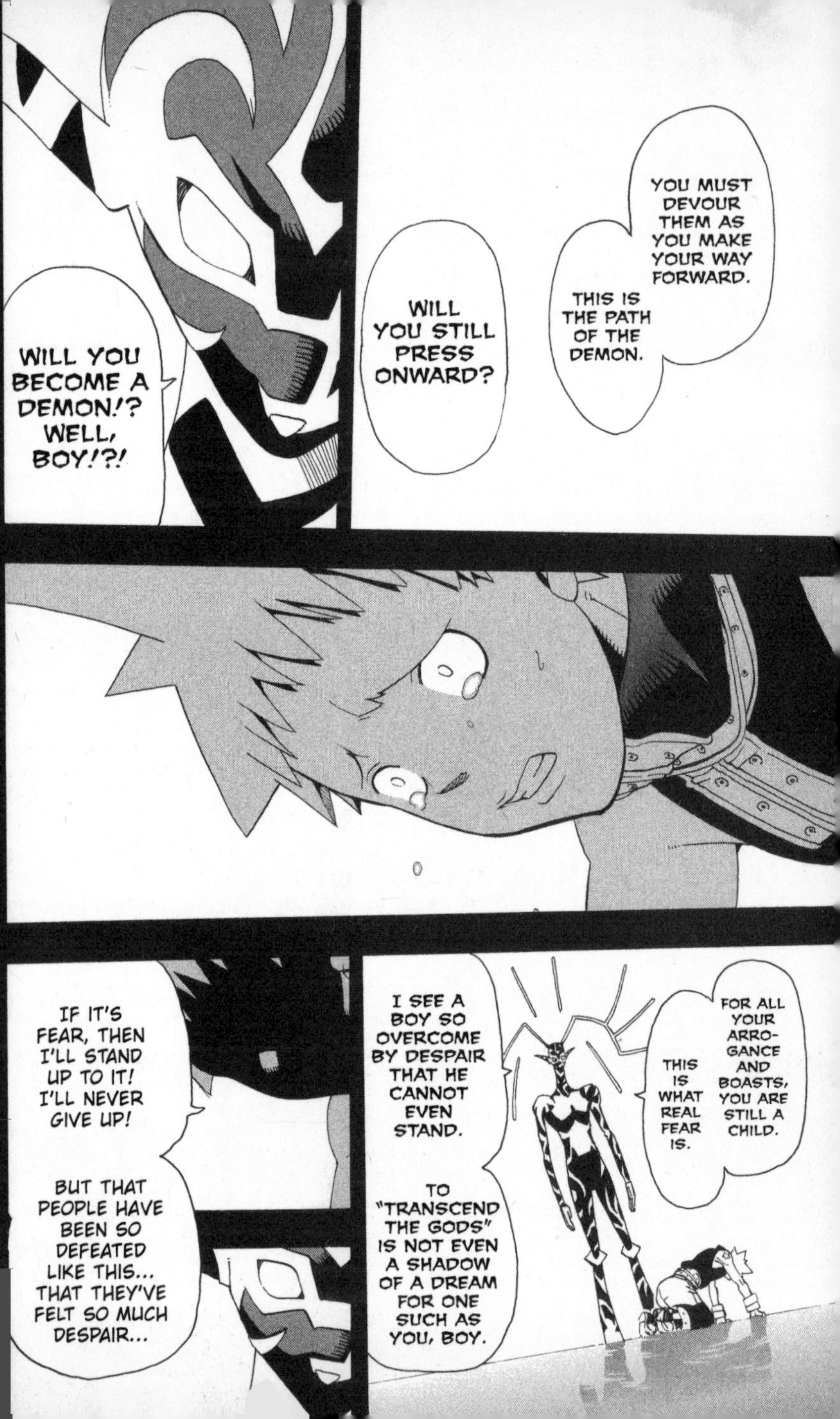
YOU MUST DEVOUR THEM AS YOU MAKE YOUR WAY FORWARD.
THIS IS THE PATH OF THE DEMON.
WILL YOU STILL PRESS ONWARD?
WILL YOU BECOME A DEMON!? WELL, BOY!?!
FOR ALL YOUR ARRO-GANCE AND BOASTS, YOU ARE STILL A CHILD.
THIS IS WHAT REAL FEAR IS.
I SEE A BOY SO OVERCOME BY DESPAIR THAT HE CANNOT EVEN STAND.
TO "TRANSCEND THE GODS" IS NOT EVEN A SHADOW OF A DREAM FOR ONE SUCH AS YOU, BOY.
IF IT'S FEAR, THEN I'LL STAND UP TO IT! I'LL NEVER GIVE UP!
BUT THAT PEOPLE HAVE BEEN SO DEFEATED LIKE THIS... THAT THEY'VE FELT SO MUCH DESPAIR...

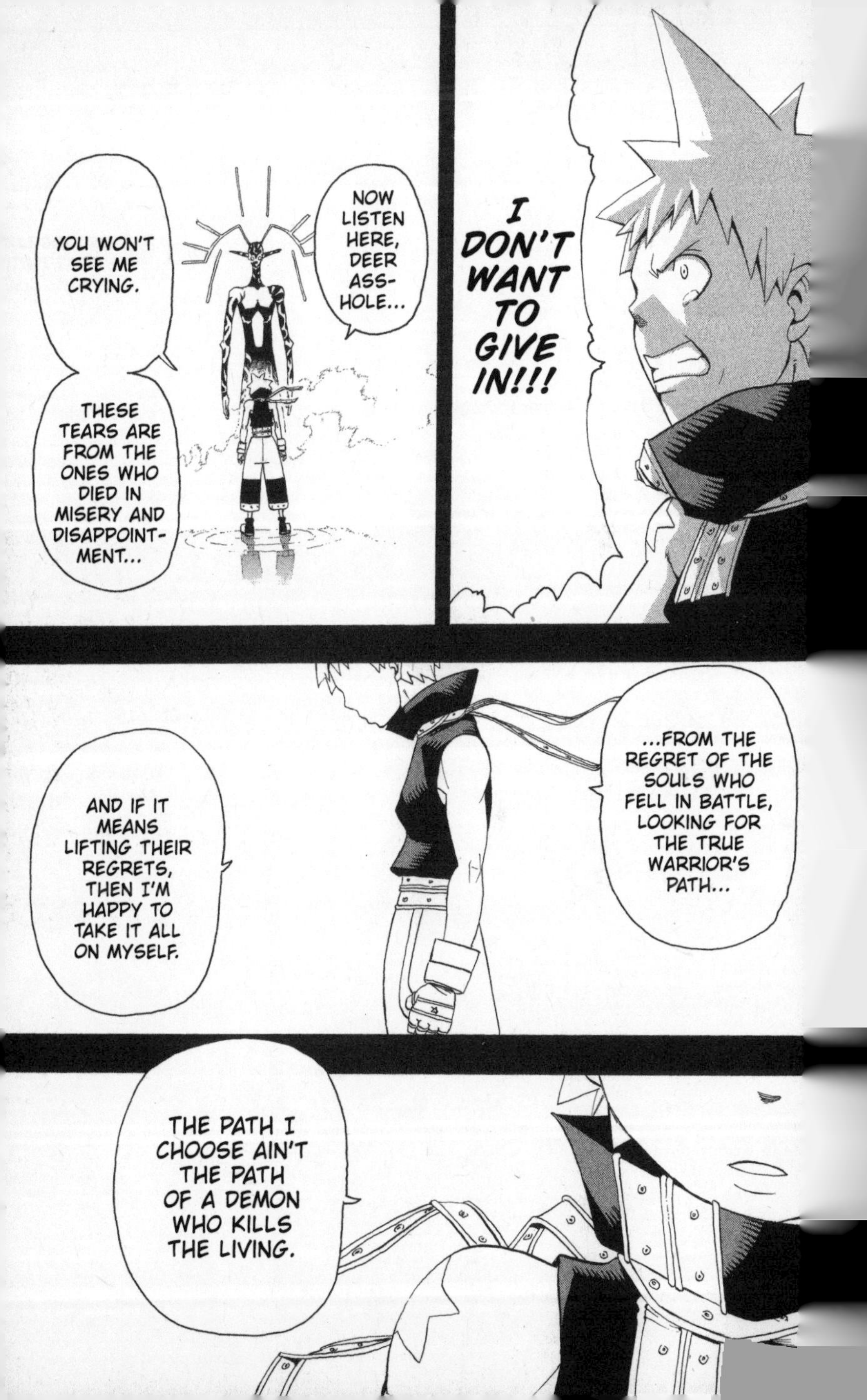
I DON'T WANT TO GIVE IN!!!
NOW LISTEN HERE, DEER ASS-HOLE...
YOU WON'T SEE ME CRYING.
THESE TEARS ARE FROM THE ONES WHO DIED IN MISERY AND DISAPPOINT-MENT...
...FROM THE REGRET OF THE SOULS WHO FELL IN BATTLE, LOOKING FOR THE TRUE WARRIOR'S PATH...
AND IF IT MEANS LIFTING THEIR REGRETS, THEN I'M HAPPY TO TAKE IT ALL ON MYSELF.
THE PATH I CHOOSE AIN'T THE PATH OF A DEMON WHO KILLS THE LIVING.

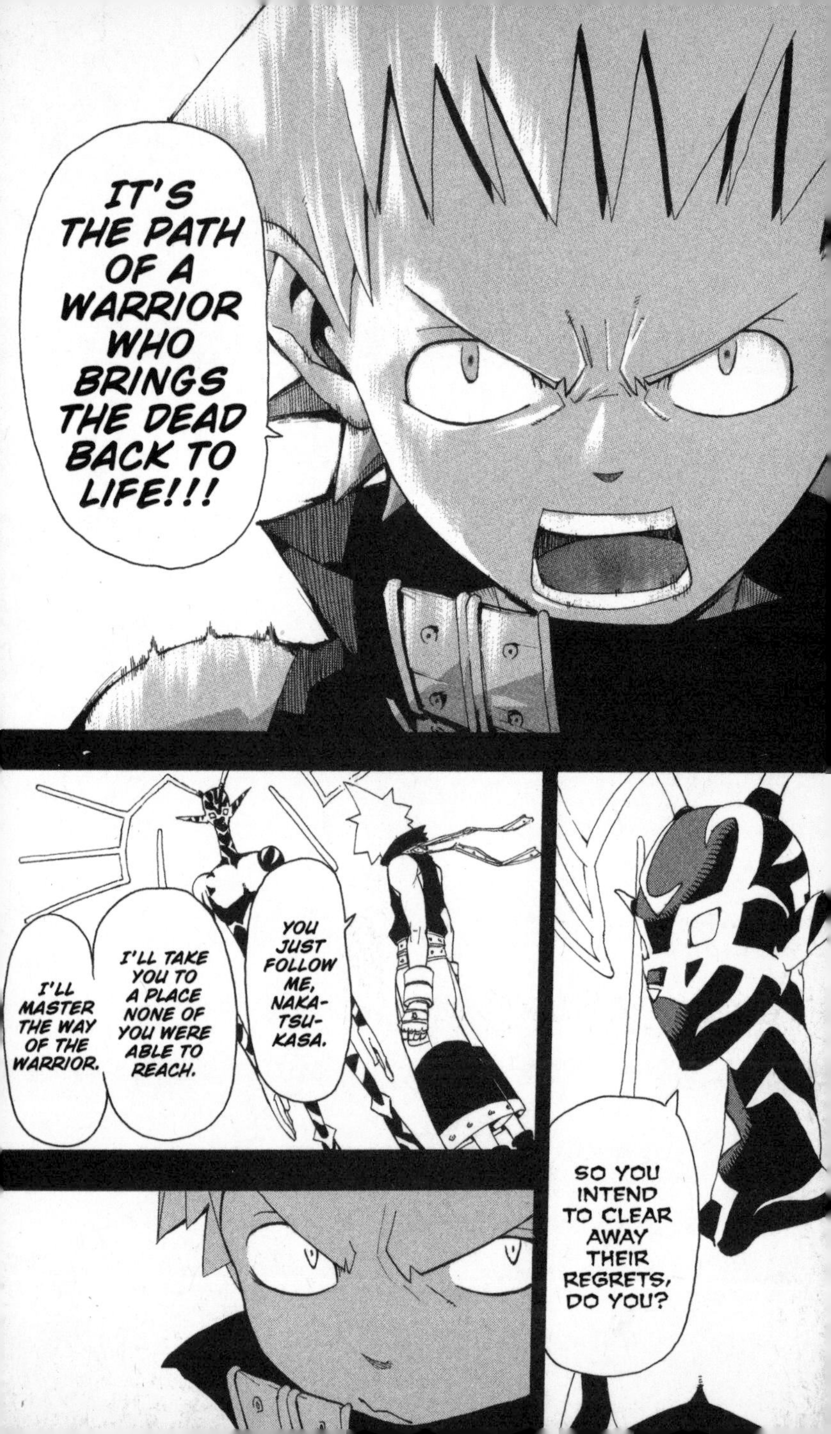
IT'S THE PATH OF A WARRIOR WHO BRINGS THE DEAD BACK TO LIFE!!!
SO YOU INTEND TO CLEAR AWAY THEIR REGRETS, DO YOU?
YOU JUST FOLLOW ME, NAKA-TSU-KASA.
I'LL TAKE YOU TO A PLACE NONE OF YOU WERE ABLE TO REACH.
I'LL MASTER THE WAY OF THE WARRIOR.

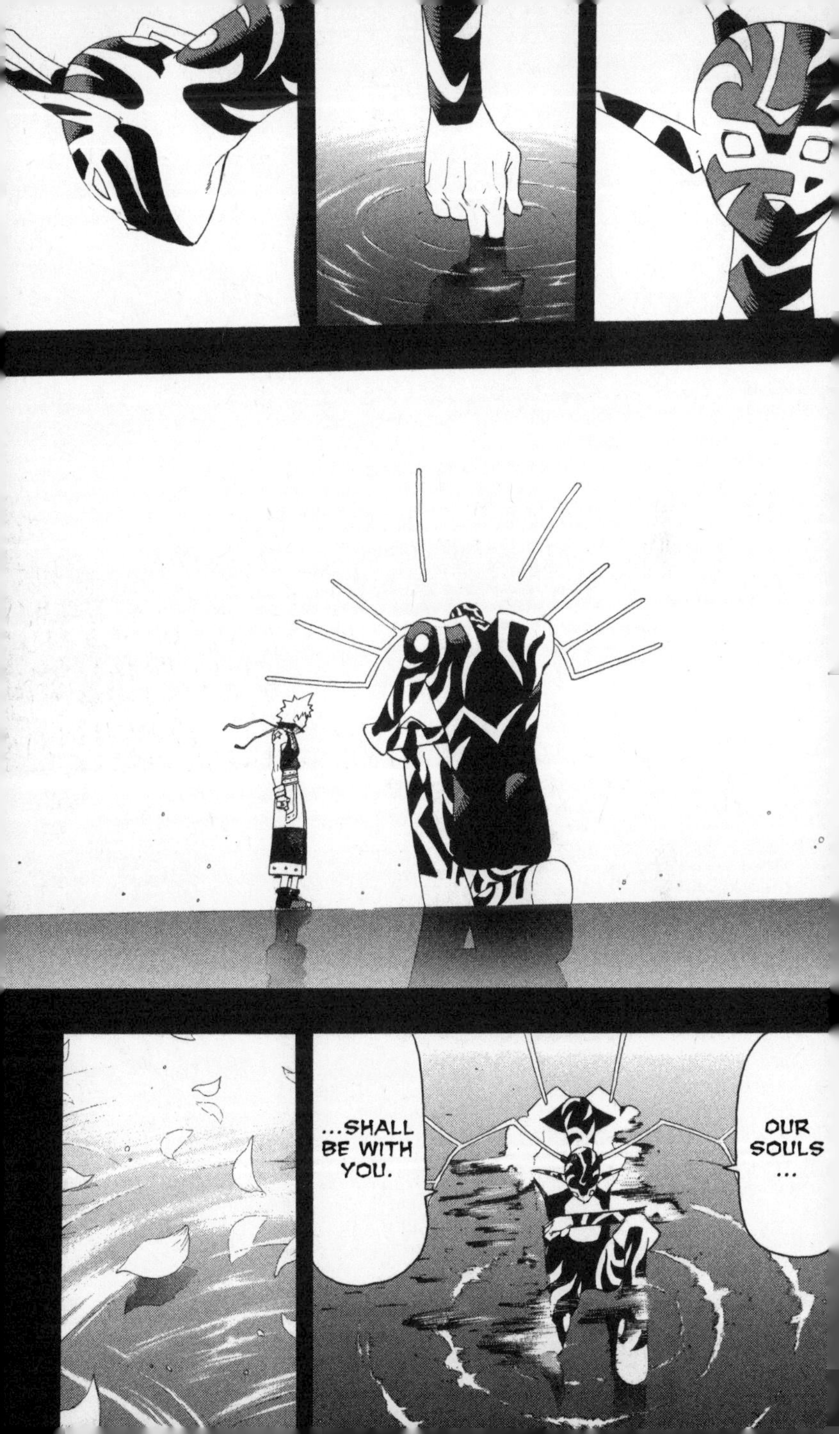
OUR SOULS ...
...SHALL BE WITH YOU.

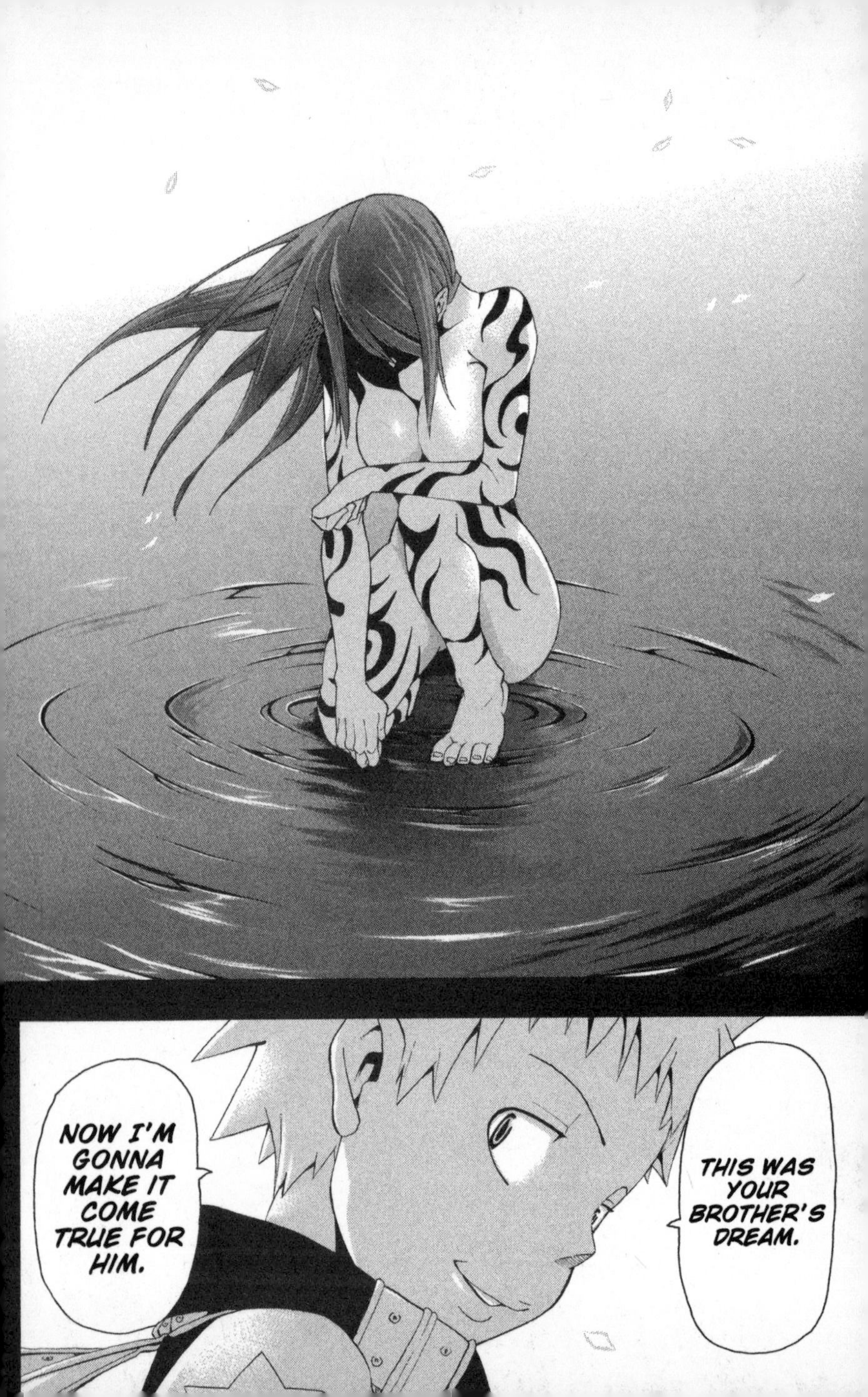
THIS WAS YOUR BROTHER'S DREAM.
NOW I'M GONNA MAKE IT COME TRUE FOR HIM.

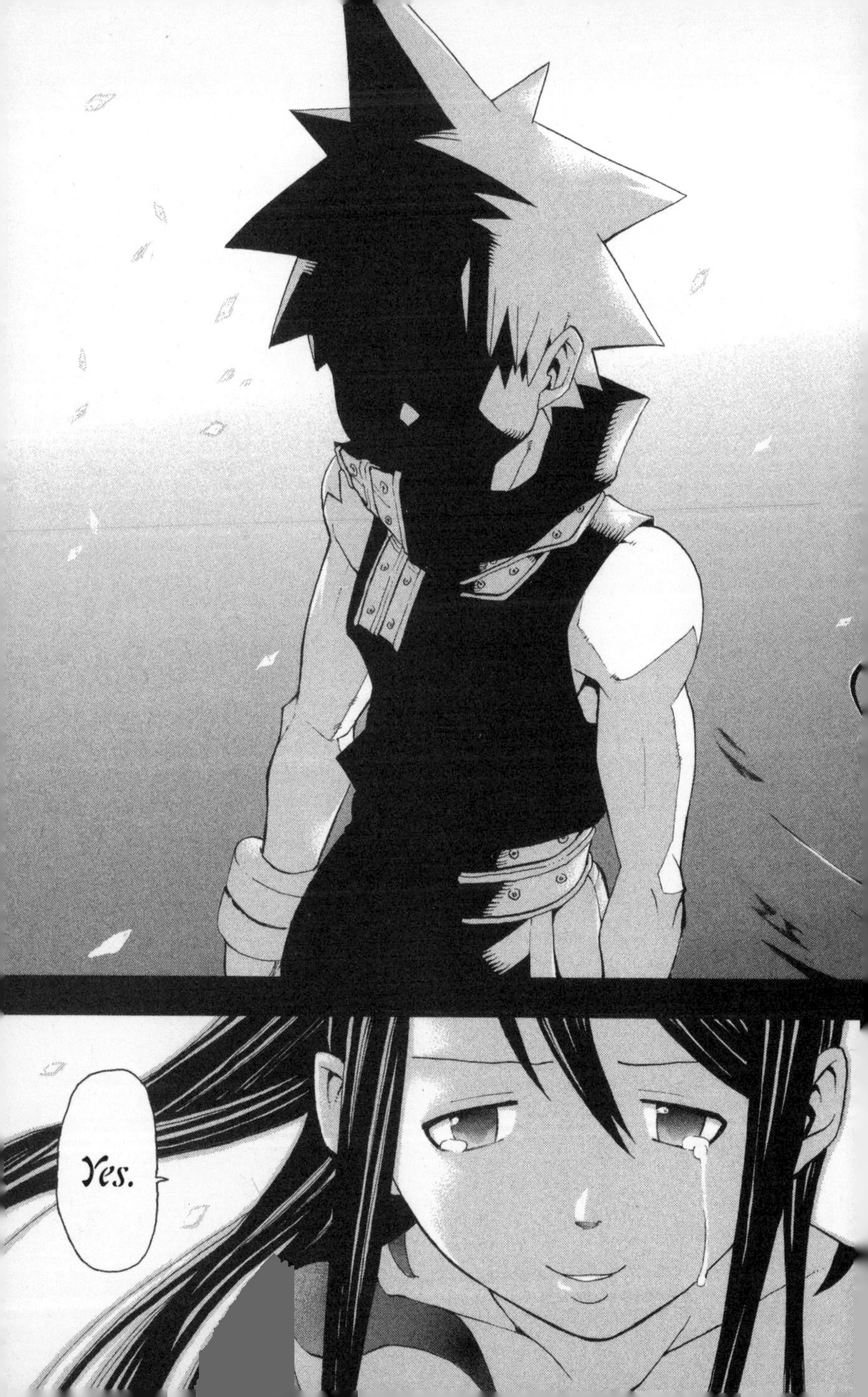
Yes.

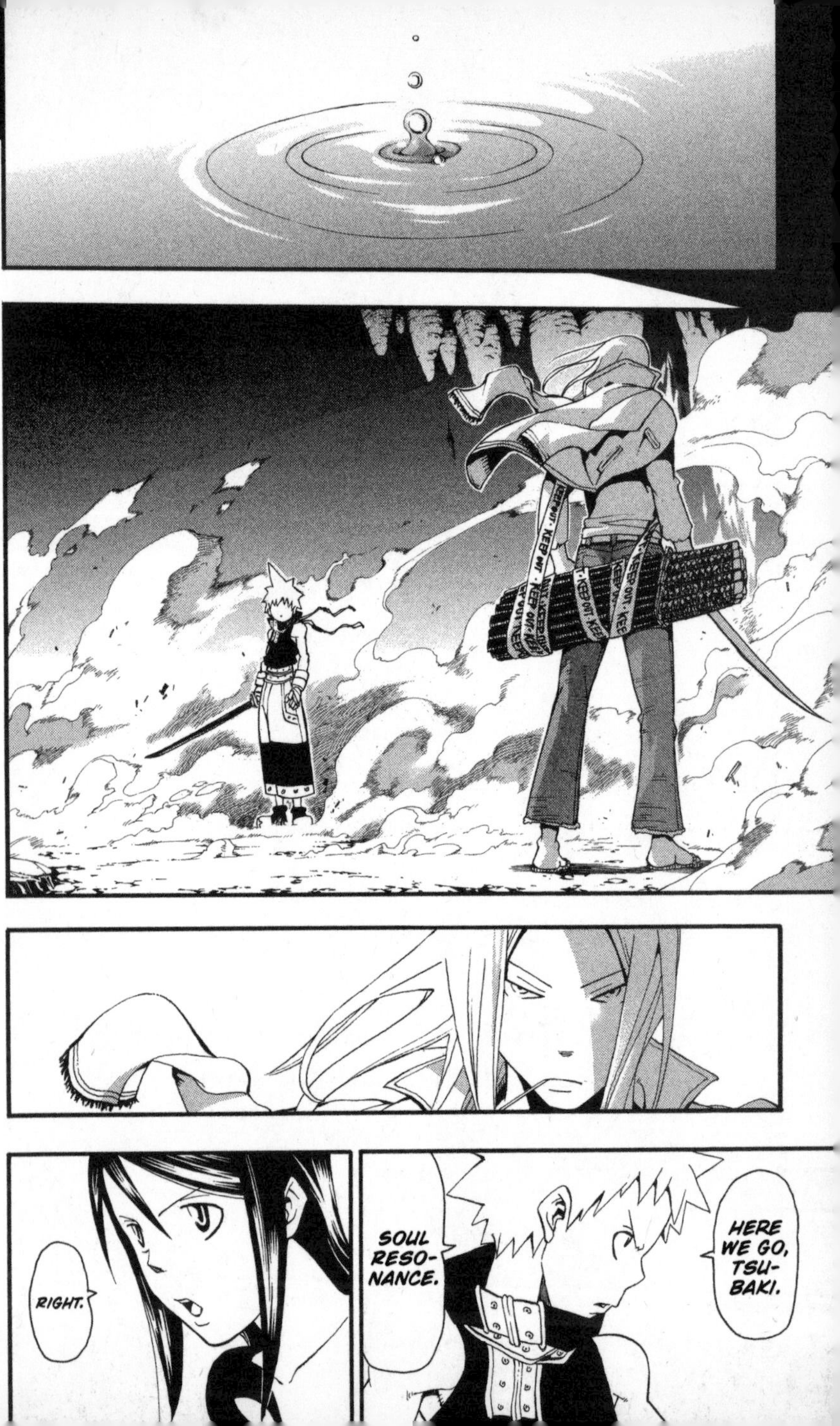
KEEP OUT
HERE WE GO, TSU-BAKI.
SOUL RESO-NANCE.
RIGHT.

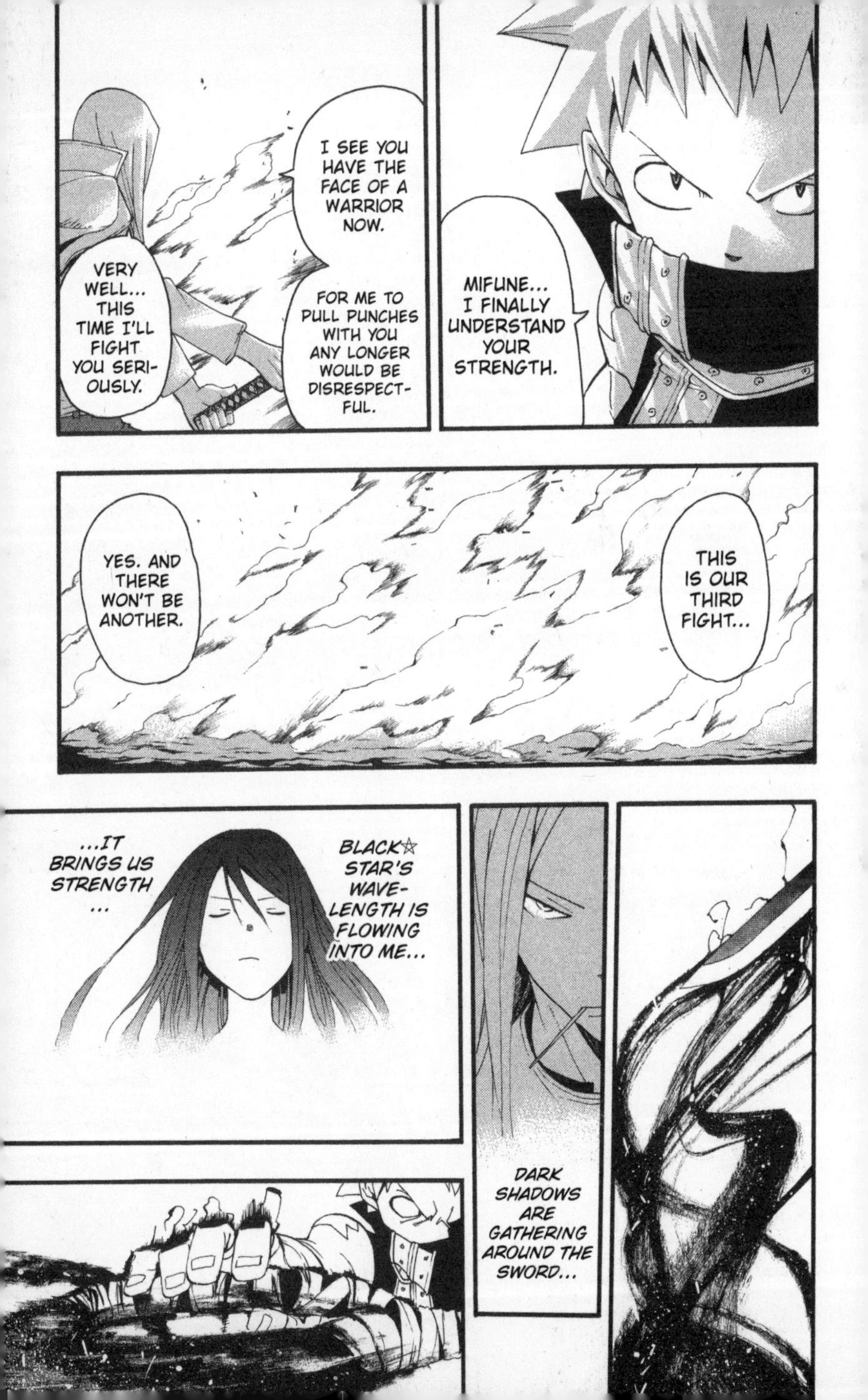
MIFUNE... I FINALLY UNDERSTAND YOUR STRENGTH.
I SEE YOU HAVE THE FACE OF A WARRIOR NOW.
FOR ME TO PULL PUNCHES WITH YOU ANY LONGER WOULD BE DISRESPECT-FUL.
VERY WELL... THIS TIME I'LL FIGHT YOU SERI-OUSLY.
THIS IS OUR THIRD FIGHT...
YES. AND THERE WON'T BE ANOTHER.
DARK SHADOWS ARE GATHERING AROUND THE SWORD...
BLACK☆STAR'S WAVE-LENGTH IS FLOWING INTO ME...
...IT BRINGS US STRENGTH...

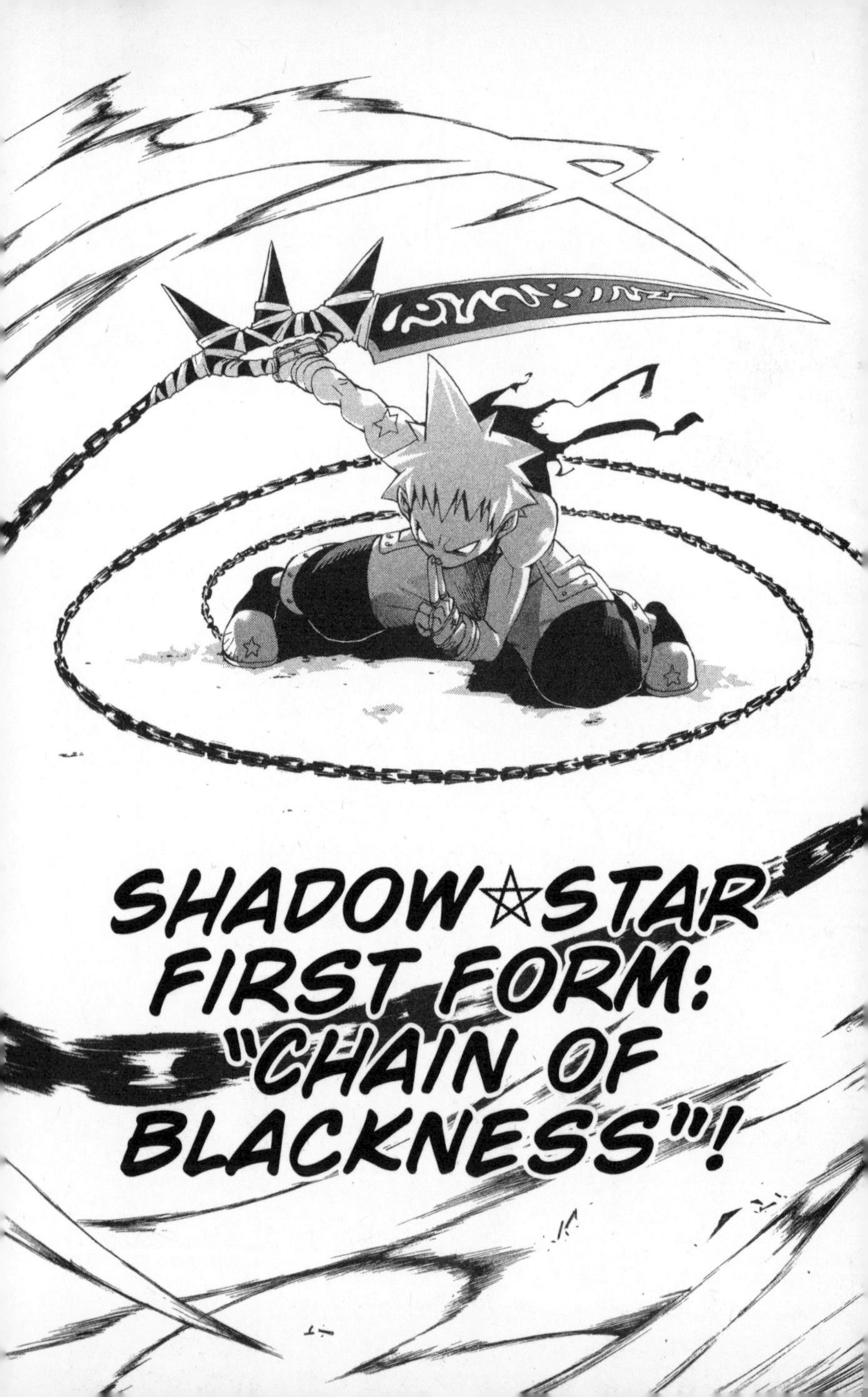
SHADOW☆STAR FIRST FORM: "CHAIN OF BLACKNESS"!

RAAAH!

OSAMURAI

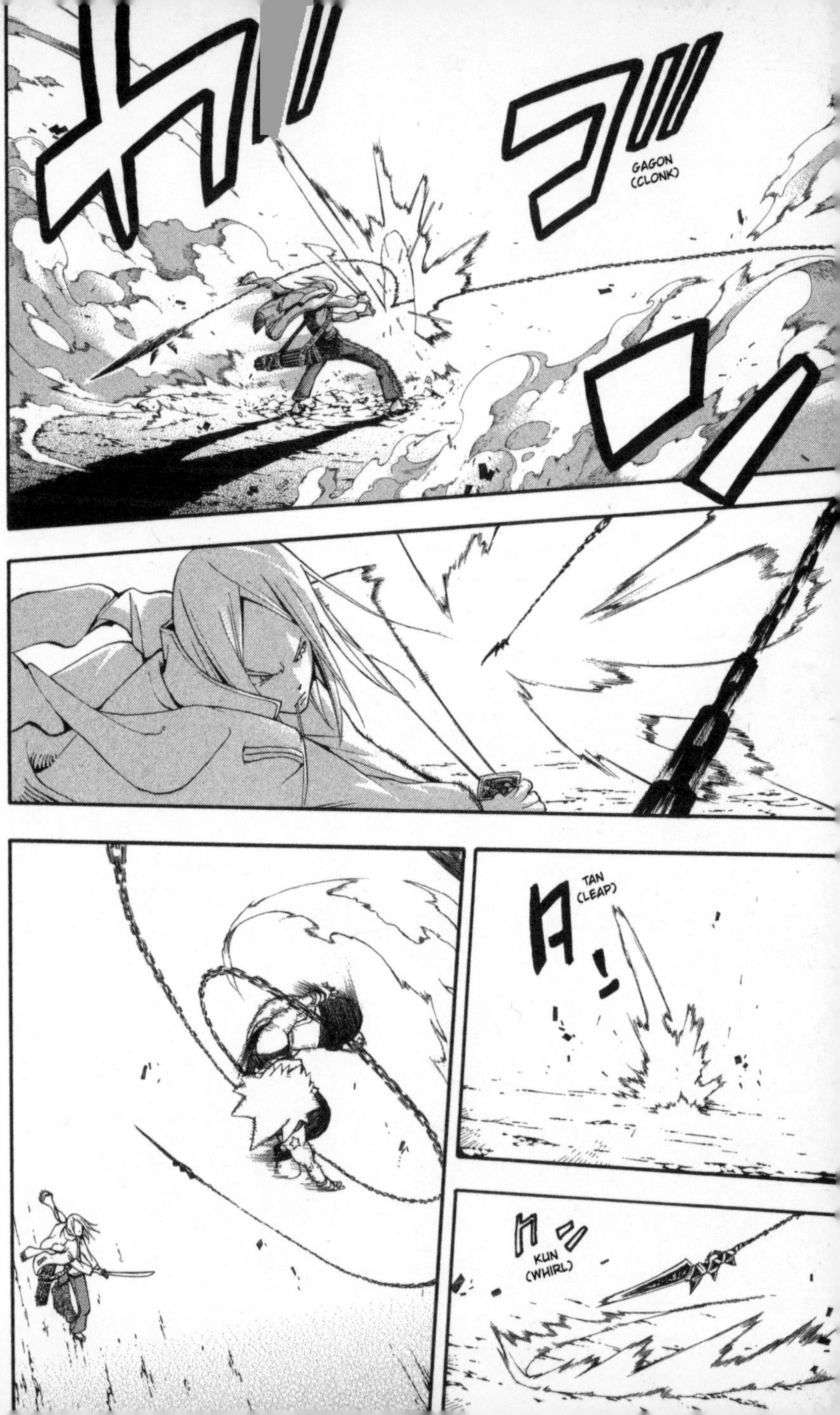
GAGON
(CLONK)
TAN
(LEAP)
KUN
(WHIRL)

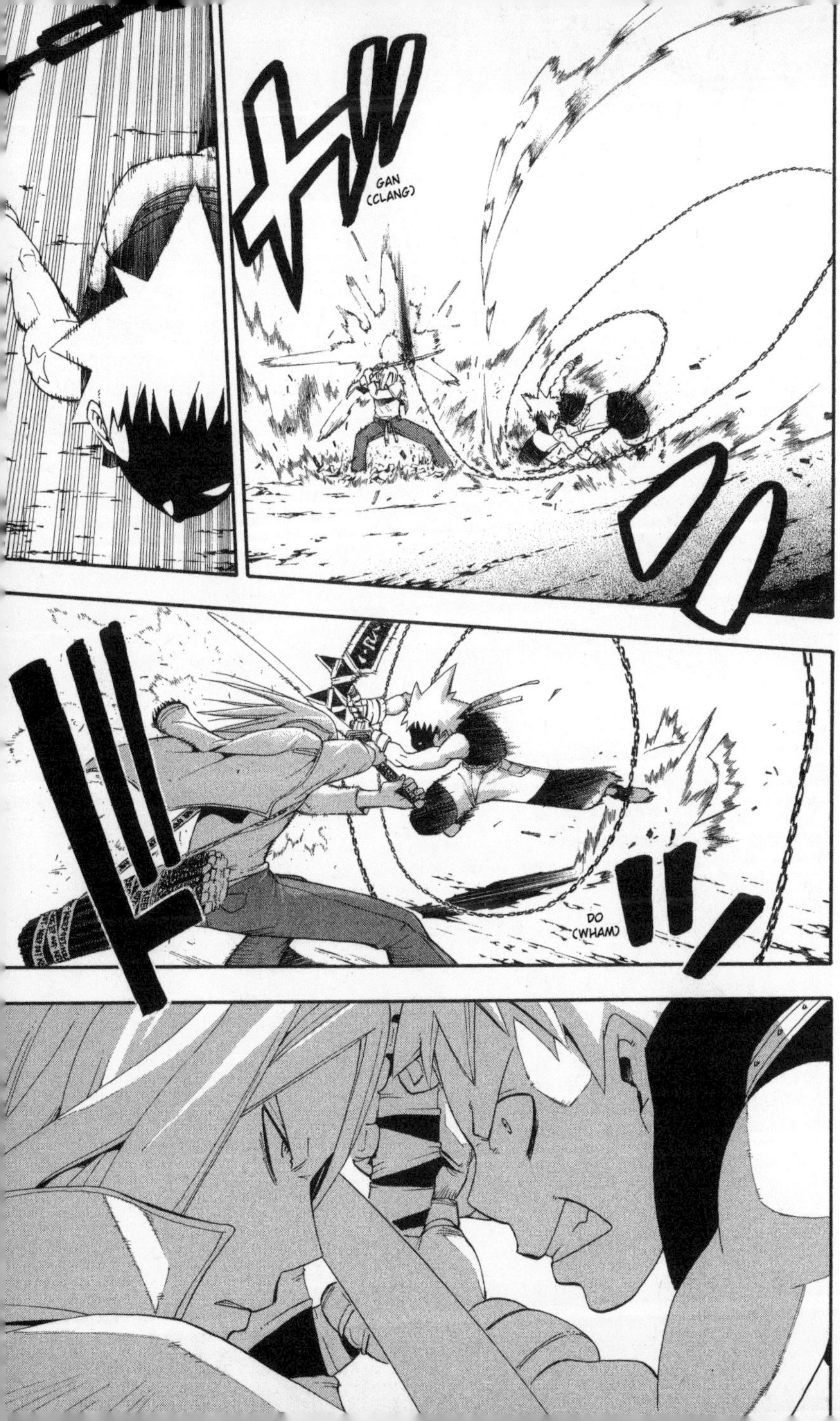
GAN
(CLANG)
DO
(WHAM)

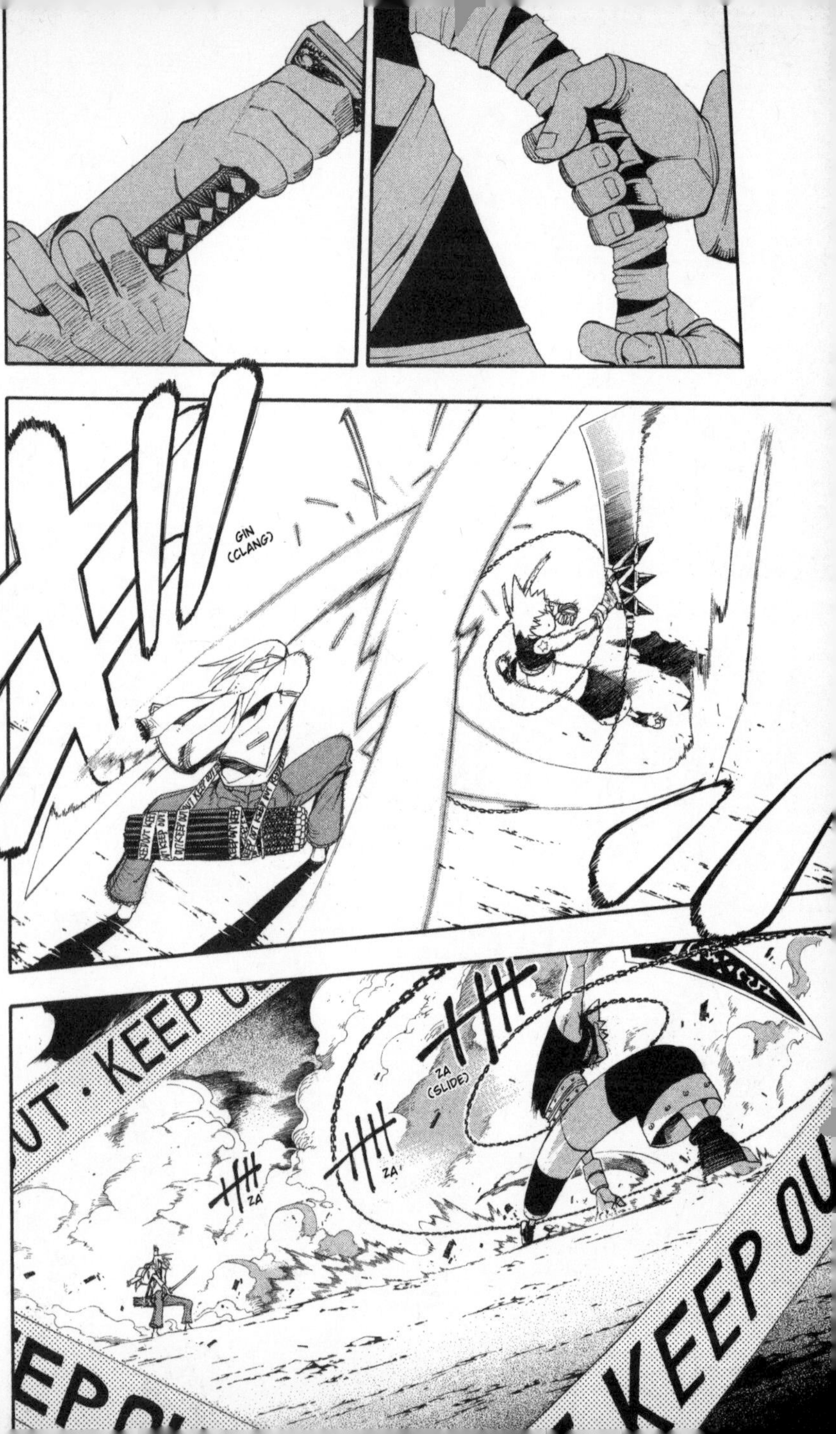
GIN
(CLANG)
ZA
(SLIDE)
ZA
ZA
UT · KEEP OU
KEEP OU
EEP O

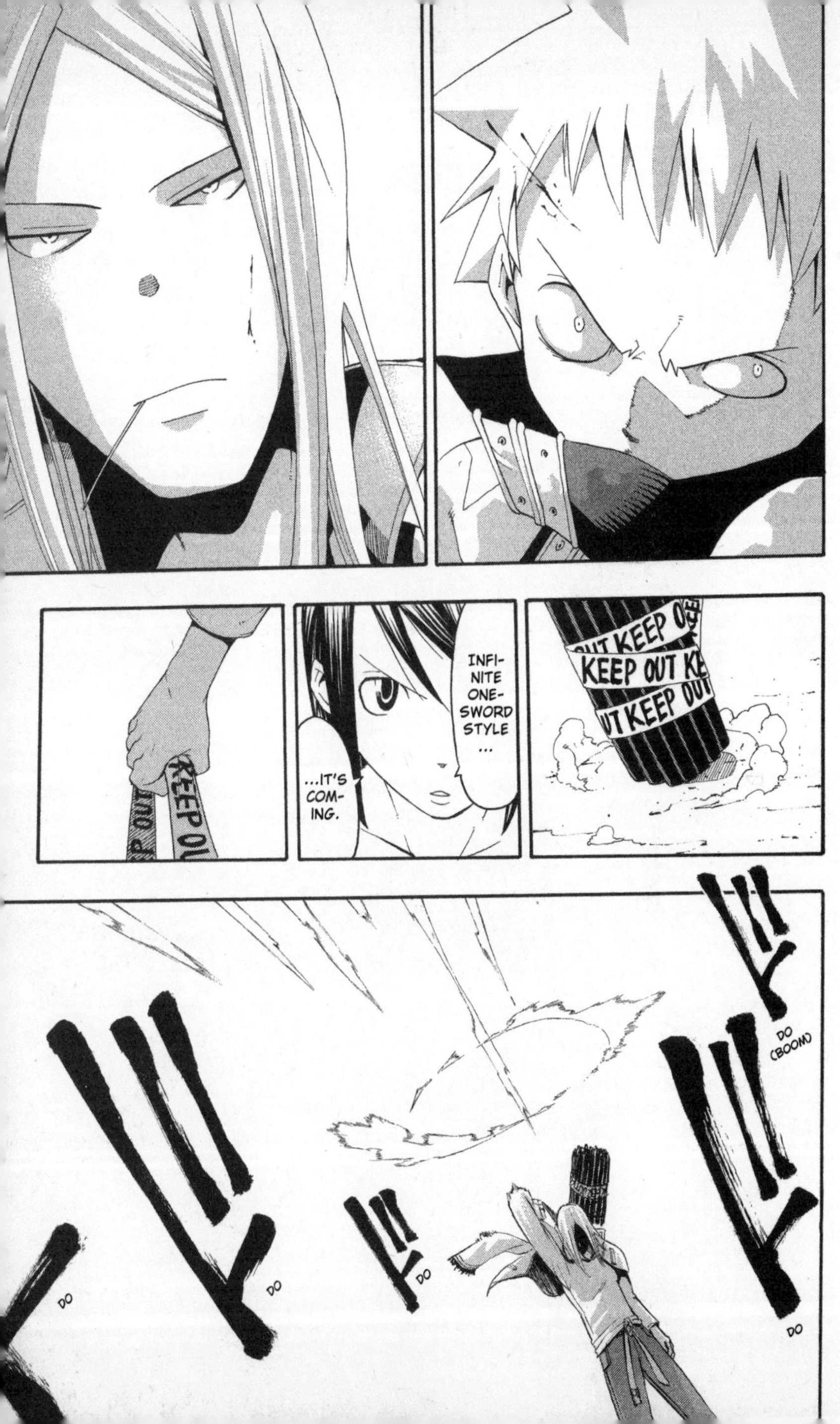
KEEP OUT
INFINITE ONE-SWORD STYLE ...
...IT'S COMING.
DO (BOOM)
DO
DO
DO
DO

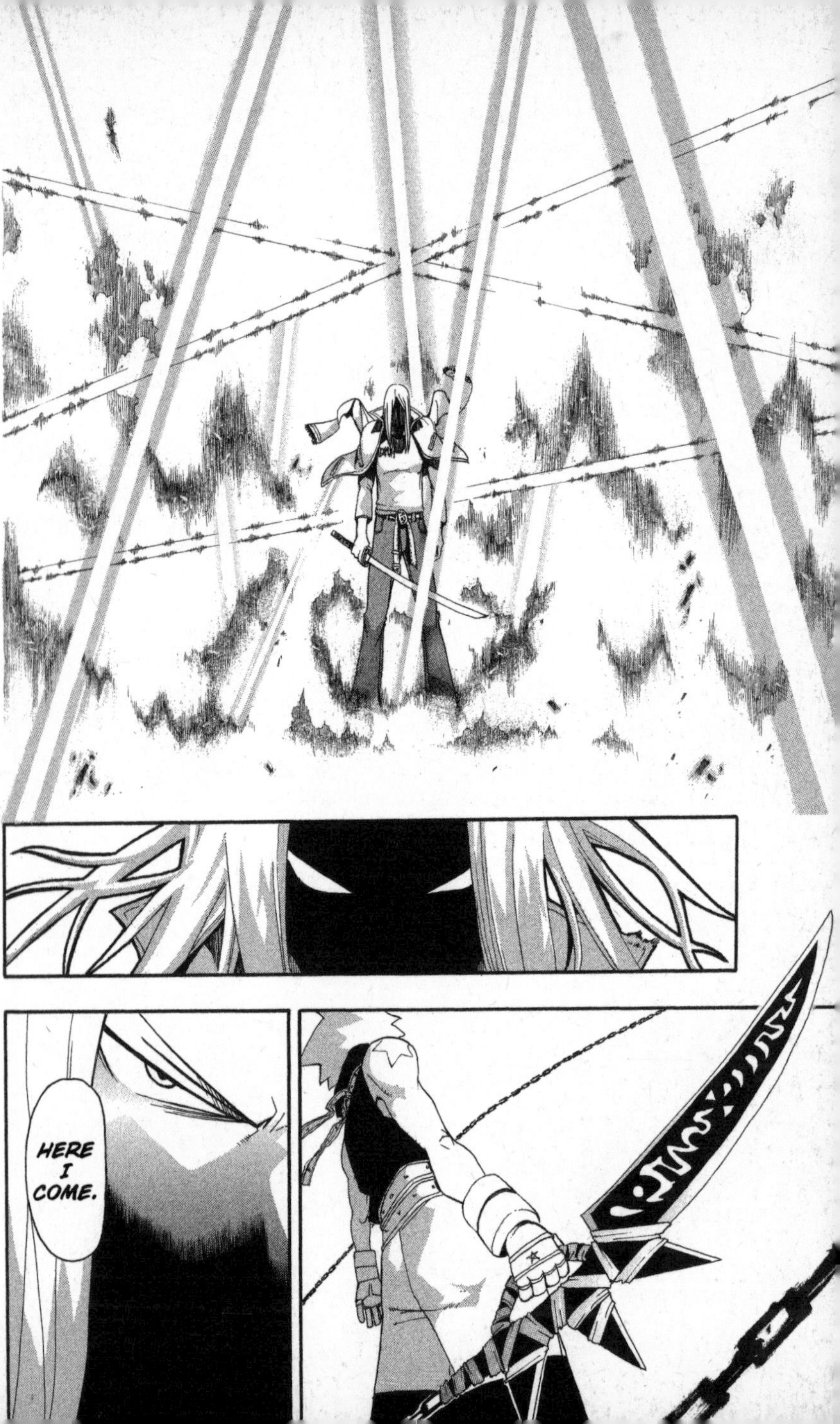
HERE I COME.

SOUL EATER

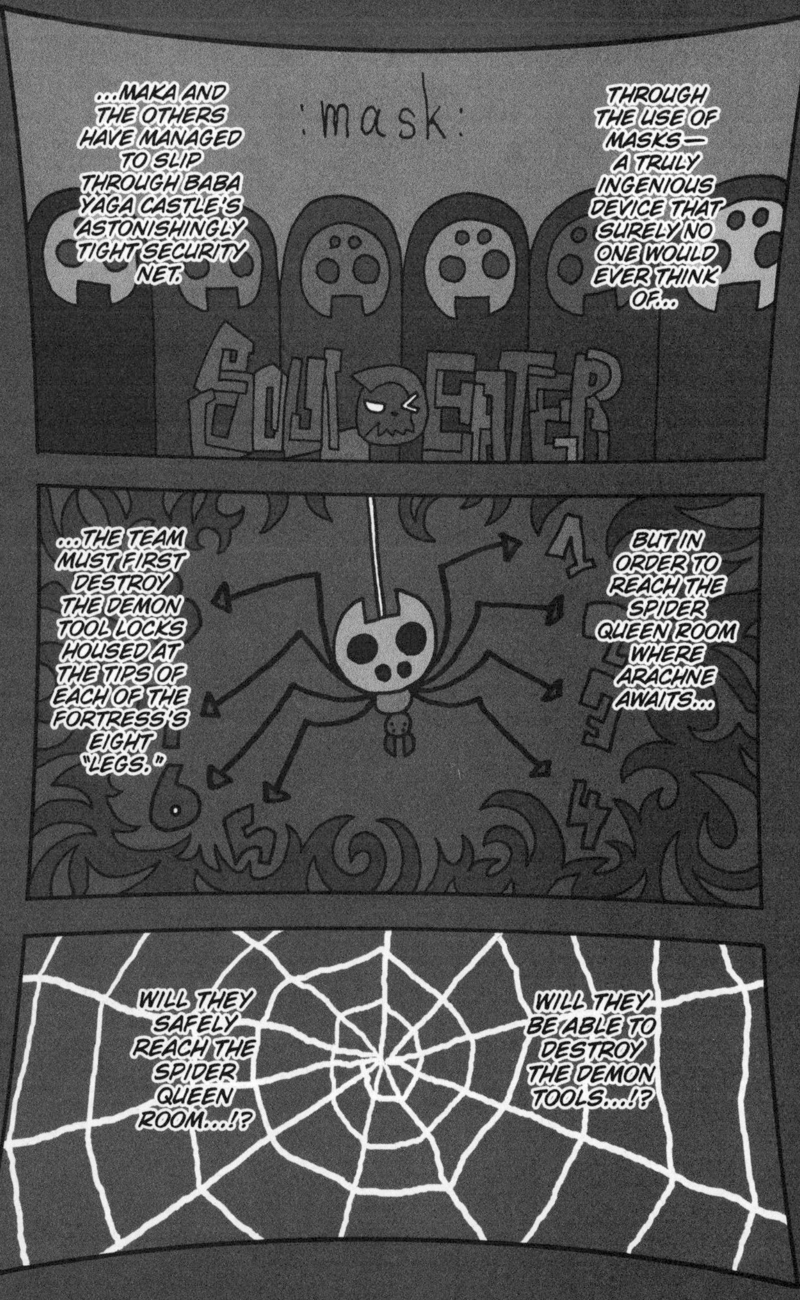
THROUGH THE USE OF MASKS— A TRULY INGENIOUS DEVICE THAT SURELY NO ONE WOULD EVER THINK OF...
:mask:
...MAKA AND THE OTHERS HAVE MANAGED TO SLIP THROUGH BABA YAGA CASTLE'S ASTONISHINGLY TIGHT SECURITY NET.
SOUL EATER
BUT IN ORDER TO REACH THE SPIDER QUEEN ROOM WHERE ARACHNE AWAITS...
...THE TEAM MUST FIRST DESTROY THE DEMON TOOL LOCKS HOUSED AT THE TIPS OF EACH OF THE FORTRESS'S EIGHT "LEGS."
WILL THEY BE ABLE TO DESTROY THE DEMON TOOLS...!?
WILL THEY SAFELY REACH THE SPIDER QUEEN ROOM...!?

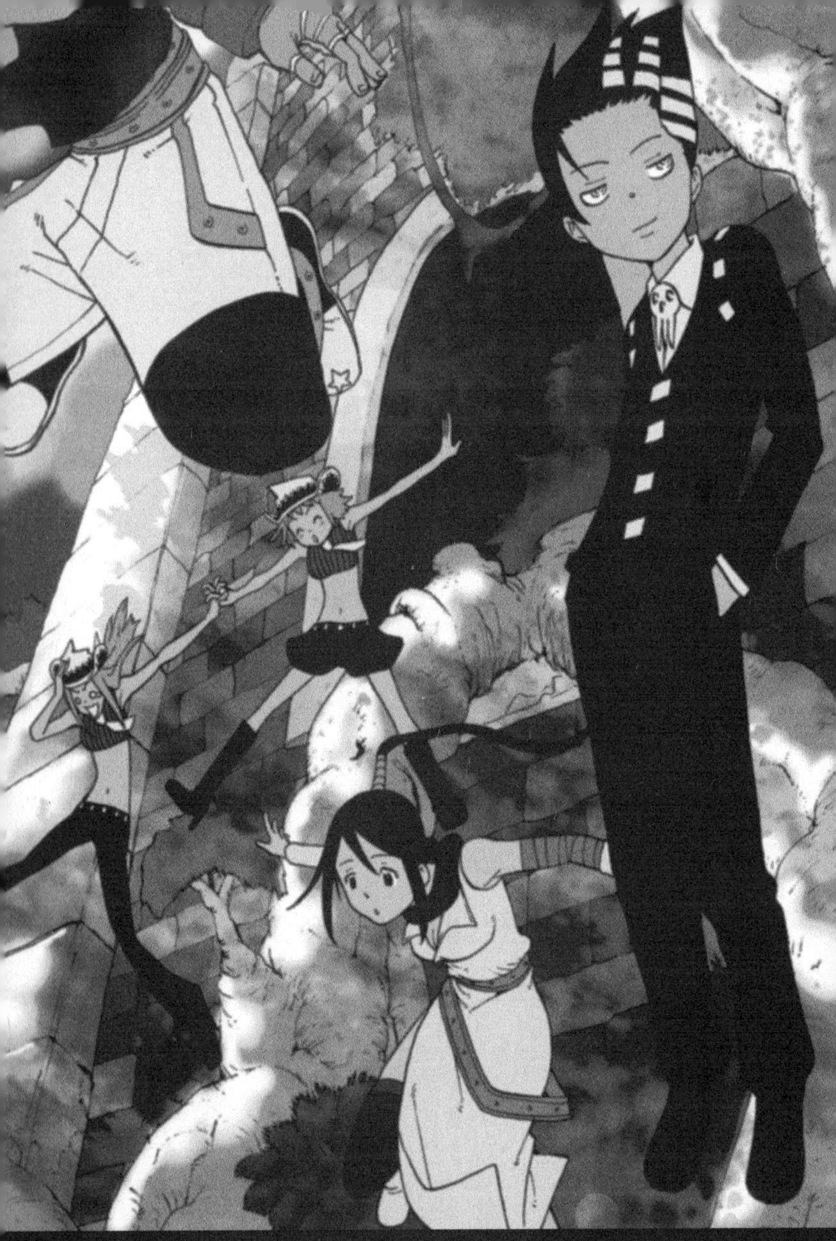

YAGA CASTLE (PART 5)

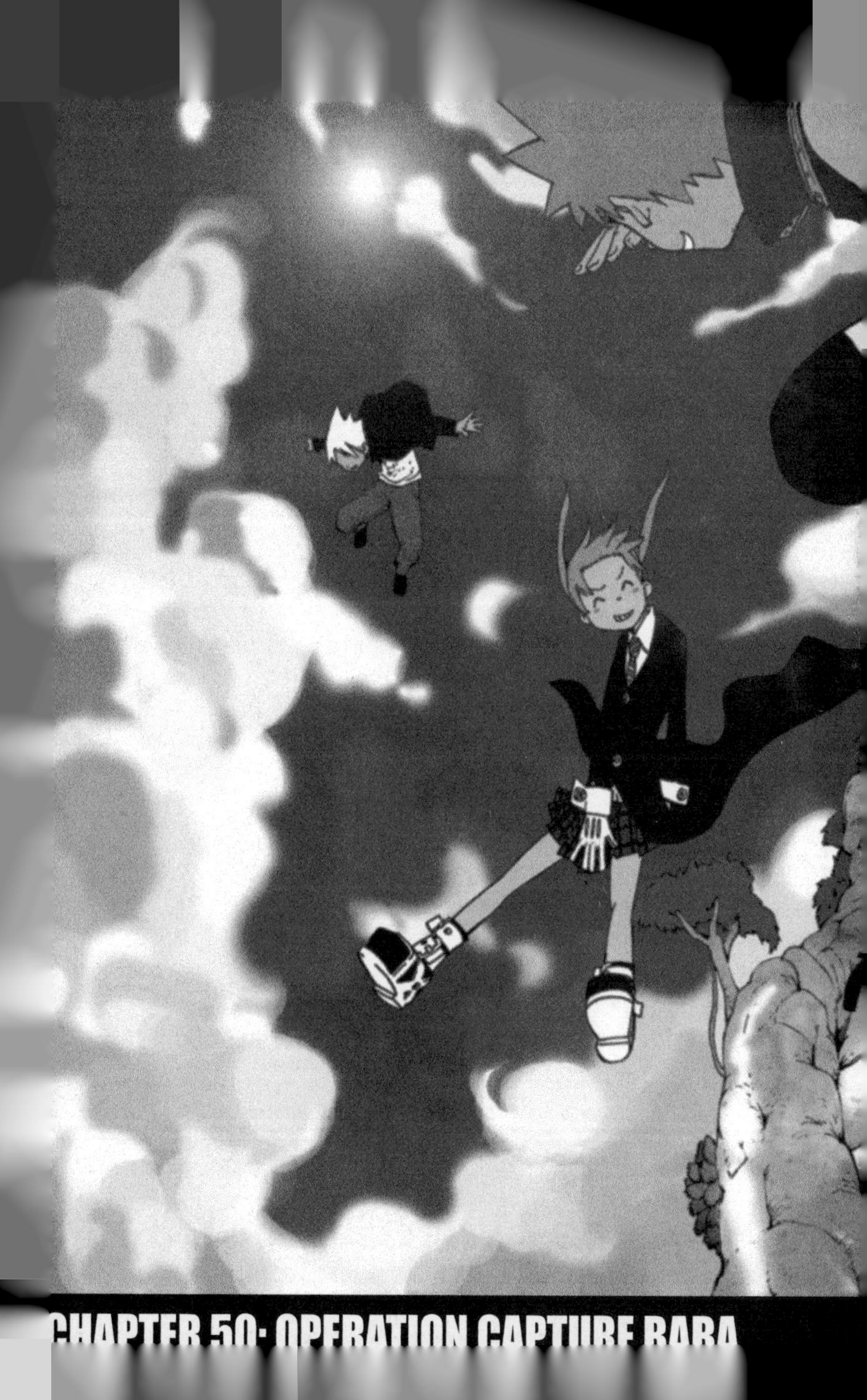

CHAPTER 50: OPERATION CAPTURE BABA

SOUL EATER

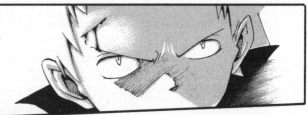

HERE I
COME.

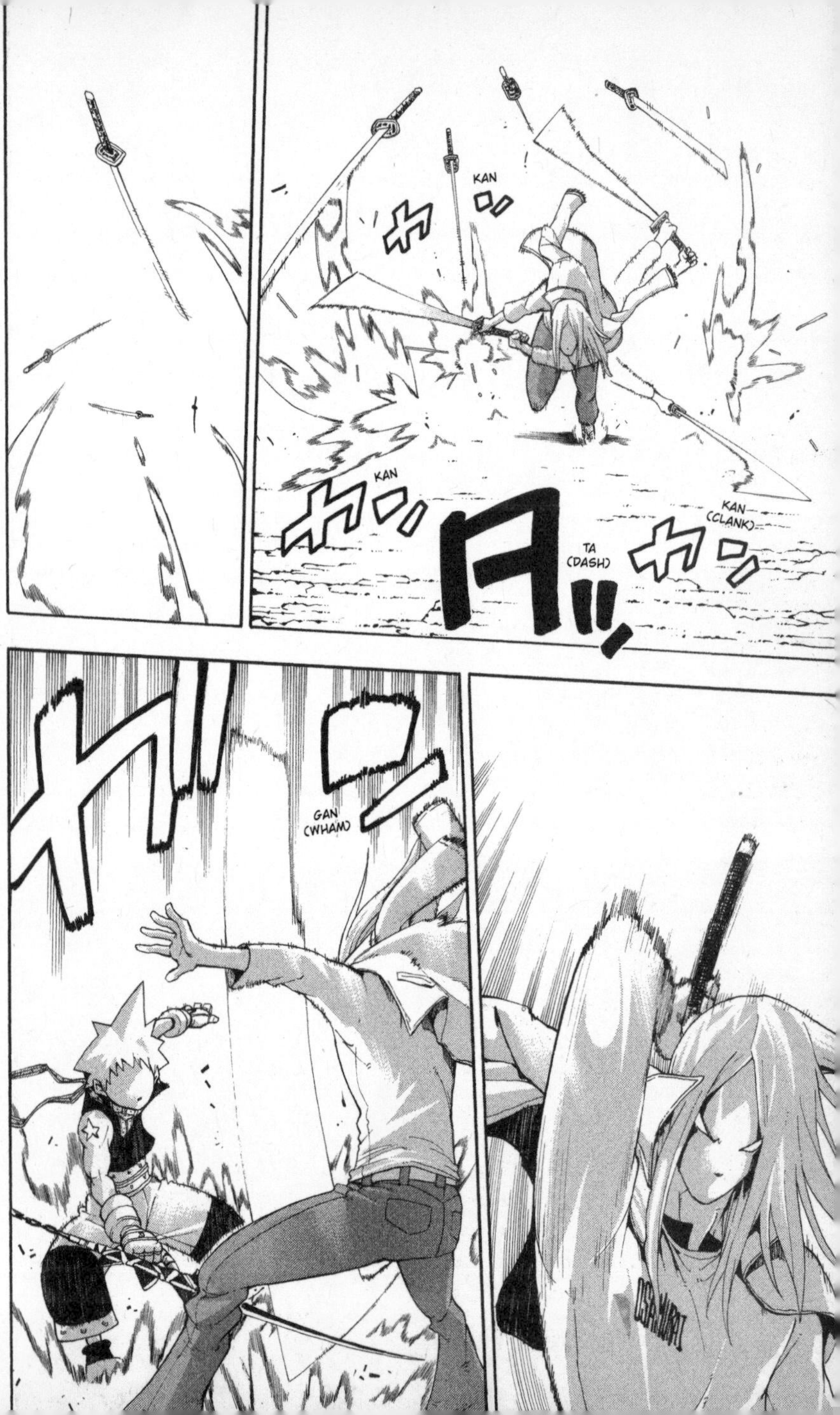
KAN
KAN (CLANK)
TA (DASH)
KAN
GAN (WHAM)

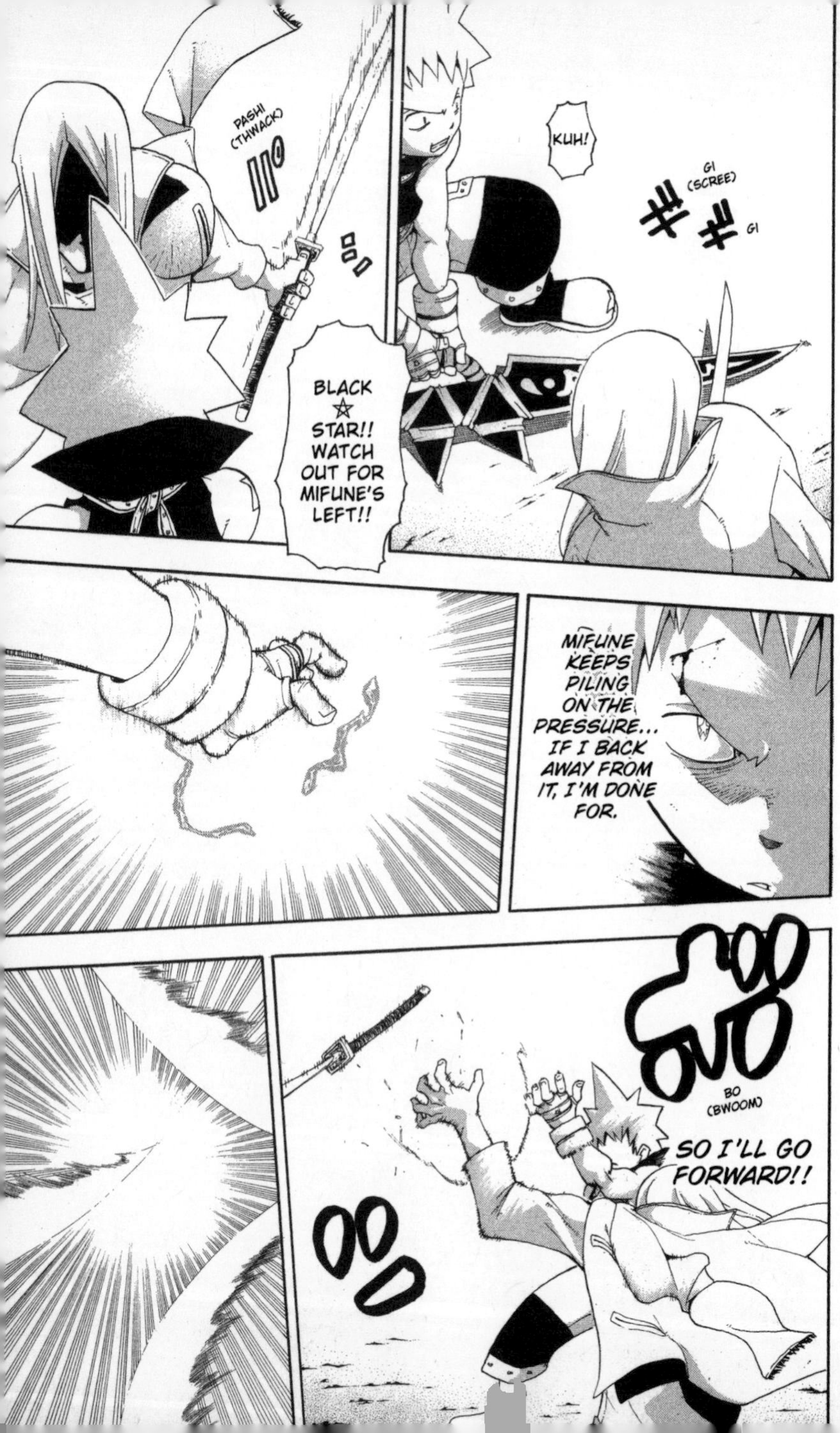
KUH!
GI (SCREE)
GI
PASHI (THWACK)
BLACK☆STAR!! WATCH OUT FOR MIFUNE'S LEFT!!
MIFUNE KEEPS PILING ON THE PRESSURE... IF I BACK AWAY FROM IT, I'M DONE FOR.
BO (BWOOM)
SO I'LL GO FORWARD!!

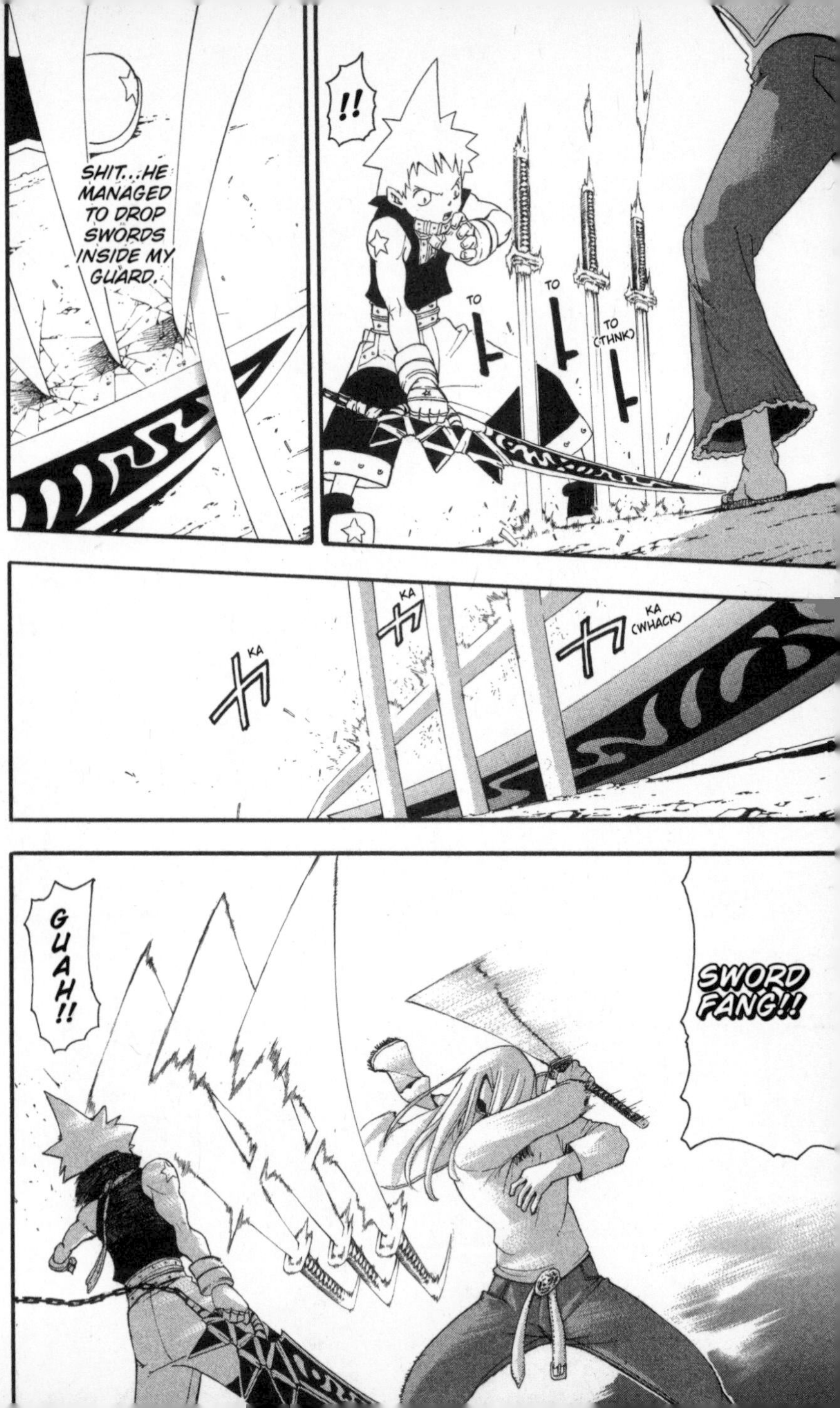
!!
TO
TO
TO (THNK)
SHIT...HE MANAGED TO DROP SWORDS INSIDE MY GUARD.
KA (WHACK)
KA
KA
SWORD FANG!!
GUAH!!

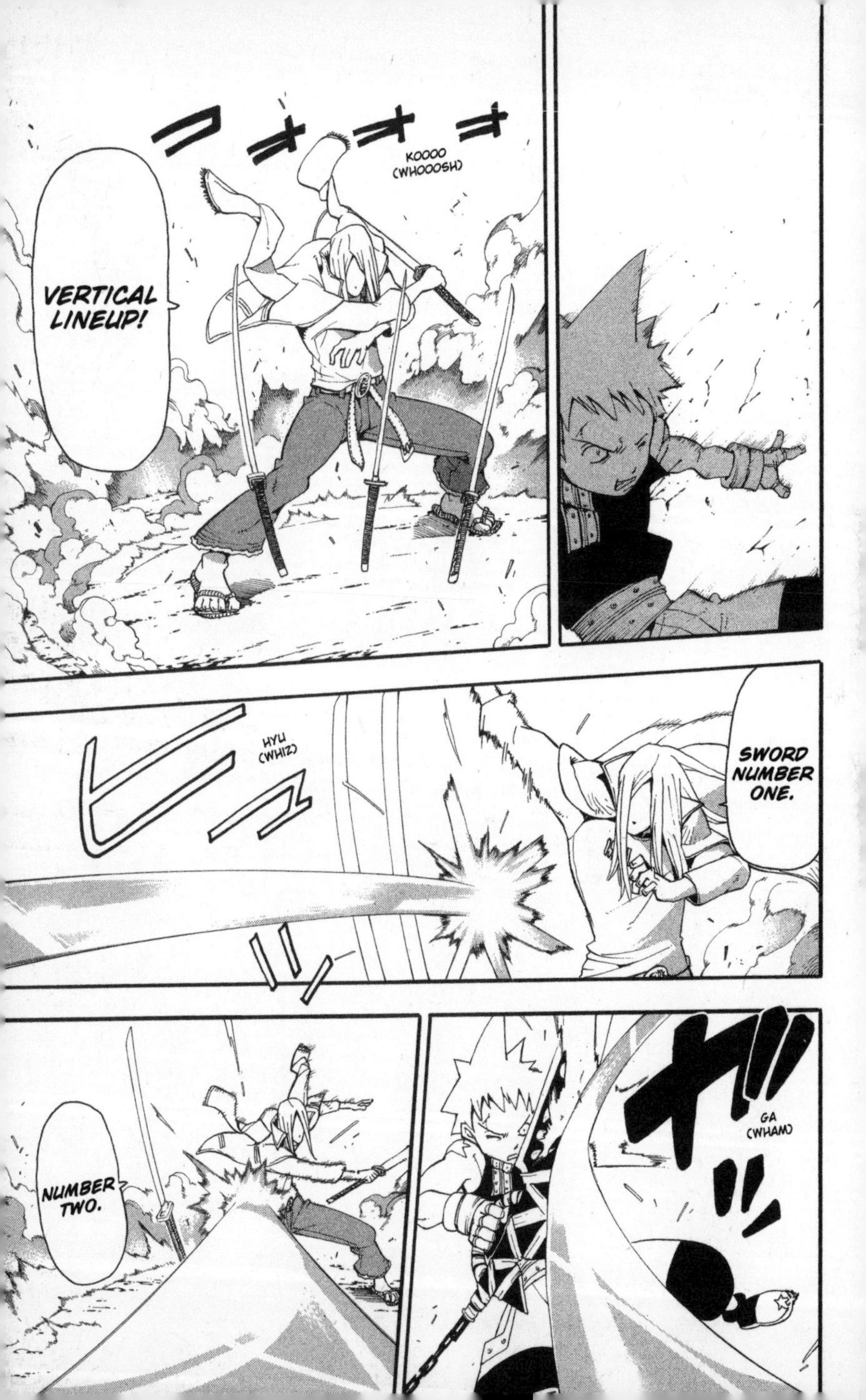
KOOOO (WHOOOSH)
VERTICAL LINEUP!
SWORD NUMBER ONE.
HYU (WHIZ)
GA (WHAM)
NUMBER TWO.

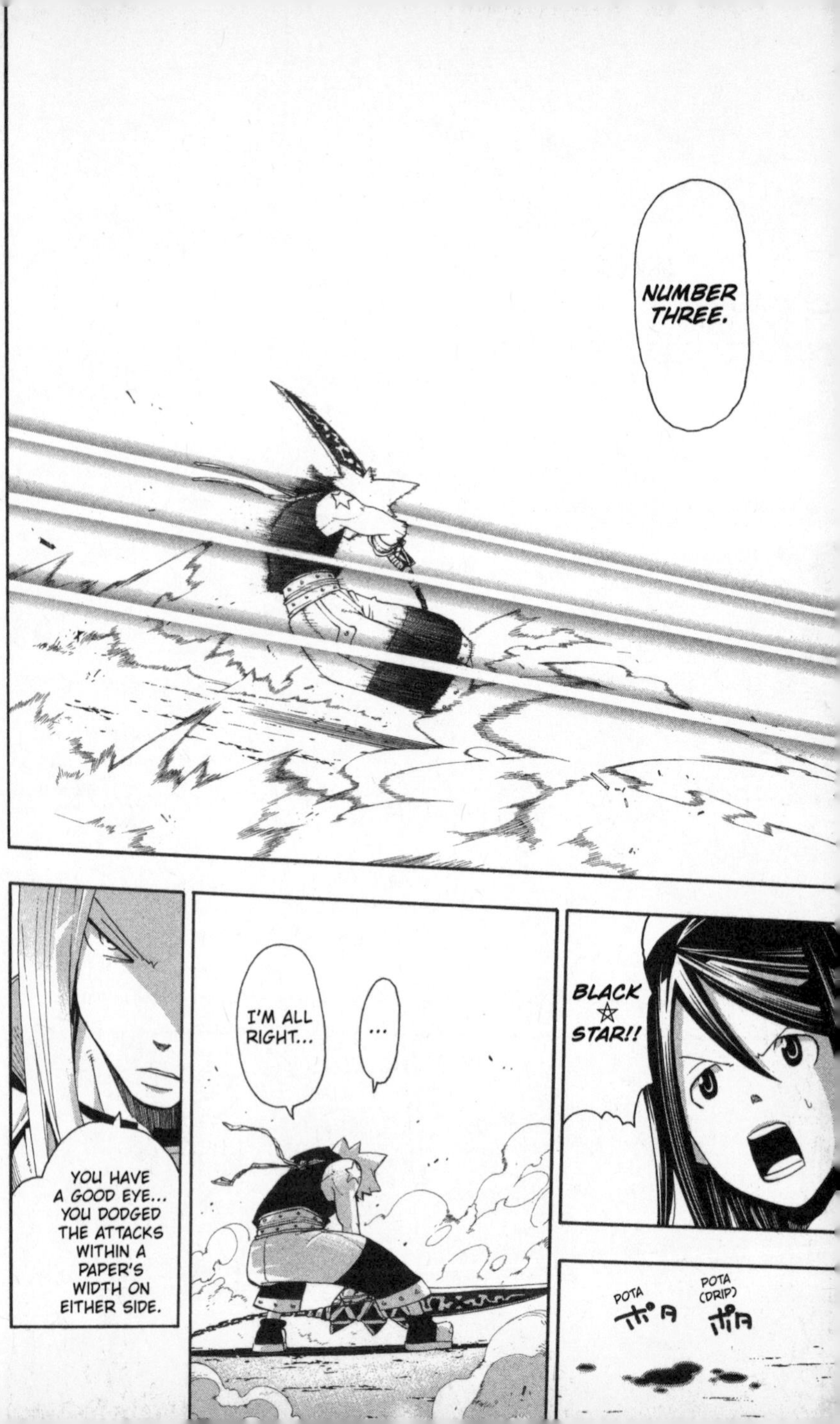

NUMBER THREE.
BLACK ☆ STAR!!
POTA
POTA (DRIP)
...
I'M ALL RIGHT...
YOU HAVE A GOOD EYE... YOU DODGED THE ATTACKS WITHIN A PAPER'S WIDTH ON EITHER SIDE.

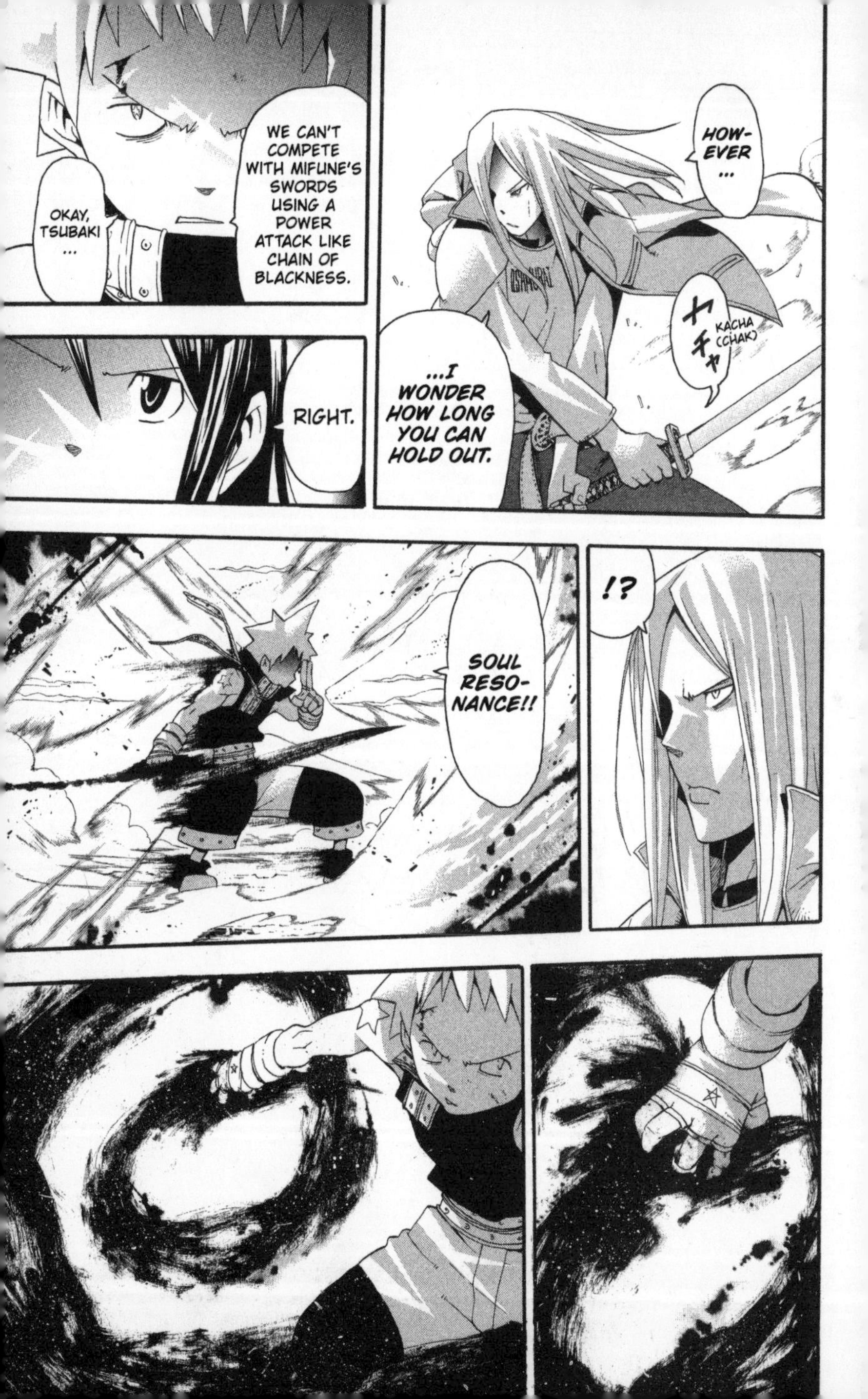
HOW-EVER...
カチャ
KACHA (CHAK)
...I WONDER HOW LONG YOU CAN HOLD OUT.
WE CAN'T COMPETE WITH MIFUNE'S SWORDS USING A POWER ATTACK LIKE CHAIN OF BLACKNESS.
OKAY, TSUBAKI...
RIGHT.
!?
SOUL RESO-NANCE!!

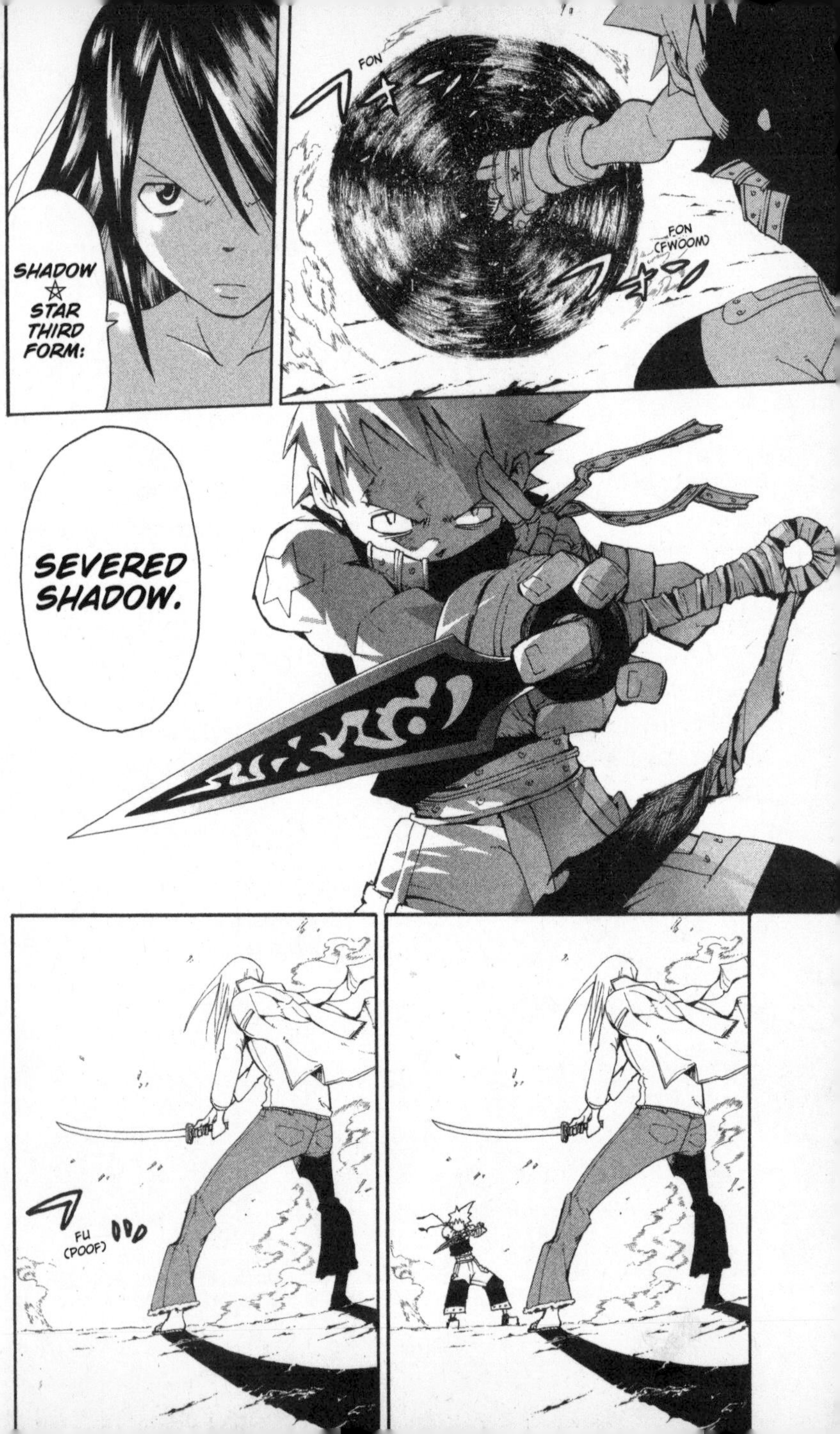
FON
FON
(FWOOM)
SHADOW ☆ STAR THIRD FORM:
SEVERED SHADOW.
FU
(POOF)

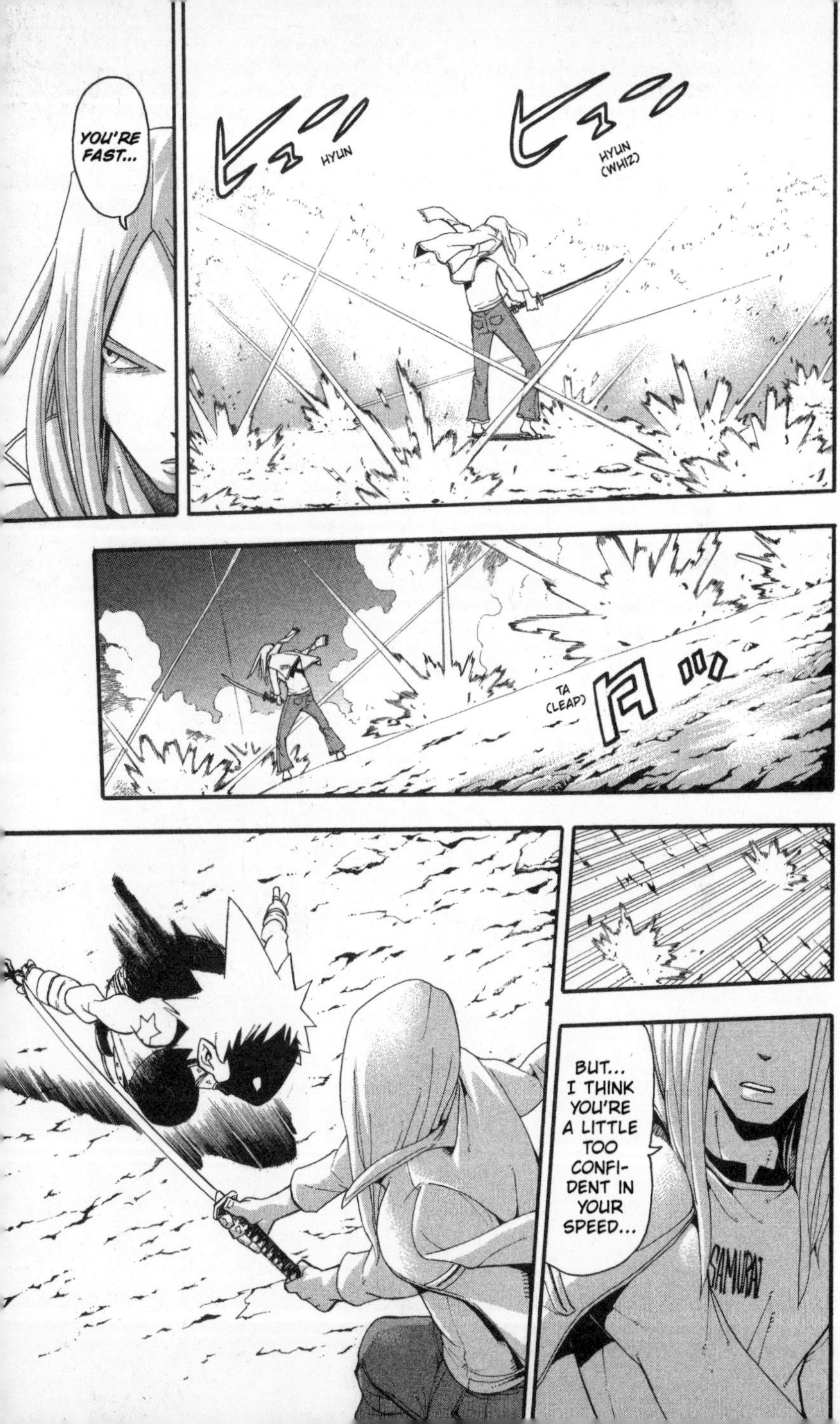
HYUN (WHIZ)
HYUN
YOU'RE FAST...
TA (LEAP)
BUT... I THINK YOU'RE A LITTLE TOO CONFIDENT IN YOUR SPEED...
SAMURAI

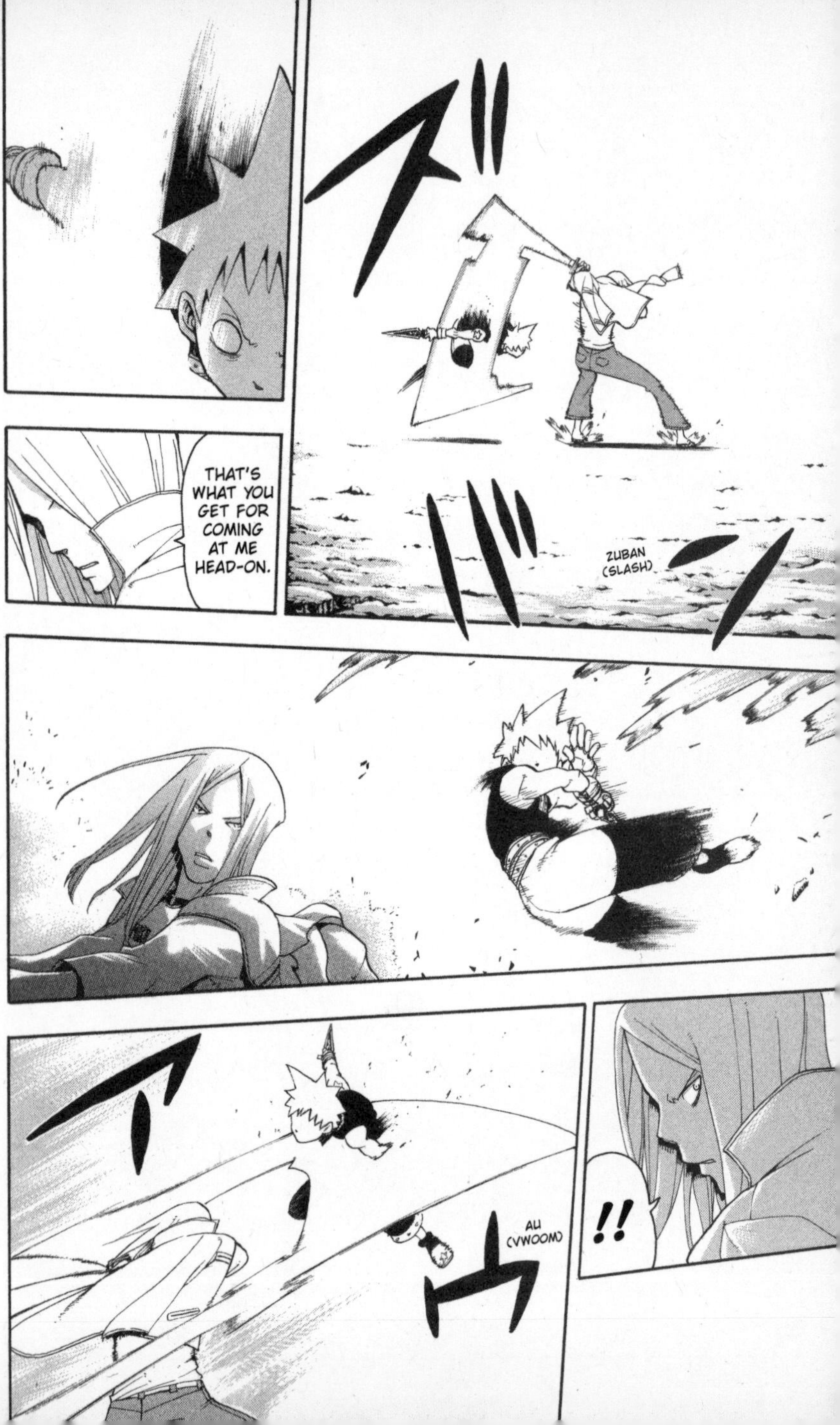
ZUBAN (SLASH)
THAT'S WHAT YOU GET FOR COMING AT ME HEAD-ON.
!!
AU (VWOOM)

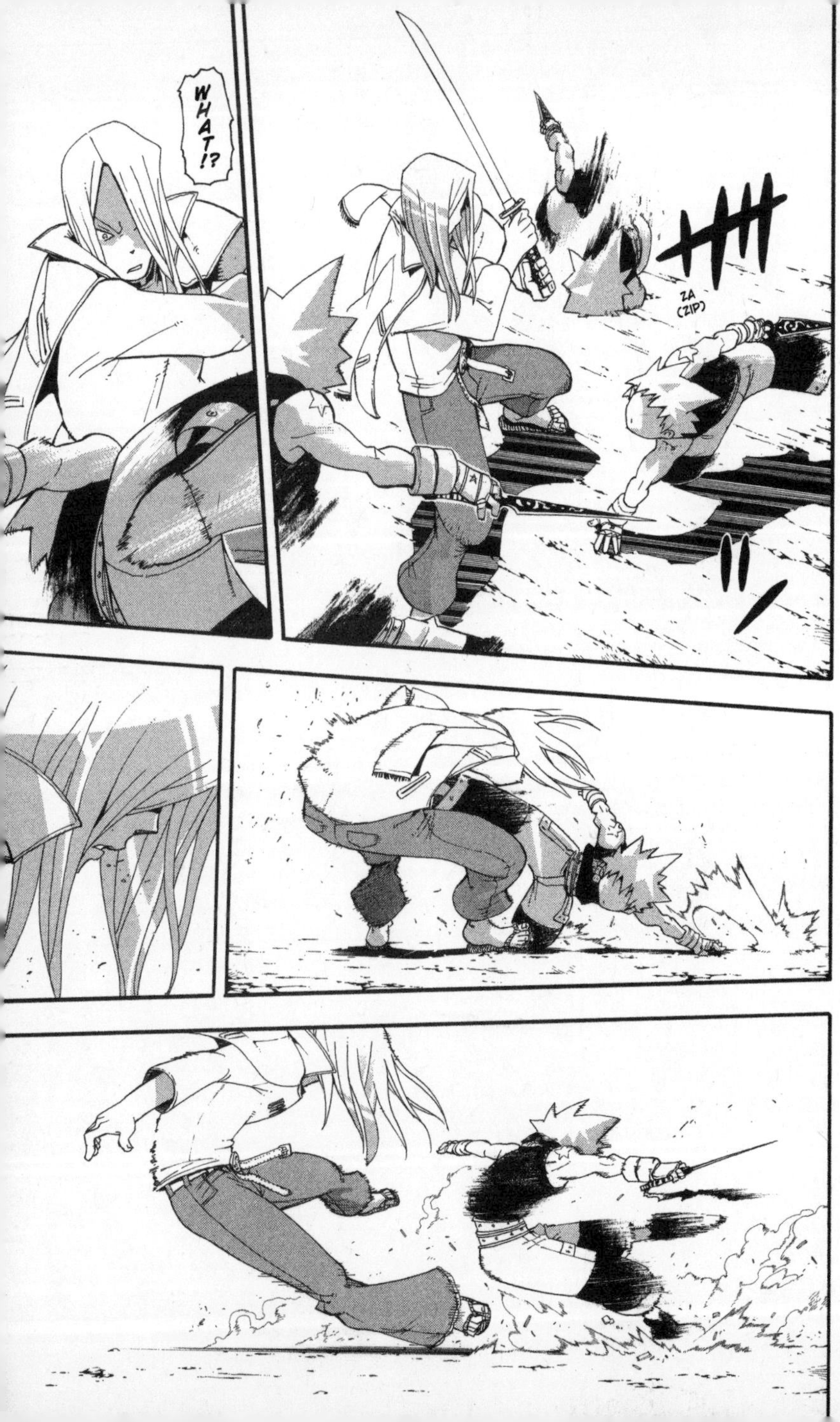
ZA
(ZIP)
WHAT!?

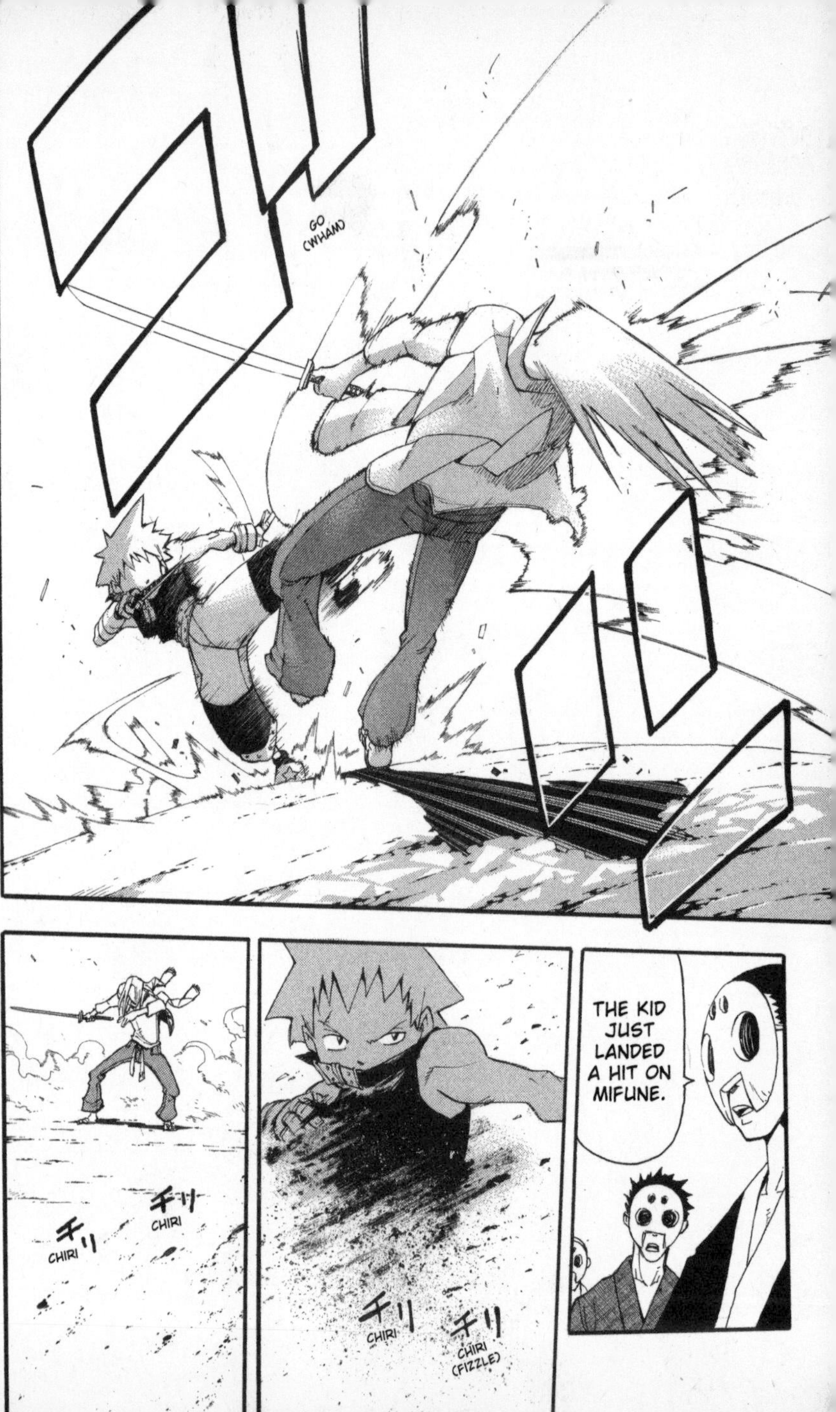
GO
(WHAM)
THE KID JUST LANDED A HIT ON MIFUNE.
チリ
CHIRI
(FIZZLE)
チリ
CHIRI
チリ
CHIRI
チリ
CHIRI

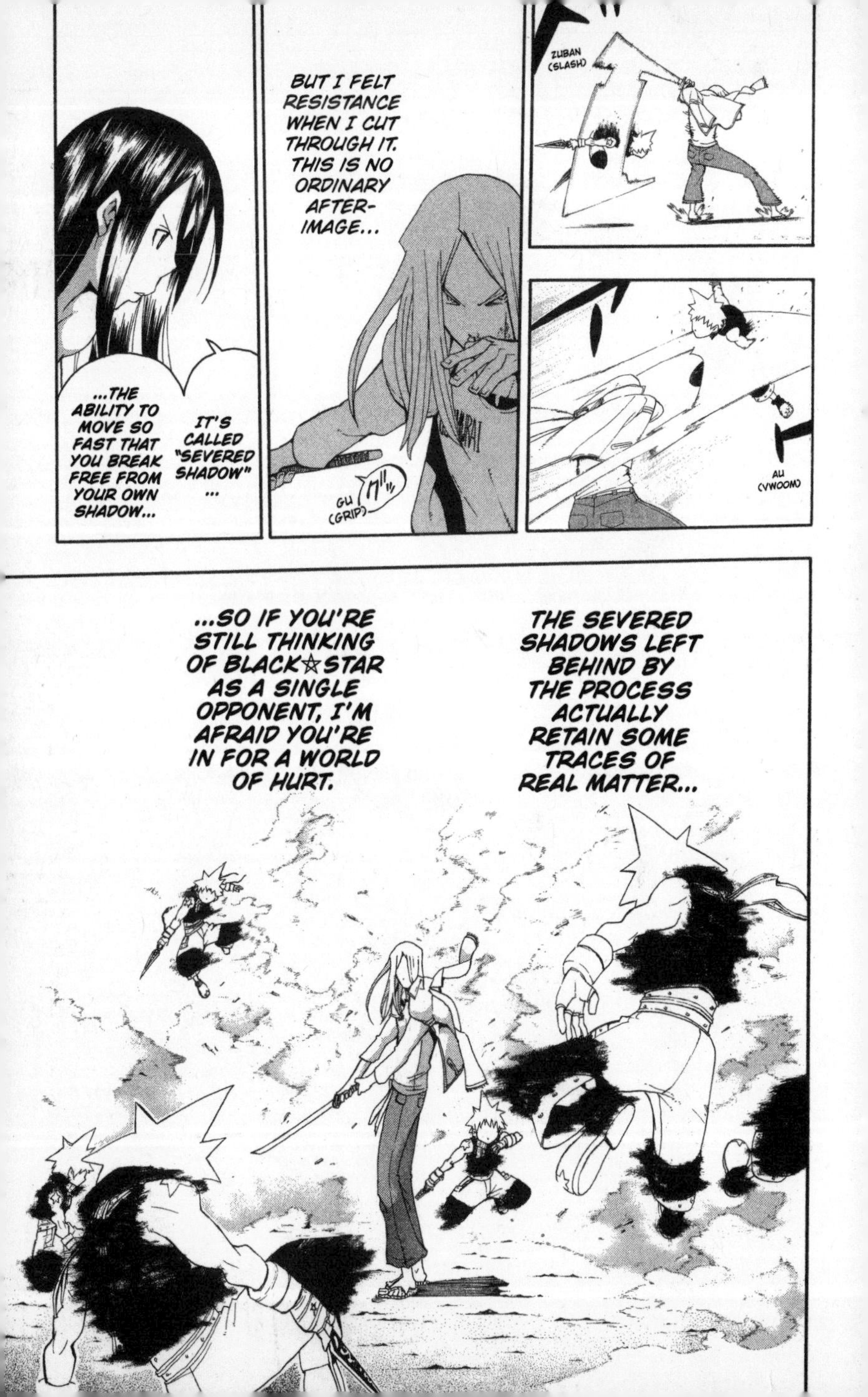
ZUBAN (SLASH)
AU (VWOOM)
BUT I FELT RESISTANCE WHEN I CUT THROUGH IT. THIS IS NO ORDINARY AFTER-IMAGE...
GU (GRIP)
IT'S CALLED "SEVERED SHADOW"...
...THE ABILITY TO MOVE SO FAST THAT YOU BREAK FREE FROM YOUR OWN SHADOW...
THE SEVERED SHADOWS LEFT BEHIND BY THE PROCESS ACTUALLY RETAIN SOME TRACES OF REAL MATTER...
...SO IF YOU'RE STILL THINKING OF BLACK☆STAR AS A SINGLE OPPONENT, I'M AFRAID YOU'RE IN FOR A WORLD OF HURT.

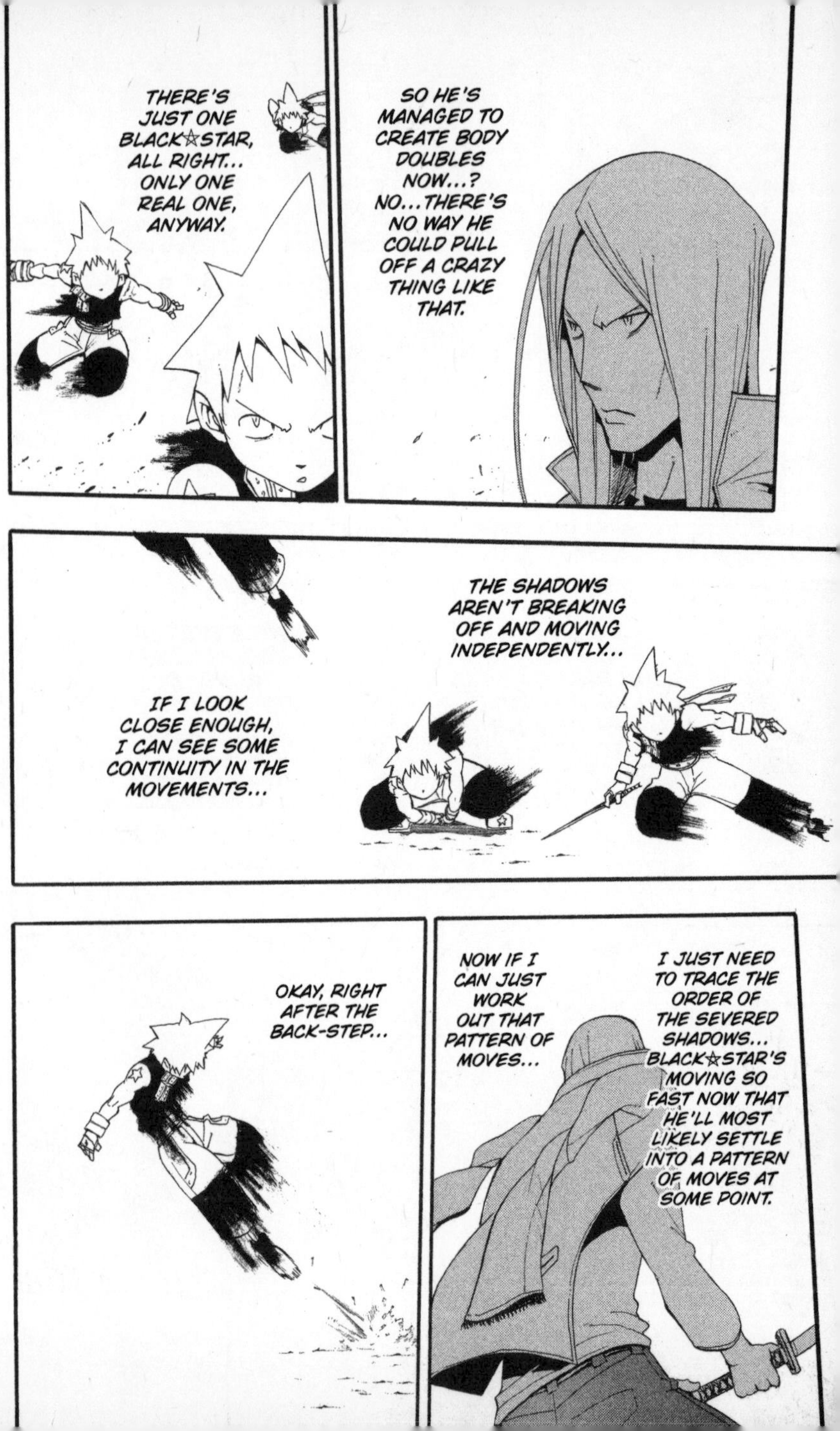
SO HE'S MANAGED TO CREATE BODY DOUBLES NOW...? NO...THERE'S NO WAY HE COULD PULL OFF A CRAZY THING LIKE THAT.
THERE'S JUST ONE BLACK☆STAR, ALL RIGHT... ONLY ONE REAL ONE, ANYWAY.
THE SHADOWS AREN'T BREAKING OFF AND MOVING INDEPENDENTLY...
IF I LOOK CLOSE ENOUGH, I CAN SEE SOME CONTINUITY IN THE MOVEMENTS...
I JUST NEED TO TRACE THE ORDER OF THE SEVERED SHADOWS... BLACK☆STAR'S MOVING SO FAST NOW THAT HE'LL MOST LIKELY SETTLE INTO A PATTERN OF MOVES AT SOME POINT.
NOW IF I CAN JUST WORK OUT THAT PATTERN OF MOVES...
OKAY, RIGHT AFTER THE BACK-STEP...

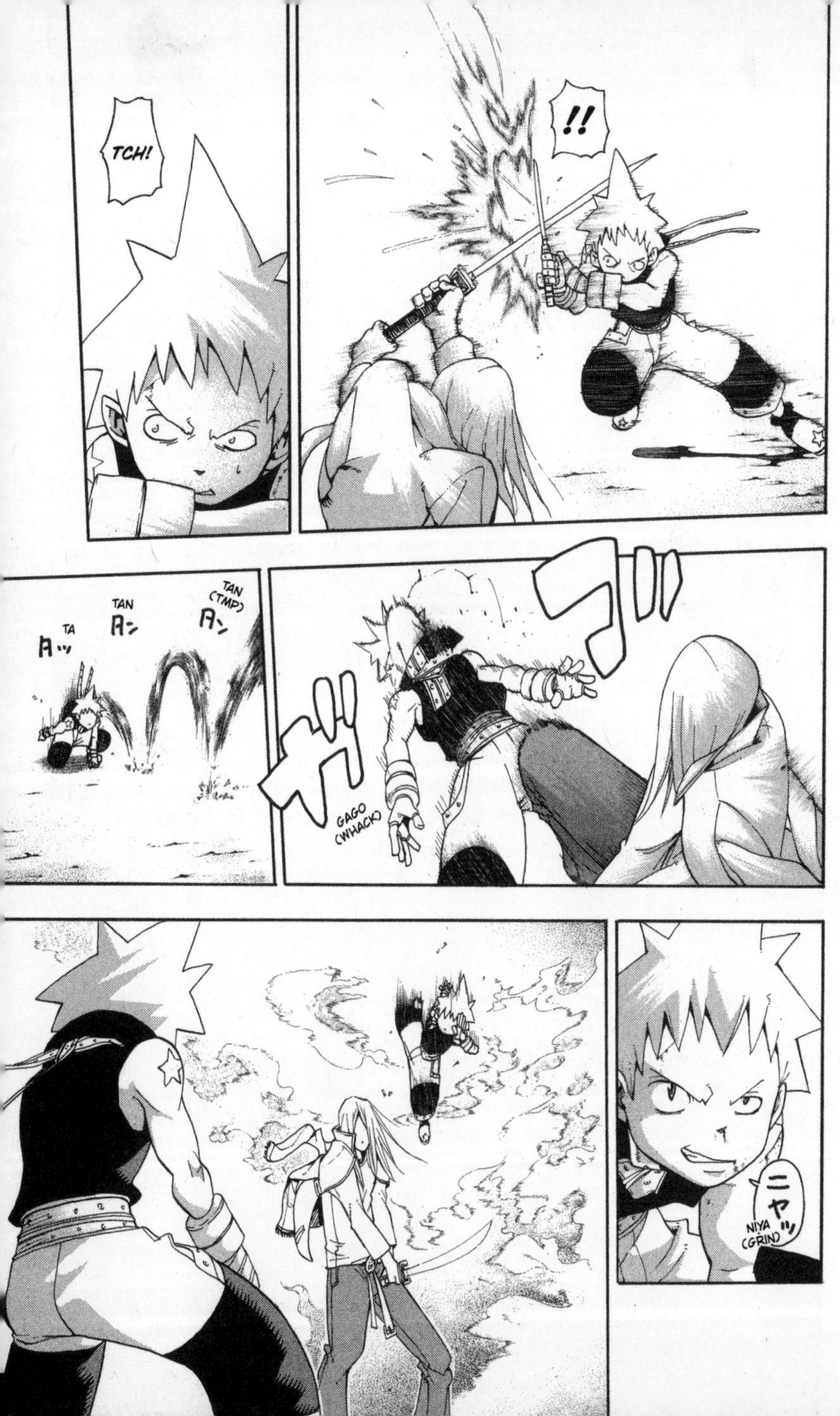
!!
TCH!
GAGO (WHACK)
タン
TAN (TMP)
タン
TAN
タッ
TA
ニヤッ
NIYA (GRIN)

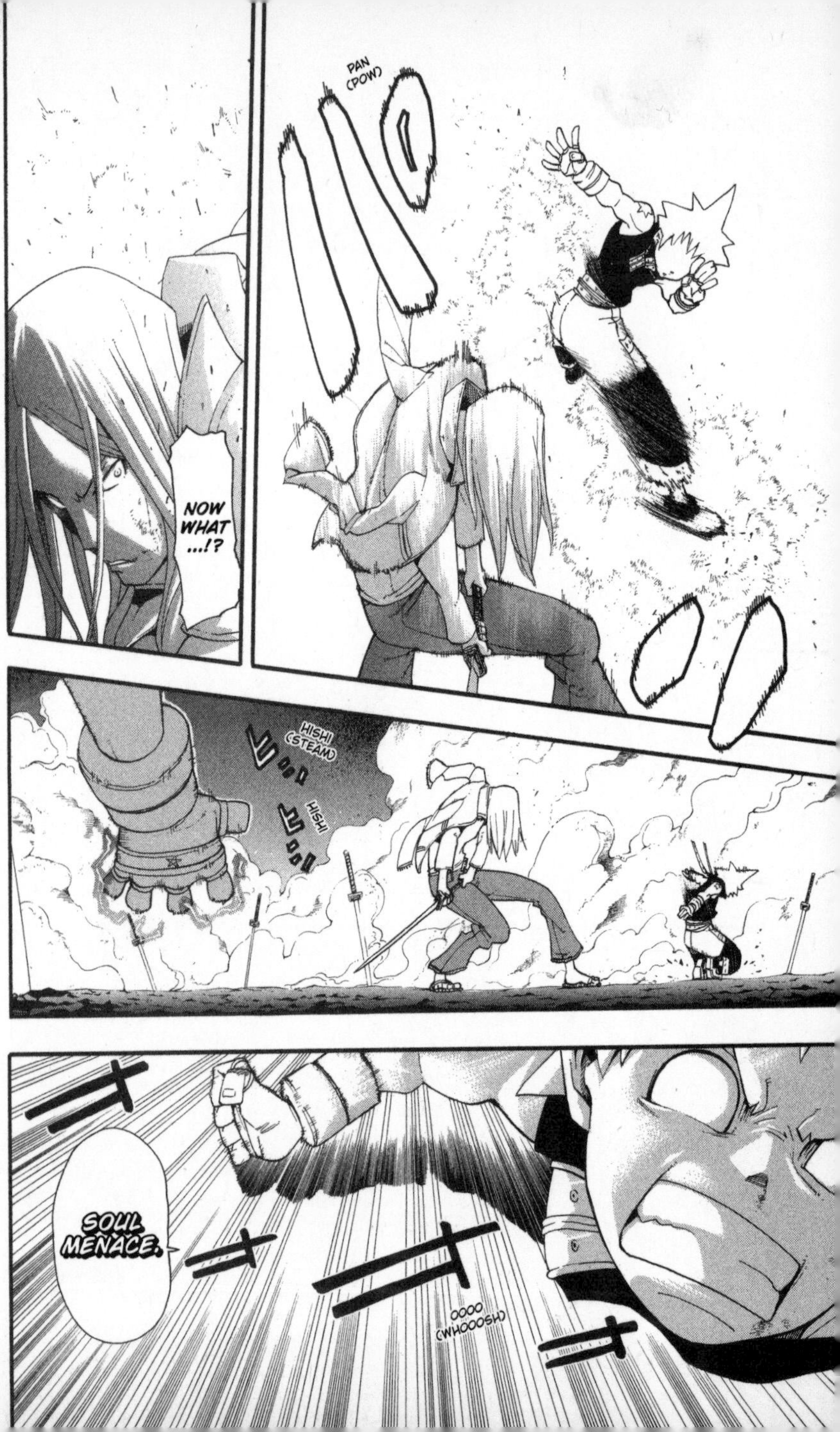

PAN (POW)
NOW WHAT ...!?
HISHI (STEAM)
HISHI
SOUL MENACE.
OOOO (WHOOOSH)

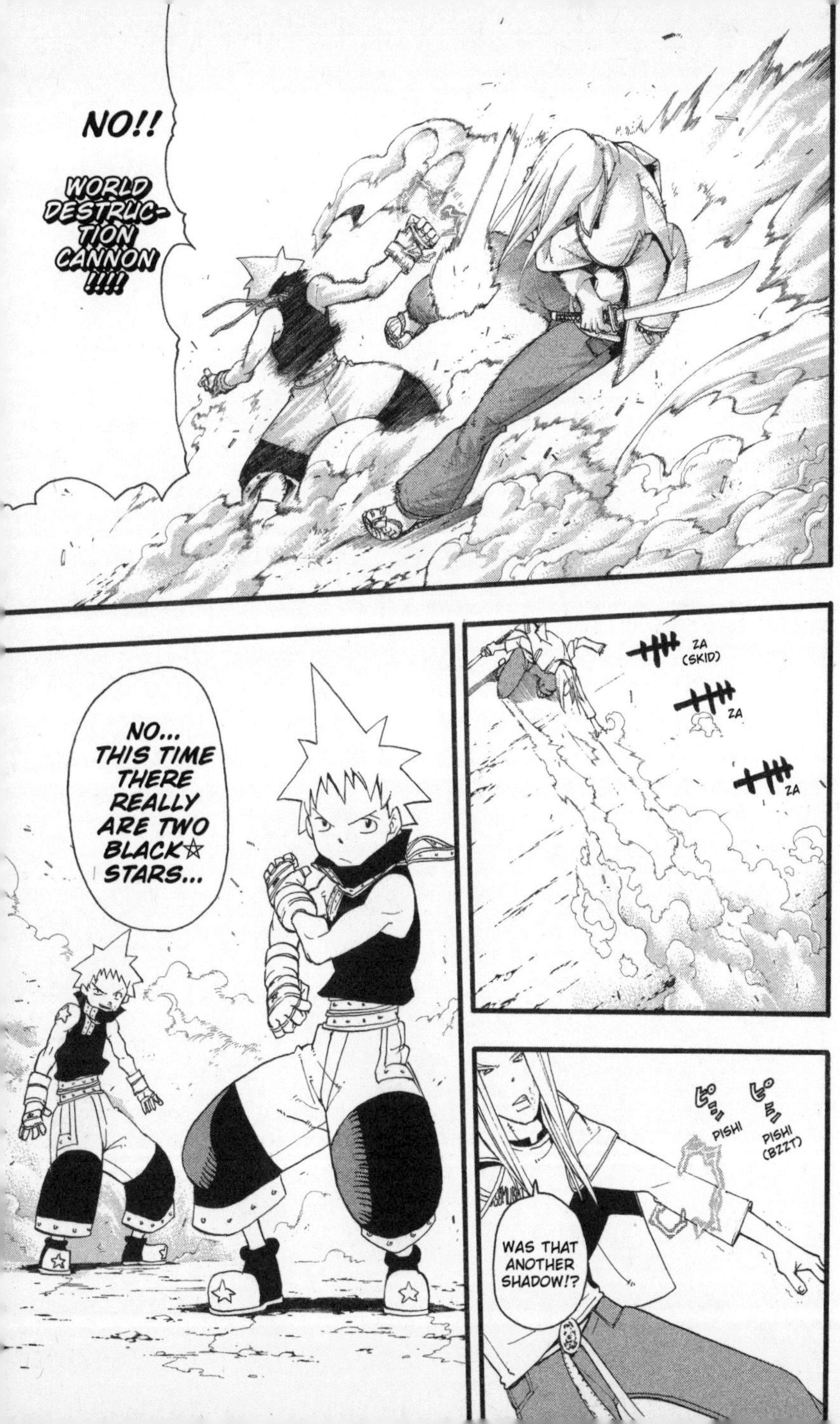
NO!!
WORLD DESTRUC-TION CANNON !!!!
ZA (SKID)
ZA
ZA
PISHI
PISHI (BZZT)
WAS THAT ANOTHER SHADOW!?
NO... THIS TIME THERE REALLY ARE TWO BLACK☆STARS...

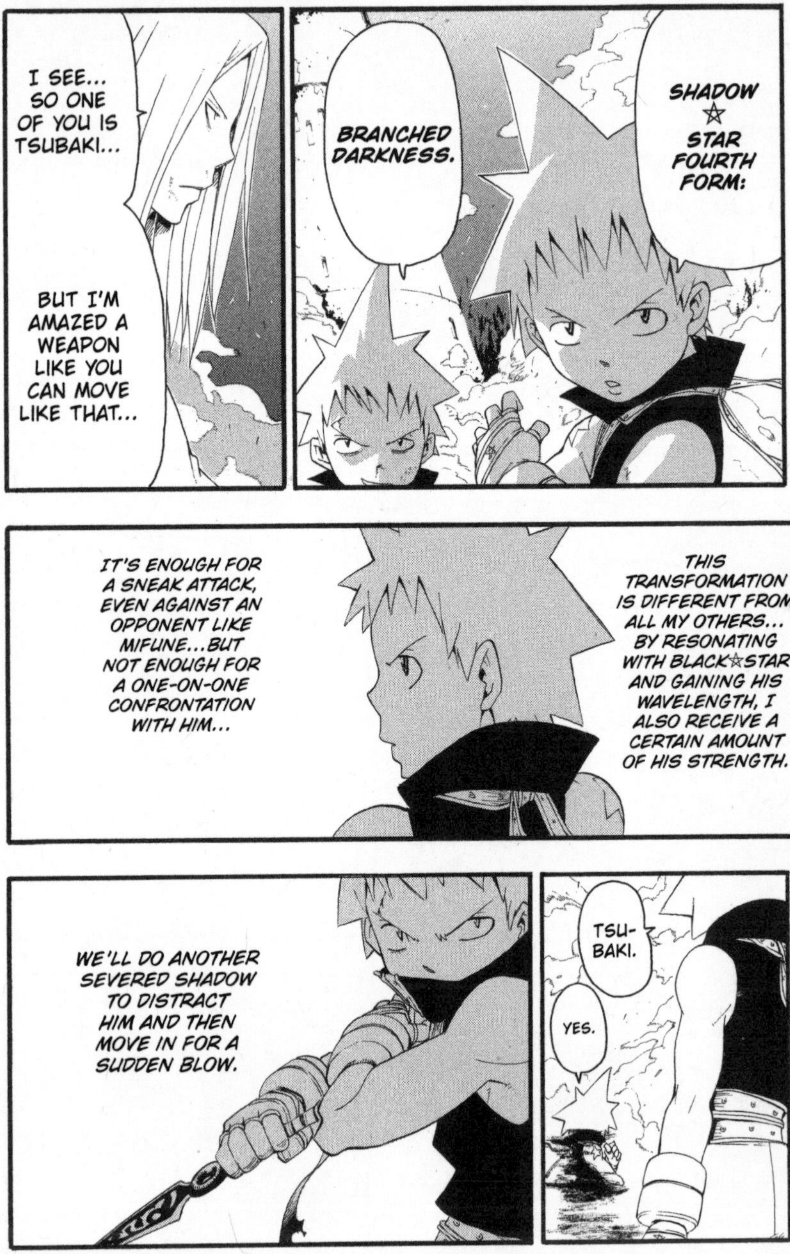
SHADOW ☆ STAR FOURTH FORM:
BRANCHED DARKNESS.
I SEE... SO ONE OF YOU IS TSUBAKI...
BUT I'M AMAZED A WEAPON LIKE YOU CAN MOVE LIKE THAT...
THIS TRANSFORMATION IS DIFFERENT FROM ALL MY OTHERS... BY RESONATING WITH BLACK☆STAR AND GAINING HIS WAVELENGTH, I ALSO RECEIVE A CERTAIN AMOUNT OF HIS STRENGTH.
IT'S ENOUGH FOR A SNEAK ATTACK, EVEN AGAINST AN OPPONENT LIKE MIFUNE...BUT NOT ENOUGH FOR A ONE-ON-ONE CONFRONTATION WITH HIM...
TSU-BAKI.
YES.
WE'LL DO ANOTHER SEVERED SHADOW TO DISTRACT HIM AND THEN MOVE IN FOR A SUDDEN BLOW.

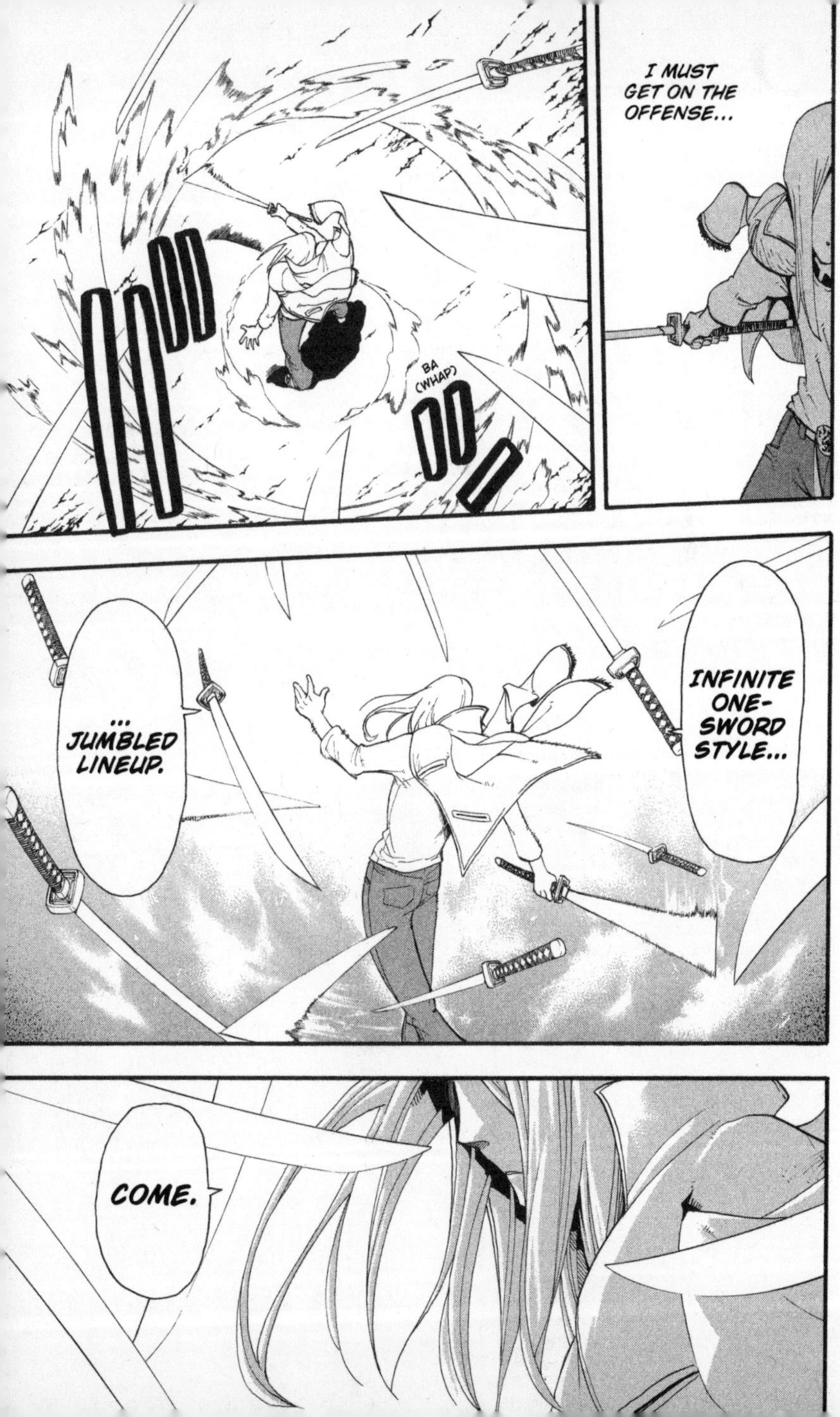
I MUST GET ON THE OFFENSE...
BA (WHAP)
INFINITE ONE-SWORD STYLE...
...JUMBLED LINEUP.
COME.

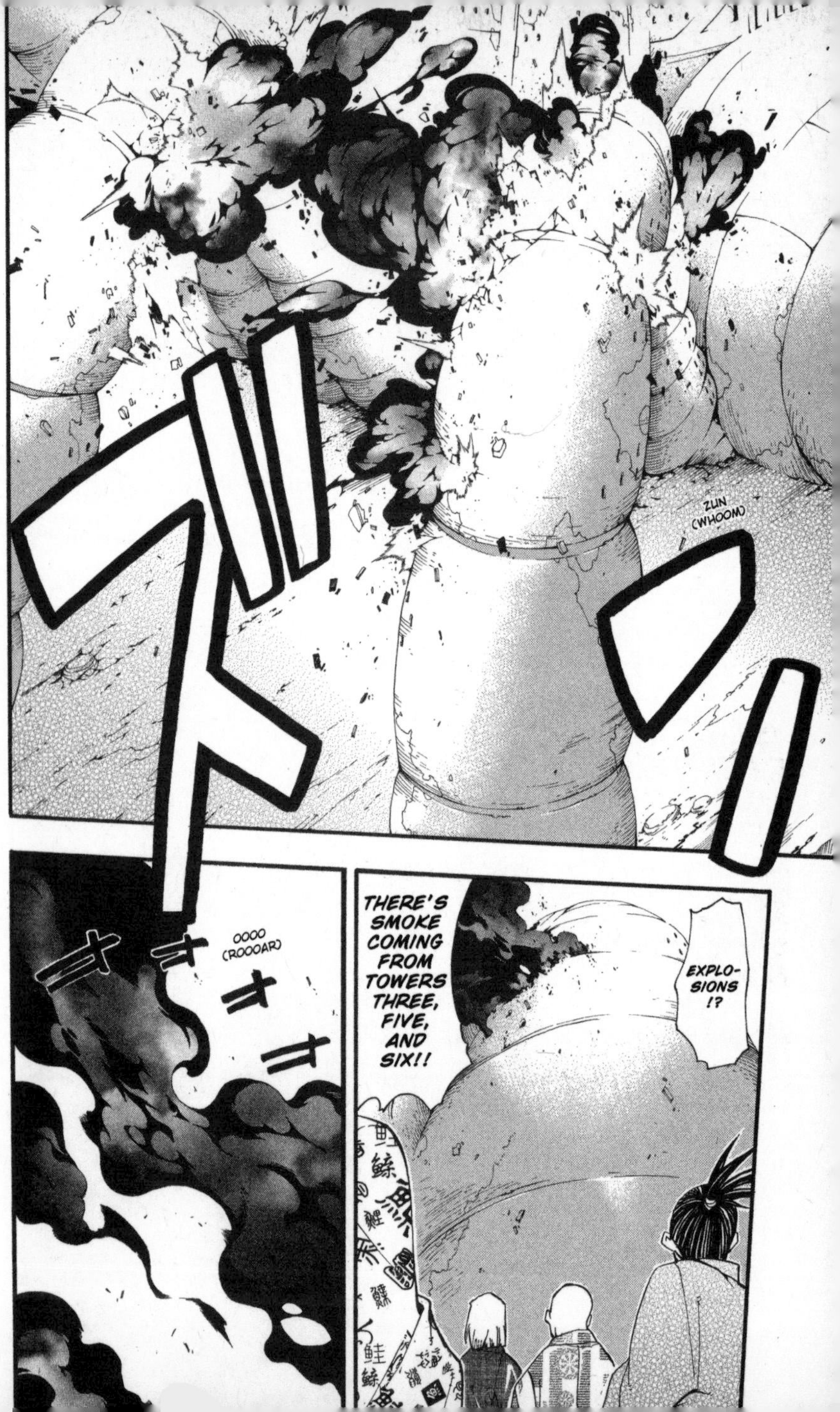
ZUN (WHOOM)
EXPLOSIONS!?
THERE'S SMOKE COMING FROM TOWERS THREE, FIVE, AND SIX!!
OOOO (ROOOAR)

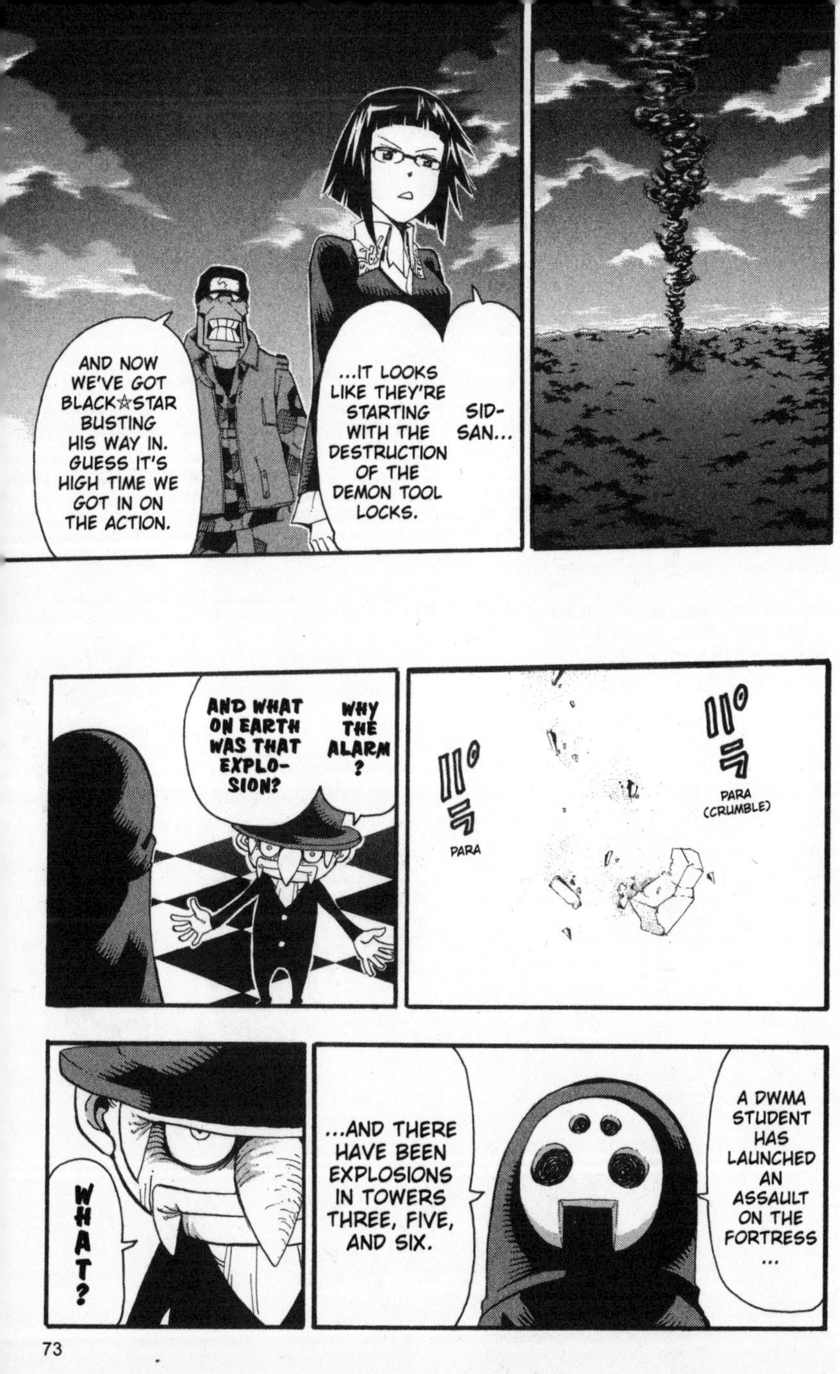
SID-SAN...
...IT LOOKS LIKE THEY'RE STARTING WITH THE DESTRUCTION OF THE DEMON TOOL LOCKS.
AND NOW WE'VE GOT BLACK☆STAR BUSTING HIS WAY IN. GUESS IT'S HIGH TIME WE GOT IN ON THE ACTION.
PARA (CRUMBLE)
PARA
WHY THE ALARM?
AND WHAT ON EARTH WAS THAT EXPLOSION?
A DWMA STUDENT HAS LAUNCHED AN ASSAULT ON THE FORTRESS...
...AND THERE HAVE BEEN EXPLOSIONS IN TOWERS THREE, FIVE, AND SIX.
WHAT?

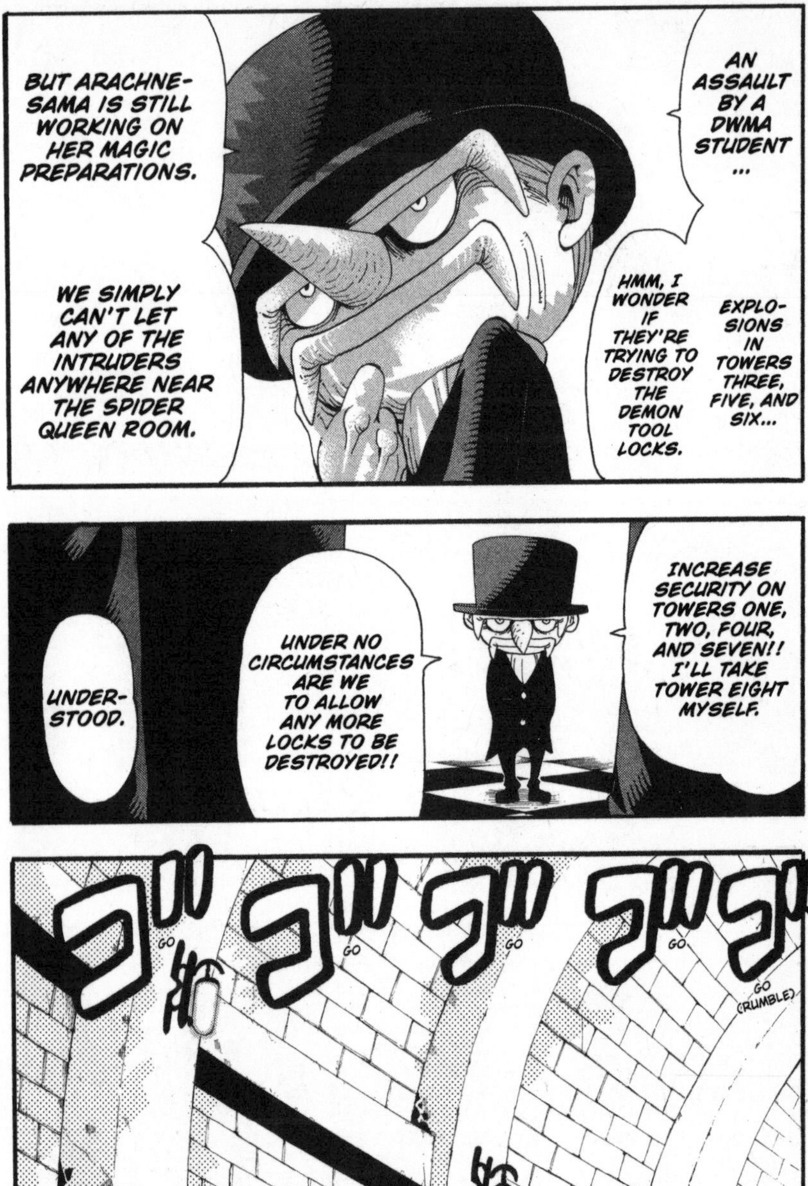
AN ASSAULT BY A DWMA STUDENT ...
EXPLOSIONS IN TOWERS THREE, FIVE, AND SIX...
HMM, I WONDER IF THEY'RE TRYING TO DESTROY THE DEMON TOOL LOCKS.
BUT ARACHNE-SAMA IS STILL WORKING ON HER MAGIC PREPARATIONS.
WE SIMPLY CAN'T LET ANY OF THE INTRUDERS ANYWHERE NEAR THE SPIDER QUEEN ROOM.
INCREASE SECURITY ON TOWERS ONE, TWO, FOUR, AND SEVEN!! I'LL TAKE TOWER EIGHT MYSELF.
UNDER NO CIRCUMSTANCES ARE WE TO ALLOW ANY MORE LOCKS TO BE DESTROYED!!
UNDER-STOOD.
GO
GO
GO
GO
GO
GO (RUMBLE)

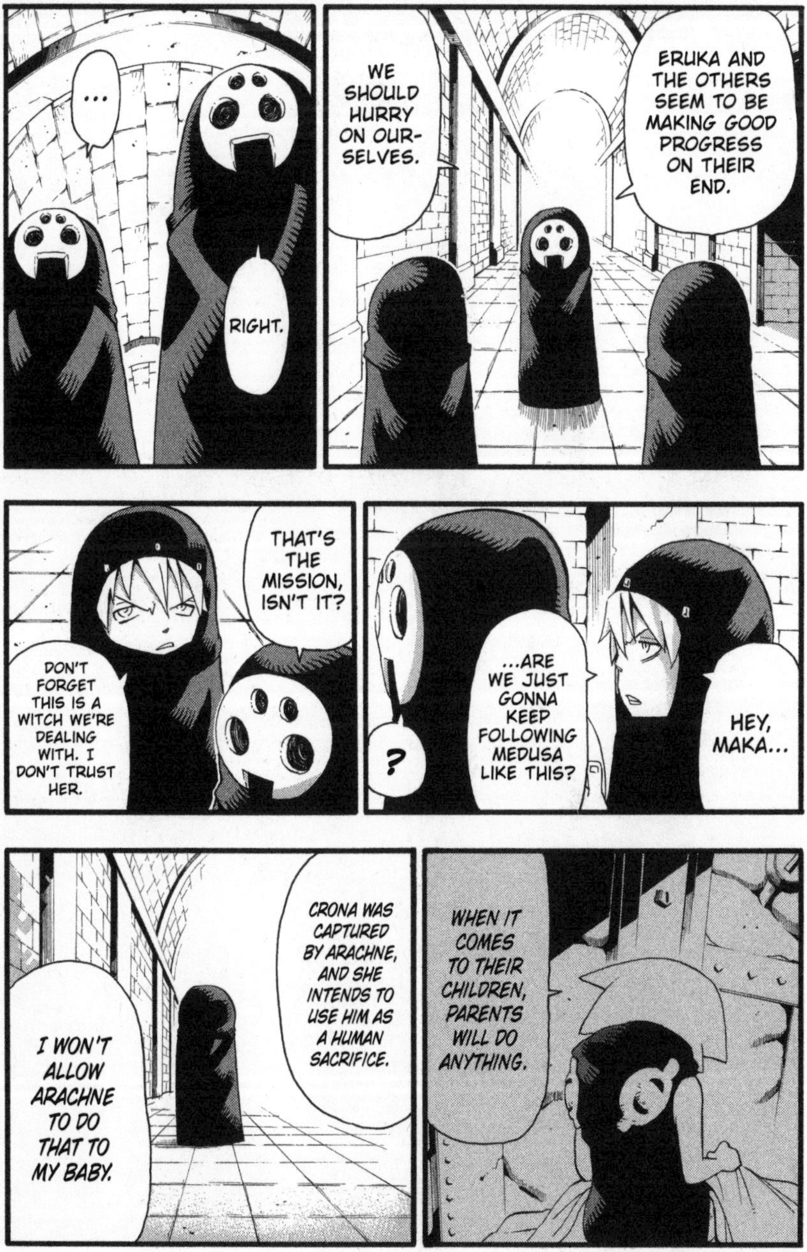
ERUKA AND THE OTHERS SEEM TO BE MAKING GOOD PROGRESS ON THEIR END.
WE SHOULD HURRY ON OURSELVES.
...
RIGHT.
HEY, MAKA...
...ARE WE JUST GONNA KEEP FOLLOWING MEDUSA LIKE THIS?
?
THAT'S THE MISSION, ISN'T IT?
DON'T FORGET THIS IS A WITCH WE'RE DEALING WITH. I DON'T TRUST HER.
WHEN IT COMES TO THEIR CHILDREN, PARENTS WILL DO ANYTHING.
CRONA WAS CAPTURED BY ARACHNE, AND SHE INTENDS TO USE HIM AS A HUMAN SACRIFICE.
I WON'T ALLOW ARACHNE TO DO THAT TO MY BABY.

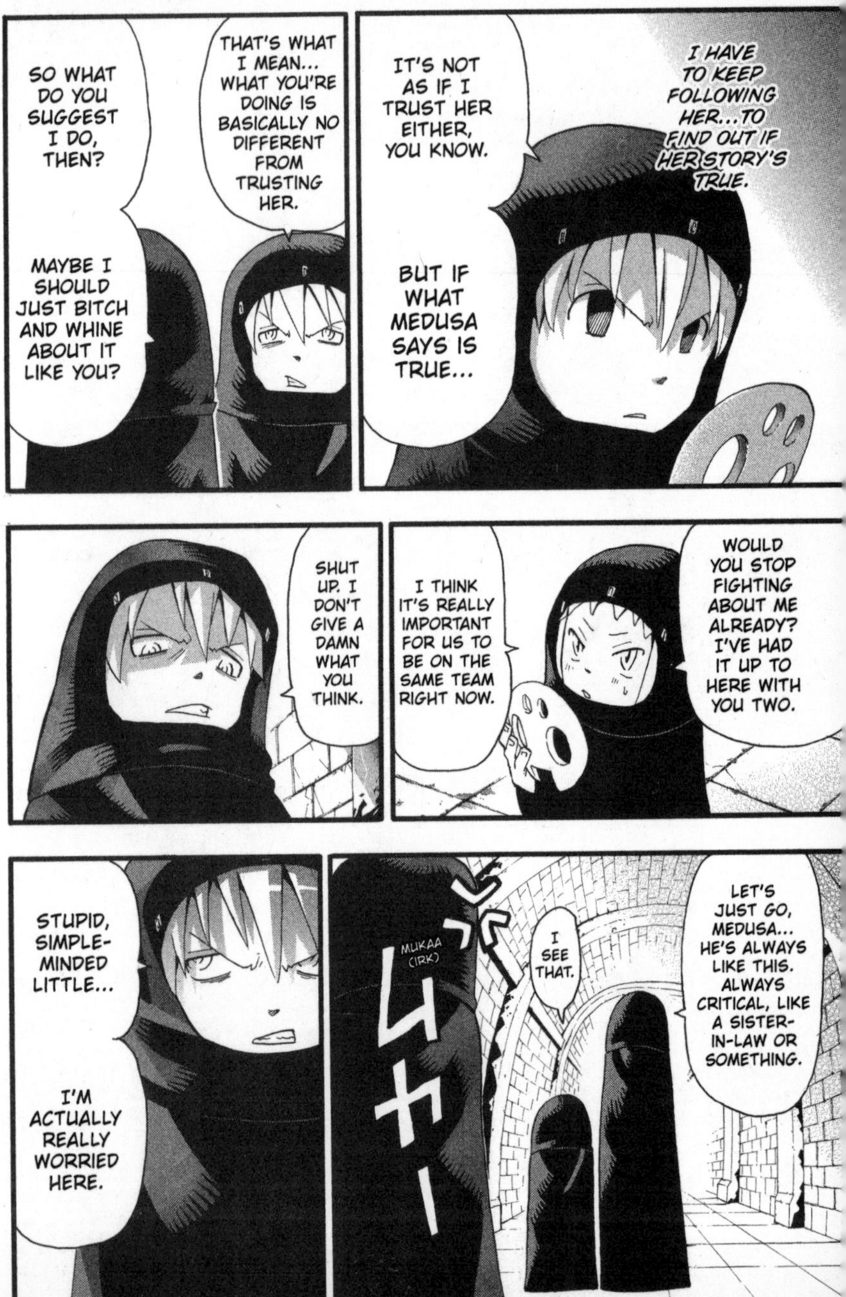
I HAVE TO KEEP FOLLOWING HER...TO FIND OUT IF HER STORY'S TRUE.
IT'S NOT AS IF I TRUST HER EITHER, YOU KNOW.
BUT IF WHAT MEDUSA SAYS IS TRUE...
THAT'S WHAT I MEAN... WHAT YOU'RE DOING IS BASICALLY NO DIFFERENT FROM TRUSTING HER.
SO WHAT DO YOU SUGGEST I DO, THEN?
MAYBE I SHOULD JUST BITCH AND WHINE ABOUT IT LIKE YOU?
WOULD YOU STOP FIGHTING ABOUT ME ALREADY? I'VE HAD IT UP TO HERE WITH YOU TWO.
I THINK IT'S REALLY IMPORTANT FOR US TO BE ON THE SAME TEAM RIGHT NOW.
SHUT UP. I DON'T GIVE A DAMN WHAT YOU THINK.
LET'S JUST GO, MEDUSA... HE'S ALWAYS LIKE THIS. ALWAYS CRITICAL, LIKE A SISTER-IN-LAW OR SOMETHING.
I SEE THAT.
MUKAA (IRK)
STUPID, SIMPLE-MINDED LITTLE...
I'M ACTUALLY REALLY WORRIED HERE.

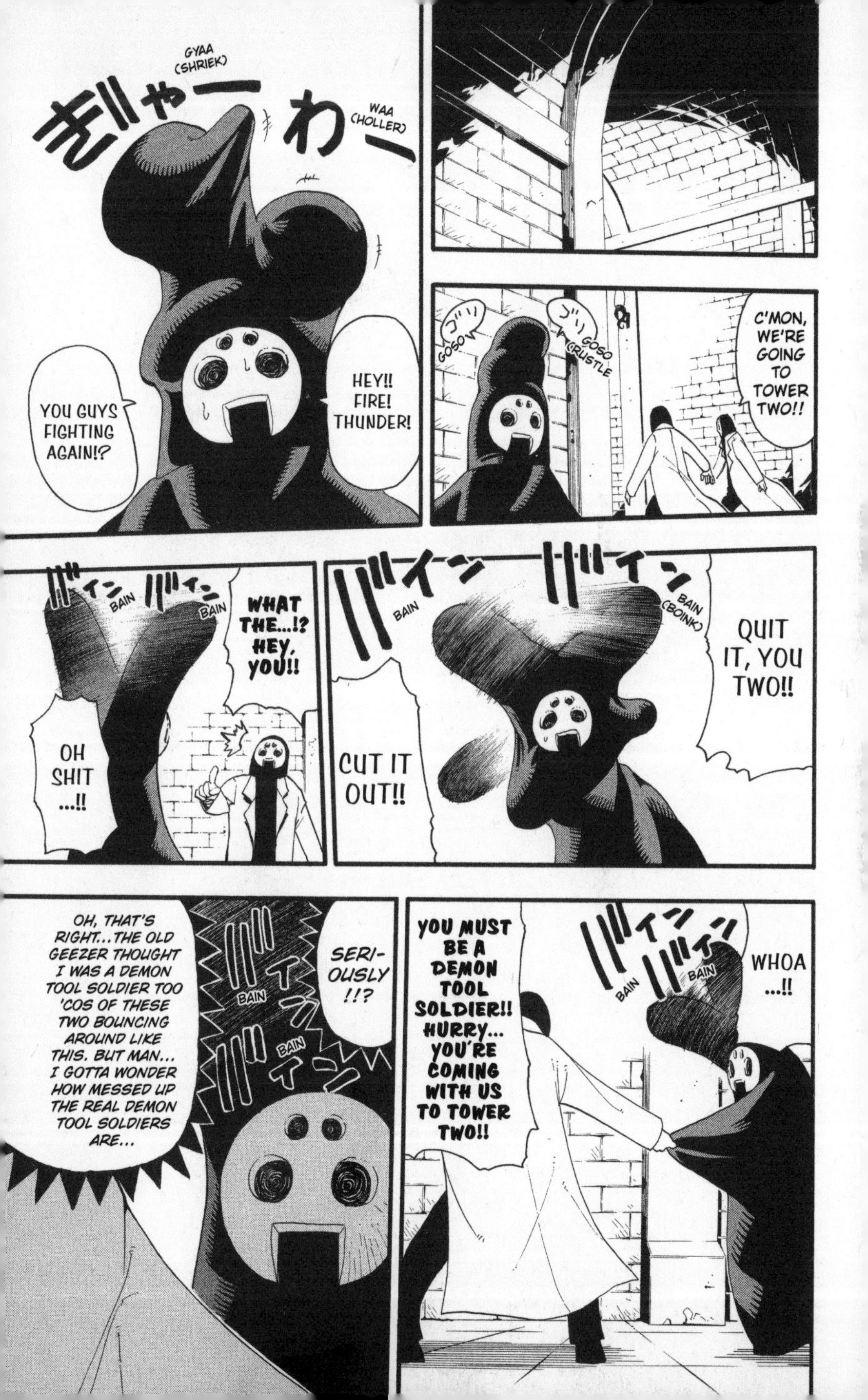
GOSO
ゴソ
GOSO (RUSTLE)
ゴソ
C'MON, WE'RE GOING TO TOWER TWO!!
GYAA (SHRIEK)
WAA (HOLLER)
HEY!! FIRE! THUNDER!
YOU GUYS FIGHTING AGAIN!?
BAIN
BAIN (BOINK)
QUIT IT, YOU TWO!!
CUT IT OUT!!
BAIN
BAIN
WHAT THE...!? HEY, YOU!!
OH SHIT ...!!
BAIN
BAIN
WHOA ...!!
YOU MUST BE A DEMON TOOL SOLDIER!! HURRY... YOU'RE COMING WITH US TO TOWER TWO!!
BAIN
BAIN
SERI-OUSLY !!?
OH, THAT'S RIGHT...THE OLD GEEZER THOUGHT I WAS A DEMON TOOL SOLDIER TOO 'COS OF THESE TWO BOUNCING AROUND LIKE THIS. BUT MAN... I GOTTA WONDER HOW MESSED UP THE REAL DEMON TOOL SOLDIERS ARE...

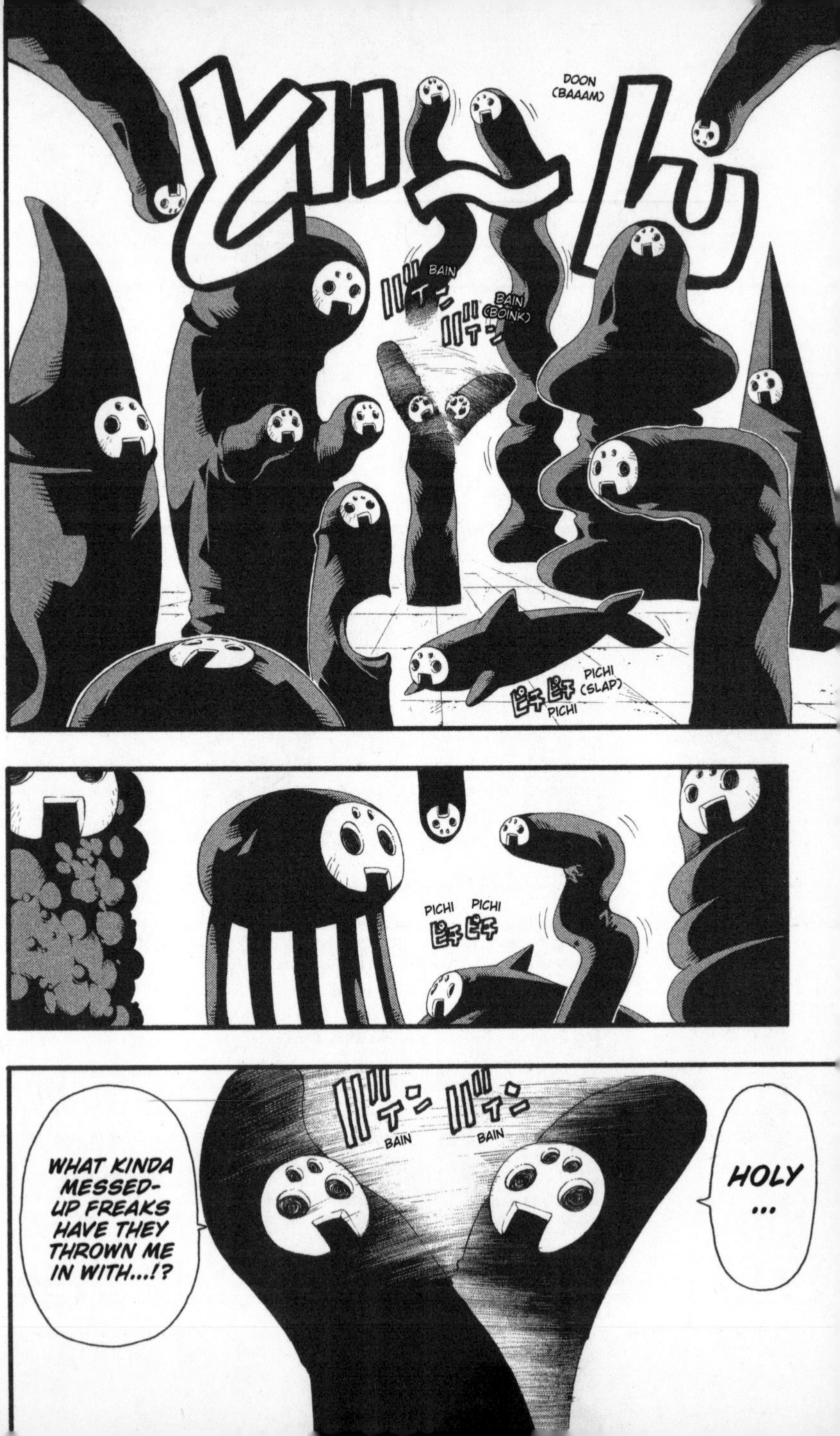
DOON (BAAAM)
BAIN
BAIN (BOINK)
PICHI (SLAP) PICHI
PICHI PICHI
BAIN
BAIN
HOLY ...
WHAT KINDA MESSED-UP FREAKS HAVE THEY THROWN ME IN WITH...!?

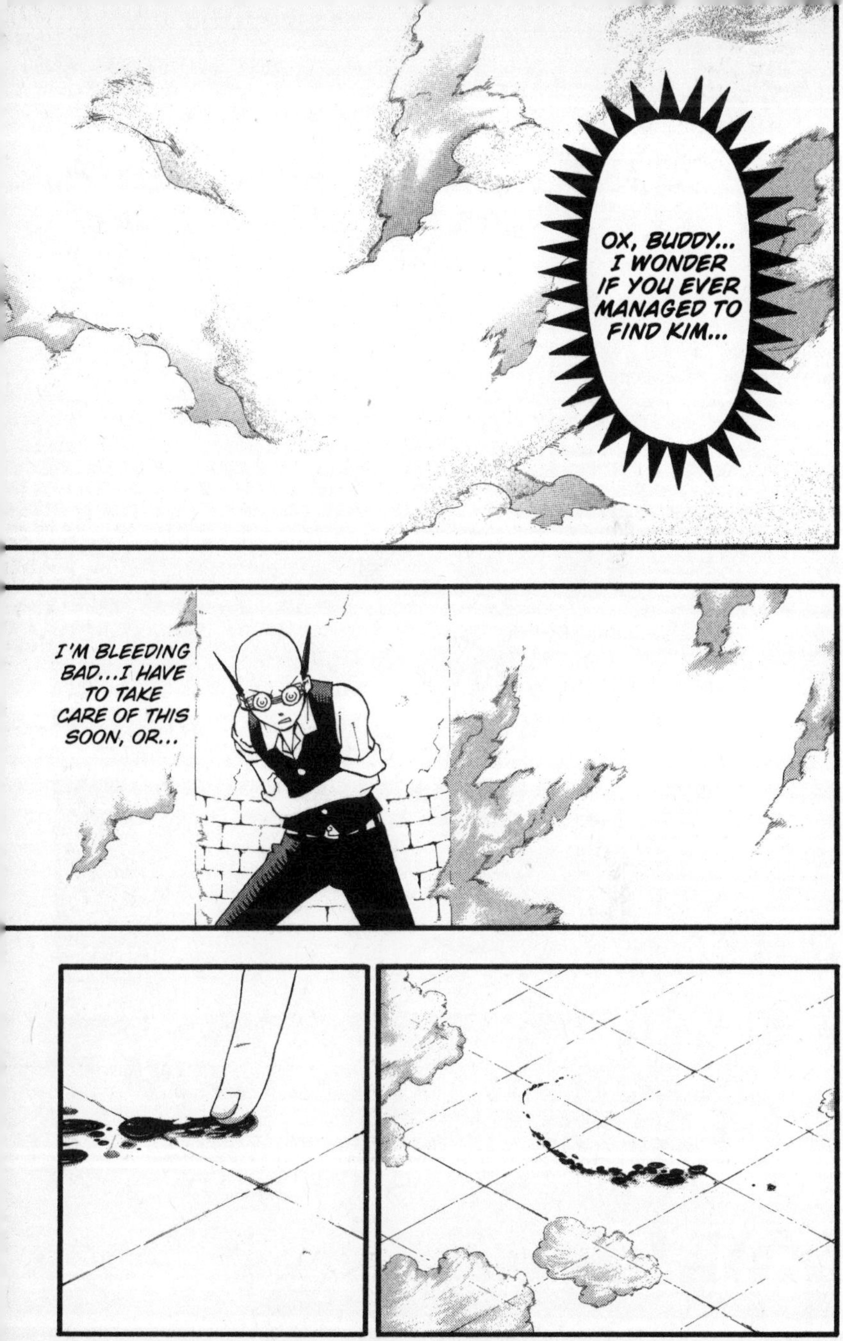
OX, BUDDY... I WONDER IF YOU EVER MANAGED TO FIND KIM...
I'M BLEEDING BAD...I HAVE TO TAKE CARE OF THIS SOON, OR...

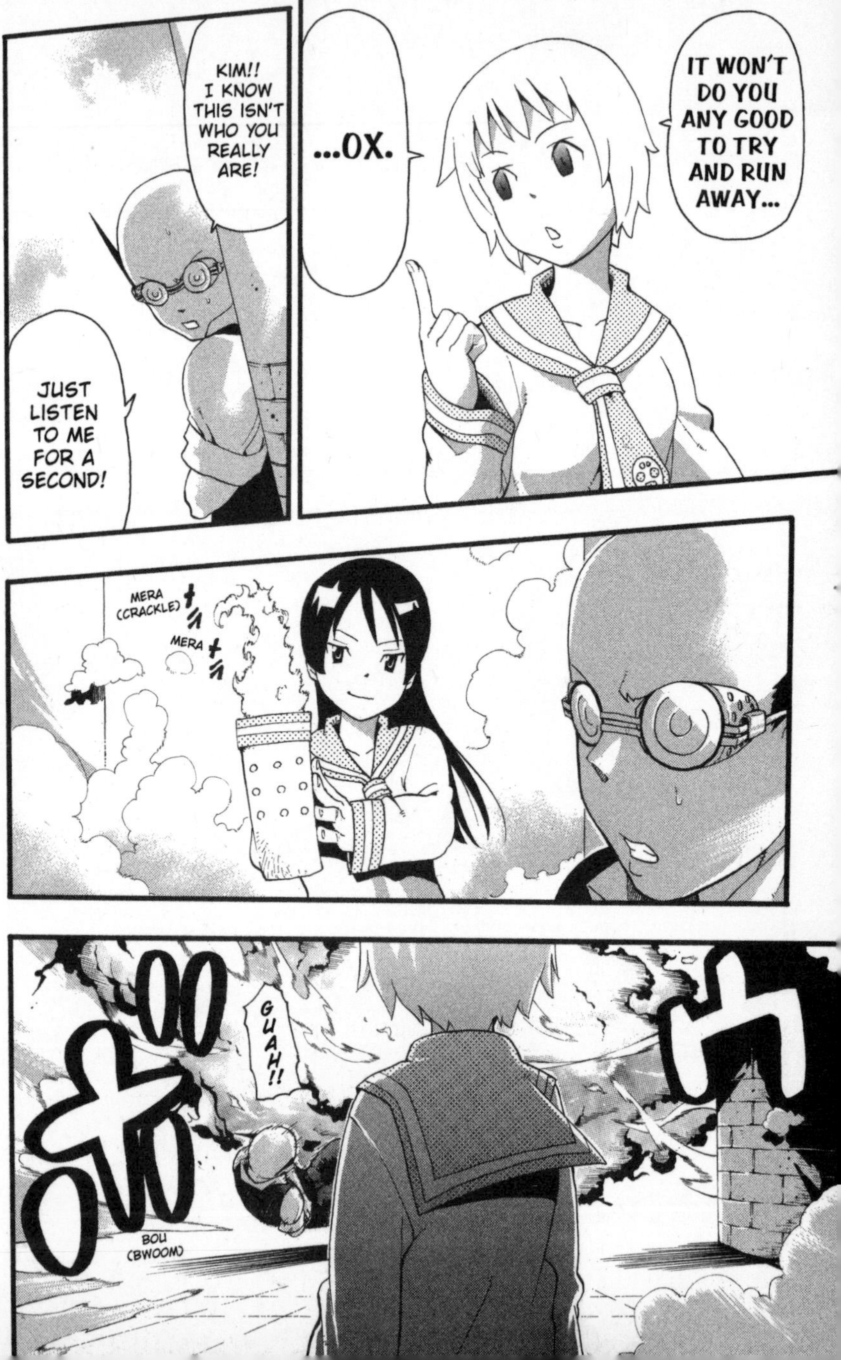
IT WON'T DO YOU ANY GOOD TO TRY AND RUN AWAY...
...OX.
KIM!! I KNOW THIS ISN'T WHO YOU REALLY ARE!
JUST LISTEN TO ME FOR A SECOND!
MERA (CRACKLE)
MERA
GUAH!!
BOU (BWOOM)

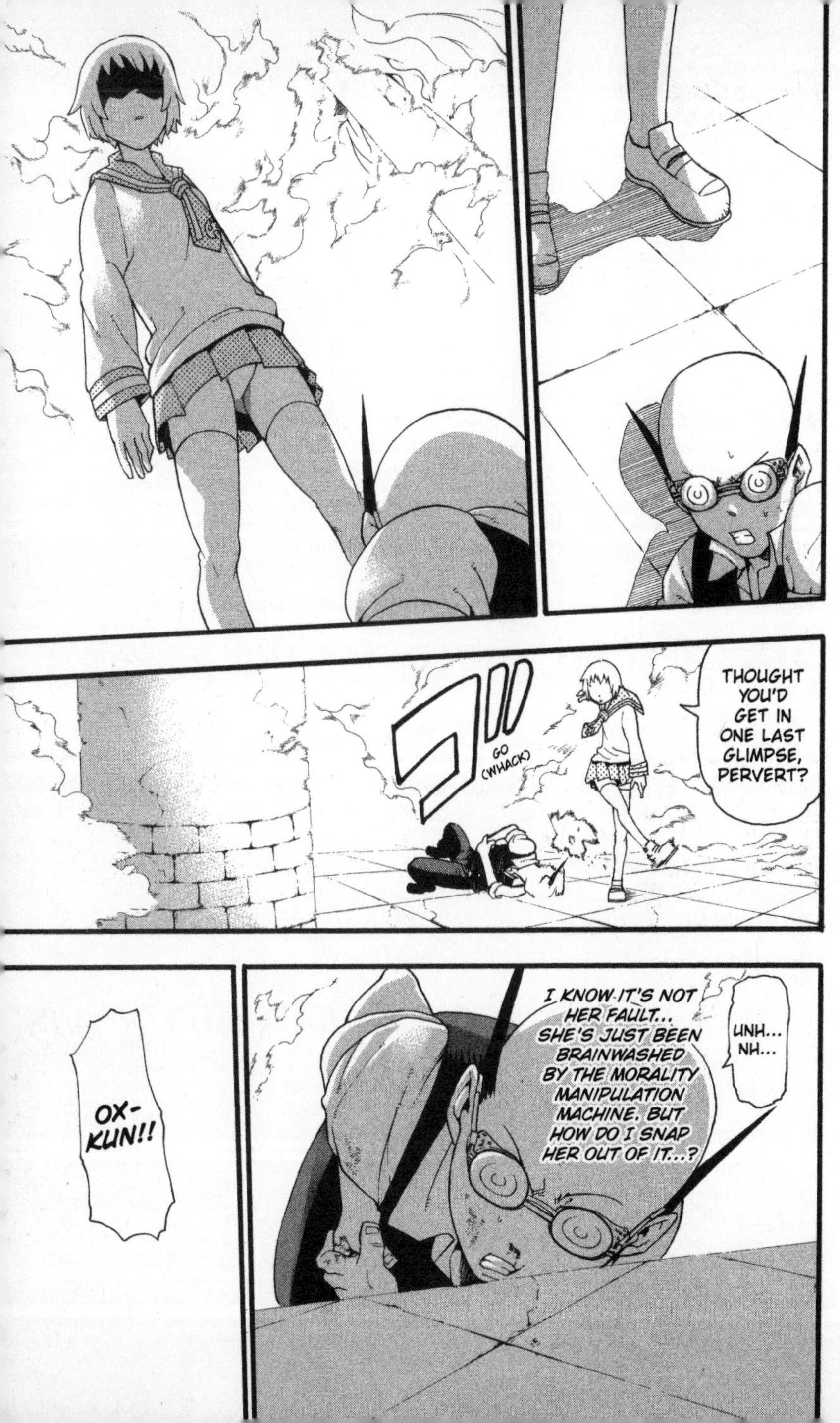
THOUGHT YOU'D GET IN ONE LAST GLIMPSE, PERVERT?
GO (WHACK)
UNH... NH...
I KNOW IT'S NOT HER FAULT... SHE'S JUST BEEN BRAINWASHED BY THE MORALITY MANIPULATION MACHINE. BUT HOW DO I SNAP HER OUT OF IT...?
OX-KUN!!

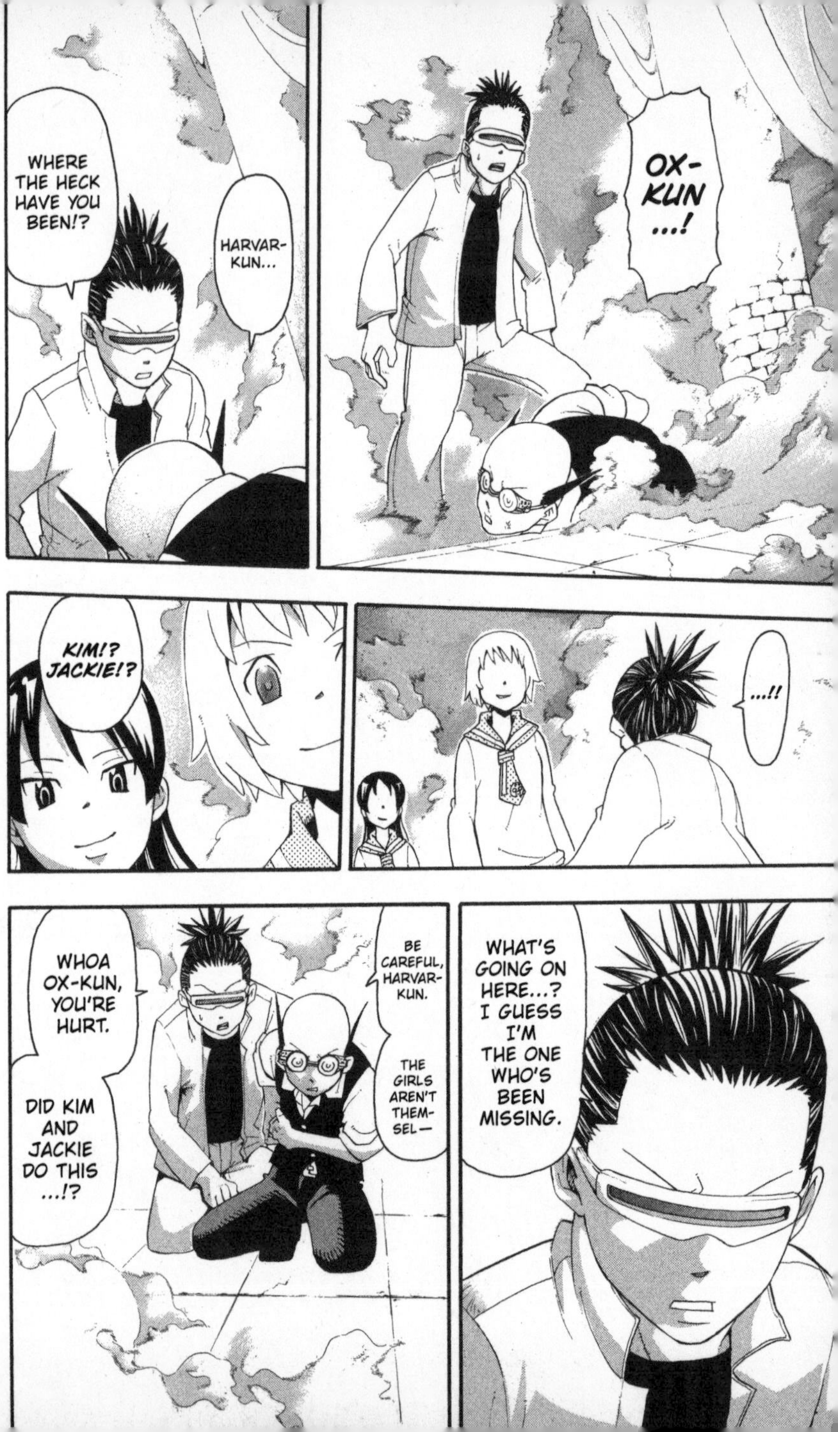
OX-KUN ...!
HARVAR-KUN...
WHERE THE HECK HAVE YOU BEEN!?
...!!
KIM!? JACKIE!?
WHAT'S GOING ON HERE...? I GUESS I'M THE ONE WHO'S BEEN MISSING.
BE CAREFUL, HARVAR-KUN.
THE GIRLS AREN'T THEMSEL—
WHOA OX-KUN, YOU'RE HURT.
DID KIM AND JACKIE DO THIS ...!?

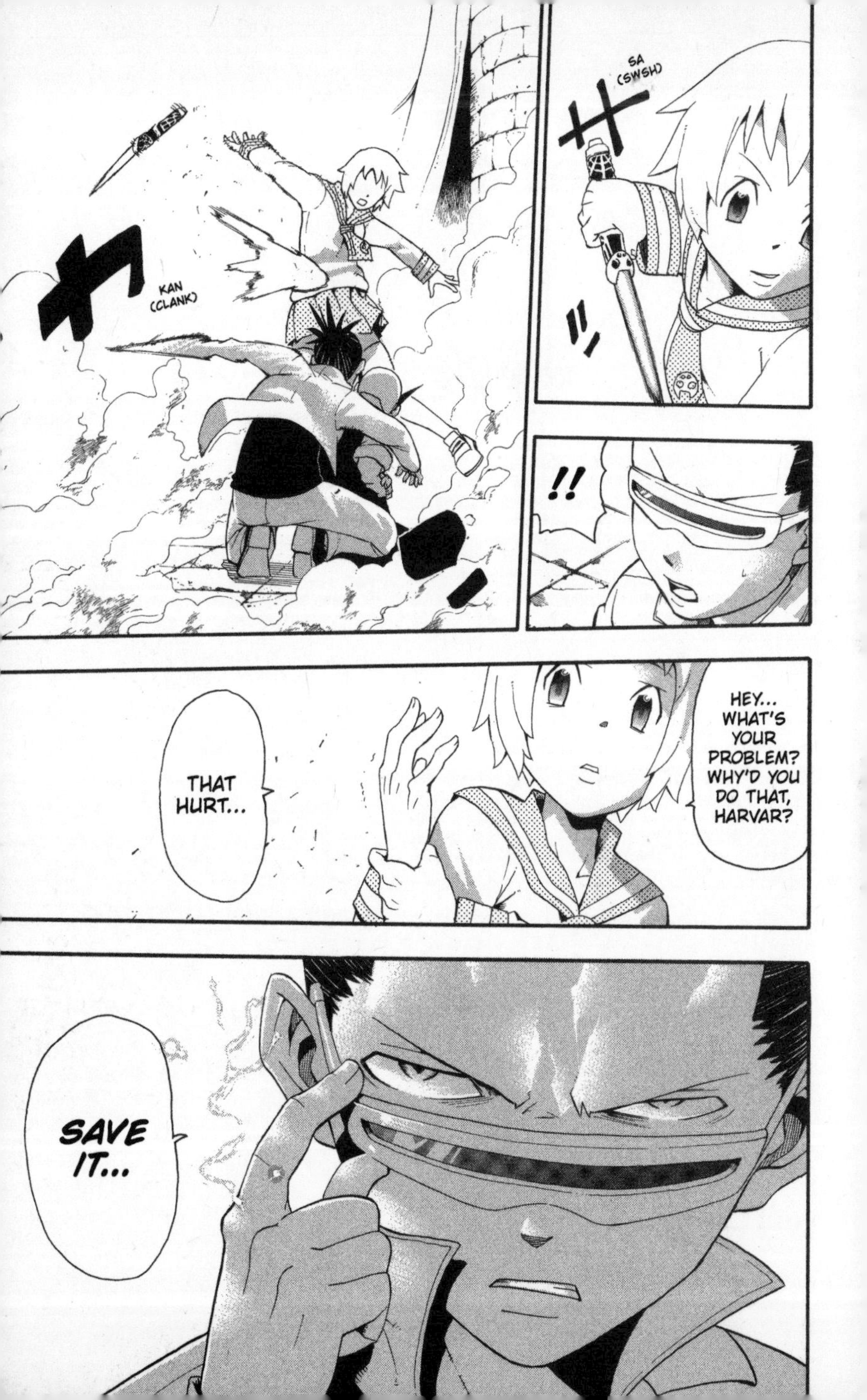
SA (SWSH)
!!
!!
KAN (CLANK)
HEY... WHAT'S YOUR PROBLEM? WHY'D YOU DO THAT, HARVAR?
THAT HURT...
SAVE IT...

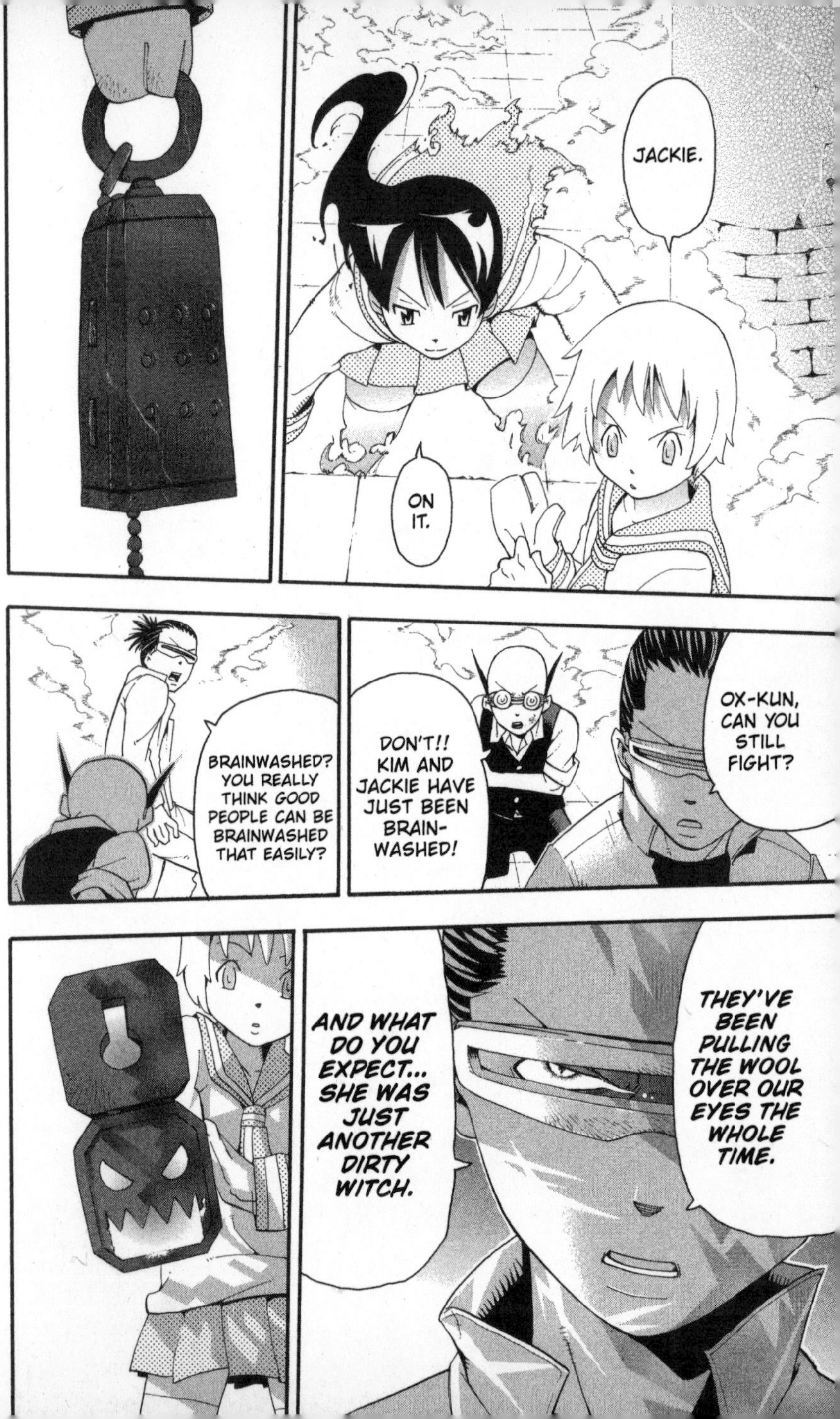
JACKIE.
ON IT.
OX-KUN, CAN YOU STILL FIGHT?
DON'T!! KIM AND JACKIE HAVE JUST BEEN BRAIN-WASHED!
BRAINWASHED? YOU REALLY THINK GOOD PEOPLE CAN BE BRAINWASHED THAT EASILY?
THEY'VE BEEN PULLING THE WOOL OVER OUR EYES THE WHOLE TIME.
AND WHAT DO YOU EXPECT... SHE WAS JUST ANOTHER DIRTY WITCH.

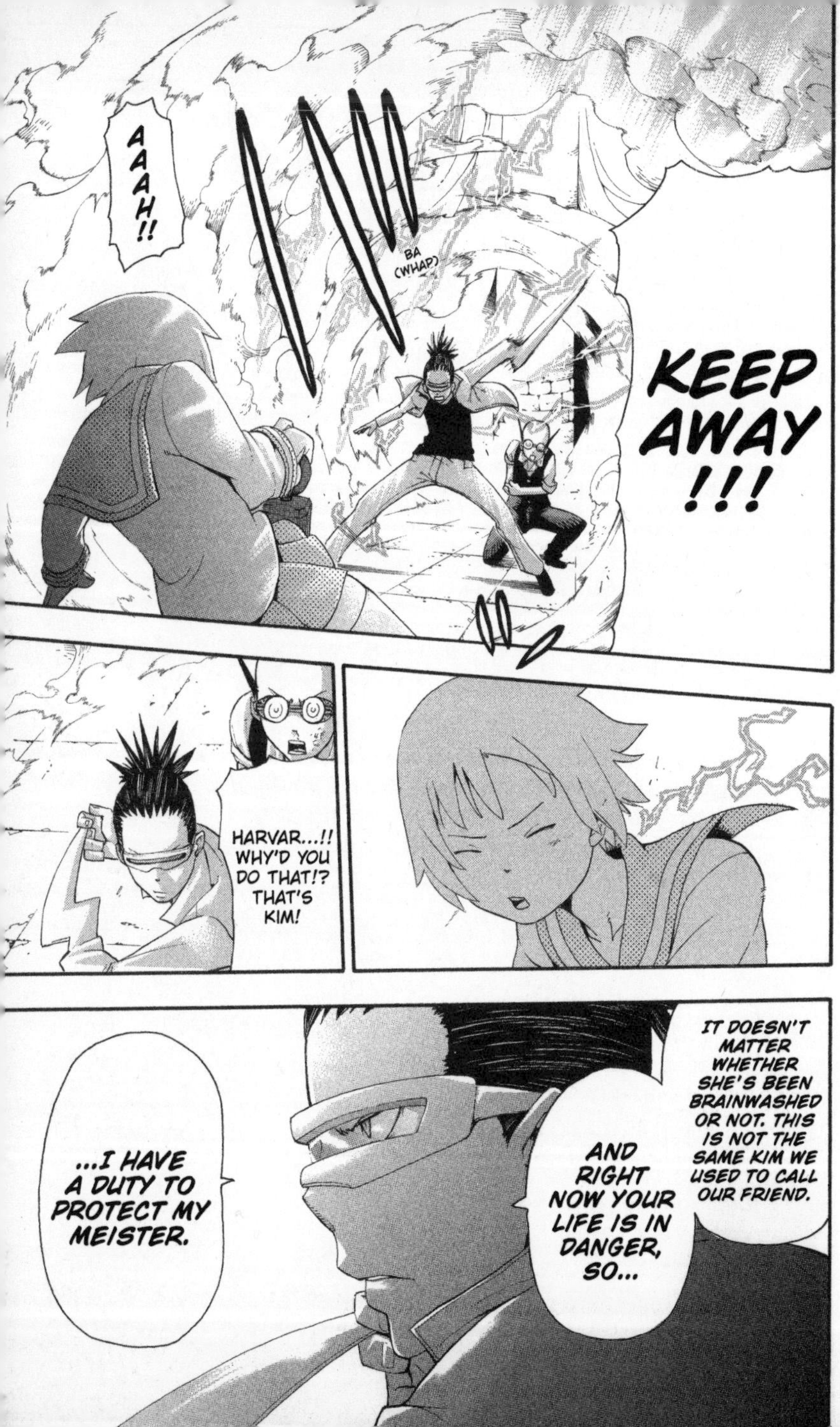
KEEP AWAY!!!
BA (WHAP)
AAAH!!
HARVAR...!! WHY'D YOU DO THAT!? THAT'S KIM!
IT DOESN'T MATTER WHETHER SHE'S BEEN BRAINWASHED OR NOT. THIS IS NOT THE SAME KIM WE USED TO CALL OUR FRIEND.
AND RIGHT NOW YOUR LIFE IS IN DANGER, SO...
...I HAVE A DUTY TO PROTECT MY MEISTER.

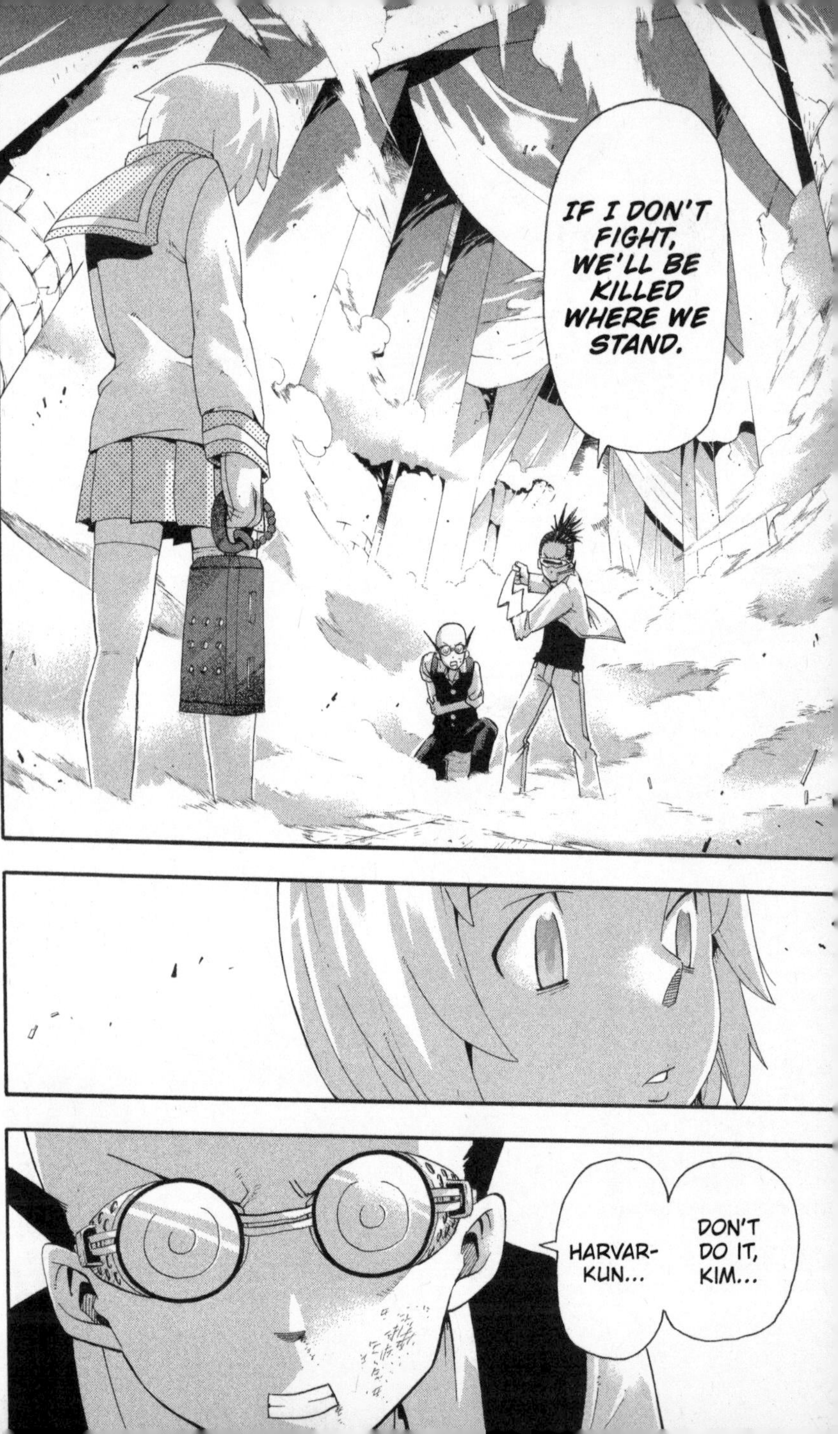
IF I DON'T FIGHT, WE'LL BE KILLED WHERE WE STAND.
DON'T DO IT, KIM...
HARVAR-KUN...

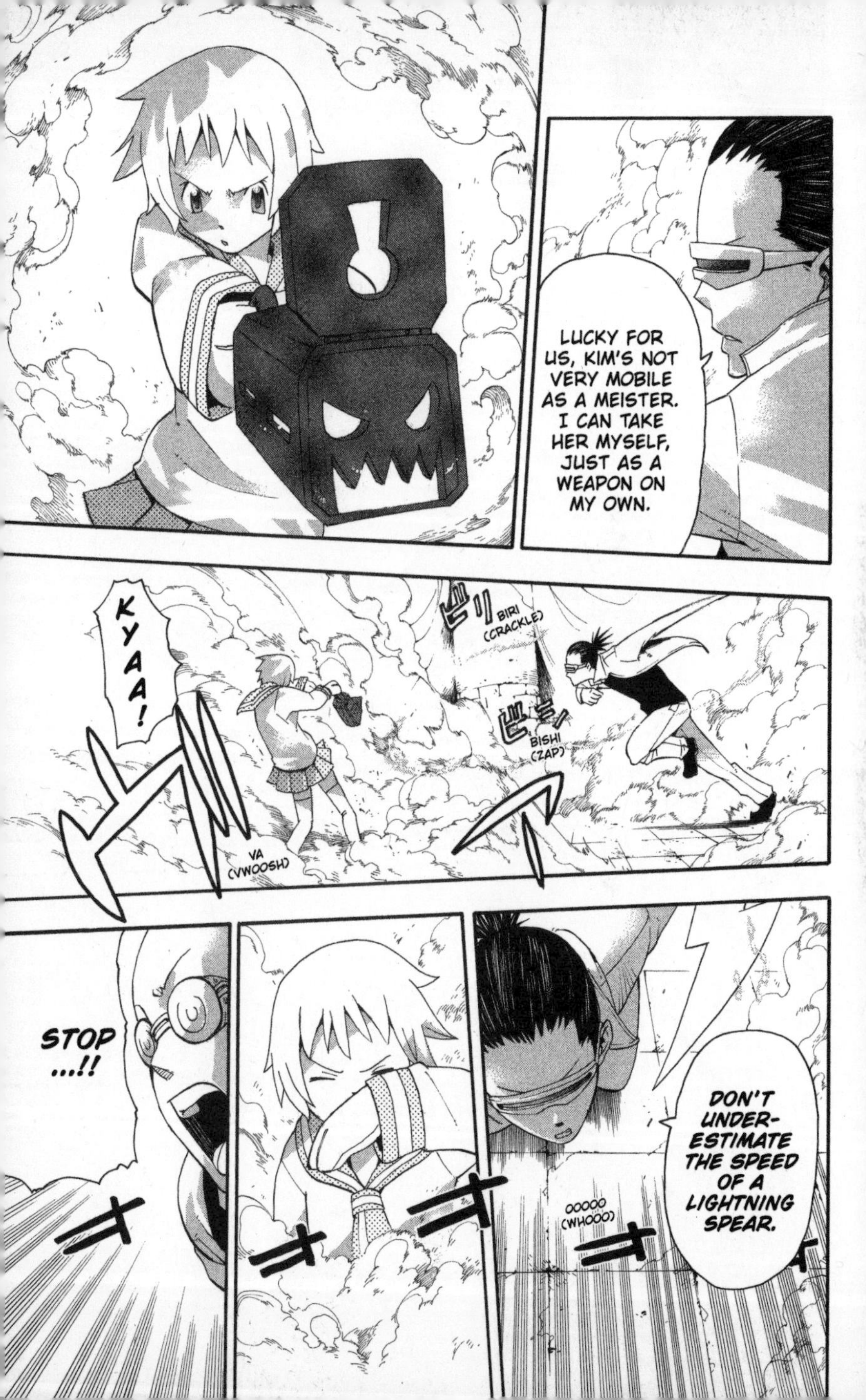
LUCKY FOR US, KIM'S NOT VERY MOBILE AS A MEISTER. I CAN TAKE HER MYSELF, JUST AS A WEAPON ON MY OWN.
BIRI (CRACKLE)
BISHI (ZAP)
KYAA!
VA (VWOOSH)
DON'T UNDER-ESTIMATE THE SPEED OF A LIGHTNING SPEAR.
OOOOO (WHOOO)
STOP ...!!

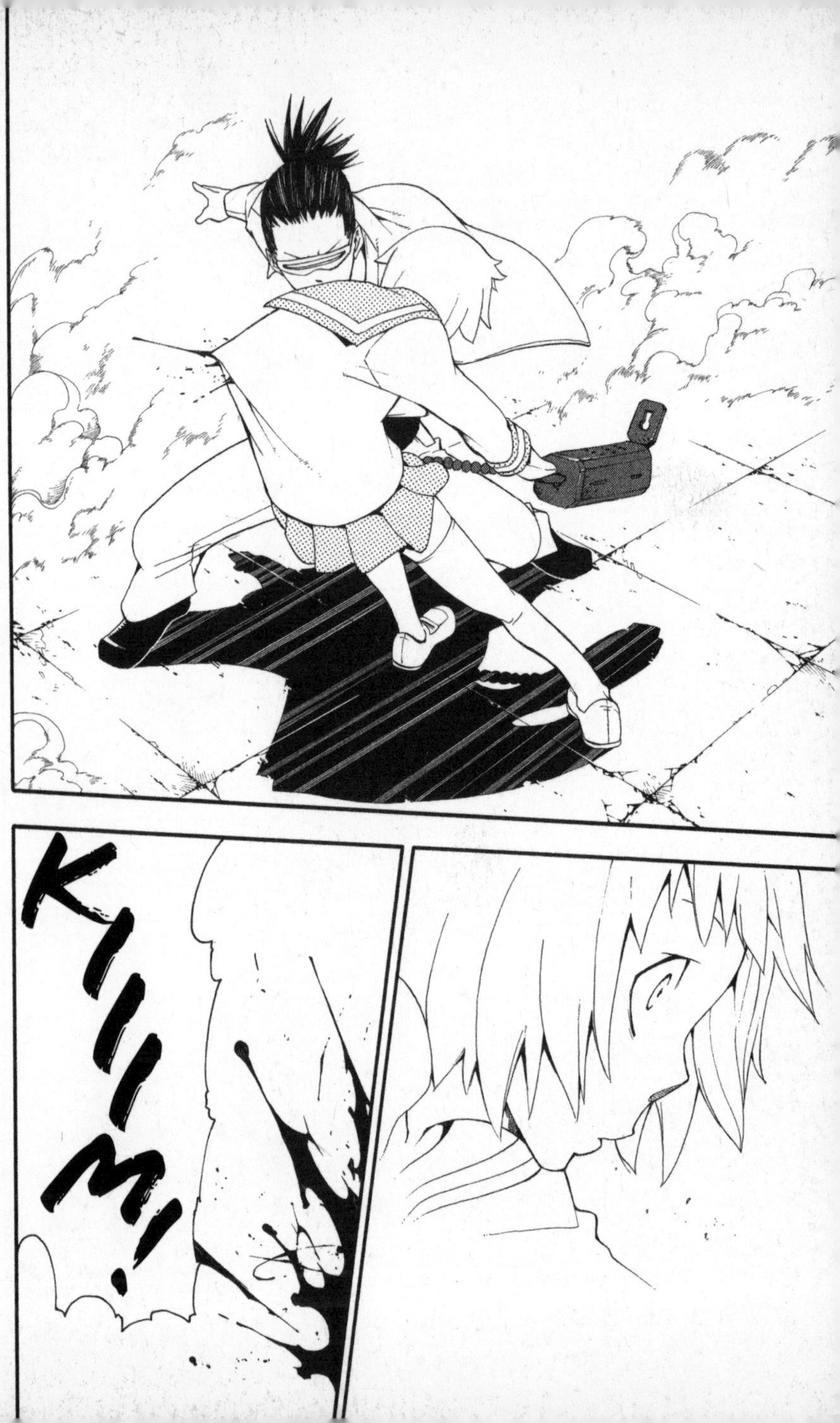
KIIIM!

SOUL EATER

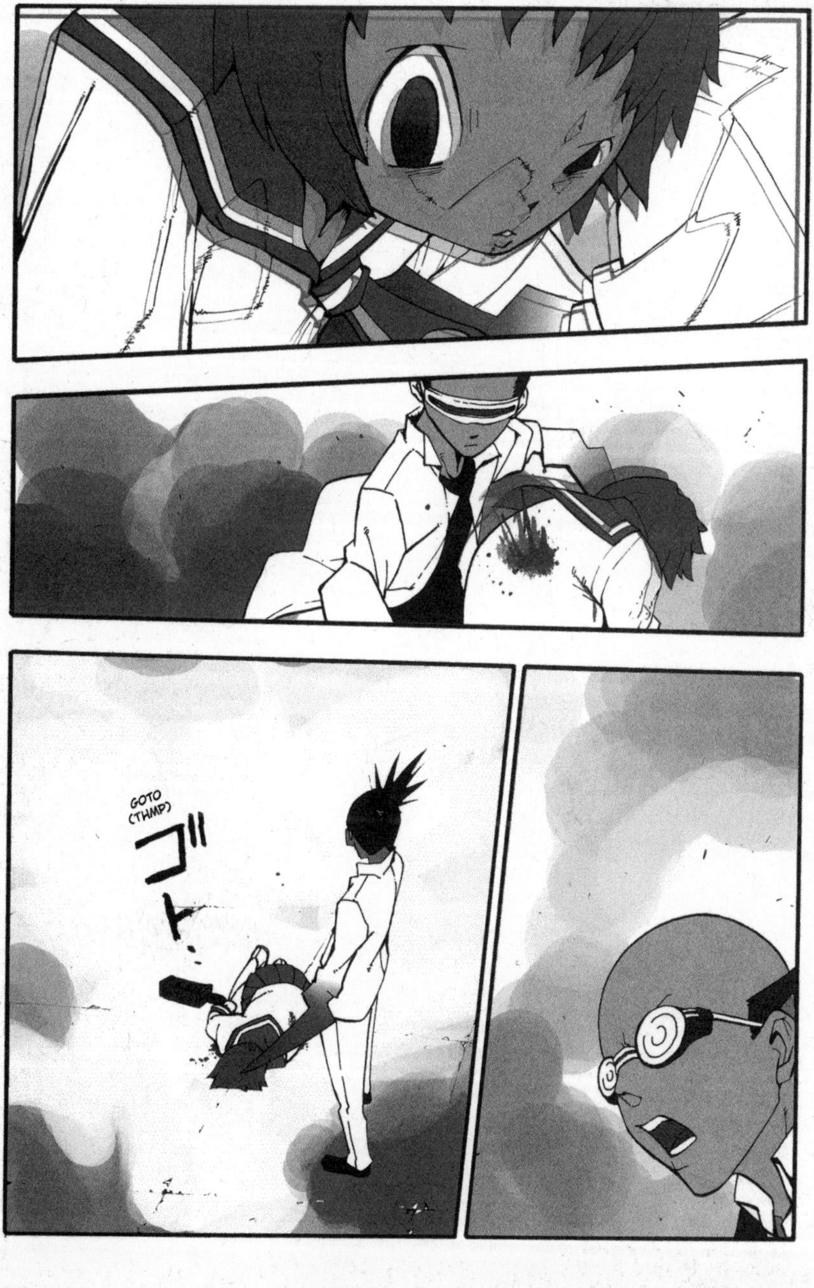
GOTO (THMP)
ゴト

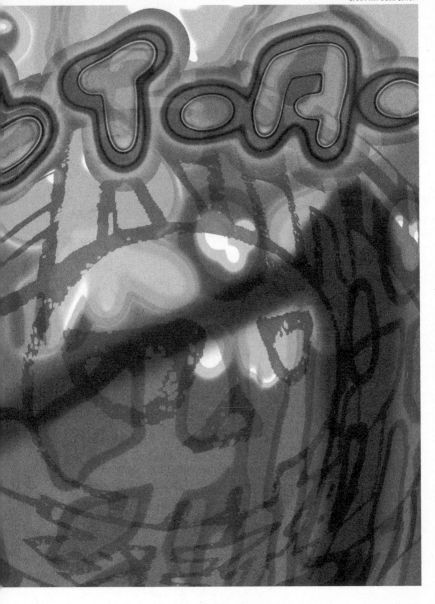

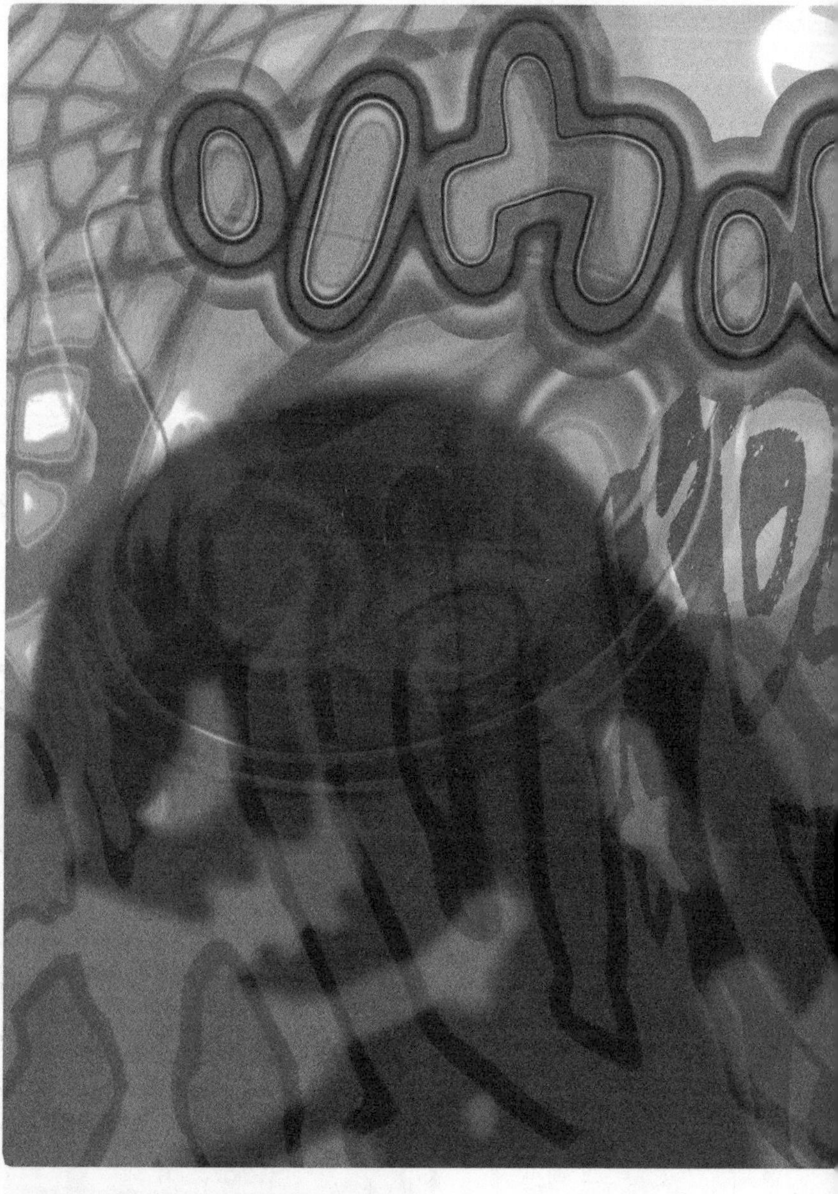

CHAPTER 51: OPERATION CAPTURE BABA YAGA CASTLE (PART 6)

SOUL EATER

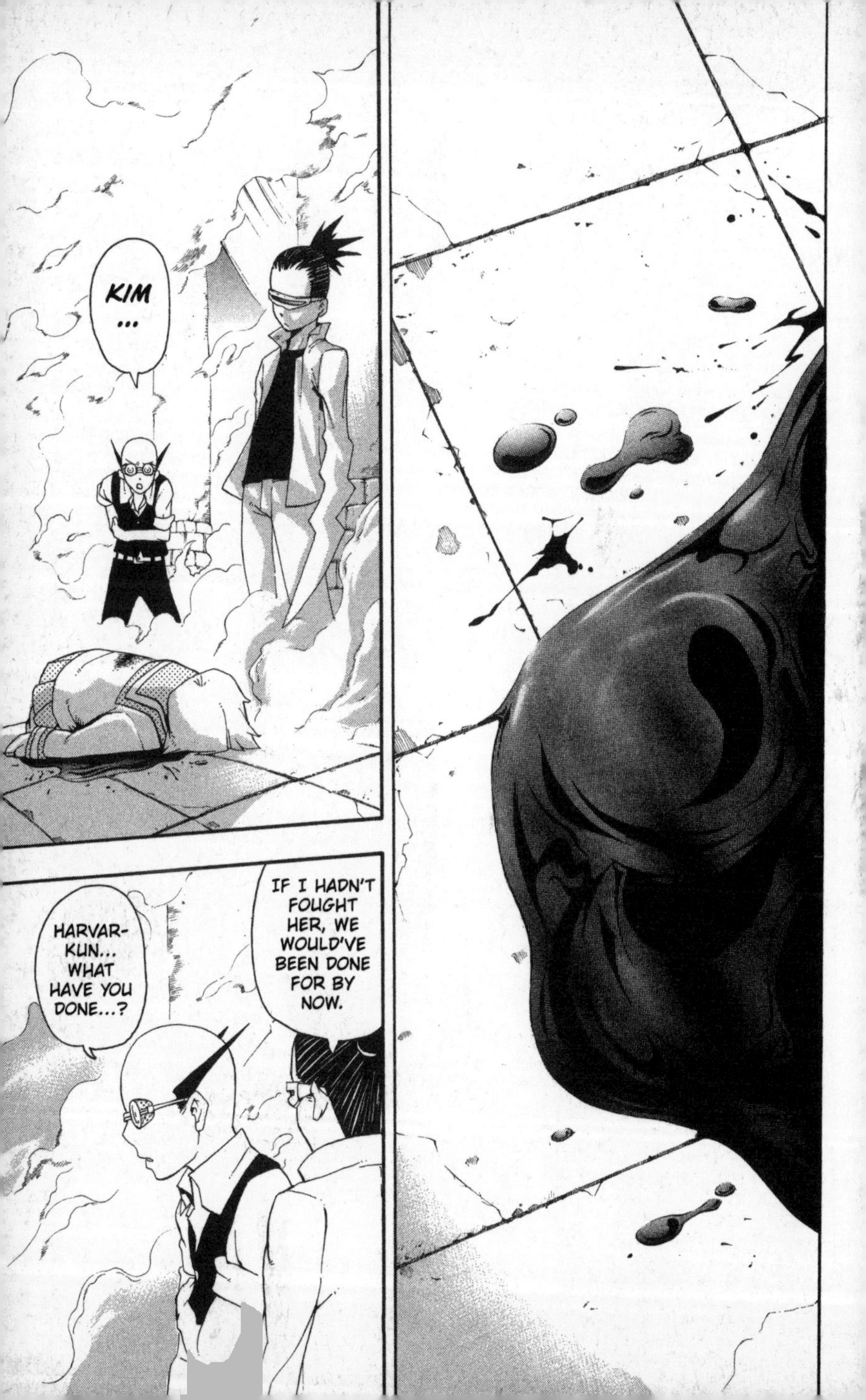
KIM ...
IF I HADN'T FOUGHT HER, WE WOULD'VE BEEN DONE FOR BY NOW.
HARVAR-KUN... WHAT HAVE YOU DONE...?

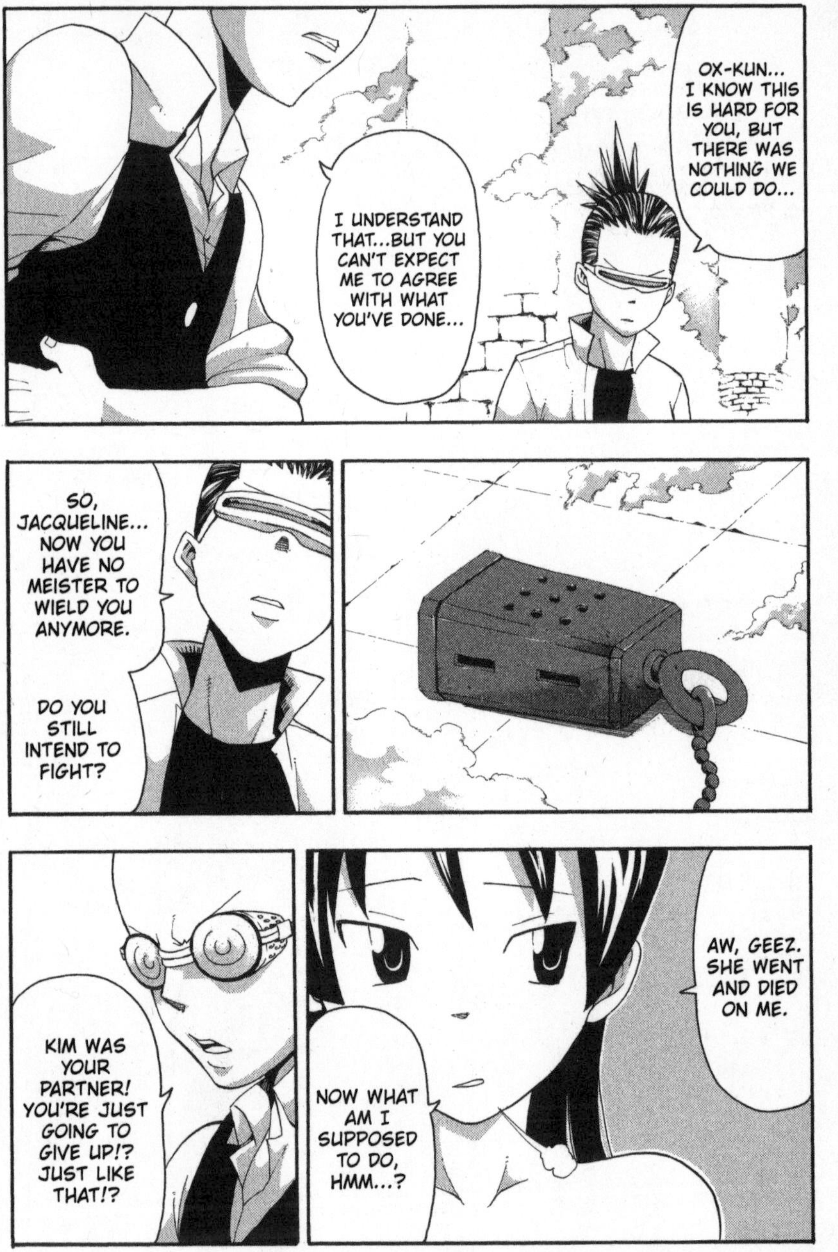
OX-KUN... I KNOW THIS IS HARD FOR YOU, BUT THERE WAS NOTHING WE COULD DO...
I UNDERSTAND THAT...BUT YOU CAN'T EXPECT ME TO AGREE WITH WHAT YOU'VE DONE...
SO, JACQUELINE... NOW YOU HAVE NO MEISTER TO WIELD YOU ANYMORE.
DO YOU STILL INTEND TO FIGHT?
AW, GEEZ. SHE WENT AND DIED ON ME.
NOW WHAT AM I SUPPOSED TO DO, HMM...?
KIM WAS YOUR PARTNER! YOU'RE JUST GOING TO GIVE UP!? JUST LIKE THAT!?

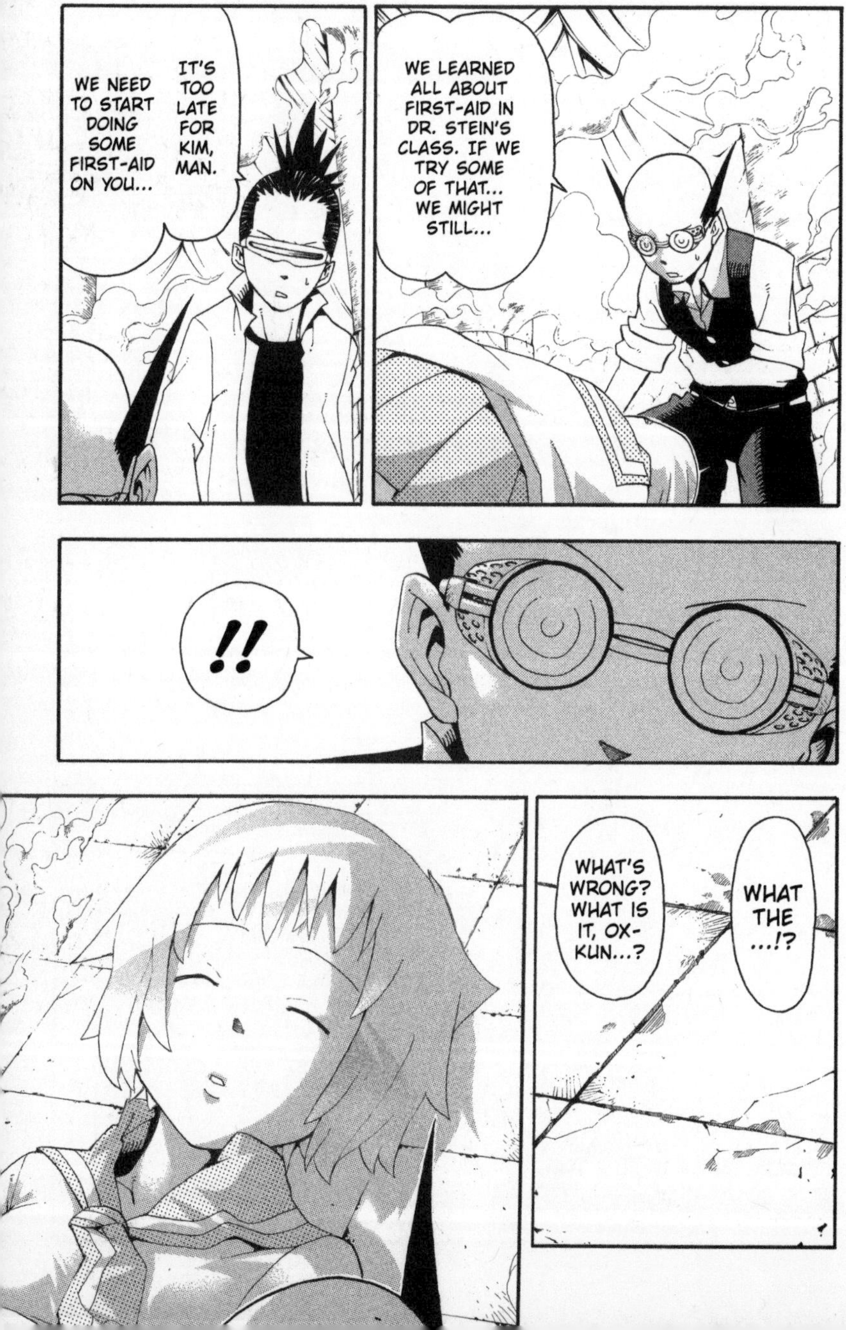
WE LEARNED ALL ABOUT FIRST-AID IN DR. STEIN'S CLASS. IF WE TRY SOME OF THAT... WE MIGHT STILL...
IT'S TOO LATE FOR KIM, MAN.
WE NEED TO START DOING SOME FIRST-AID ON YOU...
!!
WHAT THE ...!?
WHAT'S WRONG? WHAT IS IT, OX-KUN...?

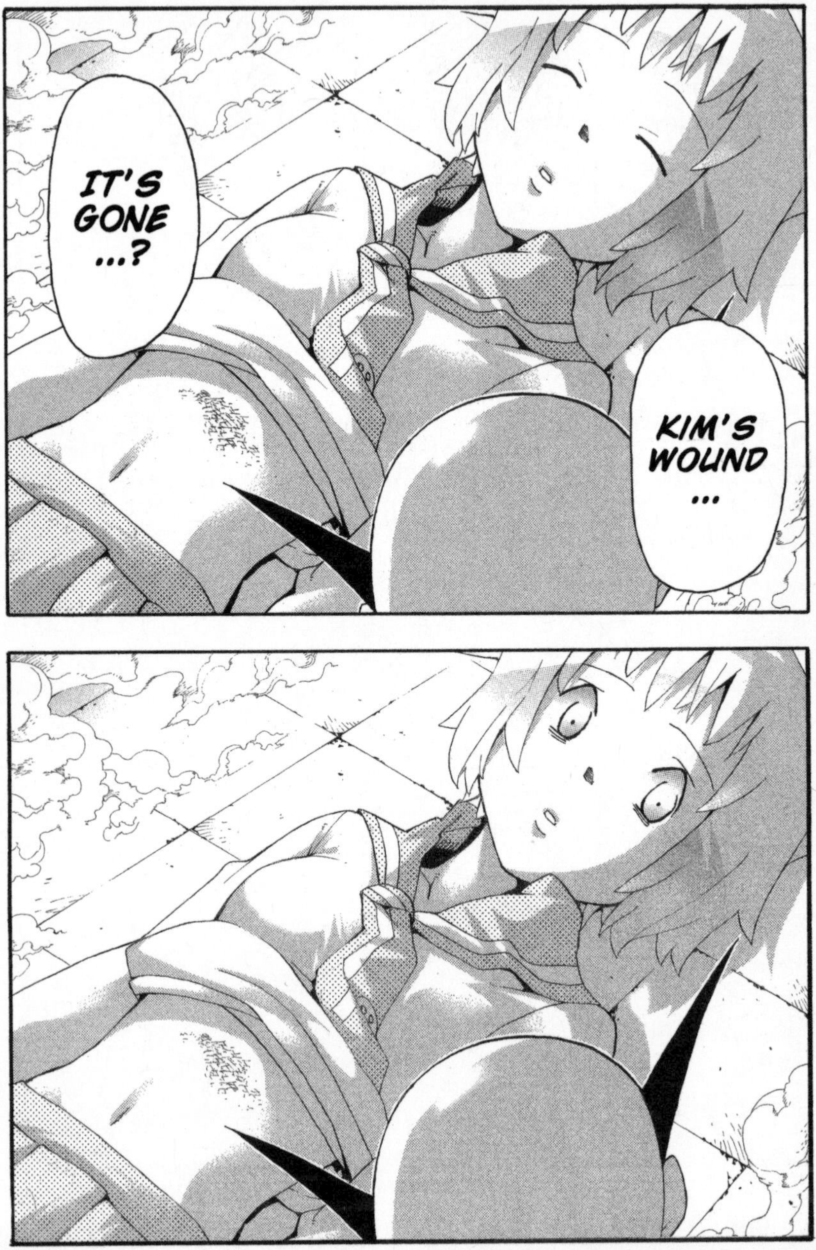
KIM'S WOUND ...
IT'S GONE ...?

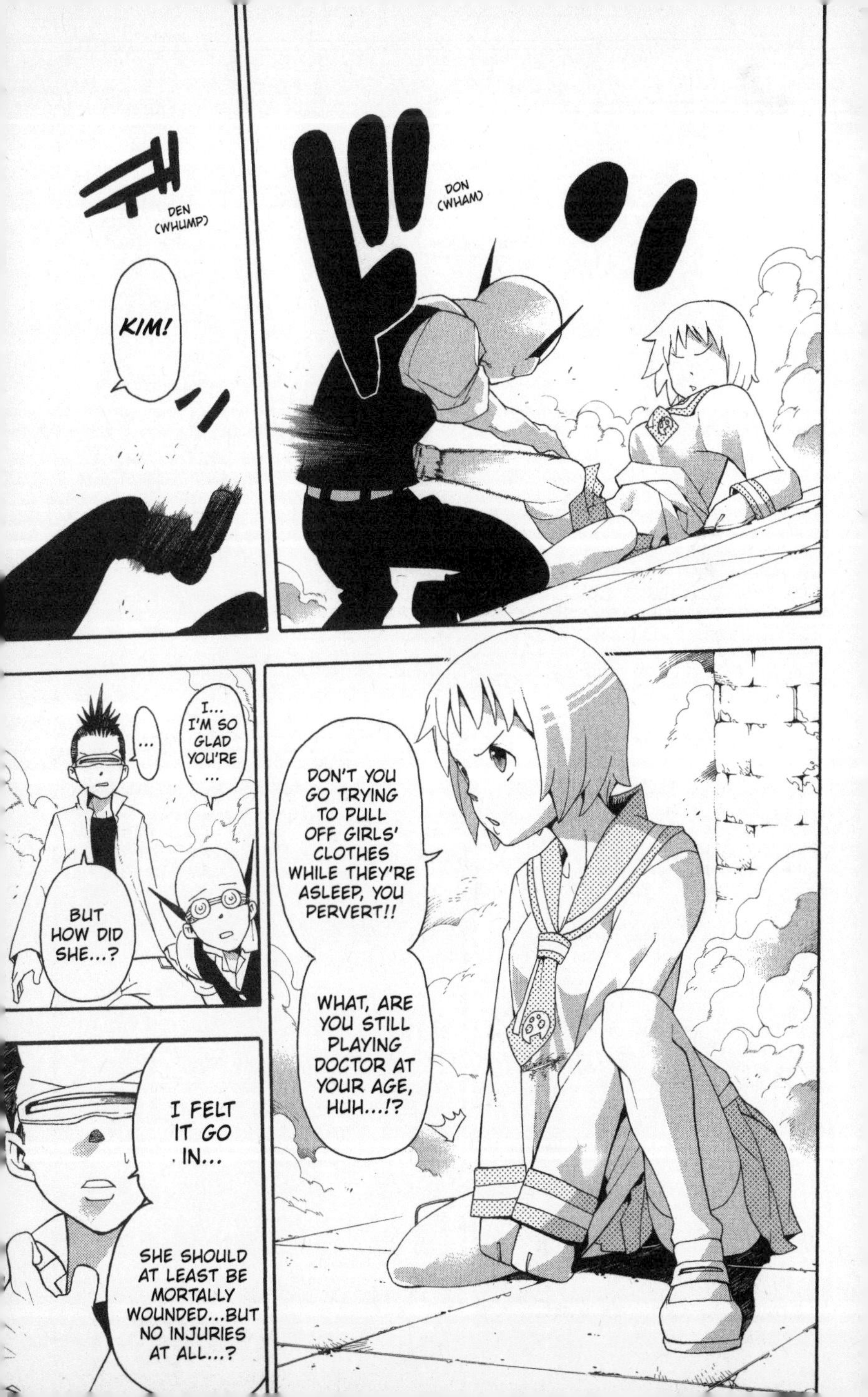
DON (WHAM)
DEN (WHUMP)
KIM!
DON'T YOU GO TRYING TO PULL OFF GIRLS' CLOTHES WHILE THEY'RE ASLEEP, YOU PERVERT!!
WHAT, ARE YOU STILL PLAYING DOCTOR AT YOUR AGE, HUH...!?
I... I'M SO GLAD YOU'RE ...
...
BUT HOW DID SHE...?
I FELT IT GO IN...
SHE SHOULD AT LEAST BE MORTALLY WOUNDED...BUT NO INJURIES AT ALL...?

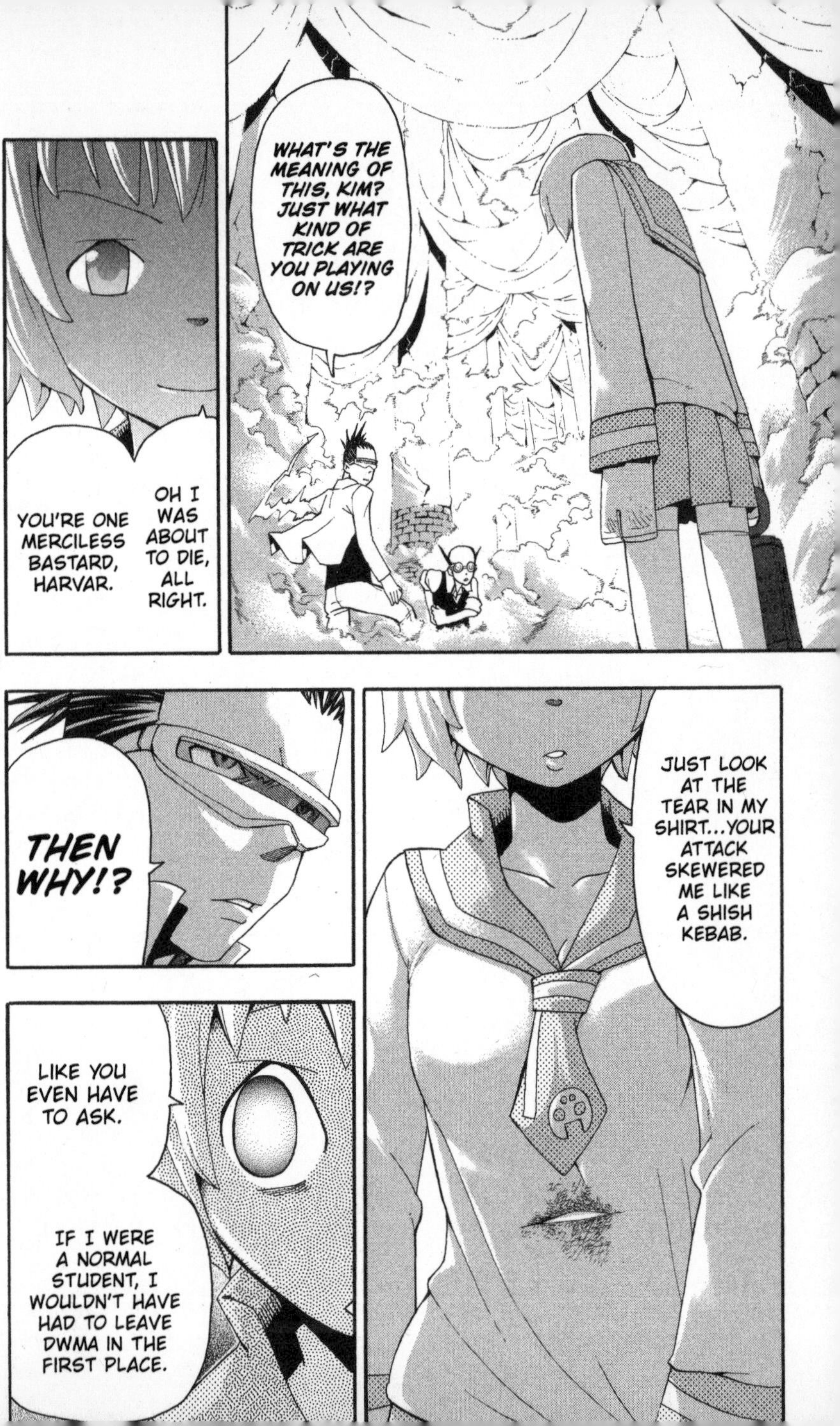
WHAT'S THE MEANING OF THIS, KIM? JUST WHAT KIND OF TRICK ARE YOU PLAYING ON US!?
OH I WAS ABOUT TO DIE, ALL RIGHT.
YOU'RE ONE MERCILESS BASTARD, HARVAR.
JUST LOOK AT THE TEAR IN MY SHIRT...YOUR ATTACK SKEWERED ME LIKE A SHISH KEBAB.
THEN WHY!?
LIKE YOU EVEN HAVE TO ASK.
IF I WERE A NORMAL STUDENT, I WOULDN'T HAVE HAD TO LEAVE DWMA IN THE FIRST PLACE.

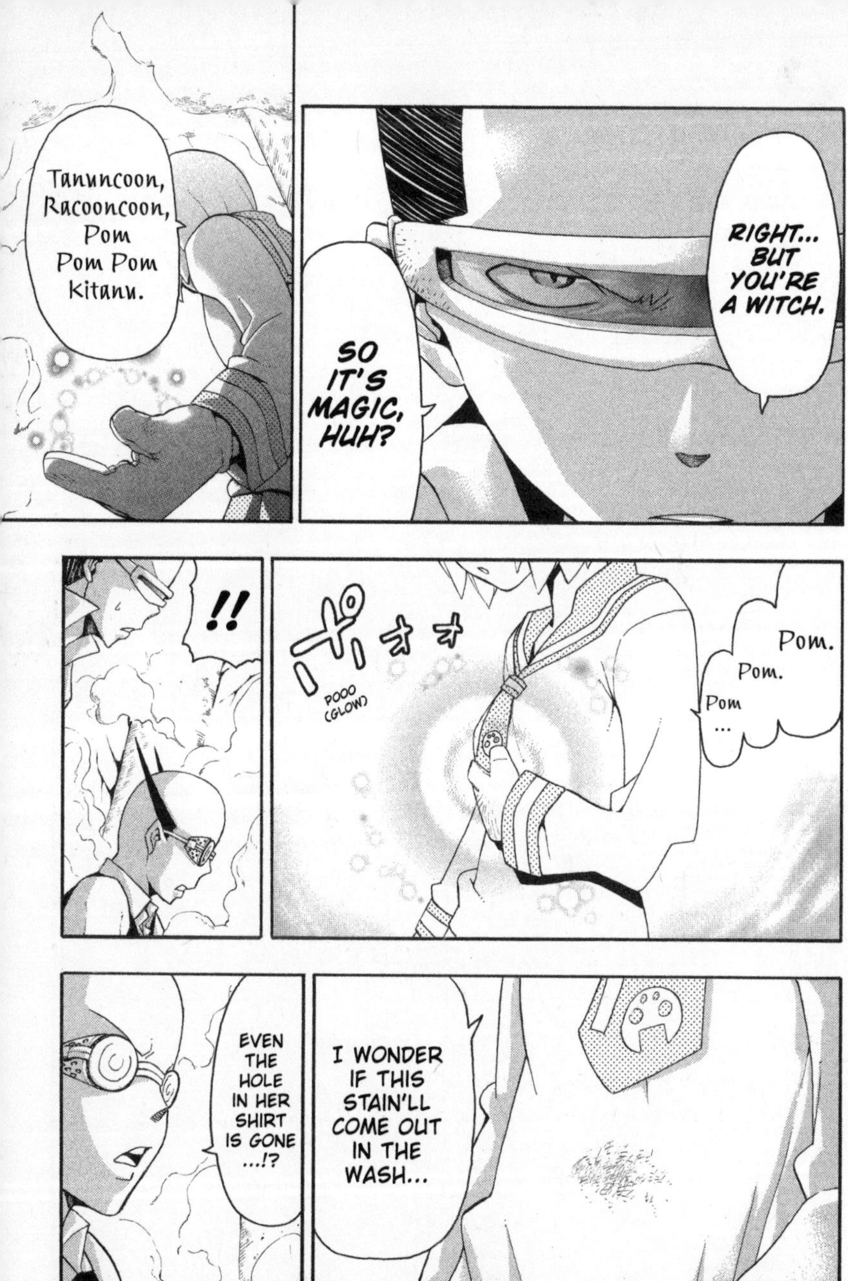
RIGHT... BUT YOU'RE A WITCH.
SO IT'S MAGIC, HUH?
Tanuncoon, Racooncoon, Pom Pom Pom Kitanu.
Pom. Pom. Pom ...
ポォォ
POOO (GLOW)
!!
I WONDER IF THIS STAIN'LL COME OUT IN THE WASH...
EVEN THE HOLE IN HER SHIRT IS GONE ...!?

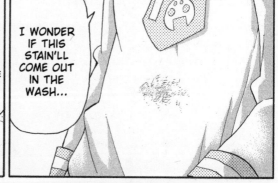

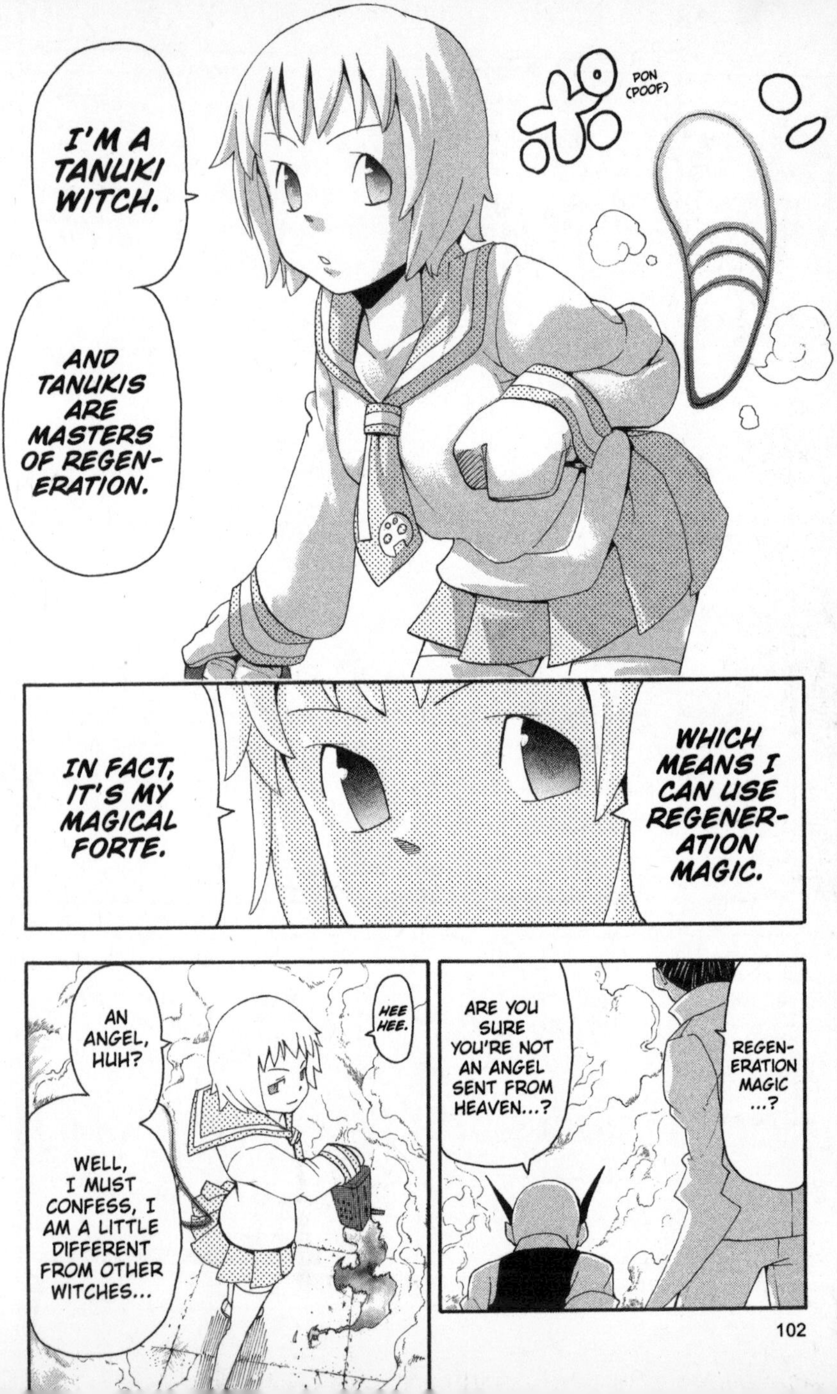
PON (POOF)
I'M A TANUKI WITCH.
AND TANUKIS ARE MASTERS OF REGEN-ERATION.
WHICH MEANS I CAN USE REGENER-ATION MAGIC.
IN FACT, IT'S MY MAGICAL FORTE.
REGEN-ERATION MAGIC ...?
ARE YOU SURE YOU'RE NOT AN ANGEL SENT FROM HEAVEN...?
HEE HEE.
AN ANGEL, HUH?
WELL, I MUST CONFESS, I AM A LITTLE DIFFERENT FROM OTHER WITCHES...

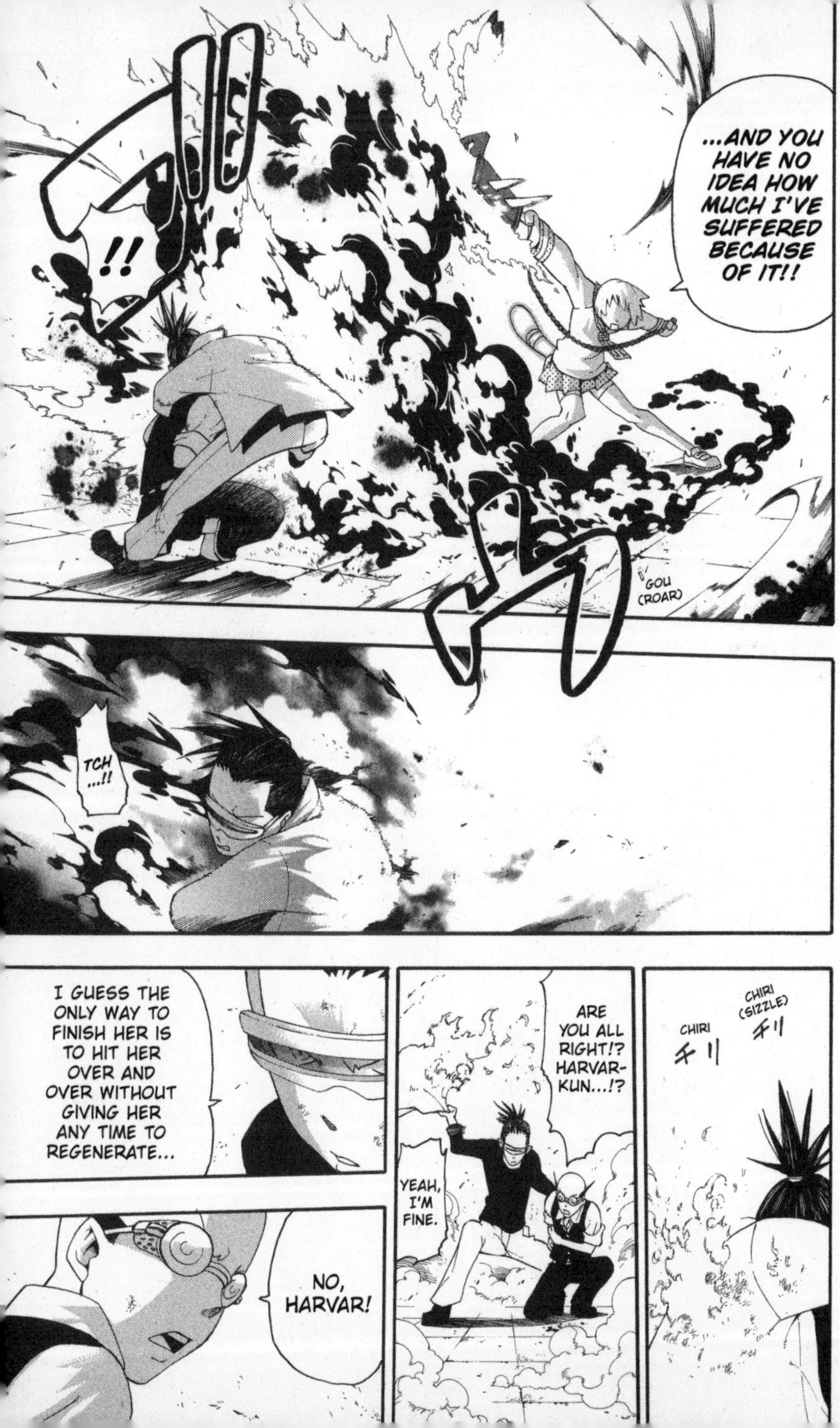
...AND YOU HAVE NO IDEA HOW MUCH I'VE SUFFERED BECAUSE OF IT!!
!!
GOU (ROAR)
TCH ...!!
CHIRI (SIZZLE)
チリ
CHIRI
チリ
ARE YOU ALL RIGHT!? HARVAR-KUN...!?
YEAH, I'M FINE.
I GUESS THE ONLY WAY TO FINISH HER IS TO HIT HER OVER AND OVER WITHOUT GIVING HER ANY TIME TO REGENERATE...
NO, HARVAR!

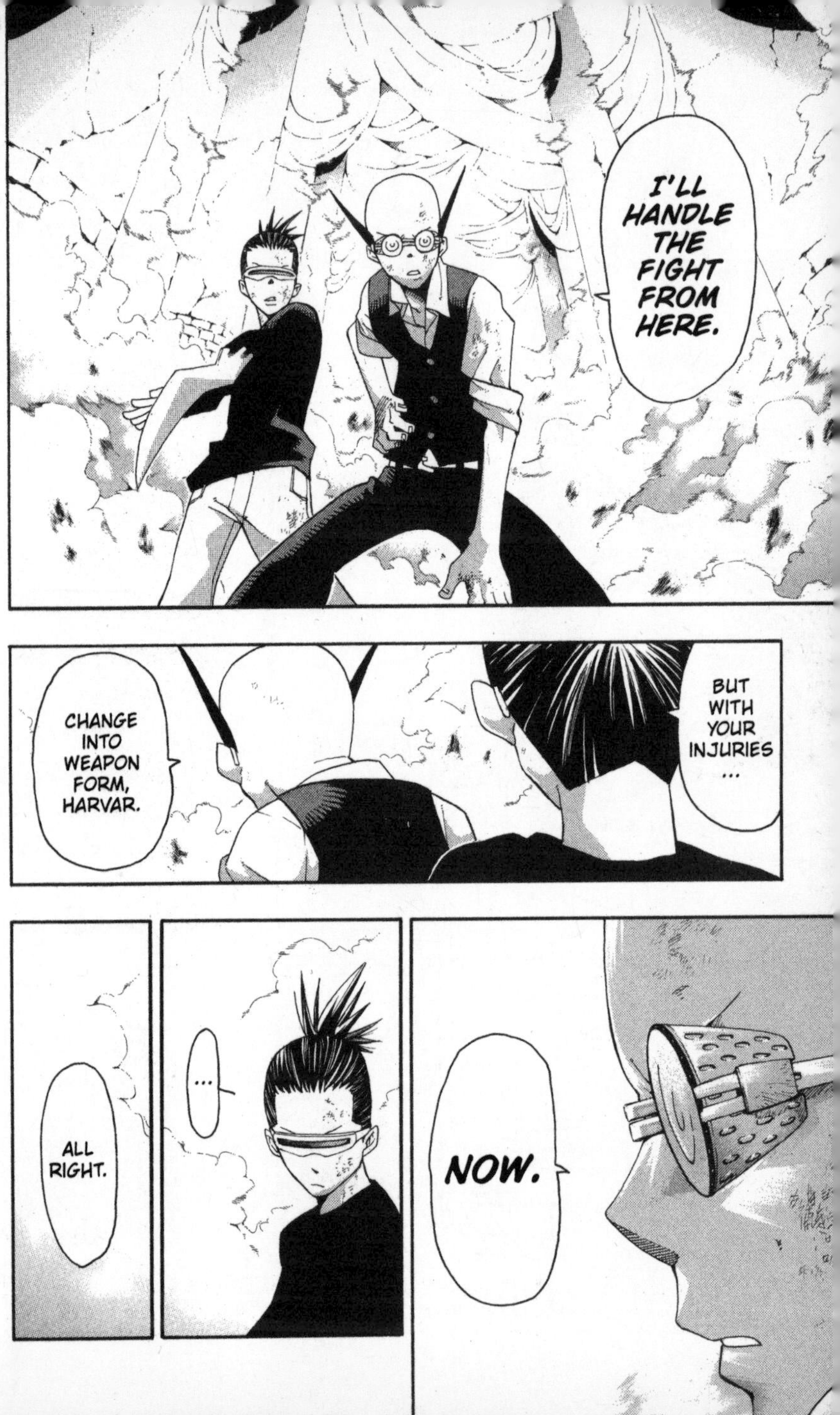
I'LL HANDLE THE FIGHT FROM HERE.
BUT WITH YOUR INJURIES...
CHANGE INTO WEAPON FORM, HARVAR.
NOW.
...
ALL RIGHT.

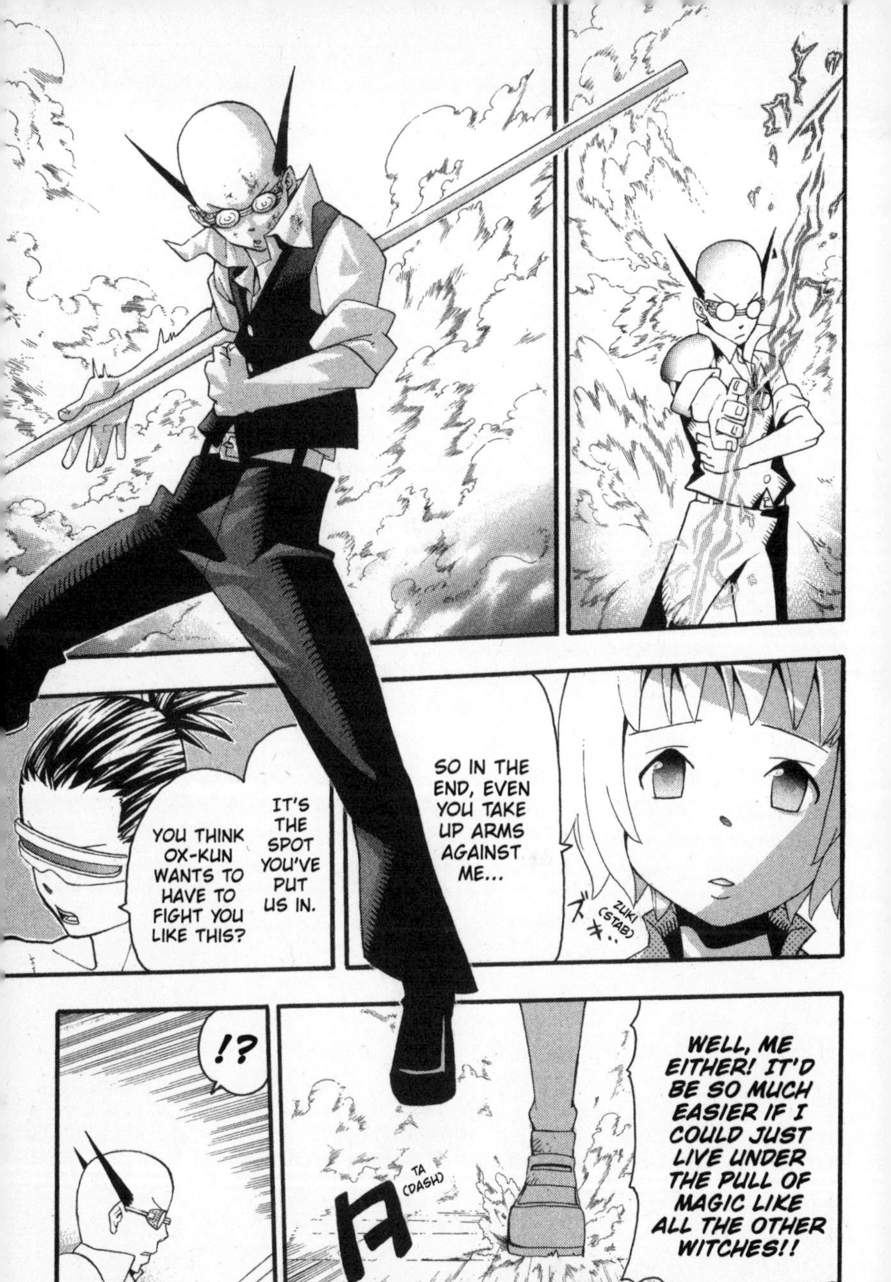
SO IN THE END, EVEN YOU TAKE UP ARMS AGAINST ME...
ZUKI (STAB)
IT'S THE SPOT YOU'VE PUT US IN.
YOU THINK OX-KUN WANTS TO HAVE TO FIGHT YOU LIKE THIS?
WELL, ME EITHER! IT'D BE SO MUCH EASIER IF I COULD JUST LIVE UNDER THE PULL OF MAGIC LIKE ALL THE OTHER WITCHES!!
TA (DASH)
!?

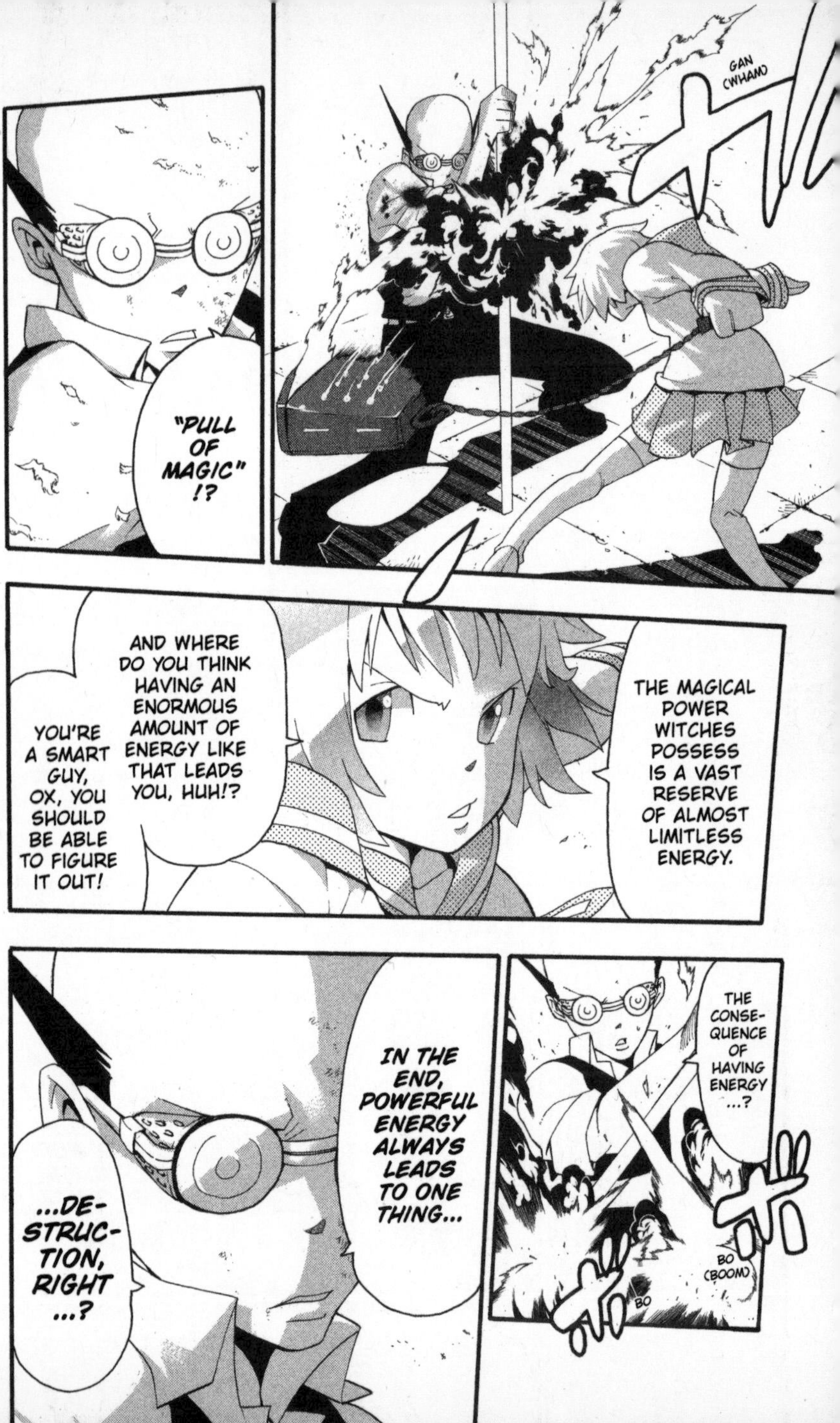
GAN (WHAM)
"PULL OF MAGIC" !?
THE MAGICAL POWER WITCHES POSSESS IS A VAST RESERVE OF ALMOST LIMITLESS ENERGY.
AND WHERE DO YOU THINK HAVING AN ENORMOUS AMOUNT OF ENERGY LIKE THAT LEADS YOU, HUH!?
YOU'RE A SMART GUY, OX, YOU SHOULD BE ABLE TO FIGURE IT OUT!
THE CONSE-QUENCE OF HAVING ENERGY ...?
BO (BOOM)
BO
IN THE END, POWERFUL ENERGY ALWAYS LEADS TO ONE THING...
...DE-STRUC-TION, RIGHT ...?

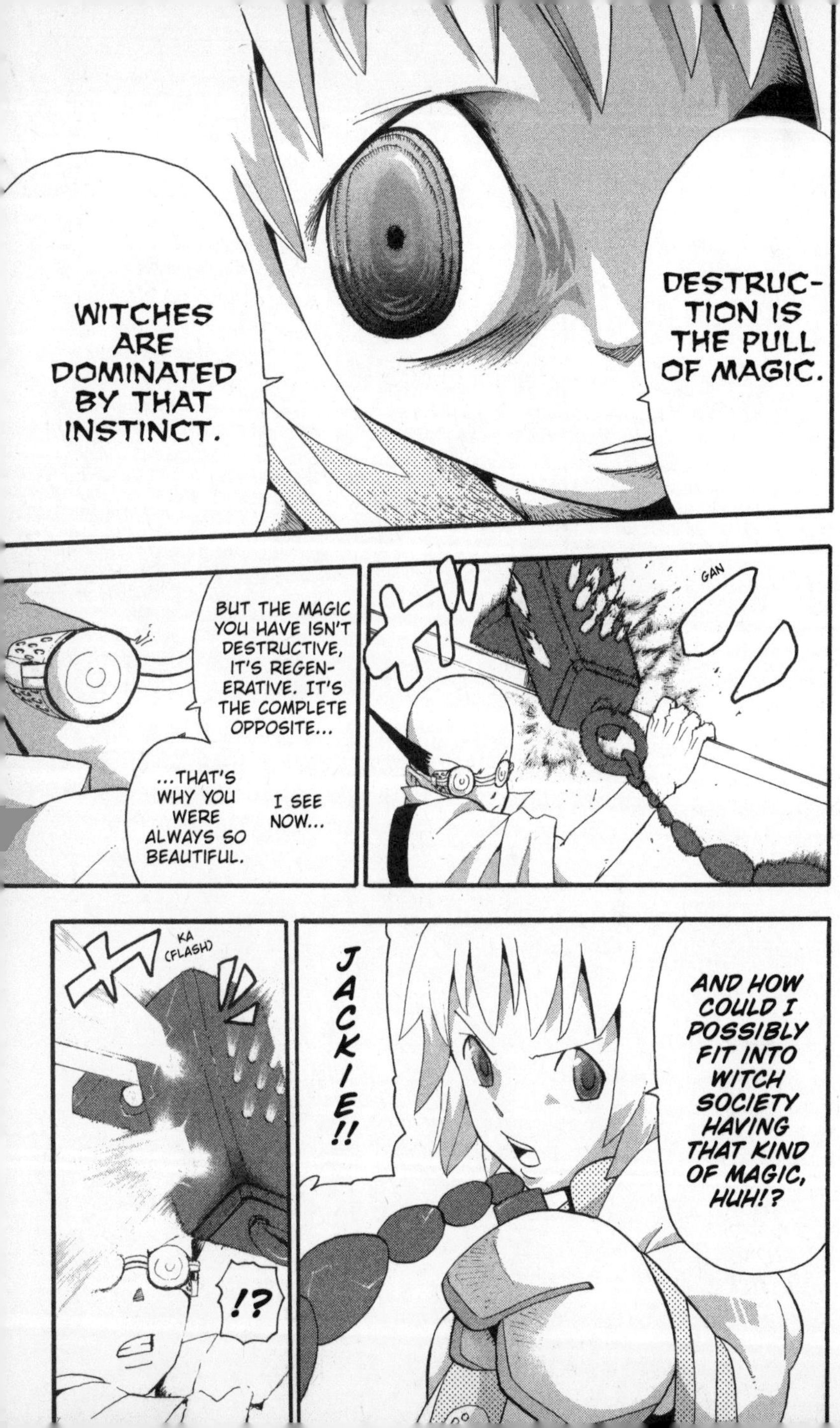
DESTRUCTION IS THE PULL OF MAGIC.
WITCHES ARE DOMINATED BY THAT INSTINCT.
GAN
BUT THE MAGIC YOU HAVE ISN'T DESTRUCTIVE, IT'S REGENERATIVE. IT'S THE COMPLETE OPPOSITE...
I SEE NOW...
...THAT'S WHY YOU WERE ALWAYS SO BEAUTIFUL.
AND HOW COULD I POSSIBLY FIT INTO WITCH SOCIETY HAVING THAT KIND OF MAGIC, HUH!?
JACKIE!!
KA (FLASH)
!?

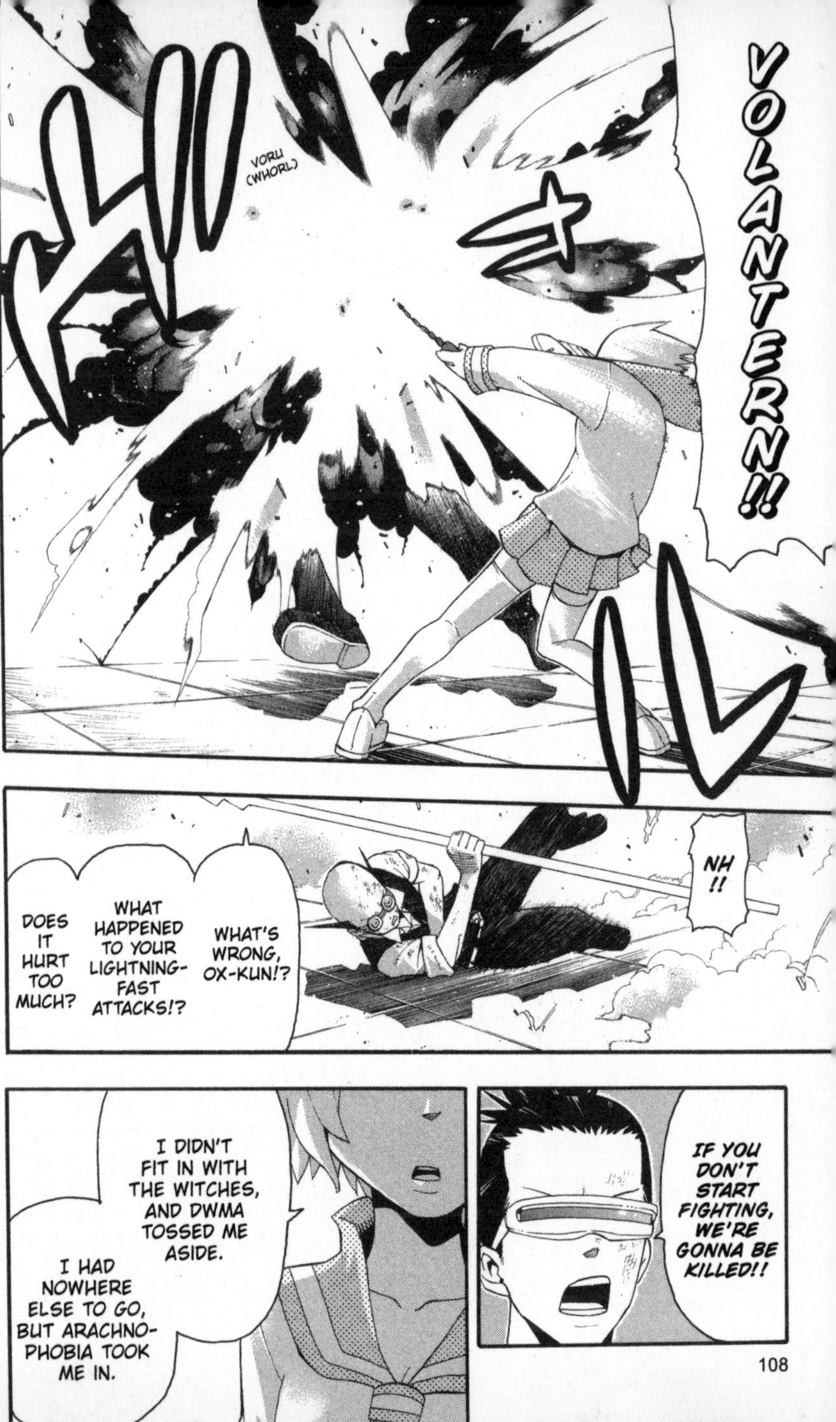
VOLANTERN!!
VORU (WHORL)
NH!!
WHAT'S WRONG, OX-KUN!?
WHAT HAPPENED TO YOUR LIGHTNING-FAST ATTACKS!?
DOES IT HURT TOO MUCH?
IF YOU DON'T START FIGHTING, WE'RE GONNA BE KILLED!!
I DIDN'T FIT IN WITH THE WITCHES, AND DWMA TOSSED ME ASIDE.
I HAD NOWHERE ELSE TO GO, BUT ARACHNOPHOBIA TOOK ME IN.

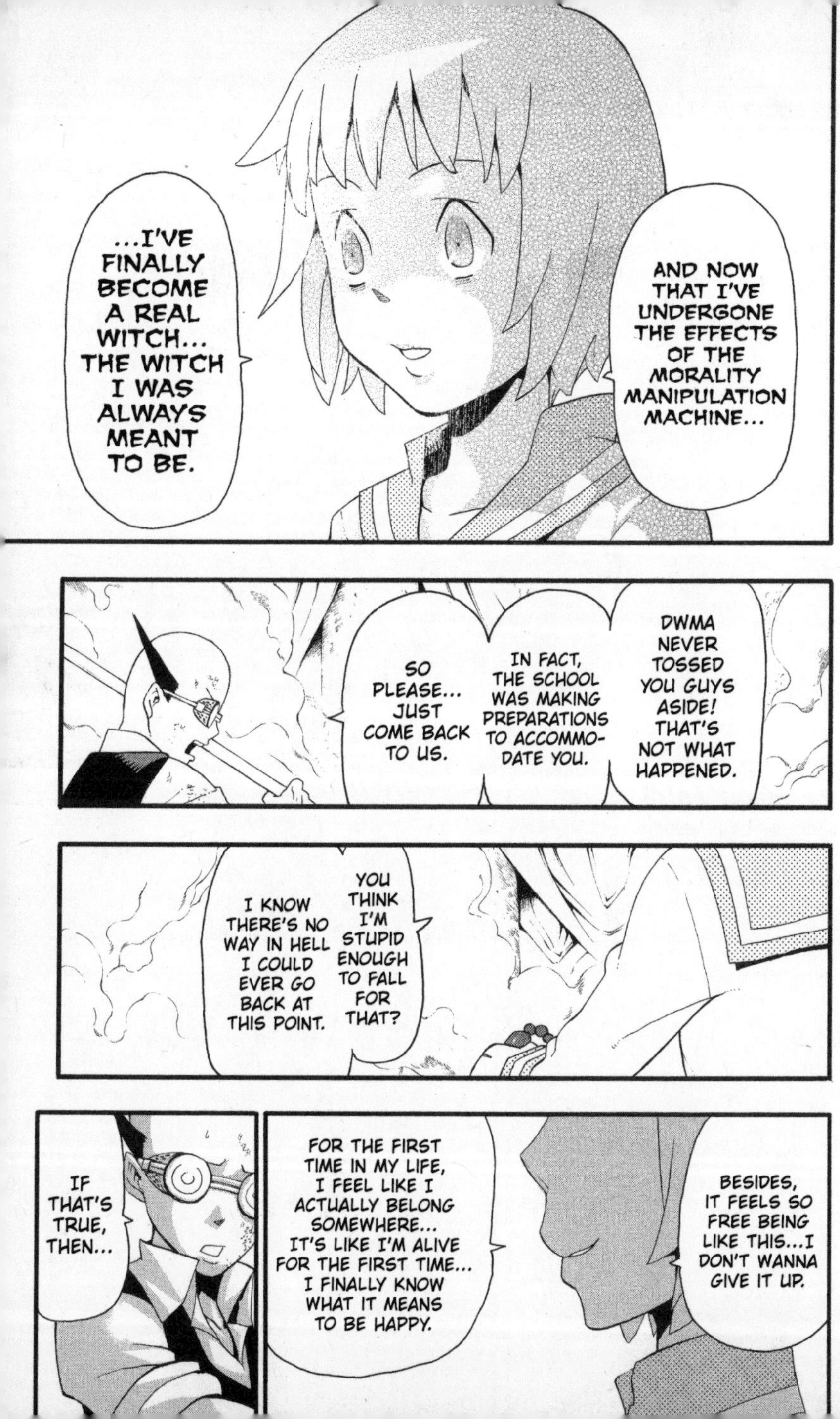
AND NOW THAT I'VE UNDERGONE THE EFFECTS OF THE MORALITY MANIPULATION MACHINE...
...I'VE FINALLY BECOME A REAL WITCH... THE WITCH I WAS ALWAYS MEANT TO BE.
DWMA NEVER TOSSED YOU GUYS ASIDE! THAT'S NOT WHAT HAPPENED.
IN FACT, THE SCHOOL WAS MAKING PREPARATIONS TO ACCOMMODATE YOU.
SO PLEASE... JUST COME BACK TO US.
YOU THINK I'M STUPID ENOUGH TO FALL FOR THAT?
I KNOW THERE'S NO WAY IN HELL I COULD EVER GO BACK AT THIS POINT.
BESIDES, IT FEELS SO FREE BEING LIKE THIS...I DON'T WANNA GIVE IT UP.
FOR THE FIRST TIME IN MY LIFE, I FEEL LIKE I ACTUALLY BELONG SOMEWHERE... IT'S LIKE I'M ALIVE FOR THE FIRST TIME... I FINALLY KNOW WHAT IT MEANS TO BE HAPPY.
IF THAT'S TRUE, THEN...

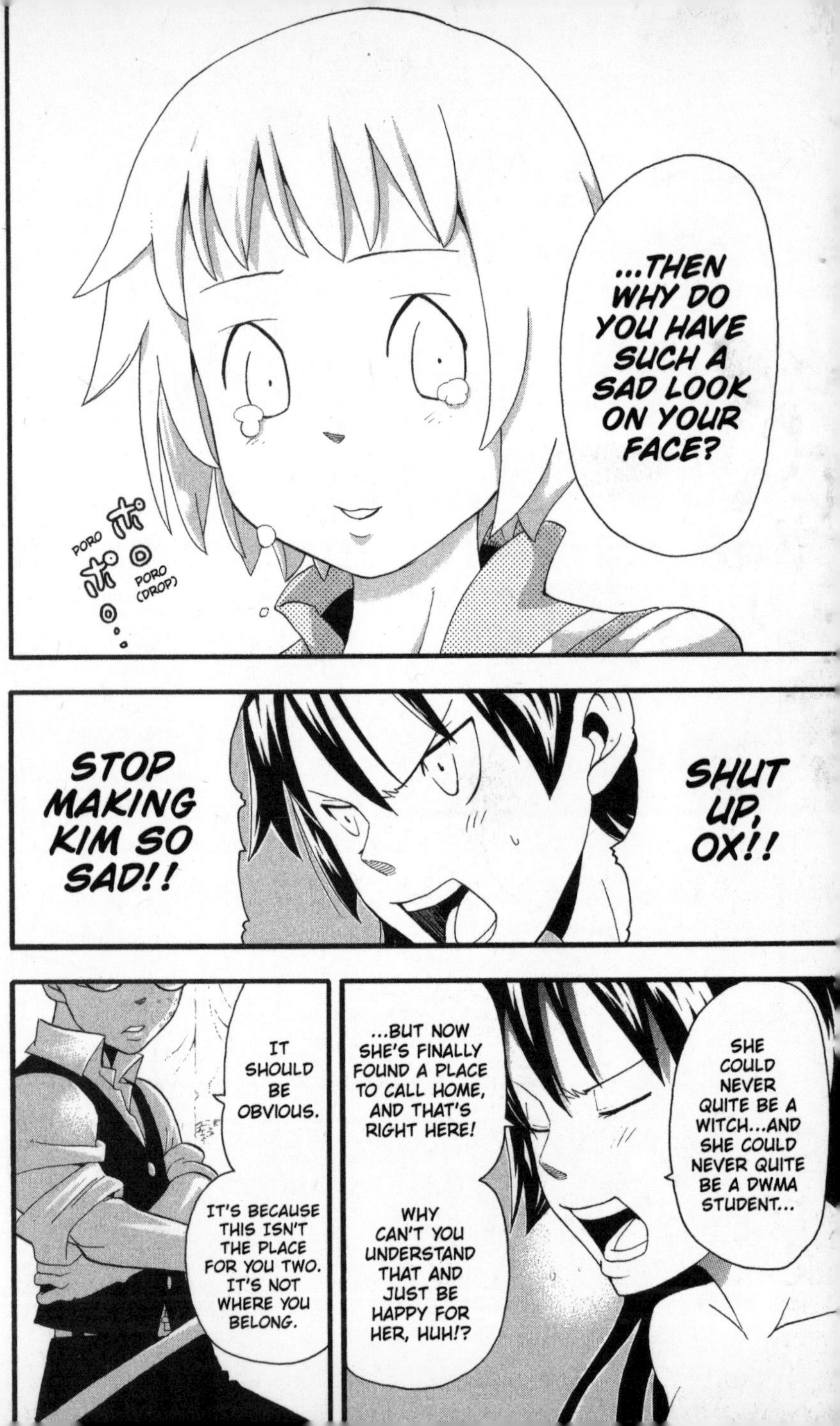
...THEN WHY DO YOU HAVE SUCH A SAD LOOK ON YOUR FACE?
PORO
PORO (DROP)
SHUT UP, OX!!
STOP MAKING KIM SO SAD!!
SHE COULD NEVER QUITE BE A WITCH...AND SHE COULD NEVER QUITE BE A DWMA STUDENT...
...BUT NOW SHE'S FINALLY FOUND A PLACE TO CALL HOME, AND THAT'S RIGHT HERE!
WHY CAN'T YOU UNDERSTAND THAT AND JUST BE HAPPY FOR HER, HUH!?
IT SHOULD BE OBVIOUS.
IT'S BECAUSE THIS ISN'T THE PLACE FOR YOU TWO. IT'S NOT WHERE YOU BELONG.

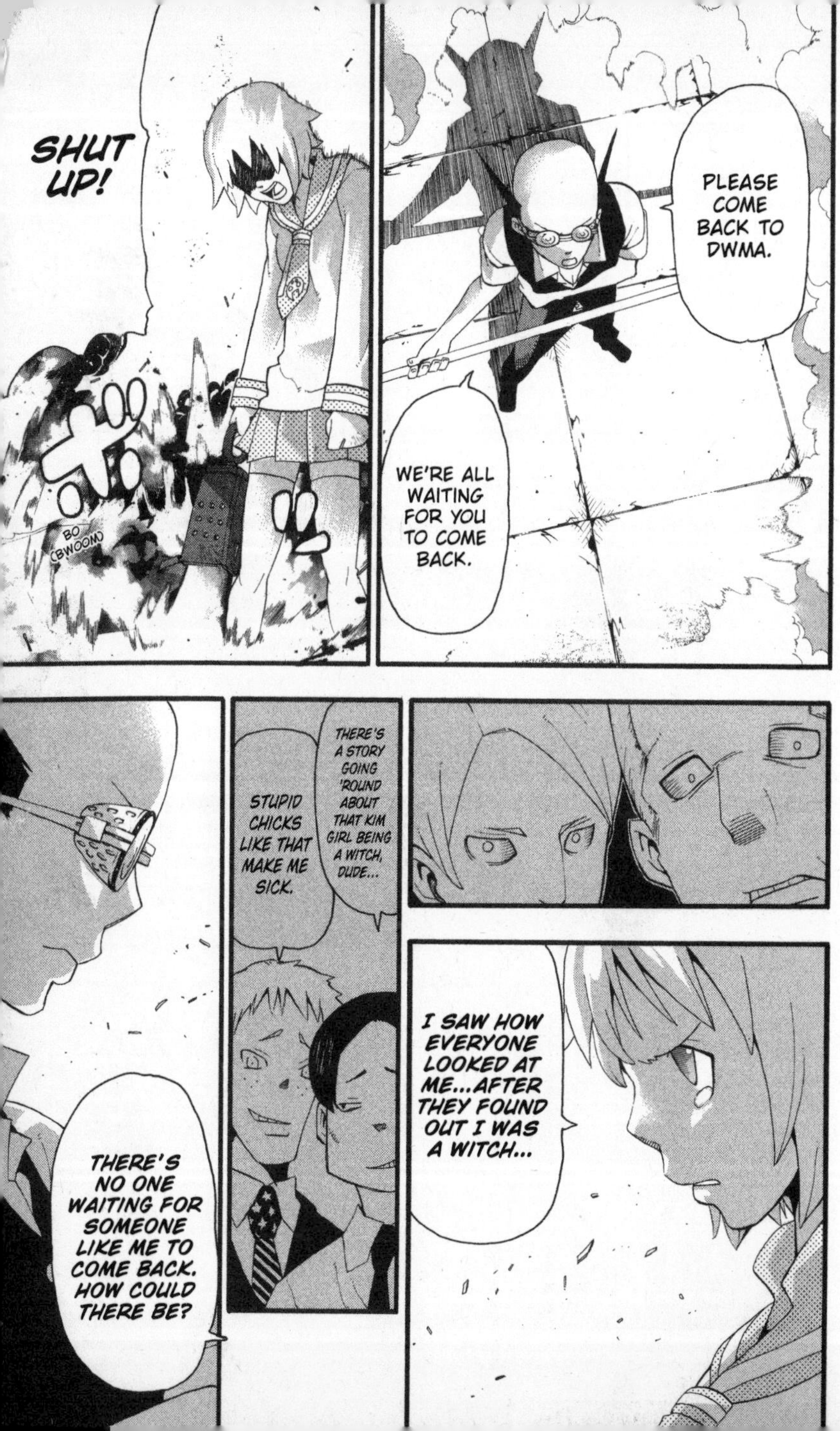
PLEASE COME BACK TO DWMA.
WE'RE ALL WAITING FOR YOU TO COME BACK.
SHUT UP!
BO (BWOOM)
I SAW HOW EVERYONE LOOKED AT ME...AFTER THEY FOUND OUT I WAS A WITCH...
THERE'S A STORY GOING 'ROUND ABOUT THAT KIM GIRL BEING A WITCH, DUDE...
STUPID CHICKS LIKE THAT MAKE ME SICK.
THERE'S NO ONE WAITING FOR SOMEONE LIKE ME TO COME BACK. HOW COULD THERE BE?

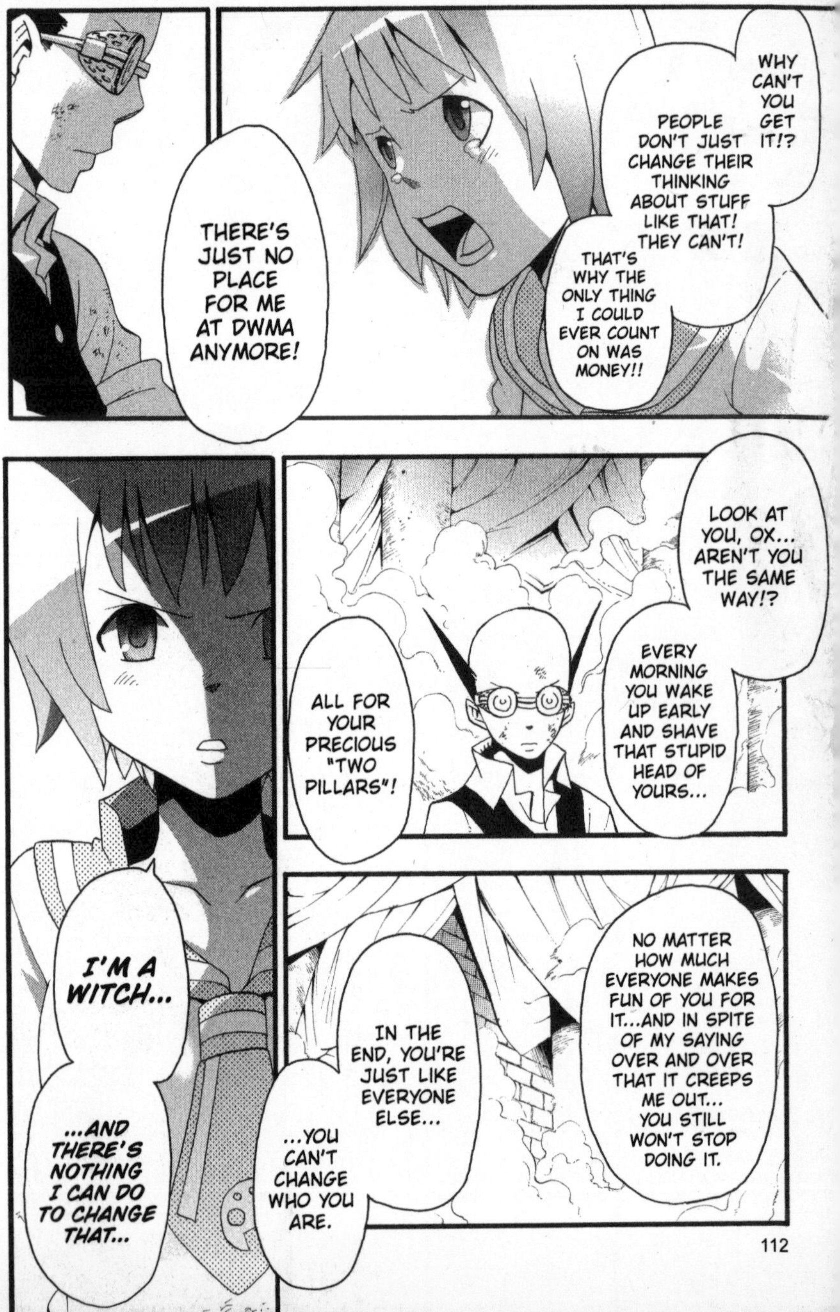
WHY CAN'T YOU GET IT!?
PEOPLE DON'T JUST CHANGE THEIR THINKING ABOUT STUFF LIKE THAT! THEY CAN'T!
THAT'S WHY THE ONLY THING I COULD EVER COUNT ON WAS MONEY!!
THERE'S JUST NO PLACE FOR ME AT DWMA ANYMORE!
LOOK AT YOU, OX... AREN'T YOU THE SAME WAY!?
EVERY MORNING YOU WAKE UP EARLY AND SHAVE THAT STUPID HEAD OF YOURS...
ALL FOR YOUR PRECIOUS "TWO PILLARS"!
NO MATTER HOW MUCH EVERYONE MAKES FUN OF YOU FOR IT...AND IN SPITE OF MY SAYING OVER AND OVER THAT IT CREEPS ME OUT... YOU STILL WON'T STOP DOING IT.
IN THE END, YOU'RE JUST LIKE EVERYONE ELSE...
...YOU CAN'T CHANGE WHO YOU ARE.
I'M A WITCH...
...AND THERE'S NOTHING I CAN DO TO CHANGE THAT...

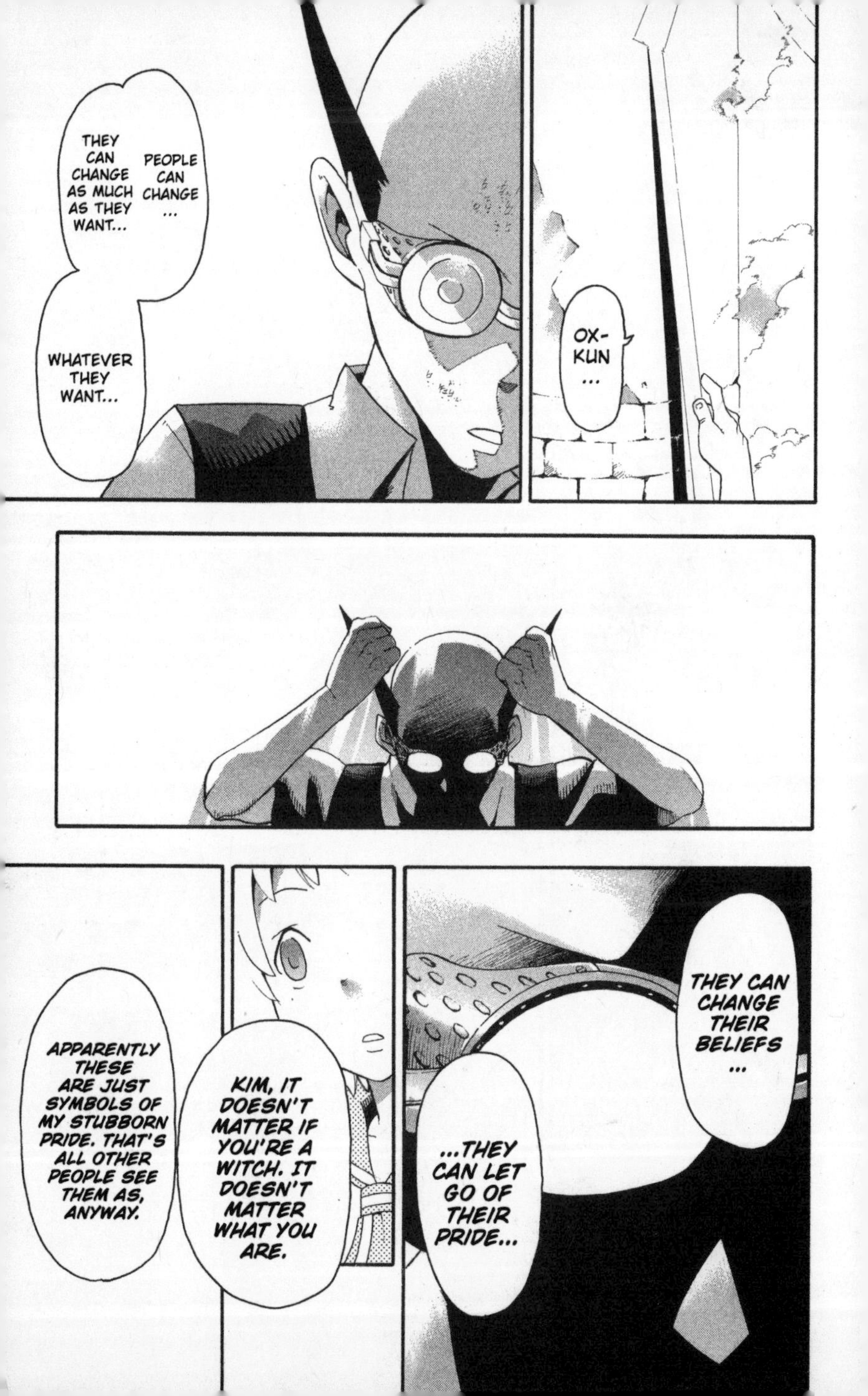
OX-KUN ...
PEOPLE CAN CHANGE ...
THEY CAN CHANGE AS MUCH AS THEY WANT...
WHATEVER THEY WANT...
THEY CAN CHANGE THEIR BELIEFS ...
...THEY CAN LET GO OF THEIR PRIDE...
KIM, IT DOESN'T MATTER IF YOU'RE A WITCH. IT DOESN'T MATTER WHAT YOU ARE.
APPARENTLY THESE ARE JUST SYMBOLS OF MY STUBBORN PRIDE. THAT'S ALL OTHER PEOPLE SEE THEM AS, ANYWAY.

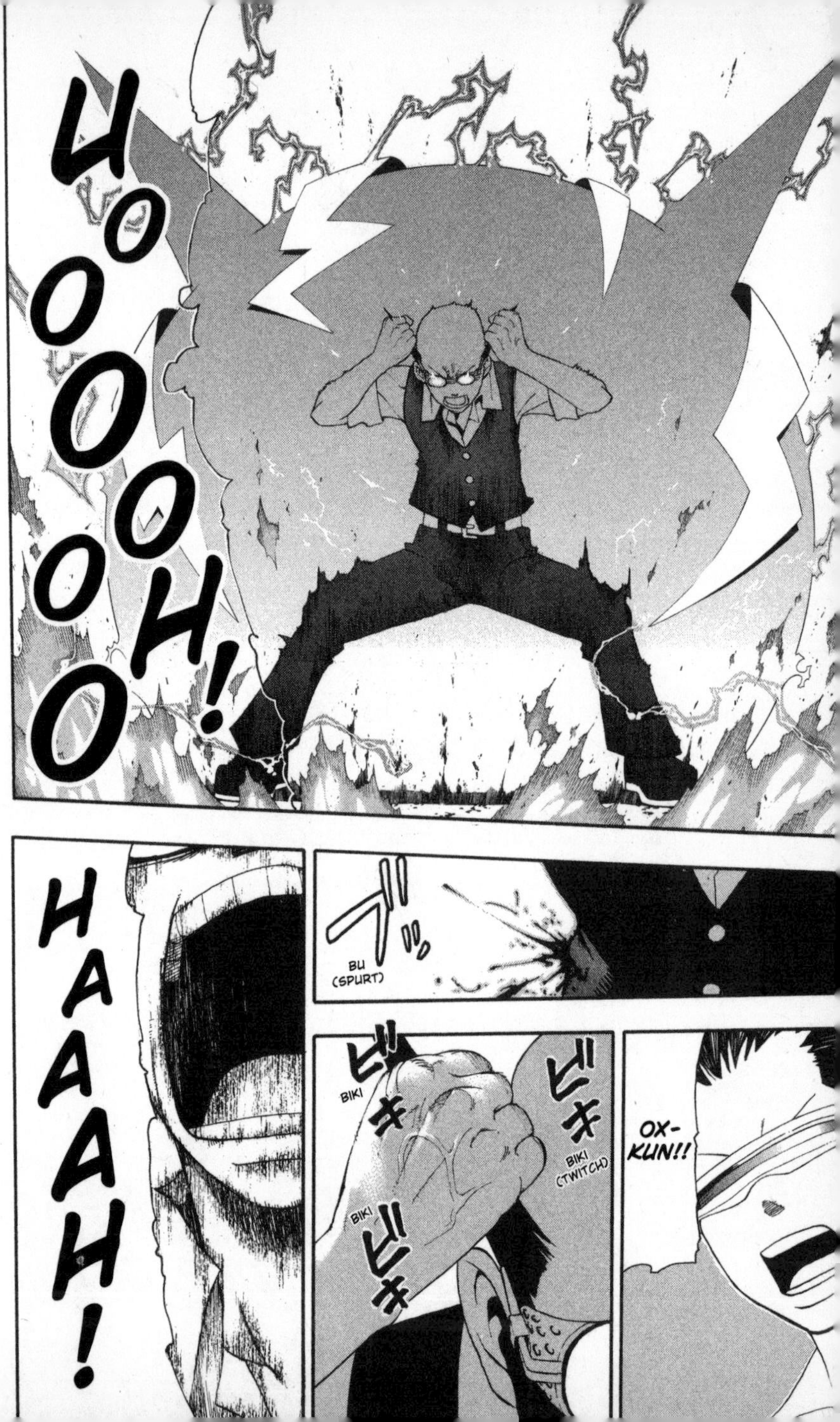
UOOOOOOH!
ブ
BU (SPURT)
OX-KUN!!
ビキ
BIKI (TWITCH)
ビキ
BIKI
ビキ
BIKI
HAAAAH!

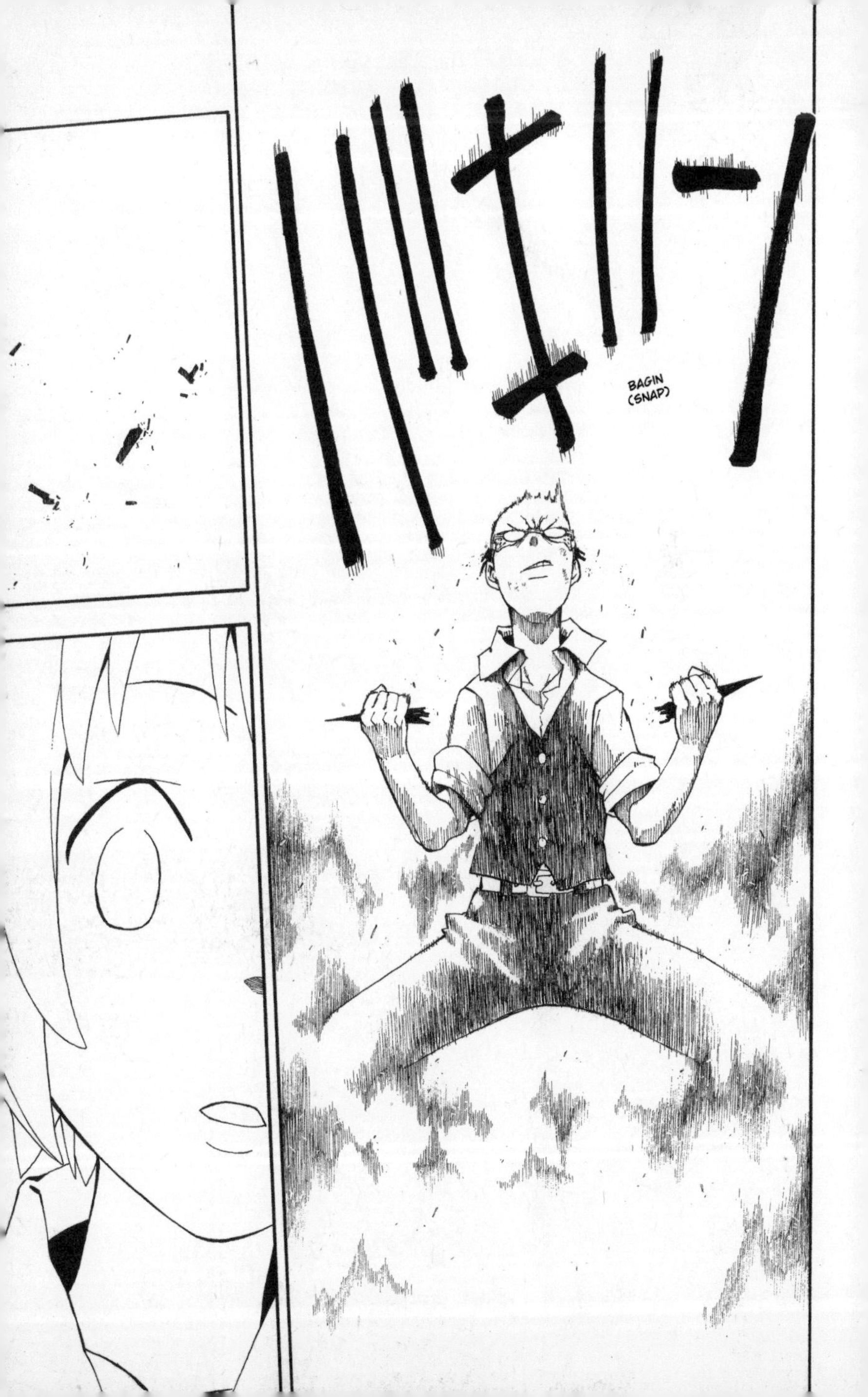
BAGIN (SNAP)

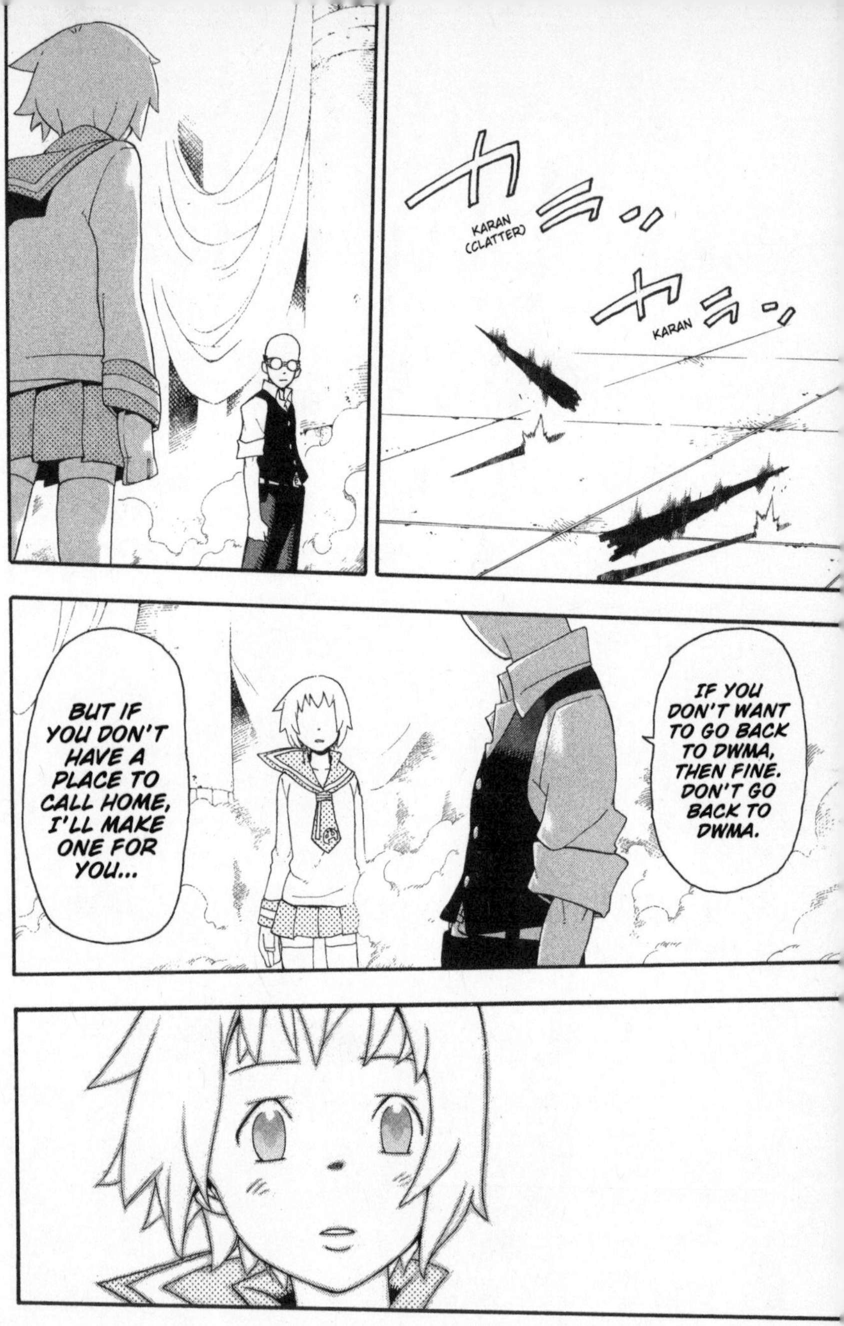
KARAN (CLATTER)
KARAN
IF YOU DON'T WANT TO GO BACK TO DWMA, THEN FINE. DON'T GO BACK TO DWMA.
BUT IF YOU DON'T HAVE A PLACE TO CALL HOME, I'LL MAKE ONE FOR YOU...

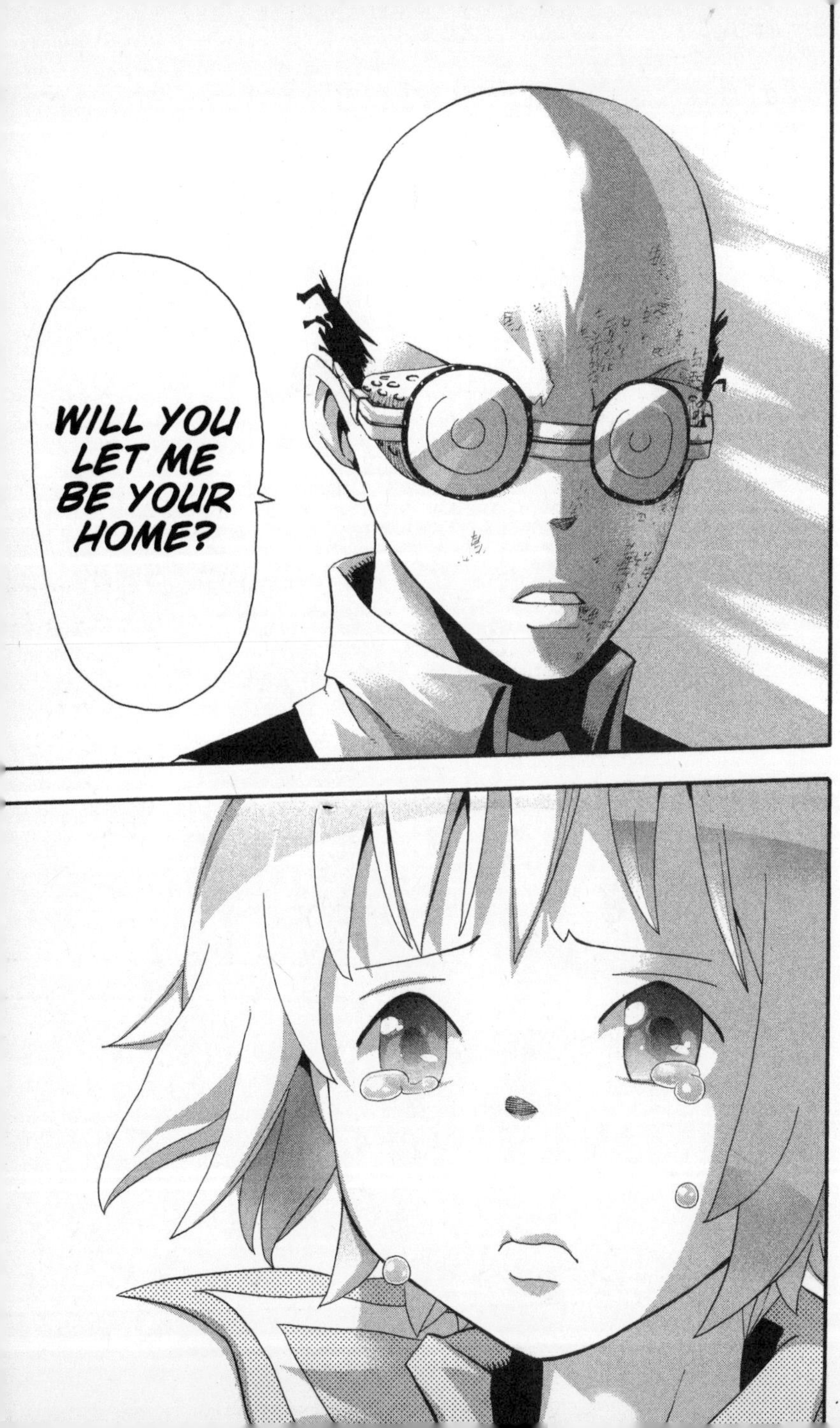
WILL YOU LET ME BE YOUR HOME?

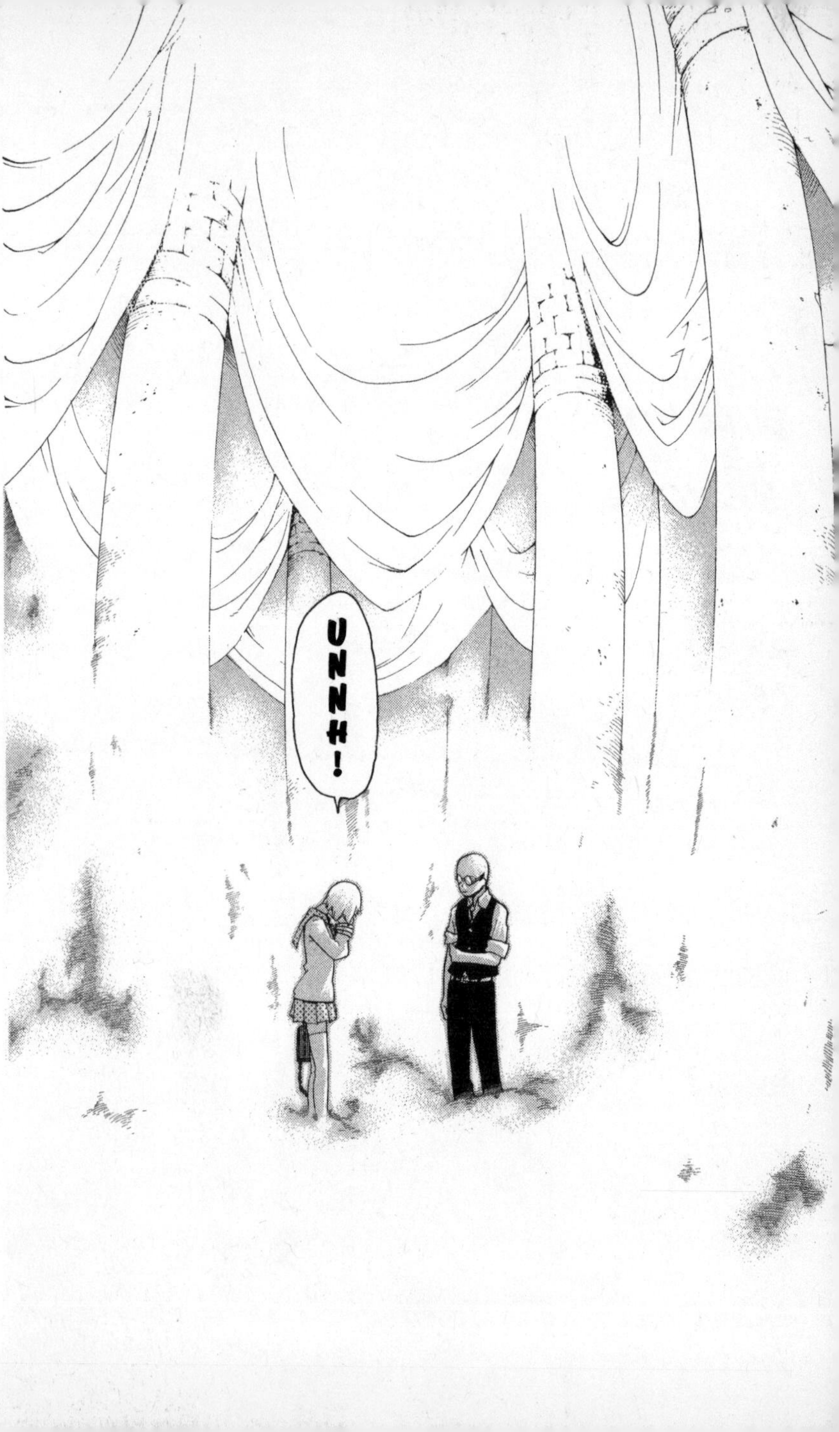
UNNH!

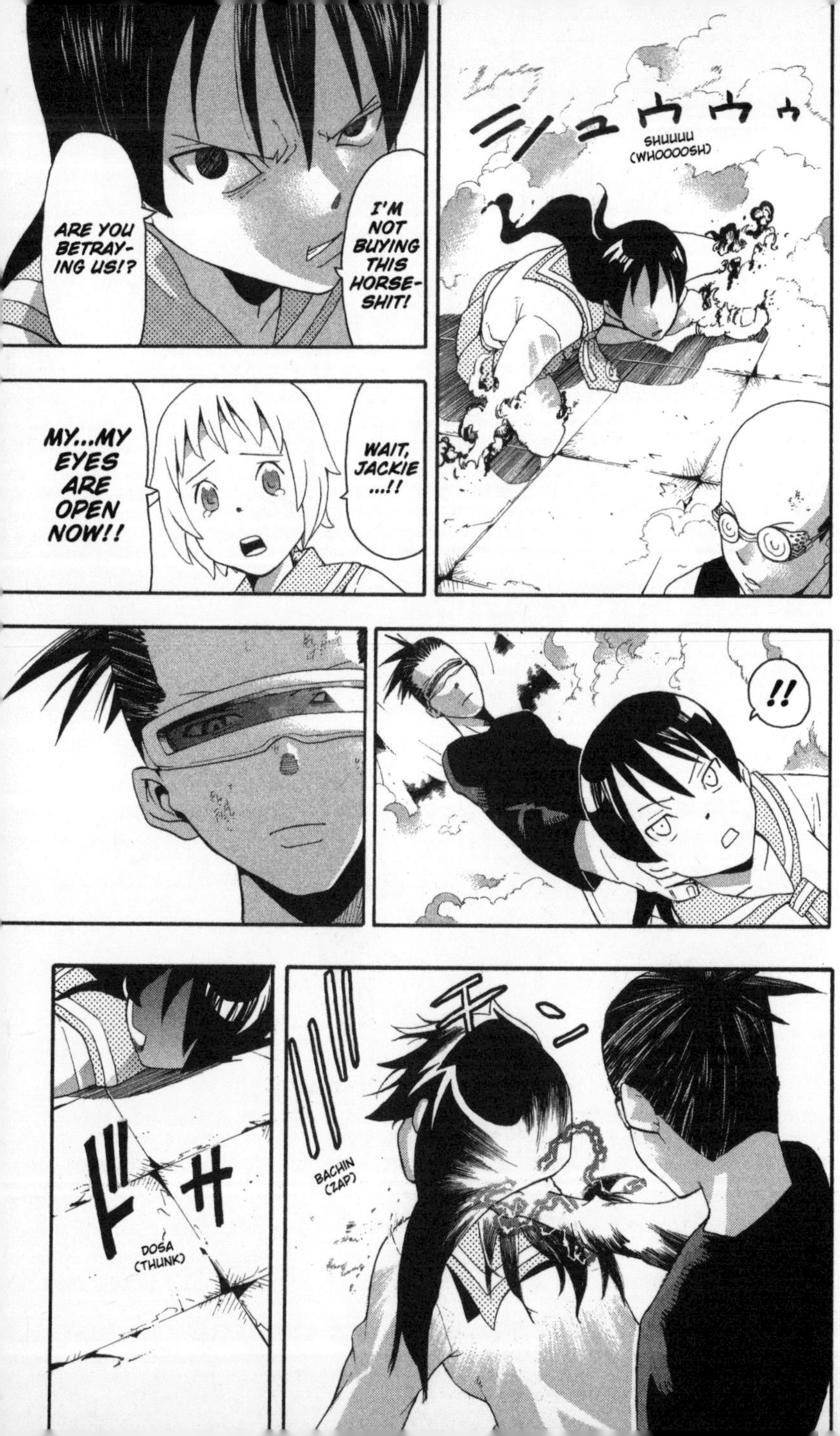
シュウウゥ
SHUUUU (WHOOOOSH)
I'M NOT BUYING THIS HORSE-SHIT!
ARE YOU BETRAY-ING US!?
WAIT, JACKIE...!!
MY...MY EYES ARE OPEN NOW!!
!!
BACHIN (ZAP)
ドサ
DOSA (THUNK)

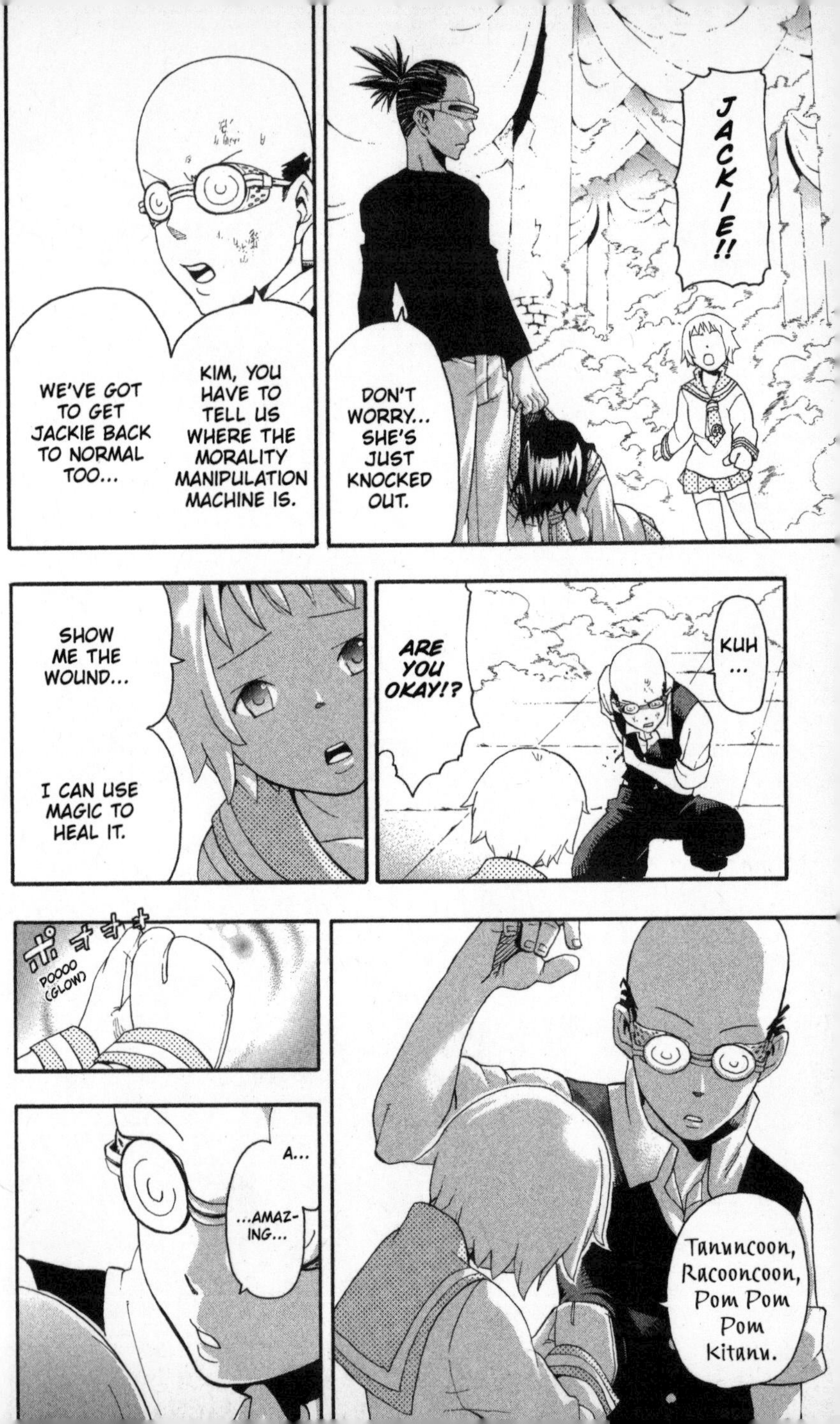
JACKIE!!
DON'T WORRY... SHE'S JUST KNOCKED OUT.
KIM, YOU HAVE TO TELL US WHERE THE MORALITY MANIPULATION MACHINE IS.
WE'VE GOT TO GET JACKIE BACK TO NORMAL TOO...
KUH ...
ARE YOU OKAY!?
SHOW ME THE WOUND...
I CAN USE MAGIC TO HEAL IT.
Tanuncoon, Racooncoon, Pom Pom Pom Kitanu.
ポォォォ
POOOO (GLOW)
A...
...AMAZ-ING...

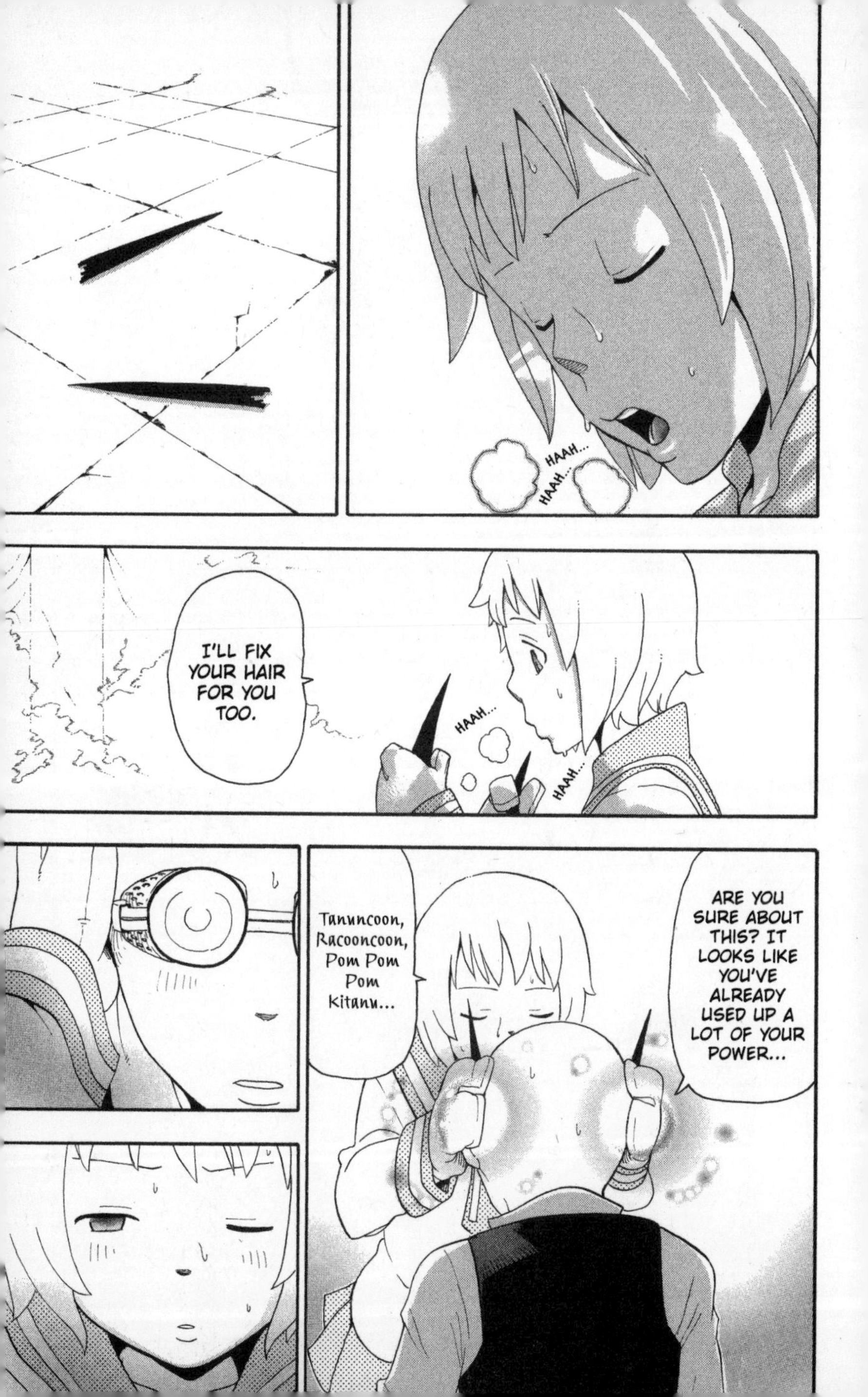
HAAH...
HAAH...
I'LL FIX YOUR HAIR FOR YOU TOO.
HAAH...
HAAH...
ARE YOU SURE ABOUT THIS? IT LOOKS LIKE YOU'VE ALREADY USED UP A LOT OF YOUR POWER...
Tanuncoon, Racooncoon, Pom Pom Pom Kitanu...

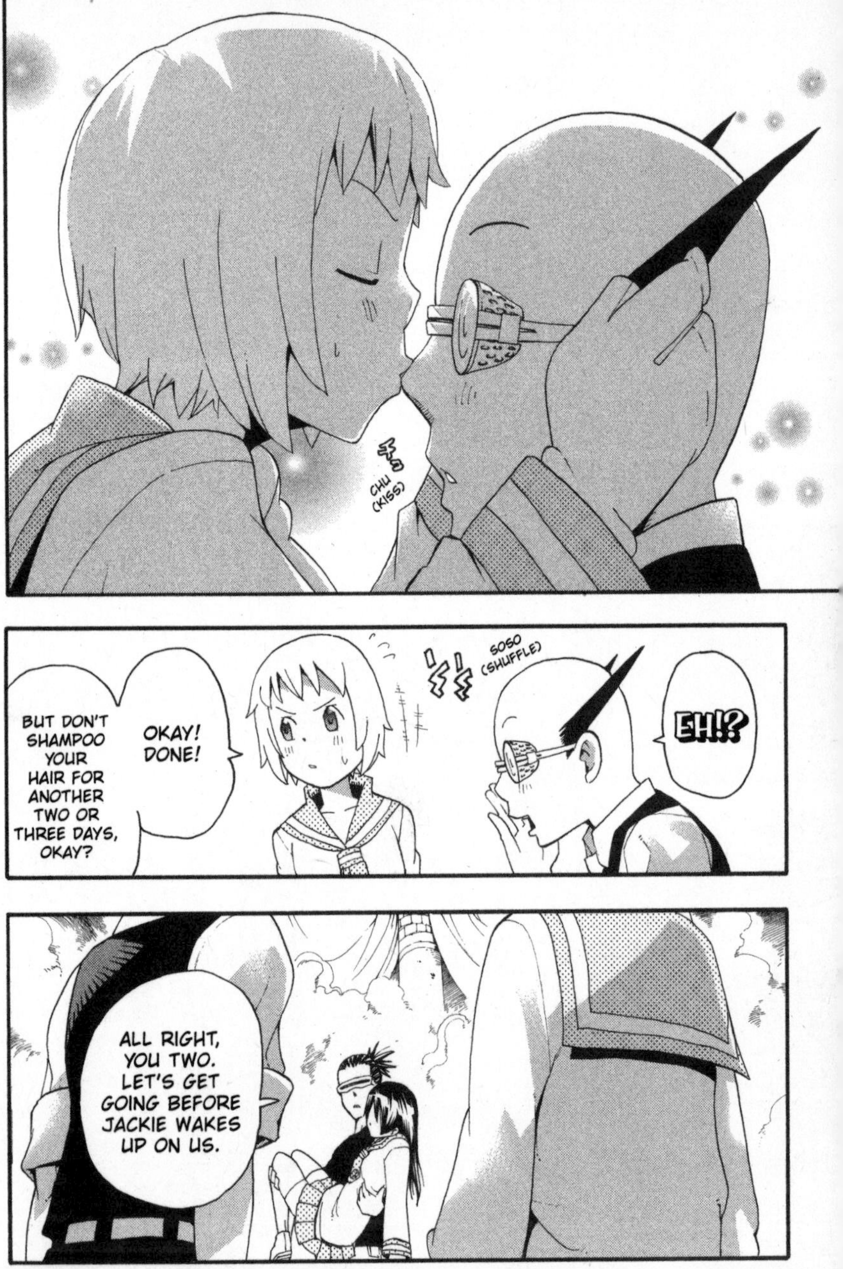
CHU (KISS)
EH!?
SOSO (SHUFFLE)
OKAY! DONE!
BUT DON'T SHAMPOO YOUR HAIR FOR ANOTHER TWO OR THREE DAYS, OKAY?
ALL RIGHT, YOU TWO. LET'S GET GOING BEFORE JACKIE WAKES UP ON US.

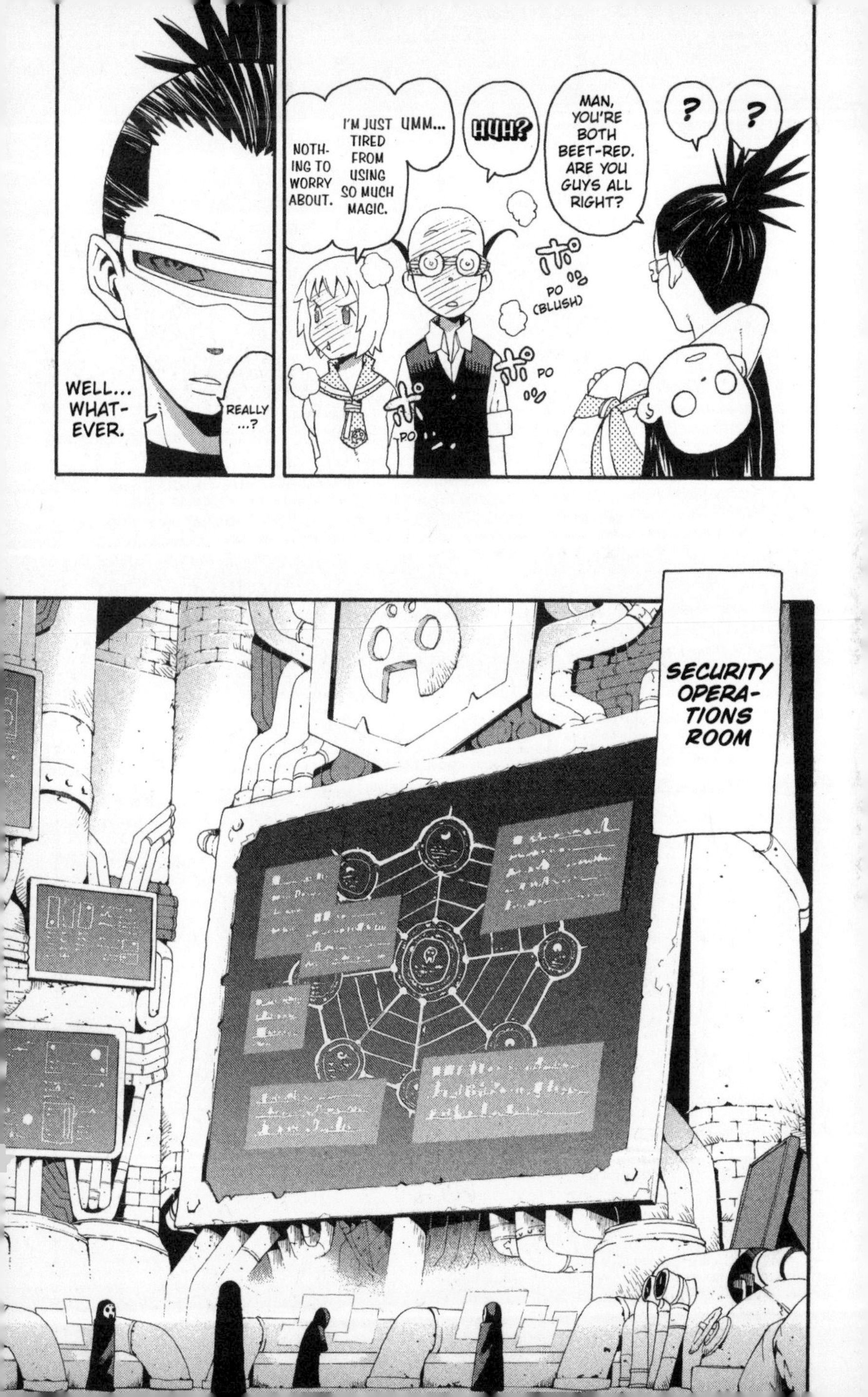
?
?
MAN, YOU'RE BOTH BEET-RED. ARE YOU GUYS ALL RIGHT?
HUH?
UMM...
I'M JUST TIRED FROM USING SO MUCH MAGIC.
NOTHING TO WORRY ABOUT.
ポ
PO (BLUSH)
ポ
PO
ポ
PO
REALLY ...?
WELL... WHATEVER.
SECURITY OPERATIONS ROOM

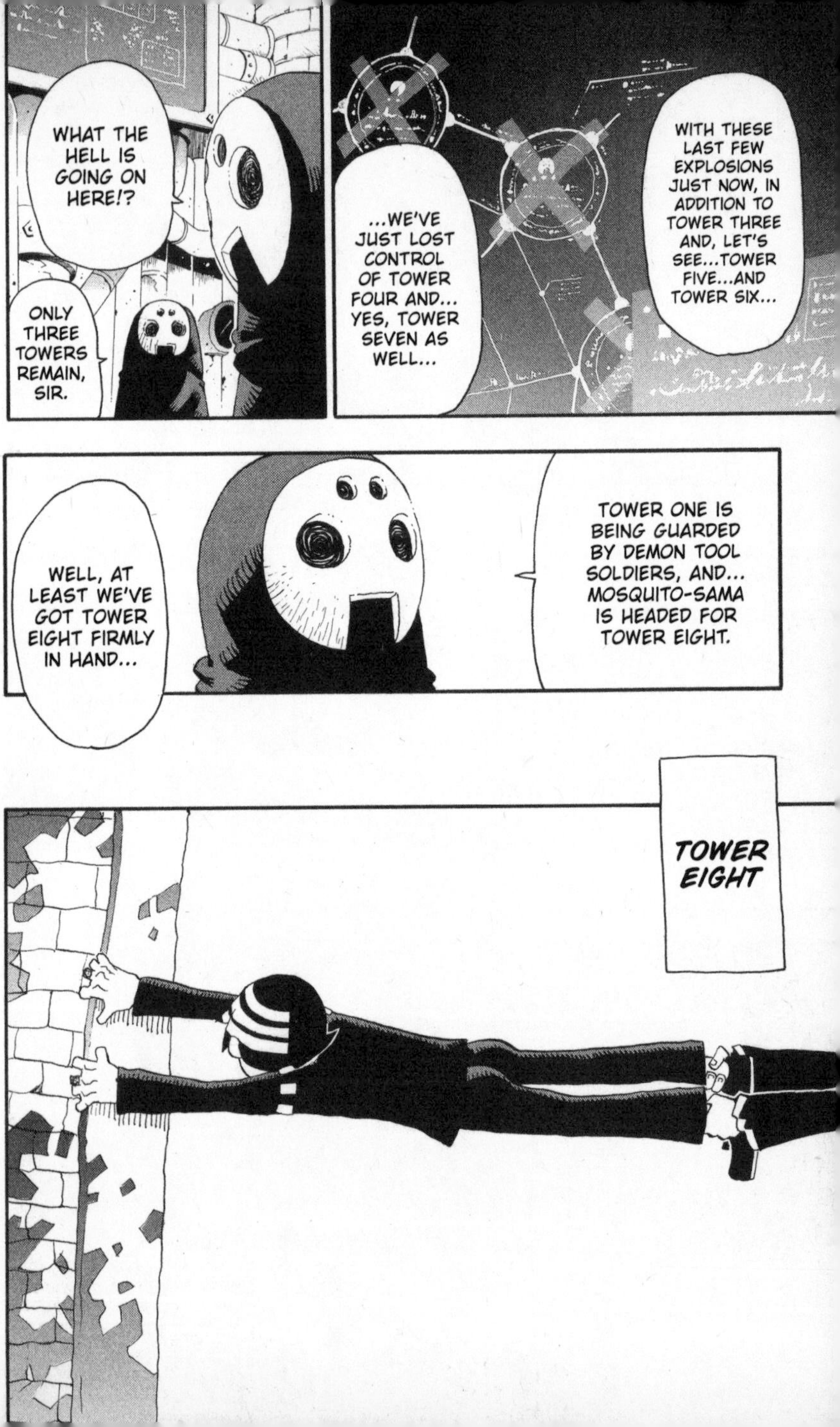
WITH THESE LAST FEW EXPLOSIONS JUST NOW, IN ADDITION TO TOWER THREE AND, LET'S SEE...TOWER FIVE...AND TOWER SIX...
...WE'VE JUST LOST CONTROL OF TOWER FOUR AND... YES, TOWER SEVEN AS WELL...
WHAT THE HELL IS GOING ON HERE!?
ONLY THREE TOWERS REMAIN, SIR.
TOWER ONE IS BEING GUARDED BY DEMON TOOL SOLDIERS, AND... MOSQUITO-SAMA IS HEADED FOR TOWER EIGHT.
WELL, AT LEAST WE'VE GOT TOWER EIGHT FIRMLY IN HAND...
TOWER EIGHT

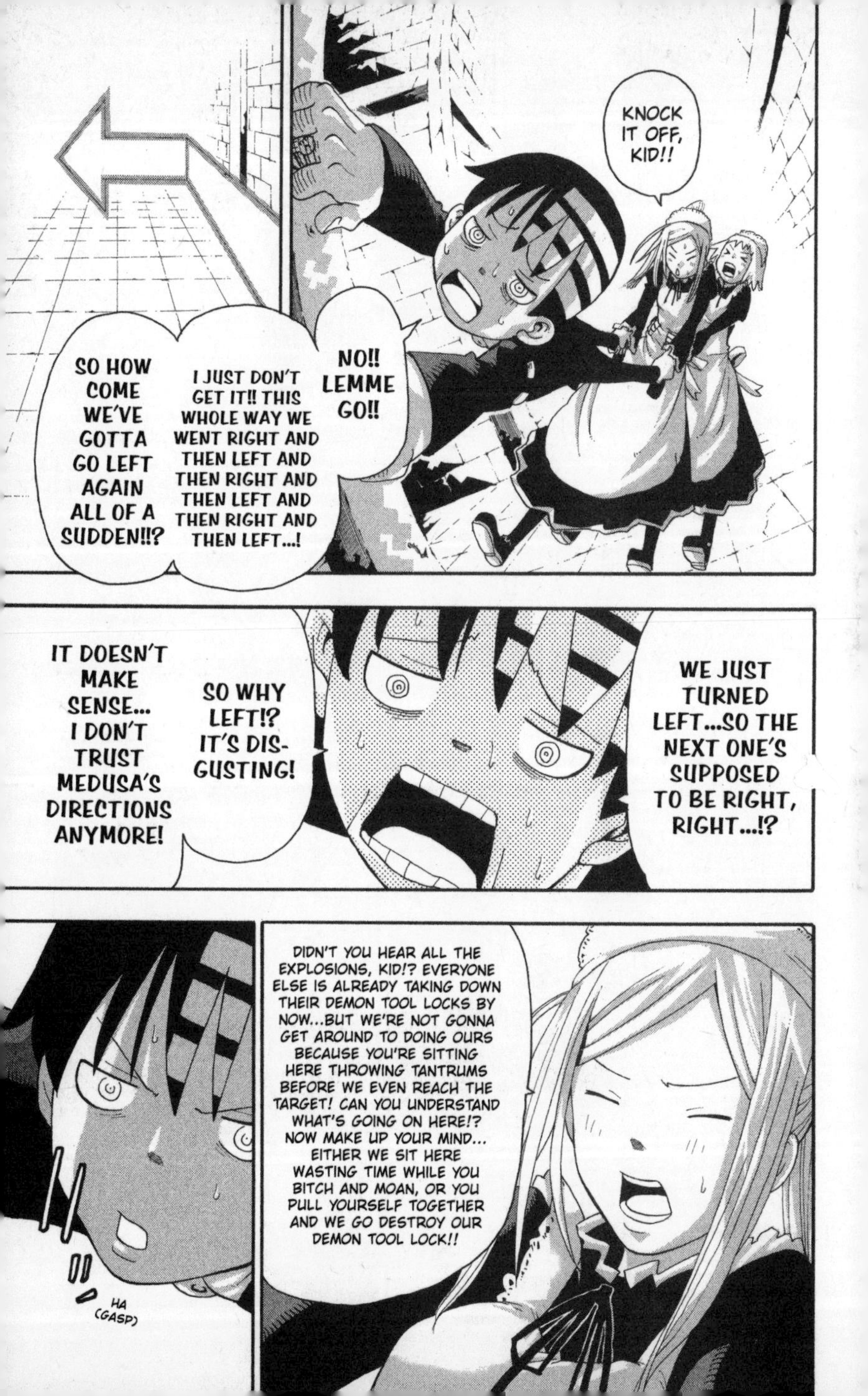
KNOCK IT OFF, KID!!
NO!! LEMME GO!!
I JUST DON'T GET IT!! THIS WHOLE WAY WE WENT RIGHT AND THEN LEFT AND THEN RIGHT AND THEN LEFT AND THEN RIGHT AND THEN LEFT...!
SO HOW COME WE'VE GOTTA GO LEFT AGAIN ALL OF A SUDDEN!!?
WE JUST TURNED LEFT...SO THE NEXT ONE'S SUPPOSED TO BE RIGHT, RIGHT...!?
SO WHY LEFT!? IT'S DIS-GUSTING!
IT DOESN'T MAKE SENSE... I DON'T TRUST MEDUSA'S DIRECTIONS ANYMORE!
DIDN'T YOU HEAR ALL THE EXPLOSIONS, KID!? EVERYONE ELSE IS ALREADY TAKING DOWN THEIR DEMON TOOL LOCKS BY NOW...BUT WE'RE NOT GONNA GET AROUND TO DOING OURS BECAUSE YOU'RE SITTING HERE THROWING TANTRUMS BEFORE WE EVEN REACH THE TARGET! CAN YOU UNDERSTAND WHAT'S GOING ON HERE!? NOW MAKE UP YOUR MIND... EITHER WE SIT HERE WASTING TIME WHILE YOU BITCH AND MOAN, OR YOU PULL YOURSELF TOGETHER AND WE GO DESTROY OUR DEMON TOOL LOCK!!
HA (GASP)

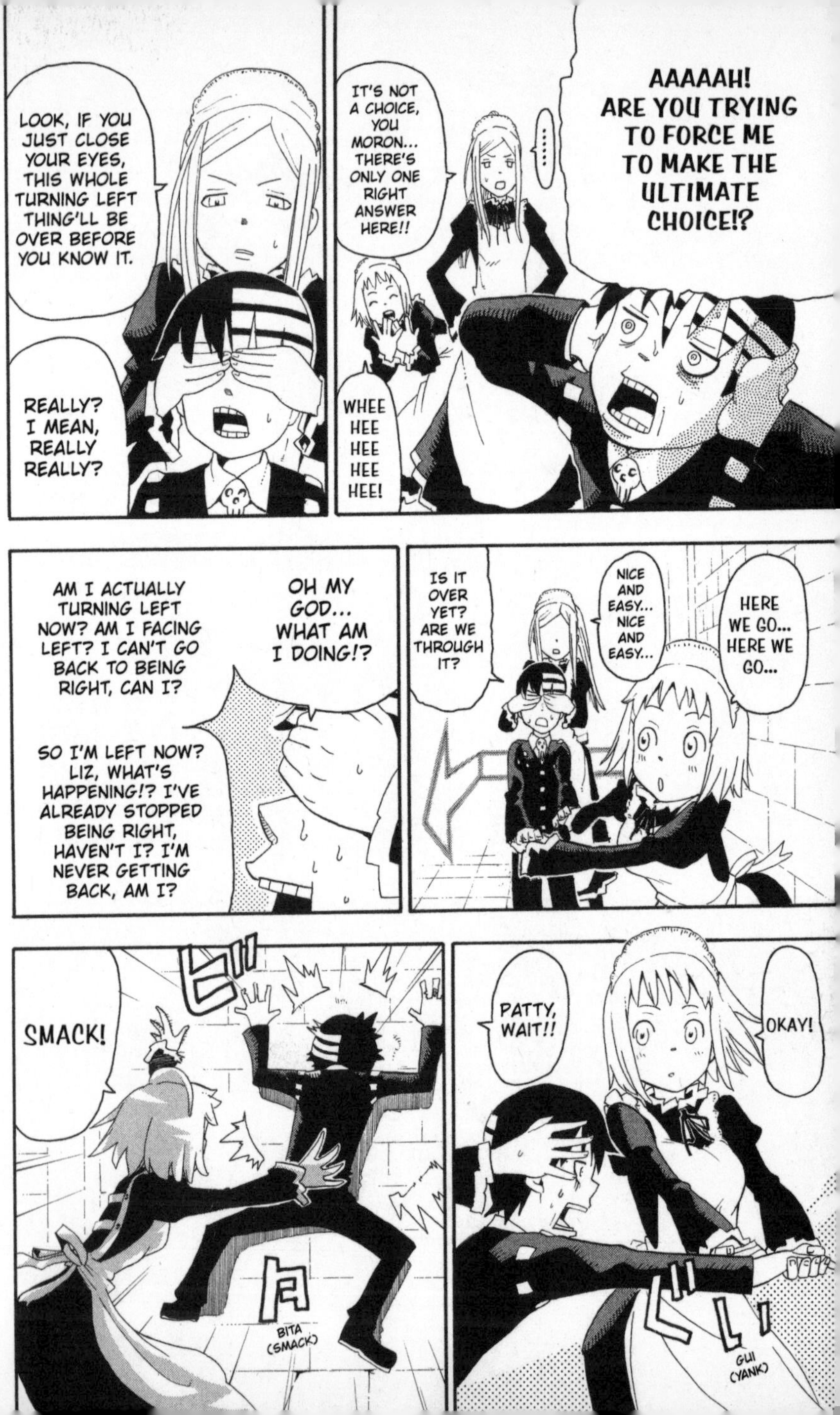

AAAAAH! ARE YOU TRYING TO FORCE ME TO MAKE THE ULTIMATE CHOICE!?
......
IT'S NOT A CHOICE, YOU MORON... THERE'S ONLY ONE RIGHT ANSWER HERE!!
WHEE HEE HEE HEE HEE!
LOOK, IF YOU JUST CLOSE YOUR EYES, THIS WHOLE TURNING LEFT THING'LL BE OVER BEFORE YOU KNOW IT.
REALLY? I MEAN, REALLY REALLY?
HERE WE GO... HERE WE GO...
NICE AND EASY... NICE AND EASY...
IS IT OVER YET? ARE WE THROUGH IT?
OH MY GOD... WHAT AM I DOING!?
AM I ACTUALLY TURNING LEFT NOW? AM I FACING LEFT? I CAN'T GO BACK TO BEING RIGHT, CAN I?
SO I'M LEFT NOW? LIZ, WHAT'S HAPPENING!? I'VE ALREADY STOPPED BEING RIGHT, HAVEN'T I? I'M NEVER GETTING BACK, AM I?
OKAY!
PATTY, WAIT!!
GUI (YANK)
SMACK!
BITA (SMACK)

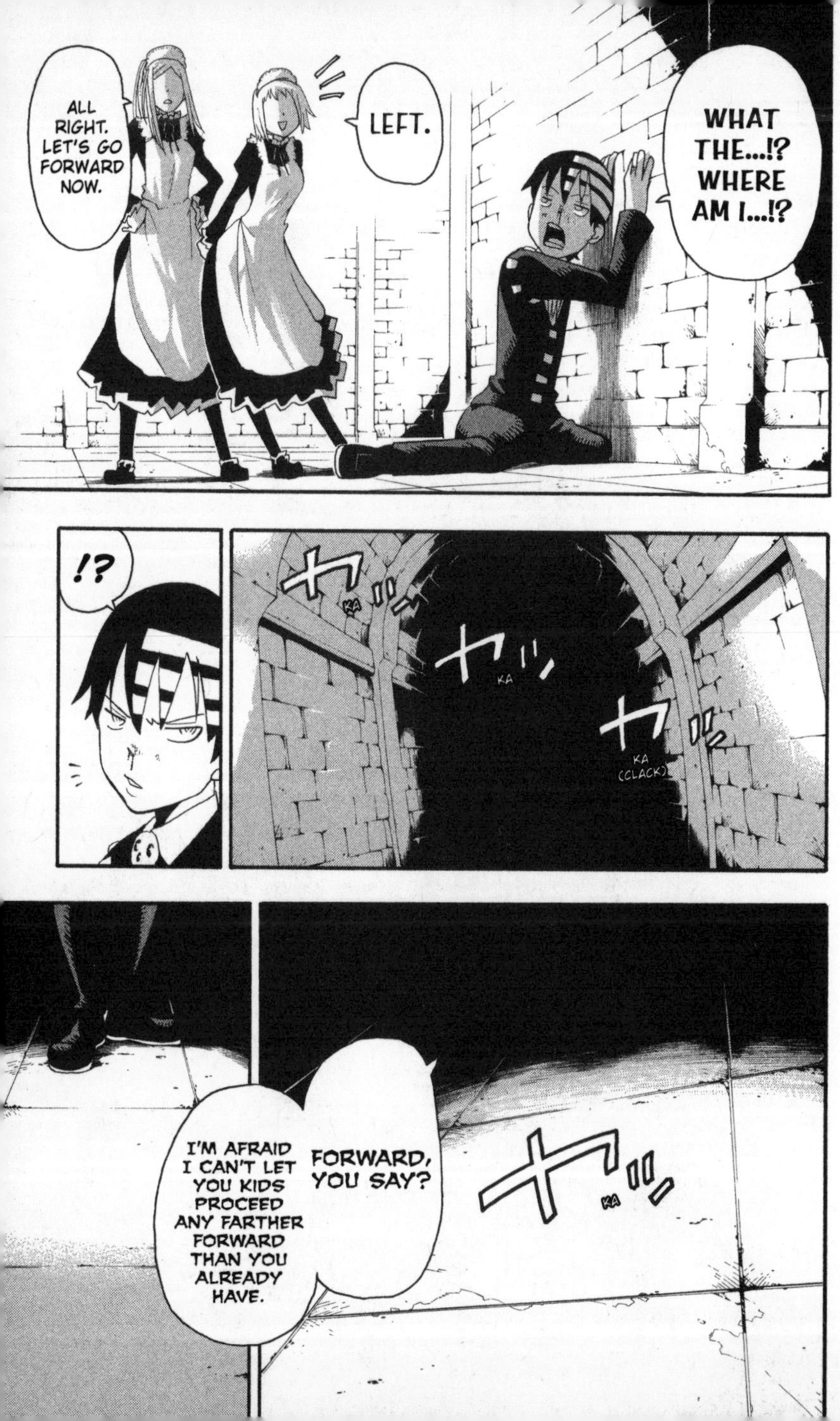
WHAT THE...!? WHERE AM I...!?
LEFT.
ALL RIGHT. LET'S GO FORWARD NOW.
KA
KA
KA (CLACK)
!?
KA
FORWARD, YOU SAY?
I'M AFRAID I CAN'T LET YOU KIDS PROCEED ANY FARTHER FORWARD THAN YOU ALREADY HAVE.

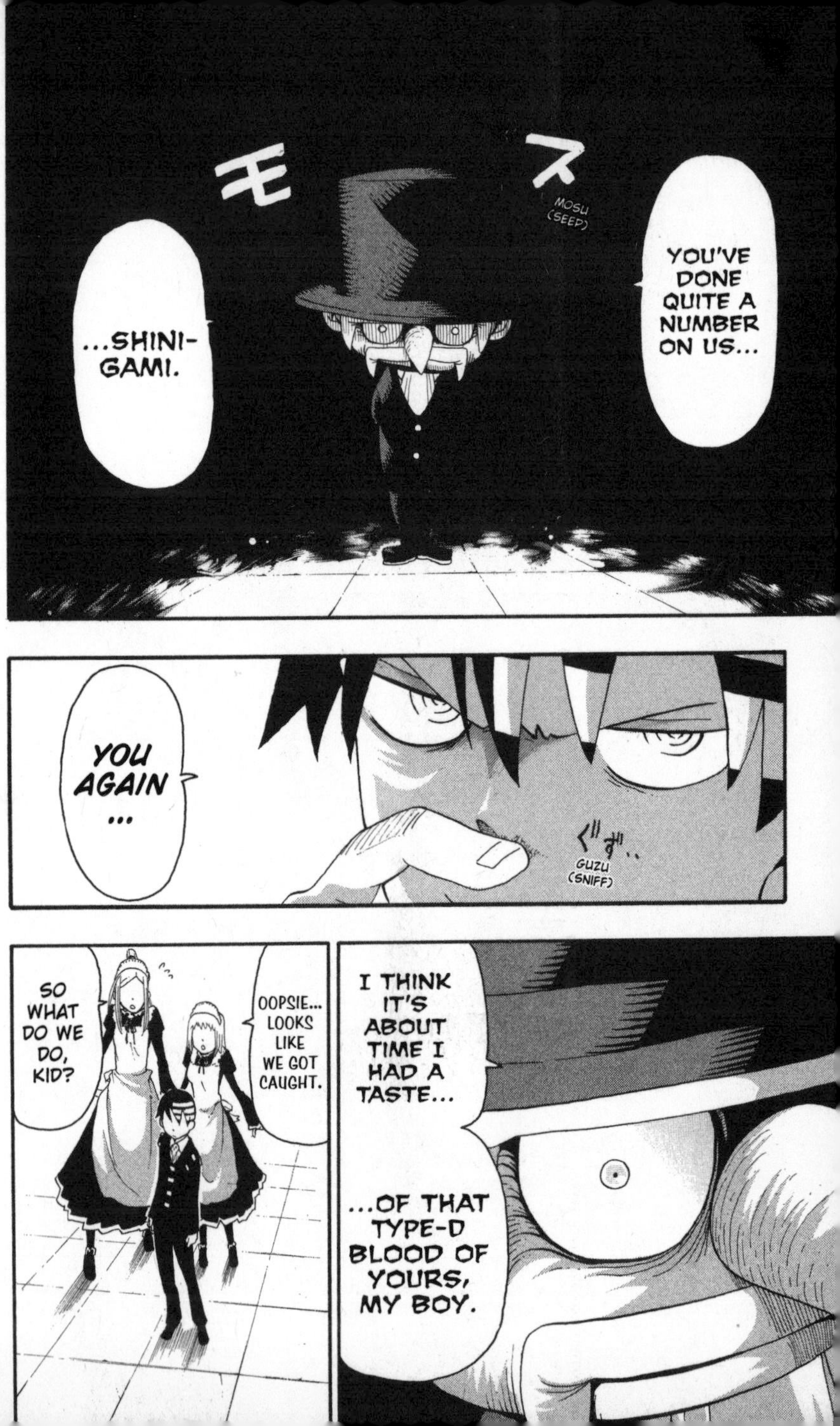
YOU'VE DONE QUITE A NUMBER ON US...
モス
MOSU (SEEP)
...SHINI-GAMI.
ぐず..
GUZU (SNIFF)
YOU AGAIN ...
I THINK IT'S ABOUT TIME I HAD A TASTE...
...OF THAT TYPE-D BLOOD OF YOURS, MY BOY.
OOPSIE... LOOKS LIKE WE GOT CAUGHT.
SO WHAT DO WE DO, KID?

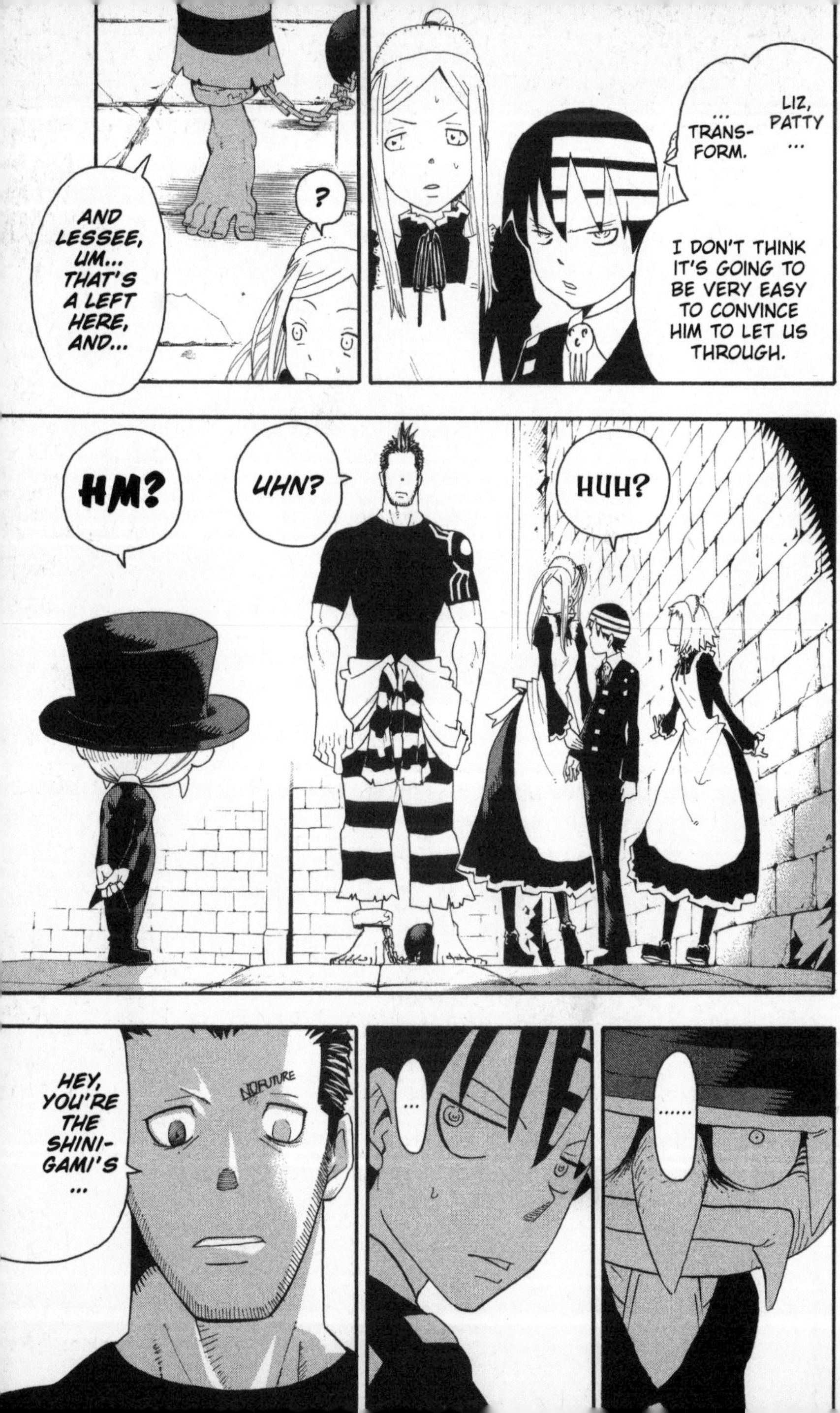
LIZ, PATTY ...
... TRANS-FORM.
I DON'T THINK IT'S GOING TO BE VERY EASY TO CONVINCE HIM TO LET US THROUGH.
?
AND LESSEE, UM... THAT'S A LEFT HERE, AND...
HUH?
UHN?
HM?
....
...
NO FUTURE
HEY, YOU'RE THE SHINI-GAMI'S ...

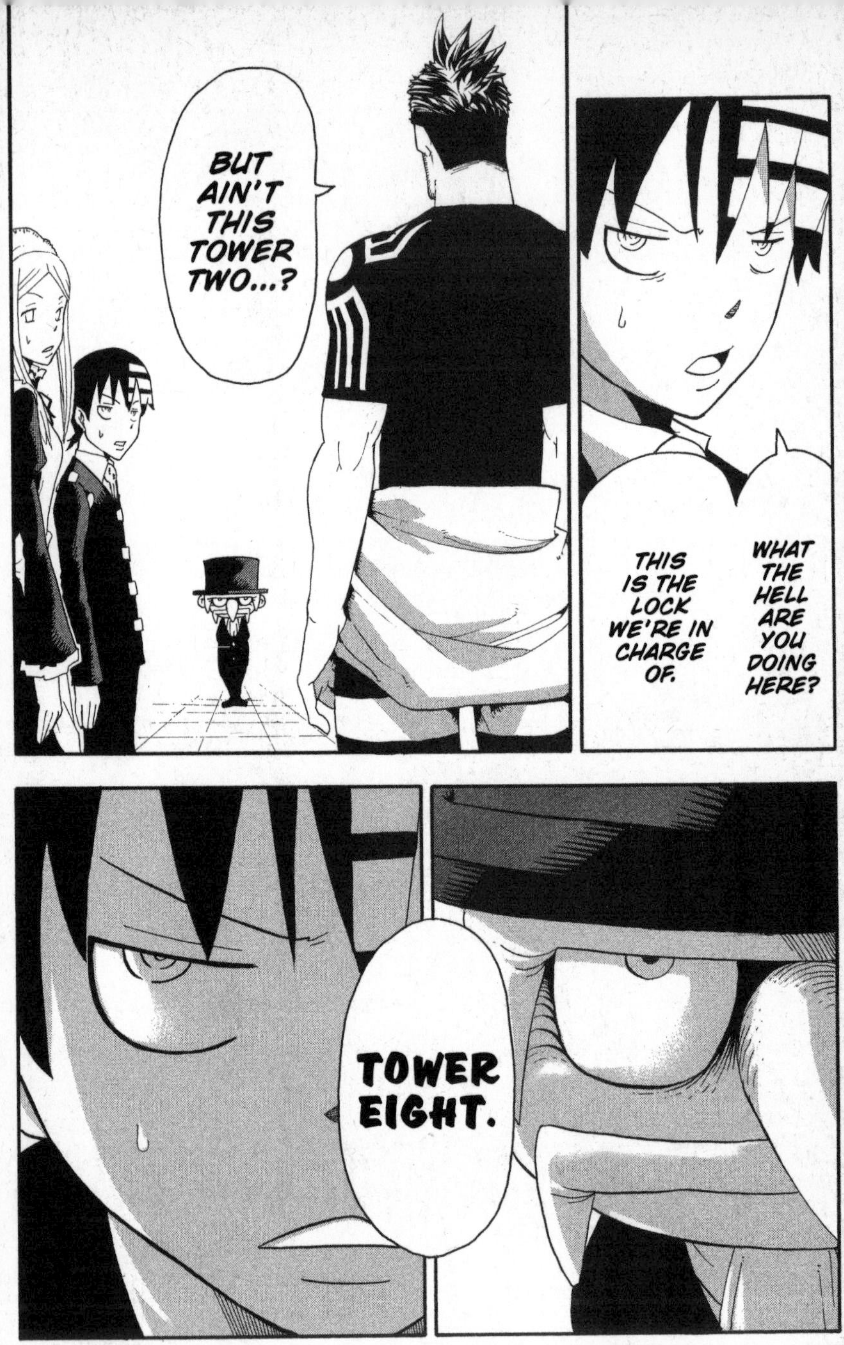
WHAT THE HELL ARE YOU DOING HERE?
THIS IS THE LOCK WE'RE IN CHARGE OF.
BUT AIN'T THIS TOWER TWO...?
TOWER EIGHT.

SOUL EATER

CHAPTER 52: OPERATION CAPTURE BABA YAGA CASTLE (PART 7)

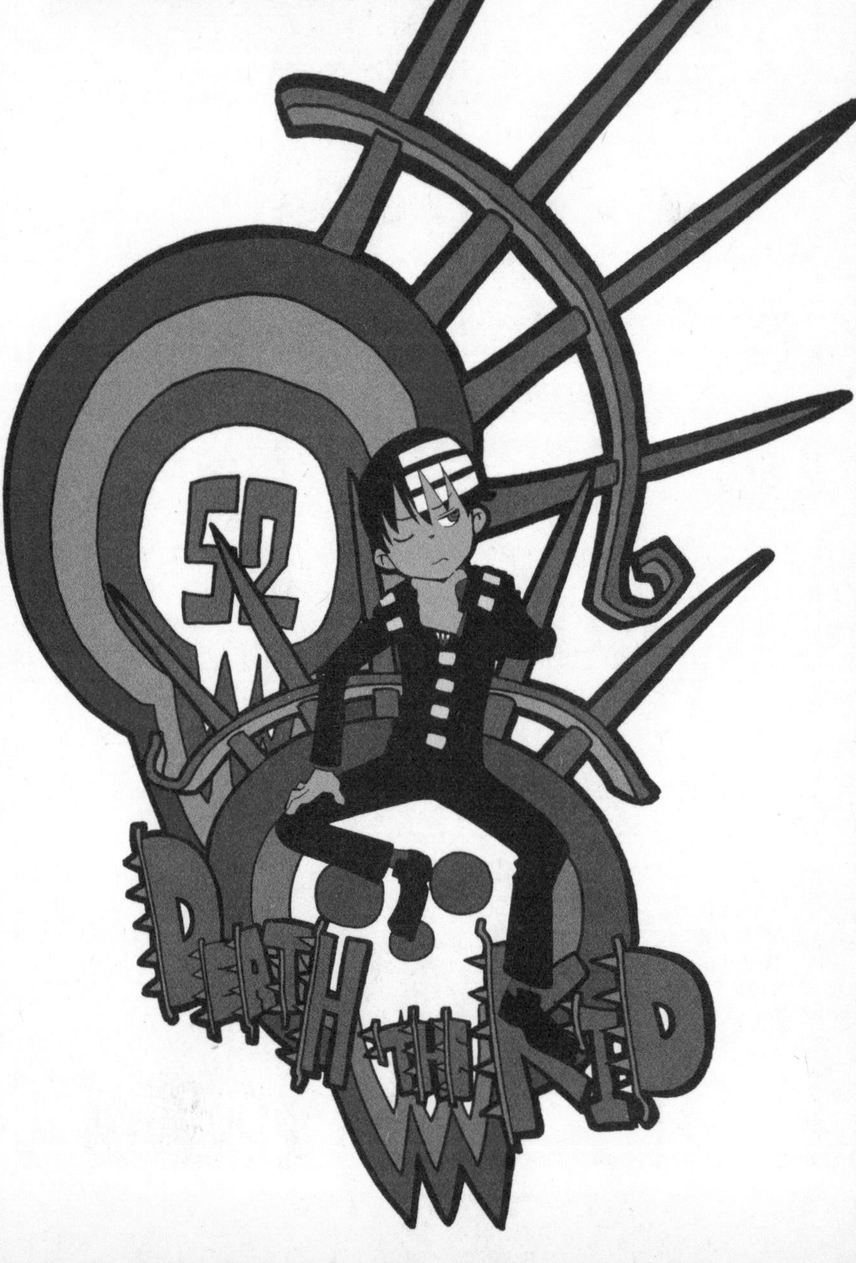
52
DEATH THE KID

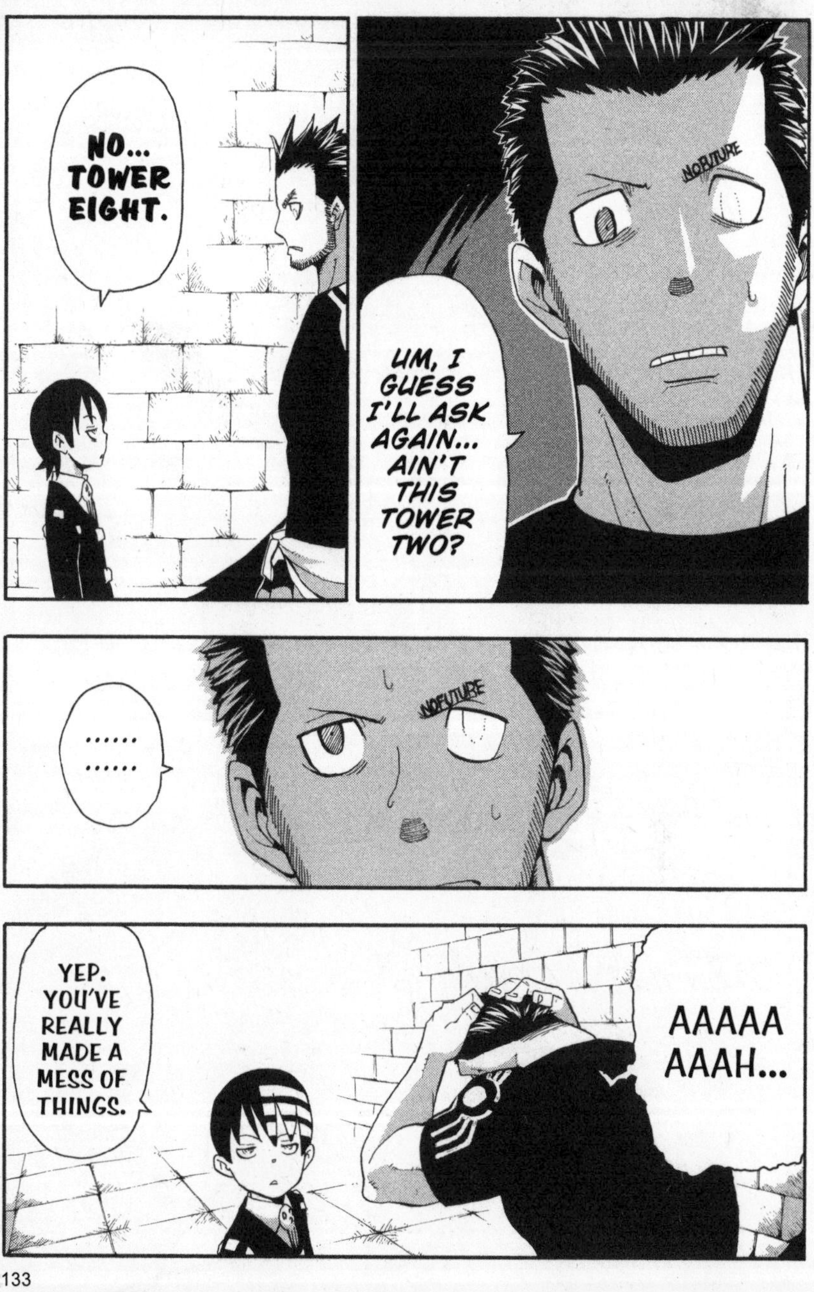
NOFUTURE
UM, I GUESS I'LL ASK AGAIN... AIN'T THIS TOWER TWO?
NO... TOWER EIGHT.
NOFUTURE
......
......
AAAAA AAAH...
YEP. YOU'VE REALLY MADE A MESS OF THINGS.

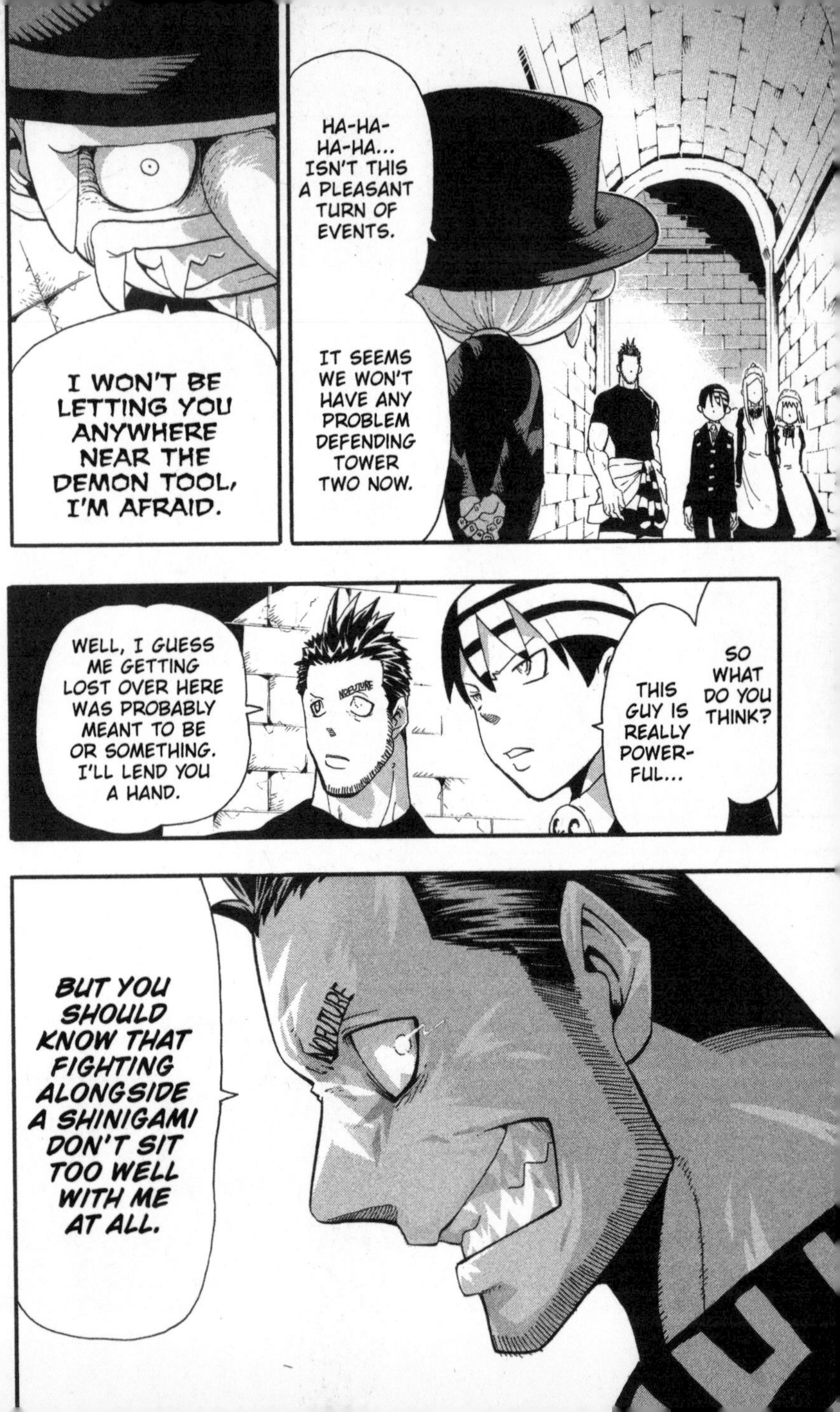
HA-HA-HA-HA... ISN'T THIS A PLEASANT TURN OF EVENTS.
IT SEEMS WE WON'T HAVE ANY PROBLEM DEFENDING TOWER TWO NOW.
I WON'T BE LETTING YOU ANYWHERE NEAR THE DEMON TOOL, I'M AFRAID.
SO WHAT DO YOU THINK?
THIS GUY IS REALLY POWER-FUL...
WELL, I GUESS ME GETTING LOST OVER HERE WAS PROBABLY MEANT TO BE OR SOMETHING. I'LL LEND YOU A HAND.
BUT YOU SHOULD KNOW THAT FIGHTING ALONGSIDE A SHINIGAMI DON'T SIT TOO WELL WITH ME AT ALL.

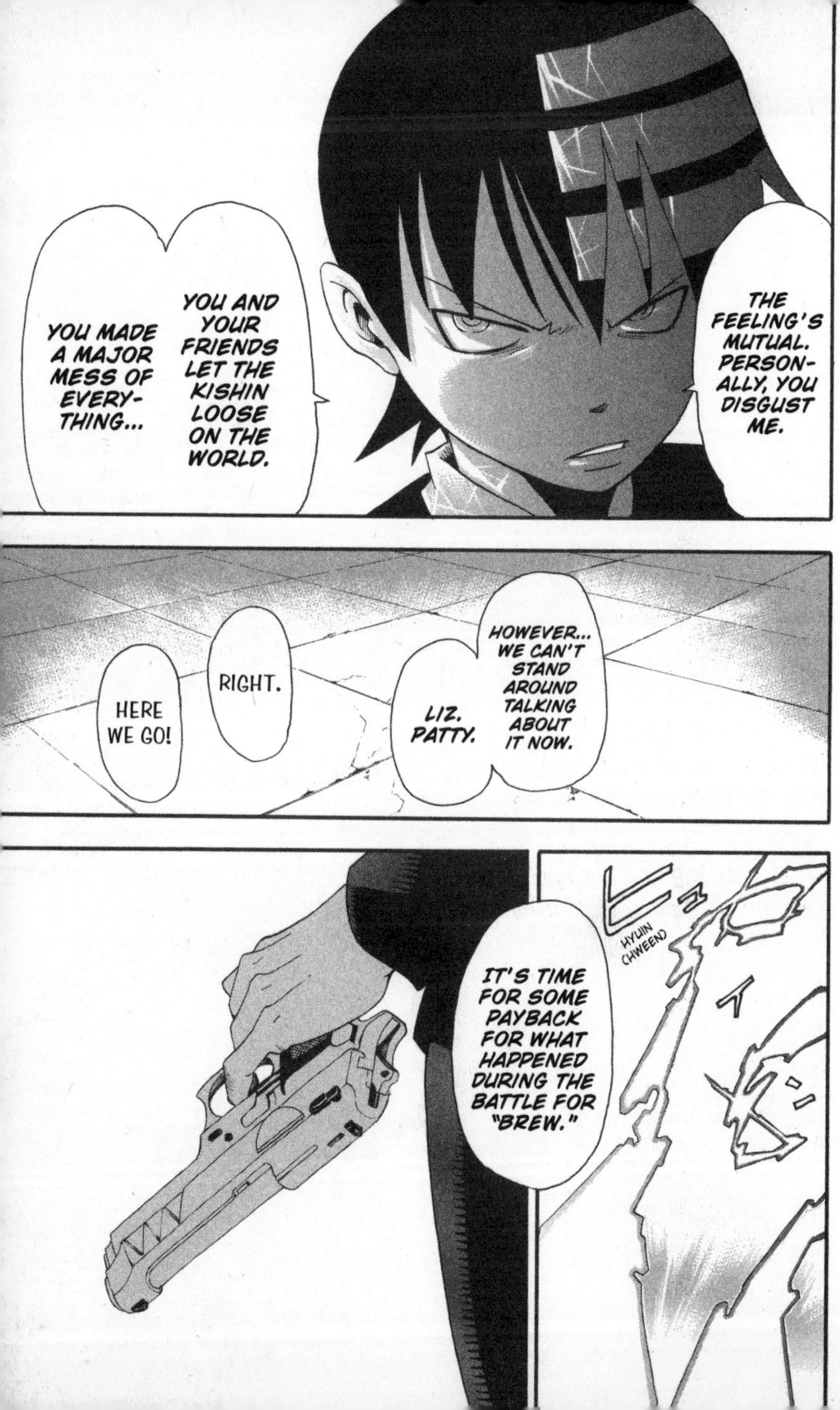
THE FEELING'S MUTUAL. PERSONALLY, YOU DISGUST ME.
YOU AND YOUR FRIENDS LET THE KISHIN LOOSE ON THE WORLD.
YOU MADE A MAJOR MESS OF EVERYTHING...
HOWEVER... WE CAN'T STAND AROUND TALKING ABOUT IT NOW.
LIZ. PATTY.
RIGHT.
HERE WE GO!
HYUIN CHWEEND
IT'S TIME FOR SOME PAYBACK FOR WHAT HAPPENED DURING THE BATTLE FOR "BREW."

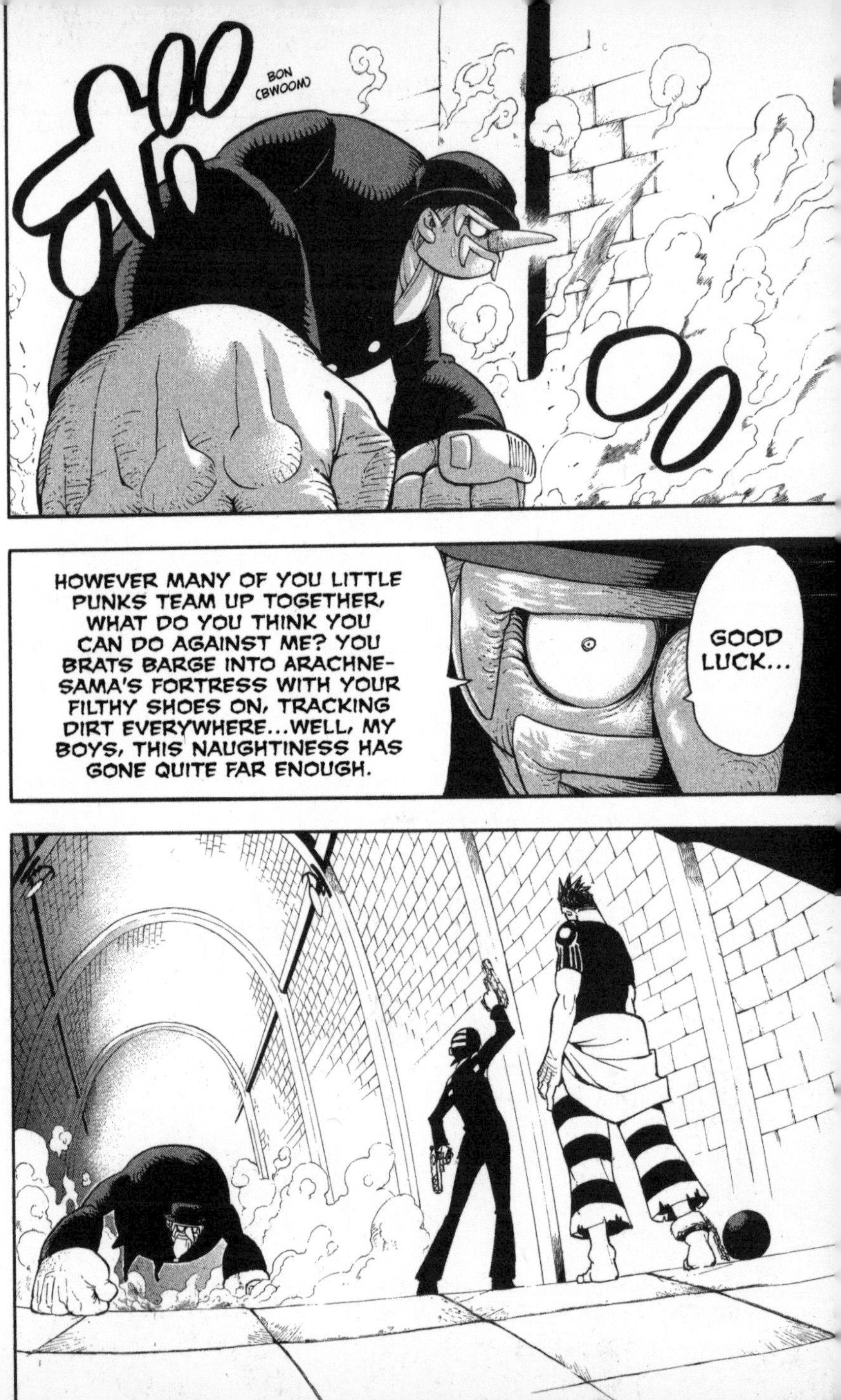
BON
(BWOOM)
GOOD LUCK...
HOWEVER MANY OF YOU LITTLE PUNKS TEAM UP TOGETHER, WHAT DO YOU THINK YOU CAN DO AGAINST ME? YOU BRATS BARGE INTO ARACHNE-SAMA'S FORTRESS WITH YOUR FILTHY SHOES ON, TRACKING DIRT EVERYWHERE...WELL, MY BOYS, THIS NAUGHTINESS HAS GONE QUITE FAR ENOUGH.

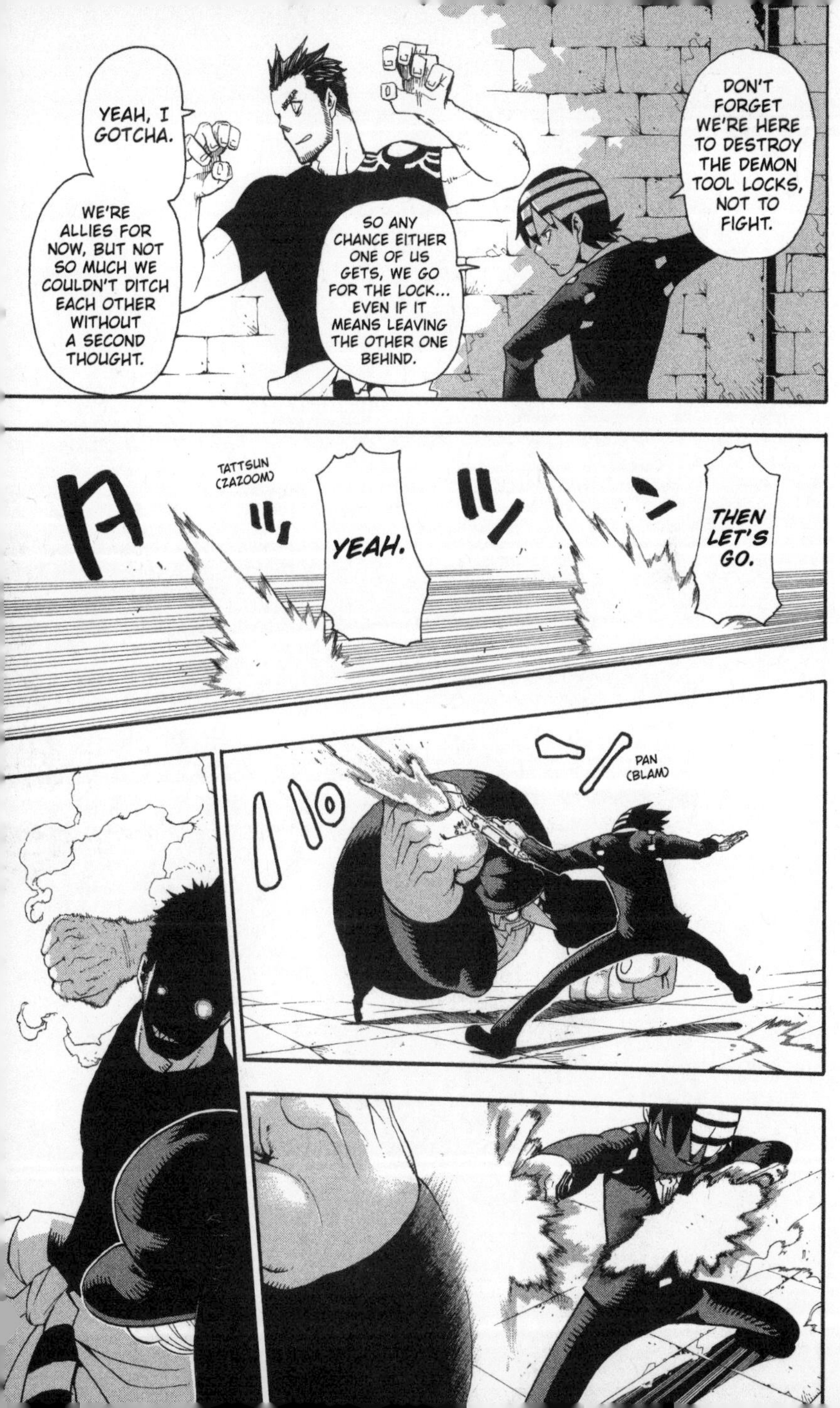
DON'T FORGET WE'RE HERE TO DESTROY THE DEMON TOOL LOCKS, NOT TO FIGHT.
YEAH, I GOTCHA.
WE'RE ALLIES FOR NOW, BUT NOT SO MUCH WE COULDN'T DITCH EACH OTHER WITHOUT A SECOND THOUGHT.
SO ANY CHANCE EITHER ONE OF US GETS, WE GO FOR THE LOCK... EVEN IF IT MEANS LEAVING THE OTHER ONE BEHIND.
THEN LET'S GO.
YEAH.
TATTSUN (ZAZOOM)
PAN (BLAM)

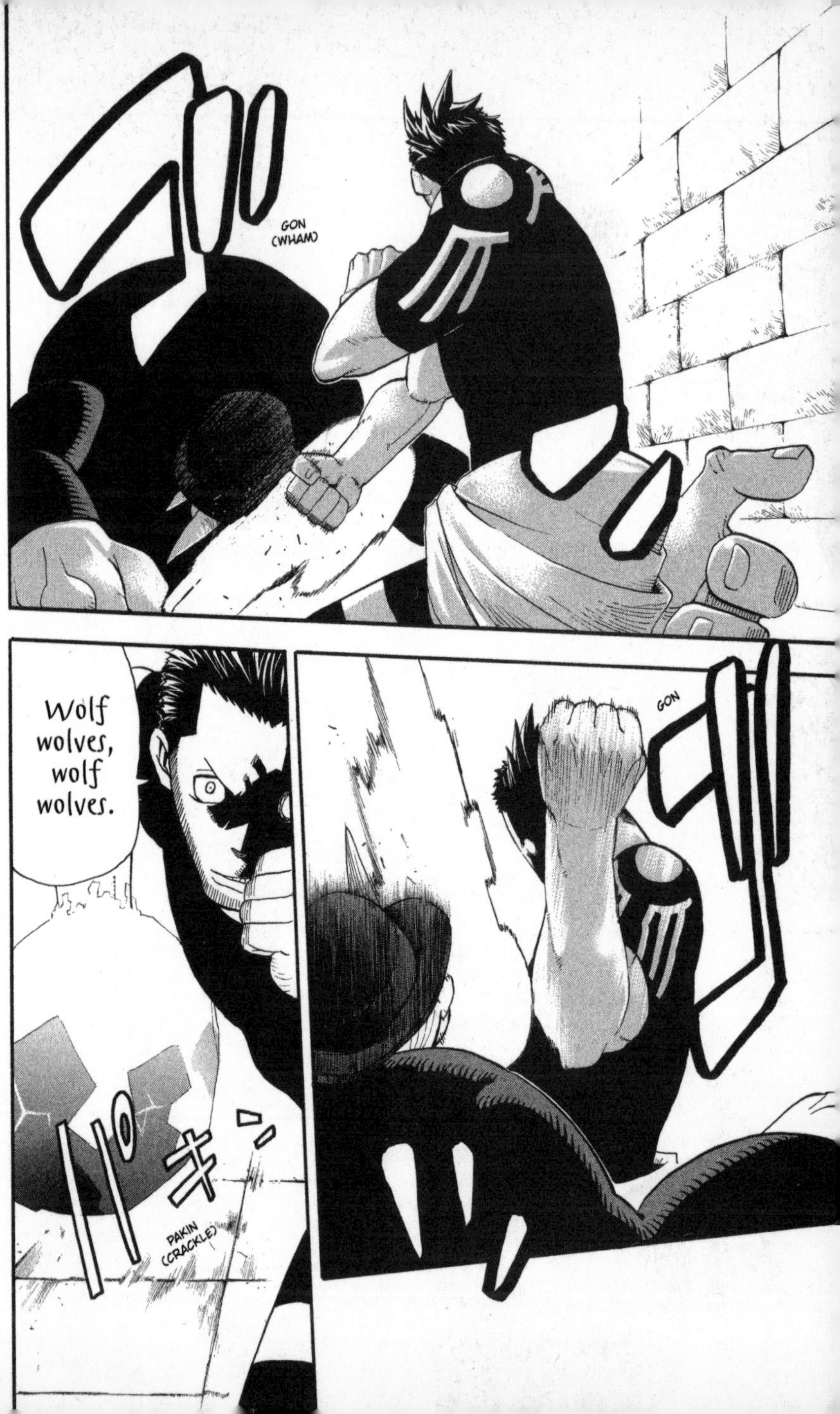
GON
(WHAM)
GON
Wolf wolves, wolf wolves.
PAKIN
(CRACKLE)

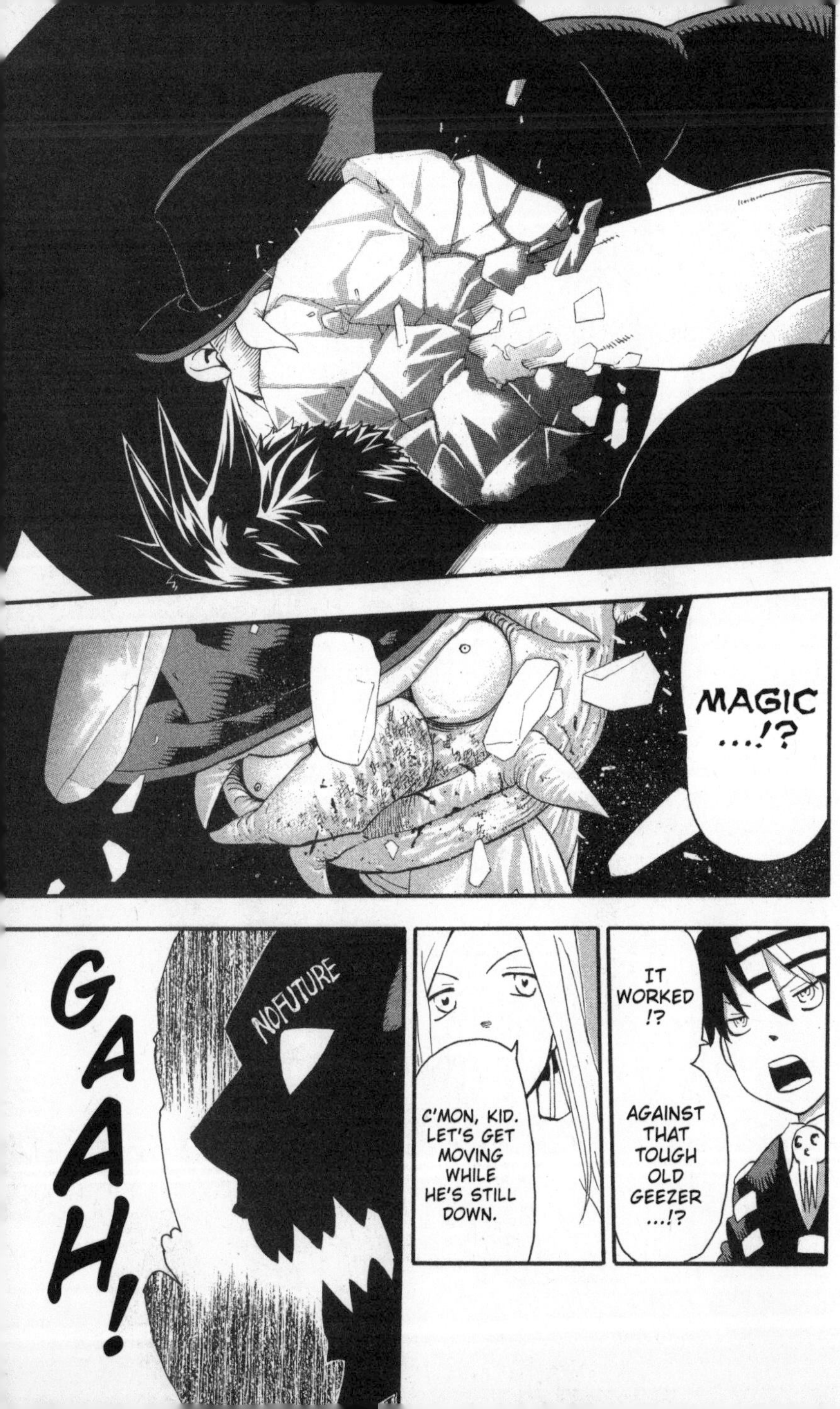
MAGIC ...!?
IT WORKED !?
AGAINST THAT TOUGH OLD GEEZER ...!?
C'MON, KID. LET'S GET MOVING WHILE HE'S STILL DOWN.
NOFUTURE
GAAH!

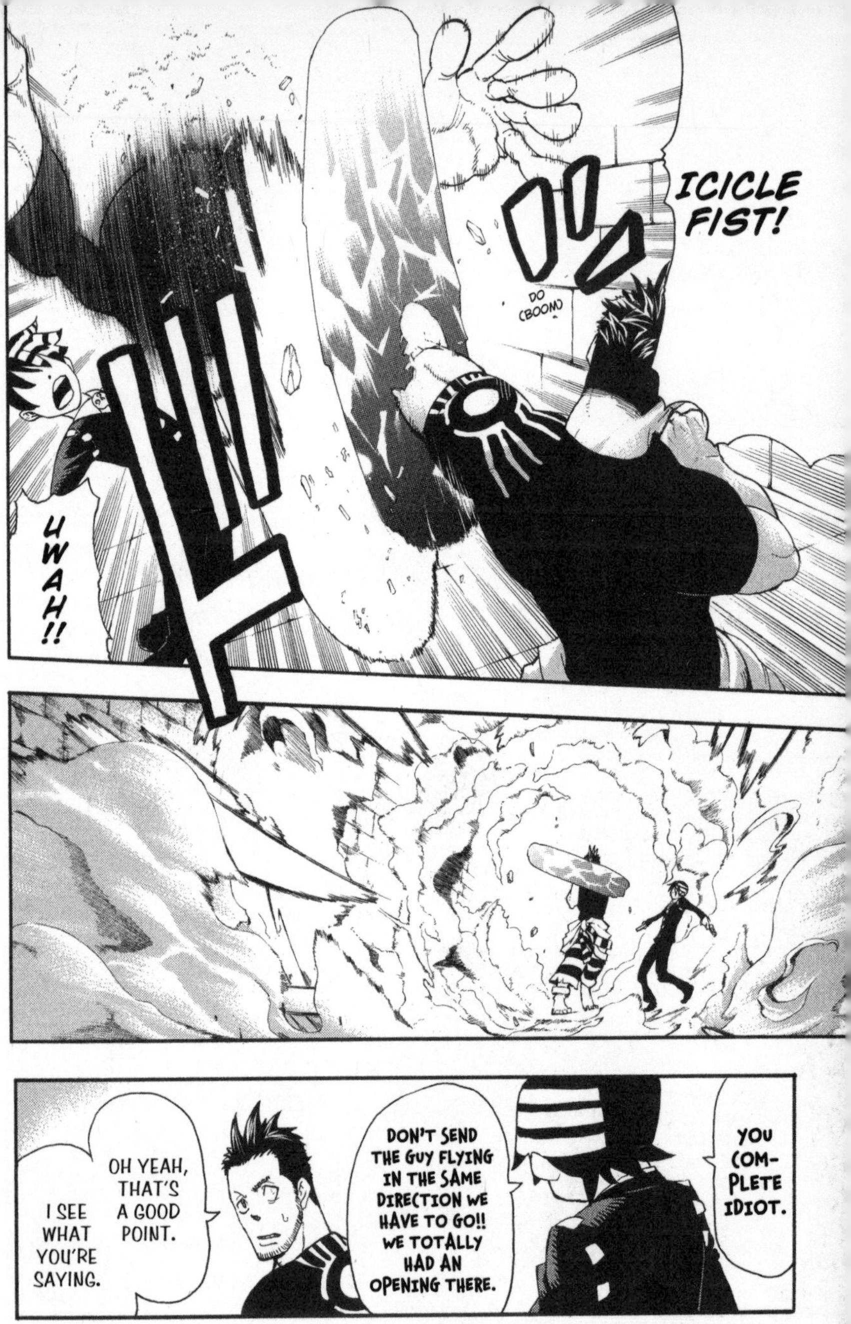
ICICLE FIST!
DO (BOOM)
UWAH!!
YOU COM- PLETE IDIOT.
DON'T SEND THE GUY FLYING IN THE SAME DIRECTION WE HAVE TO GO!! WE TOTALLY HAD AN OPENING THERE.
OH YEAH, THAT'S A GOOD POINT.
I SEE WHAT YOU'RE SAYING.

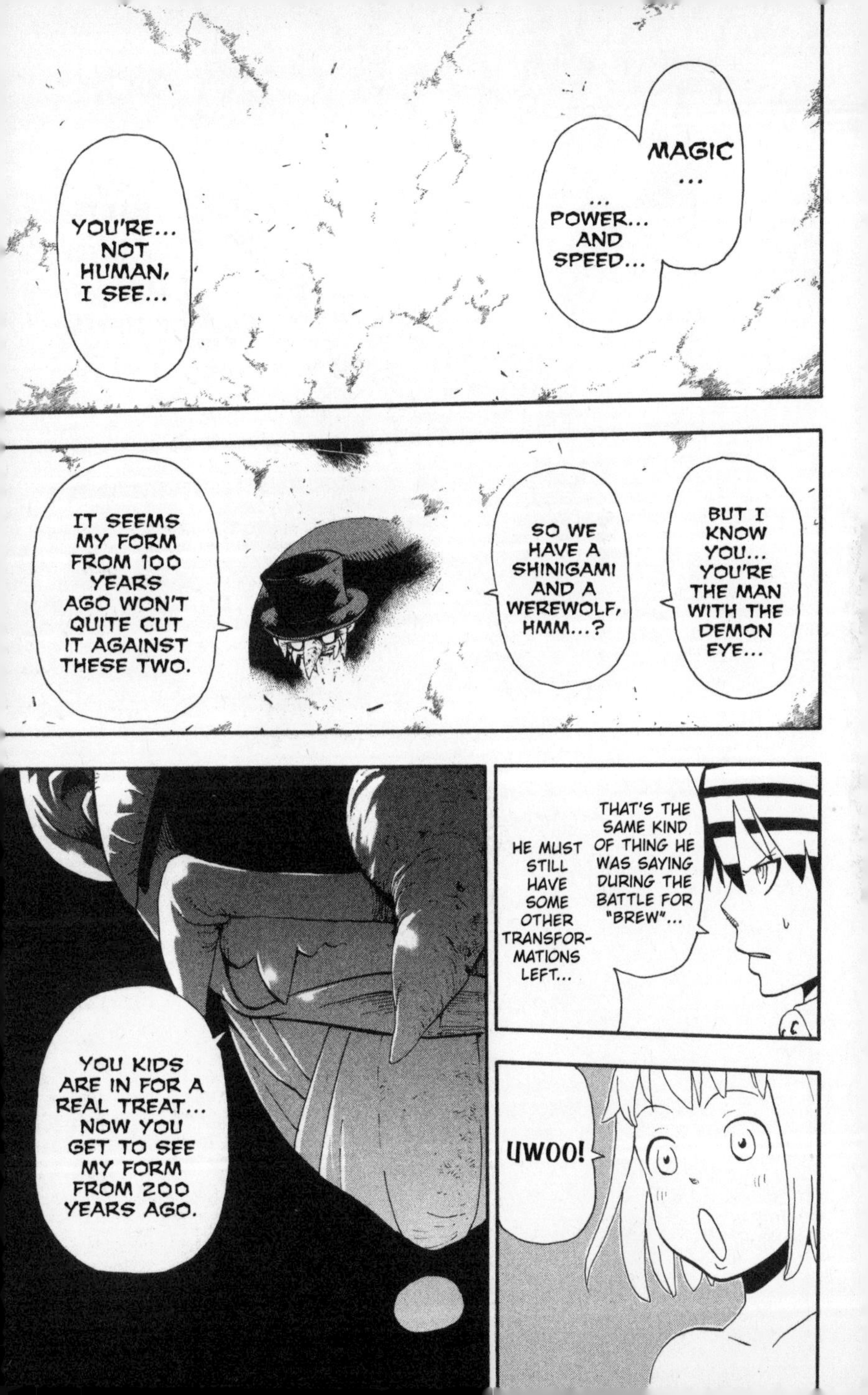
MAGIC... ... POWER... AND SPEED...
YOU'RE... NOT HUMAN, I SEE...
BUT I KNOW YOU... YOU'RE THE MAN WITH THE DEMON EYE...
SO WE HAVE A SHINIGAMI AND A WEREWOLF, HMM...?
IT SEEMS MY FORM FROM 100 YEARS AGO WON'T QUITE CUT IT AGAINST THESE TWO.
THAT'S THE SAME KIND OF THING HE WAS SAYING DURING THE BATTLE FOR "BREW"...
HE MUST STILL HAVE SOME OTHER TRANSFORMATIONS LEFT...
UWOO!
YOU KIDS ARE IN FOR A REAL TREAT... NOW YOU GET TO SEE MY FORM FROM 200 YEARS AGO.

GUH-
NU-
NU-
NU-
NU-NU-
NU-NU-
NU-NU!

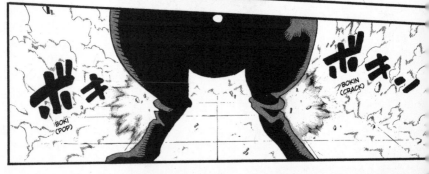

ボキ
BOKI
(POP)

ボキン
BOKIN
(CRACK)

びょ〜ん
BYOON
(BOING)

AGAAAAH!

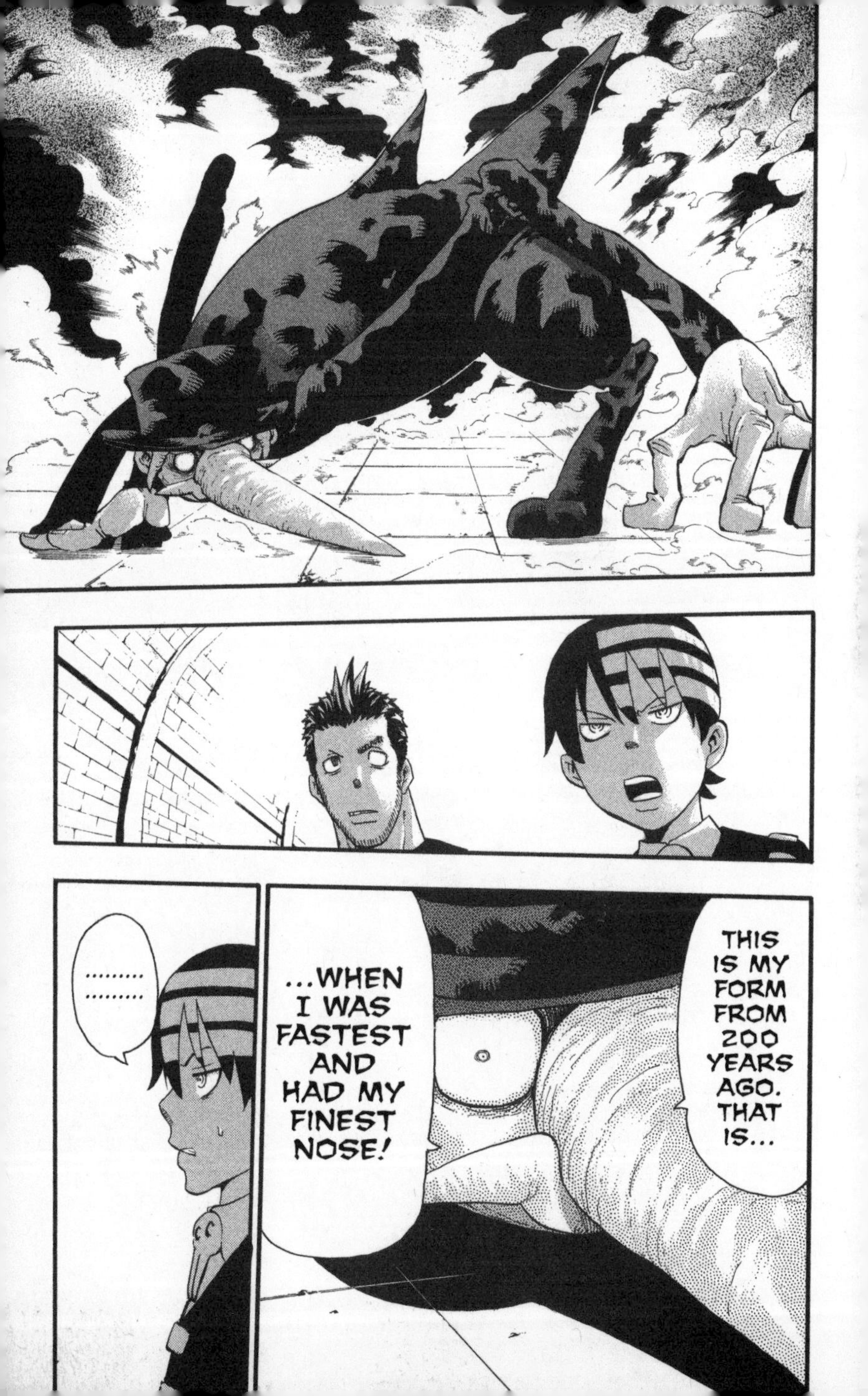
THIS IS MY FORM FROM 200 YEARS AGO. THAT IS...
...WHEN I WAS FASTEST AND HAD MY FINEST NOSE!
....
....

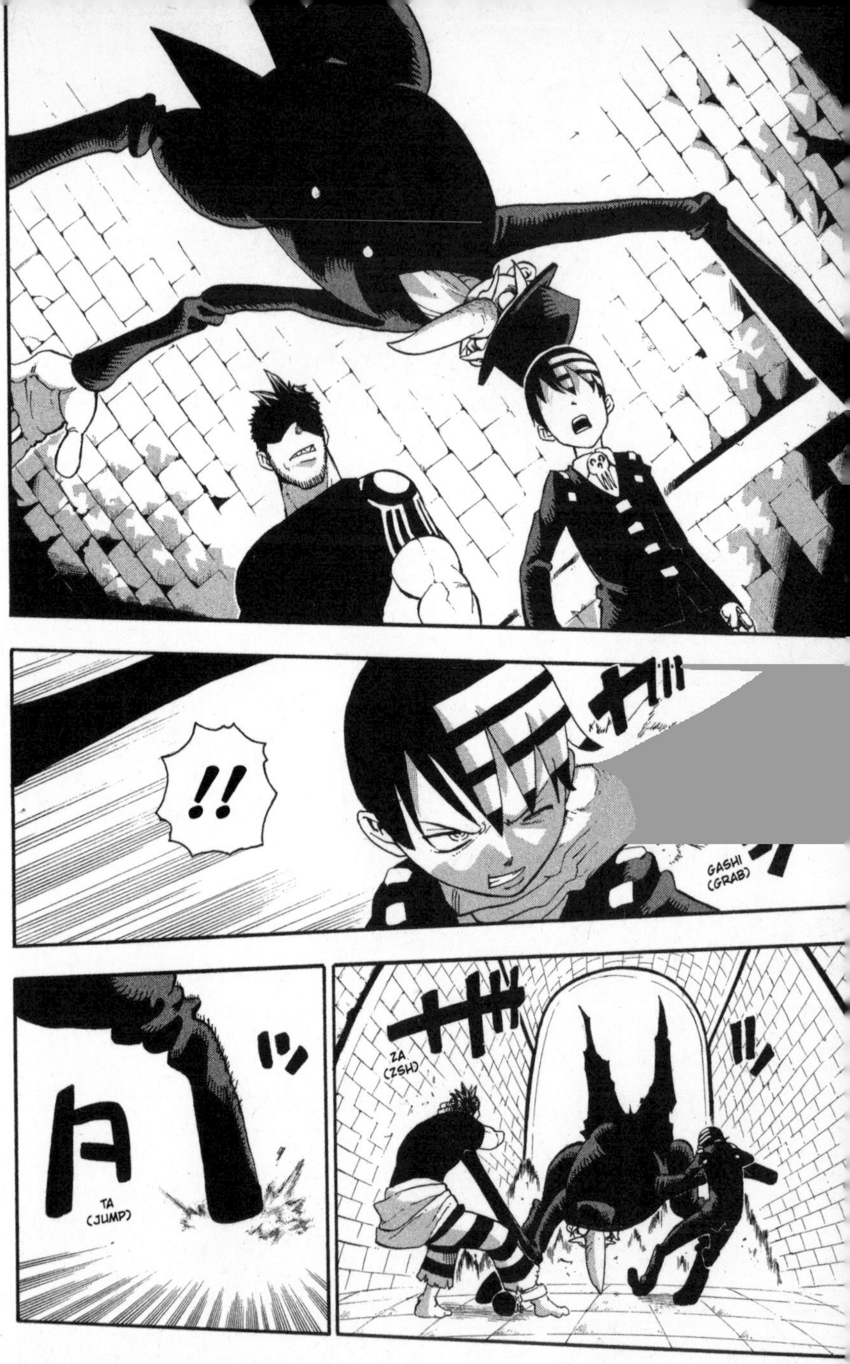
GASHI (GRAB)
!!
ZA (ZSH)
TA (JUMP)

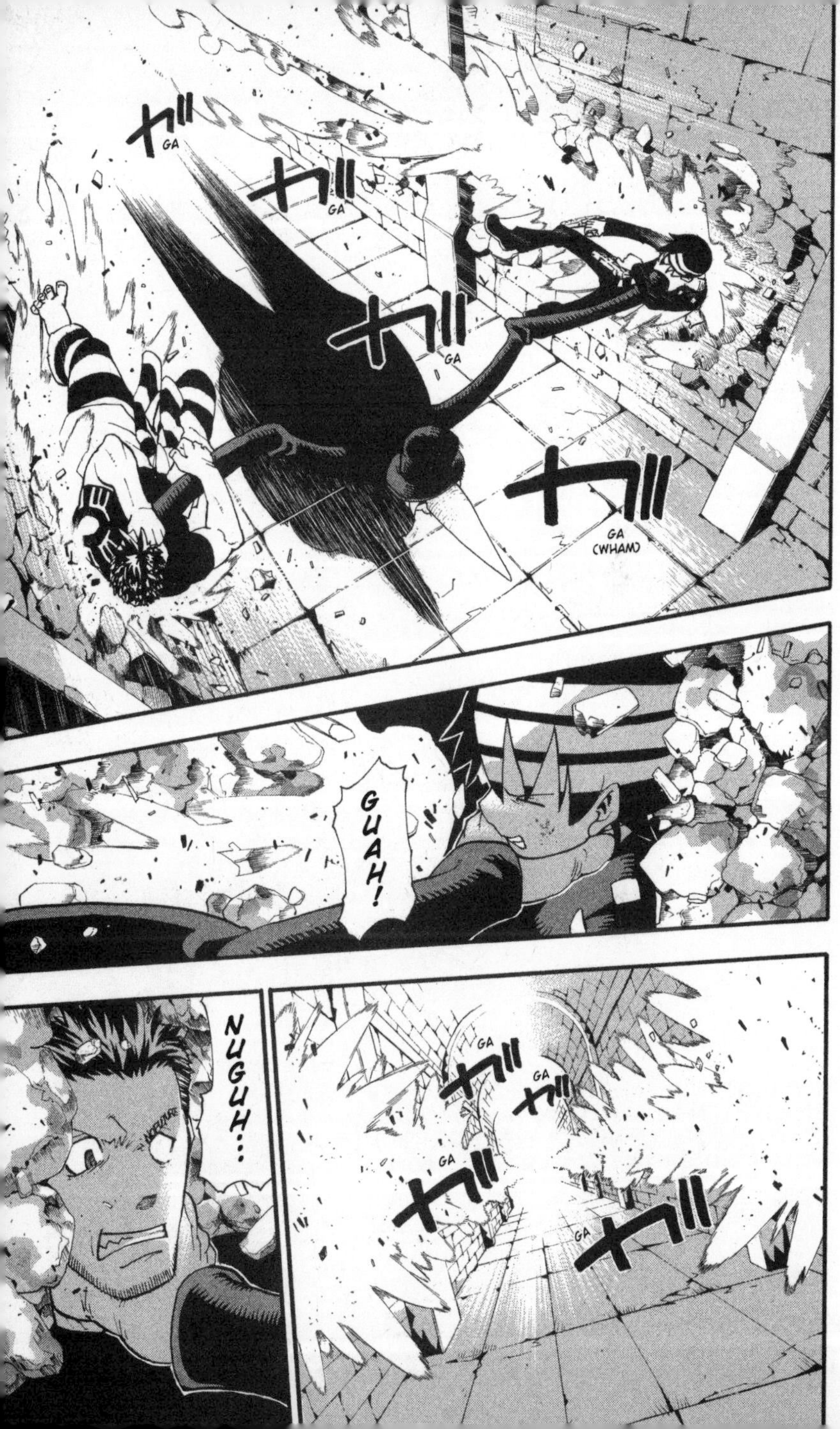
GA
GA
GA
GA
(WHAM)
GUAH!
GA
GA
GA
GA
NUGUH...

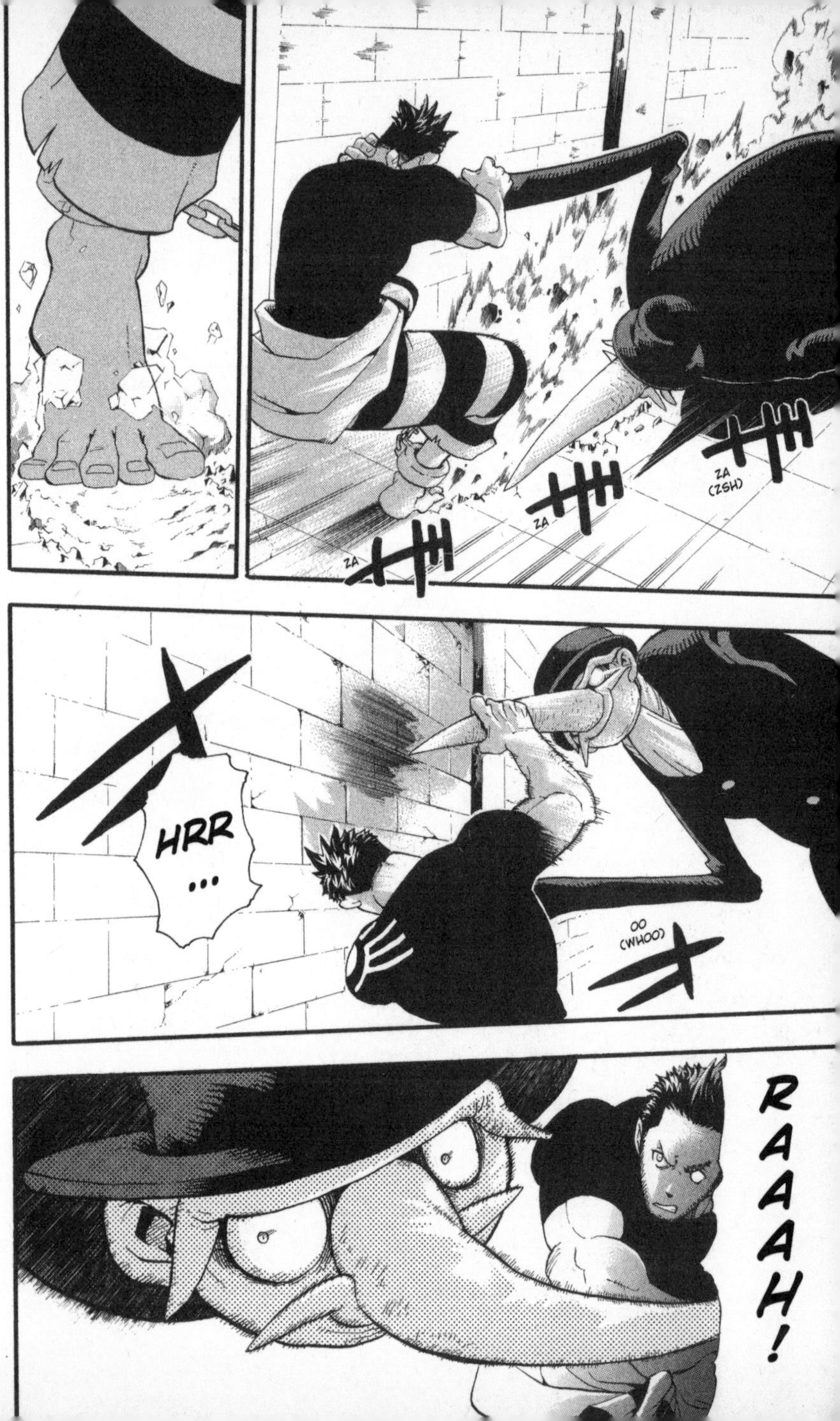
ZA (ZSH)
ZA
ZA
HRR ...
OO (WHOO)
RAAAAH!

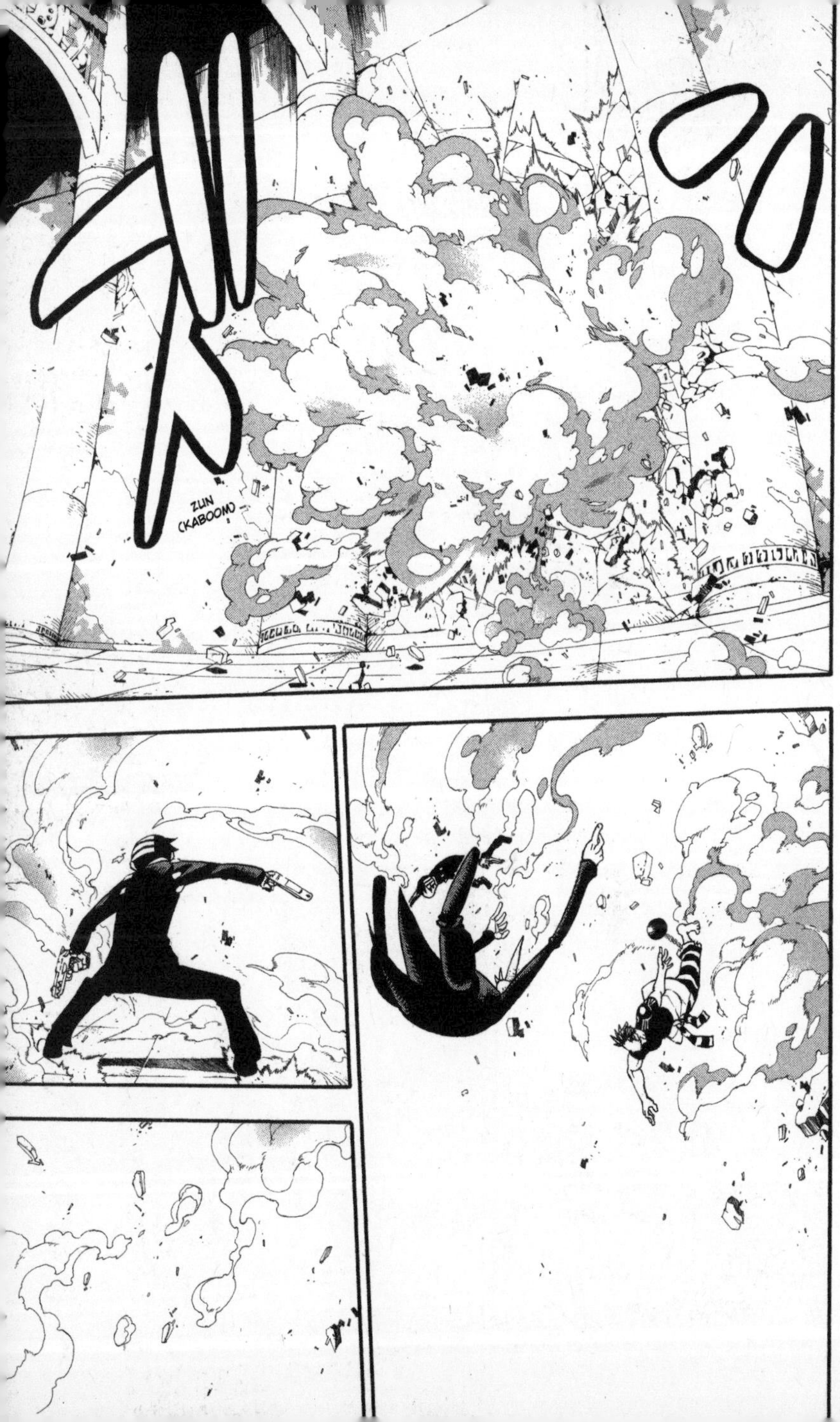
ZUN
(KABOOM)

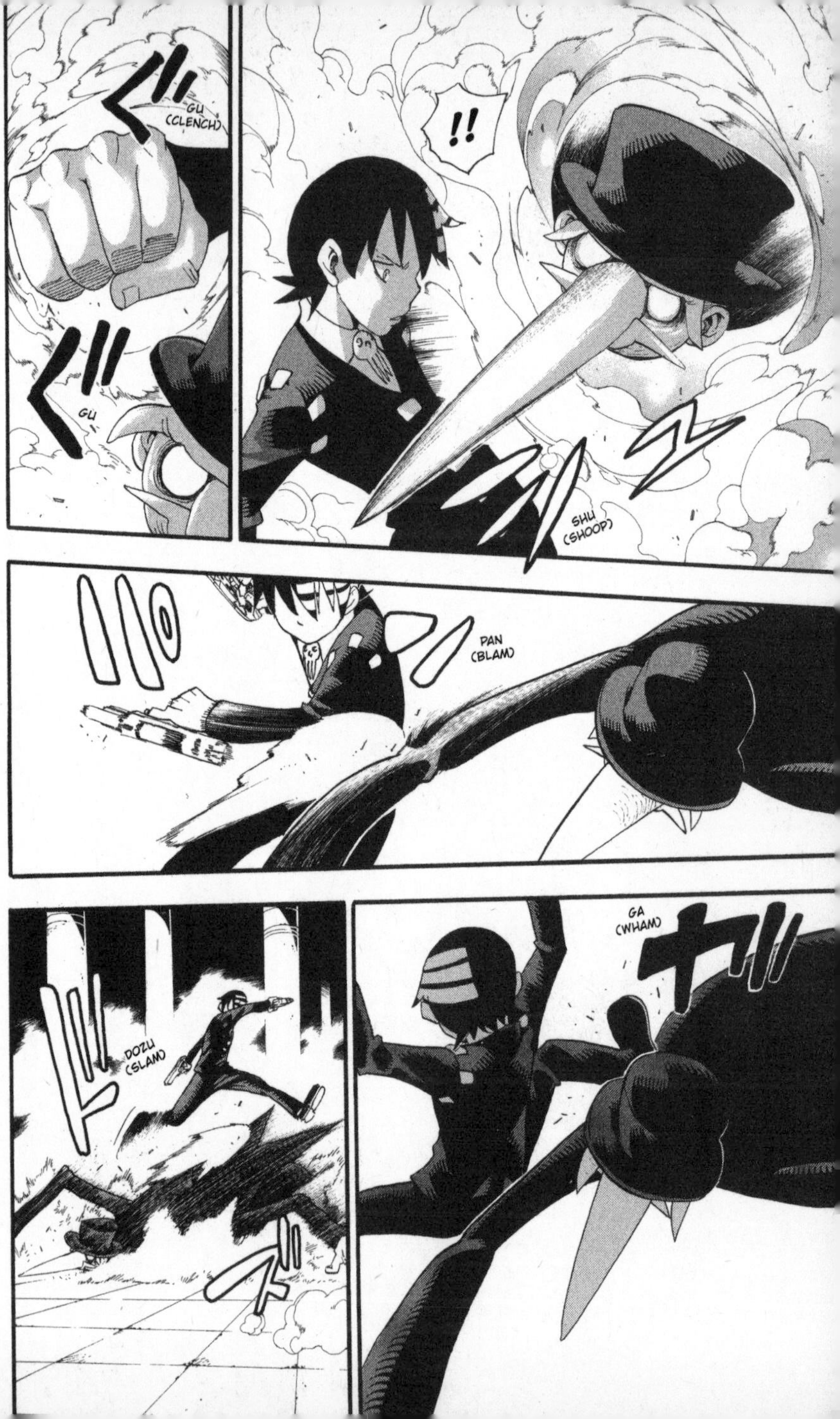
!!
SHU (SHOOP)
GU (CLENCH)
GU
PAN (BLAM)
GA (WHAM)
DOZU (SLAM)

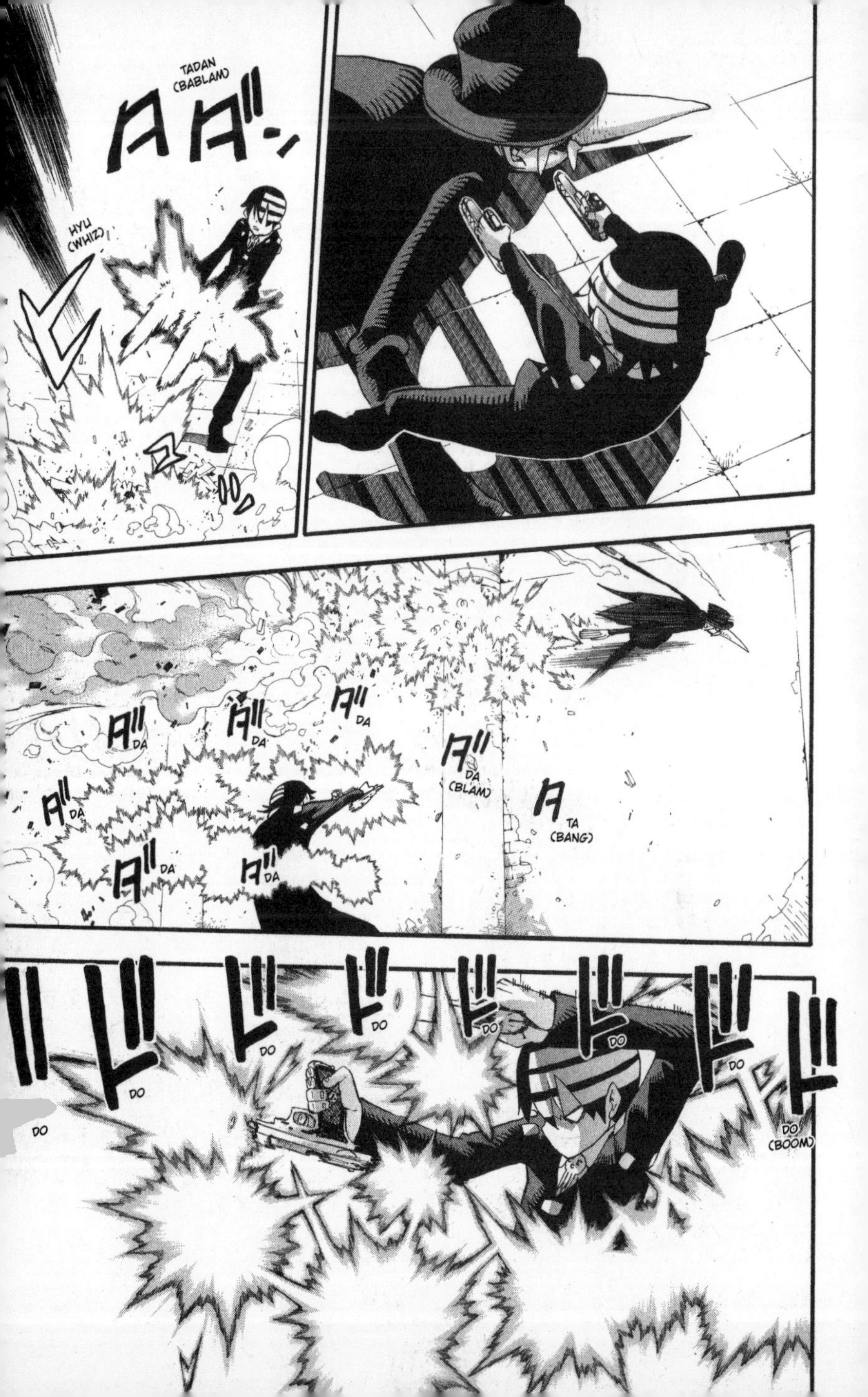
TADAN
(BABLAM)
HYU
(WHIZ)
TA
(BANG)
DA
(BLAM)
DA
DA
DA
DA
DA
DA
DO
(BOOM)
DO
DO
DO
DO
DO
DO

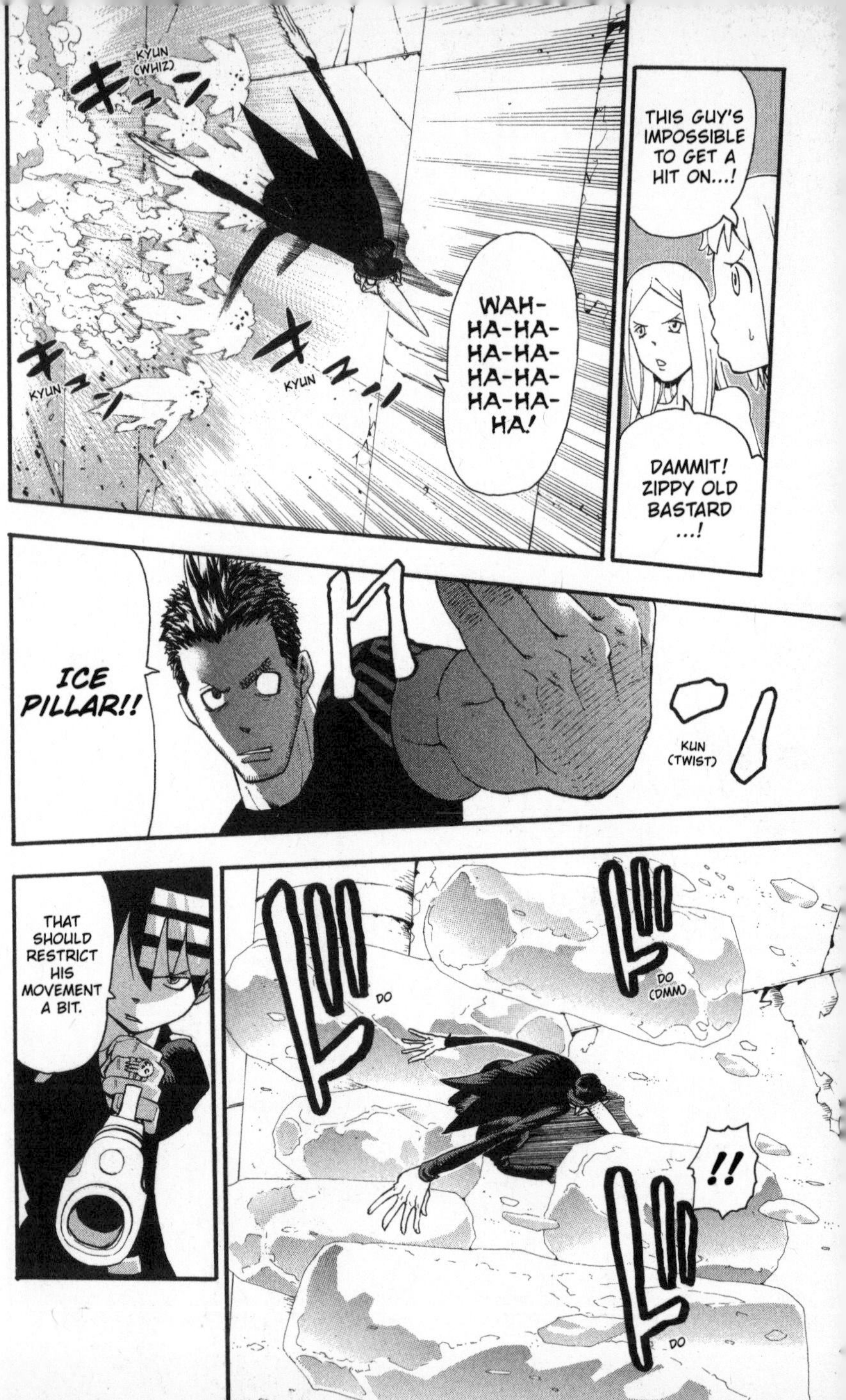
THIS GUY'S IMPOSSIBLE TO GET A HIT ON...!
DAMMIT! ZIPPY OLD BASTARD ...!
KYUN (WHIZ)
WAH-HA-HA-HA-HA-HA-HA-HA-HA-HA-HA!
KYUN
KYUN
KUN (TWIST)
ICE PILLAR!!
DO (DMM)
DO
!!
DO
THAT SHOULD RESTRICT HIS MOVEMENT A BIT.

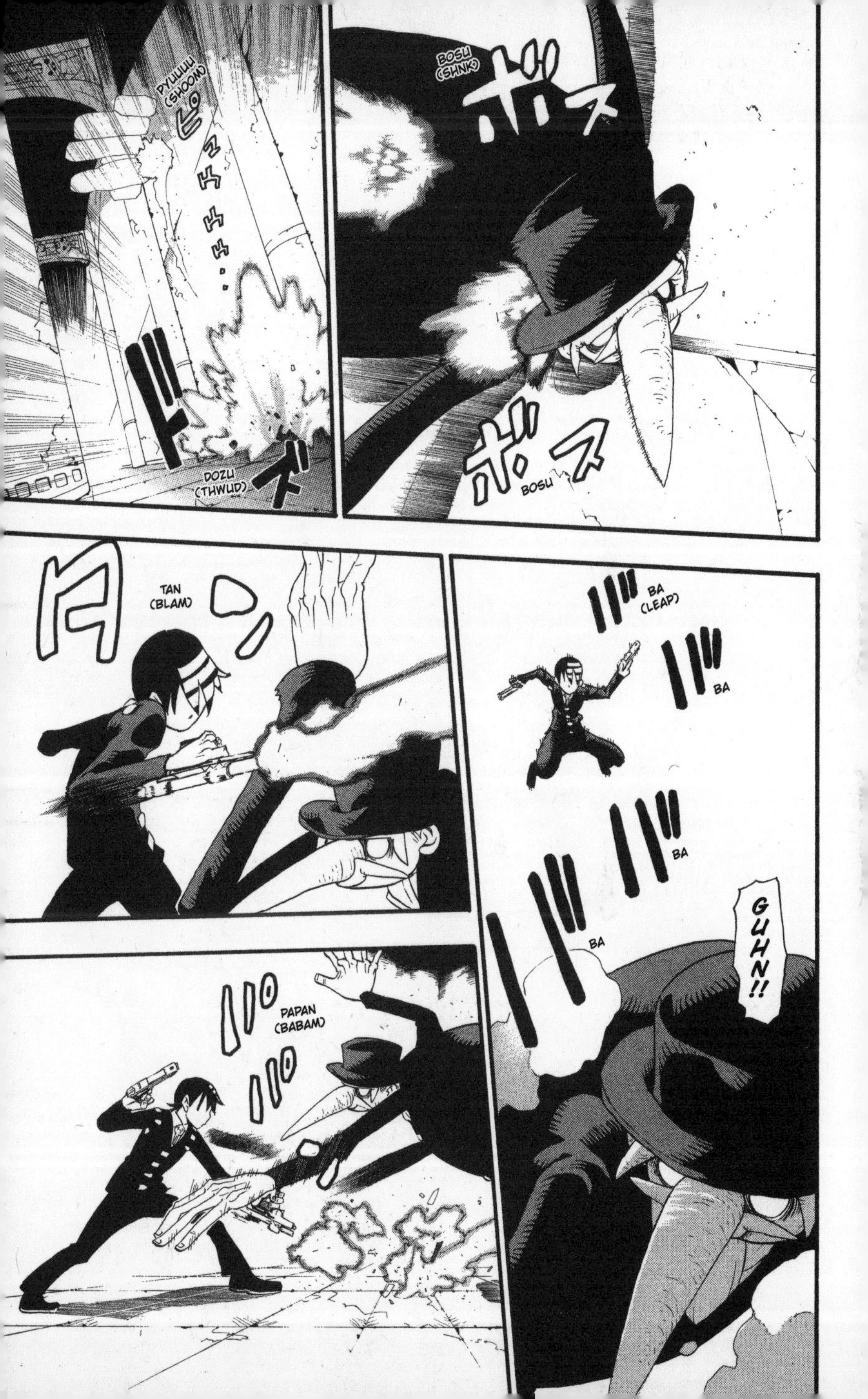
BOSU (SHNK)
BOSU
PYUUUU (SHOOM)
DOZU (THWUD)
BA (LEAP)
BA
BA
BA
GUHN!!
TAN (BLAM)
PAPAN (BABAM)

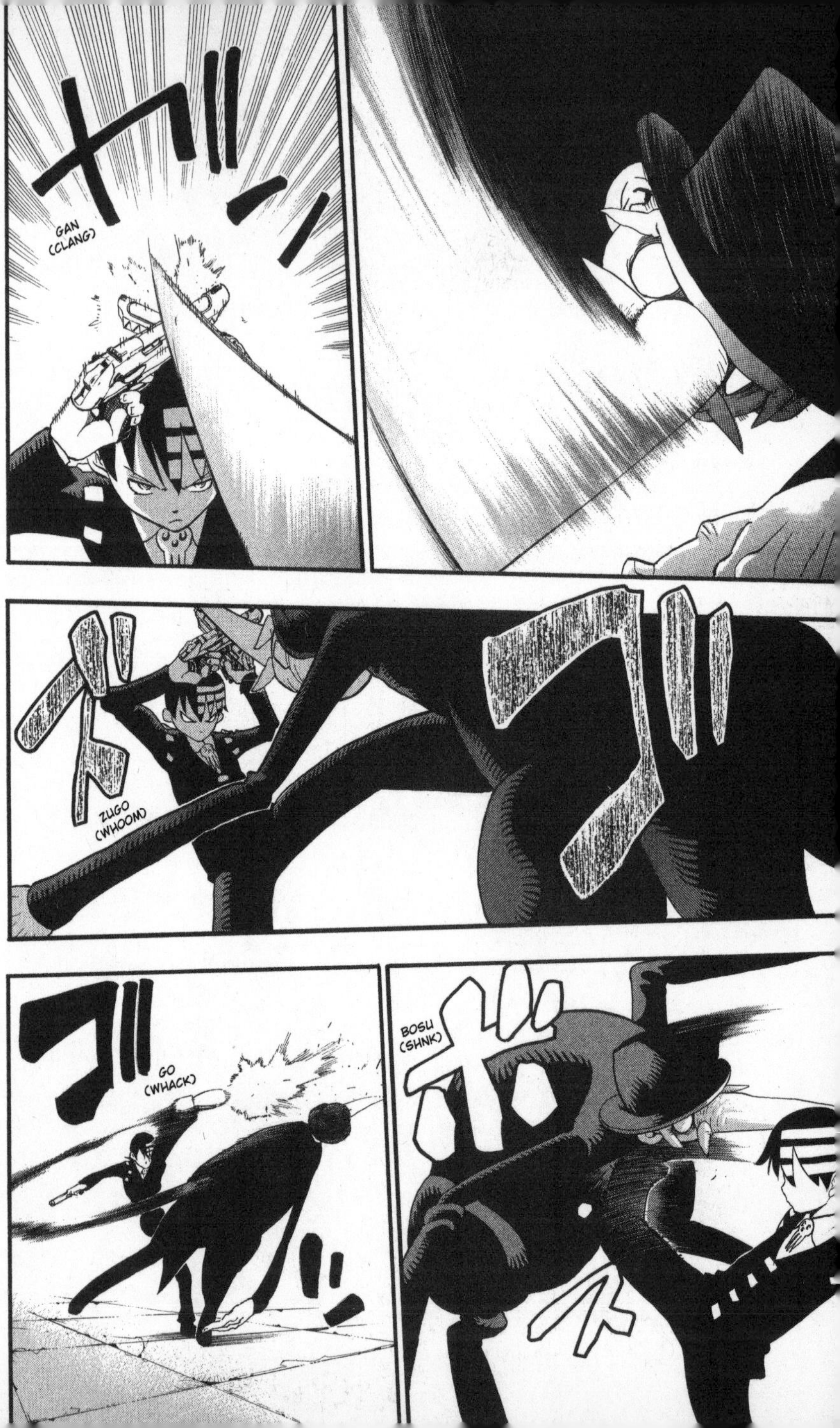
GAN
(CLANG)
ZUGO
(WHOOM)
BOSU
(SHNK)
GO
(WHACK)

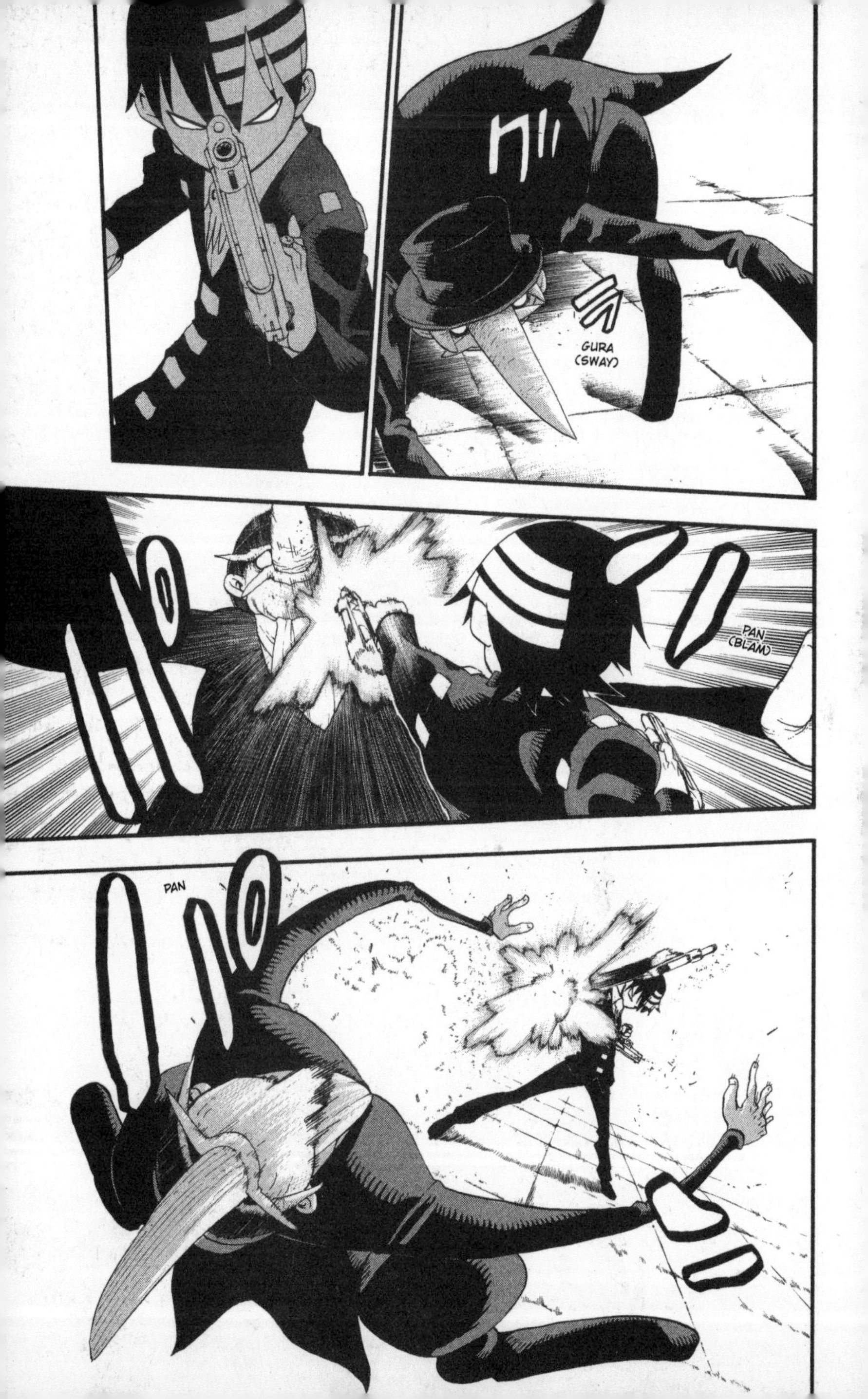
GURA
(SWAY)
PAN
(BLAM)
PAN

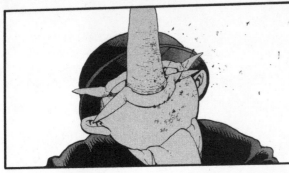

THIS IS A REAL ONSLAUGHT... MAYBE I SHOULD PULL BACK FOR A BIT...

ICE BIND.

!?

PAKIKI
(CRACKLE)

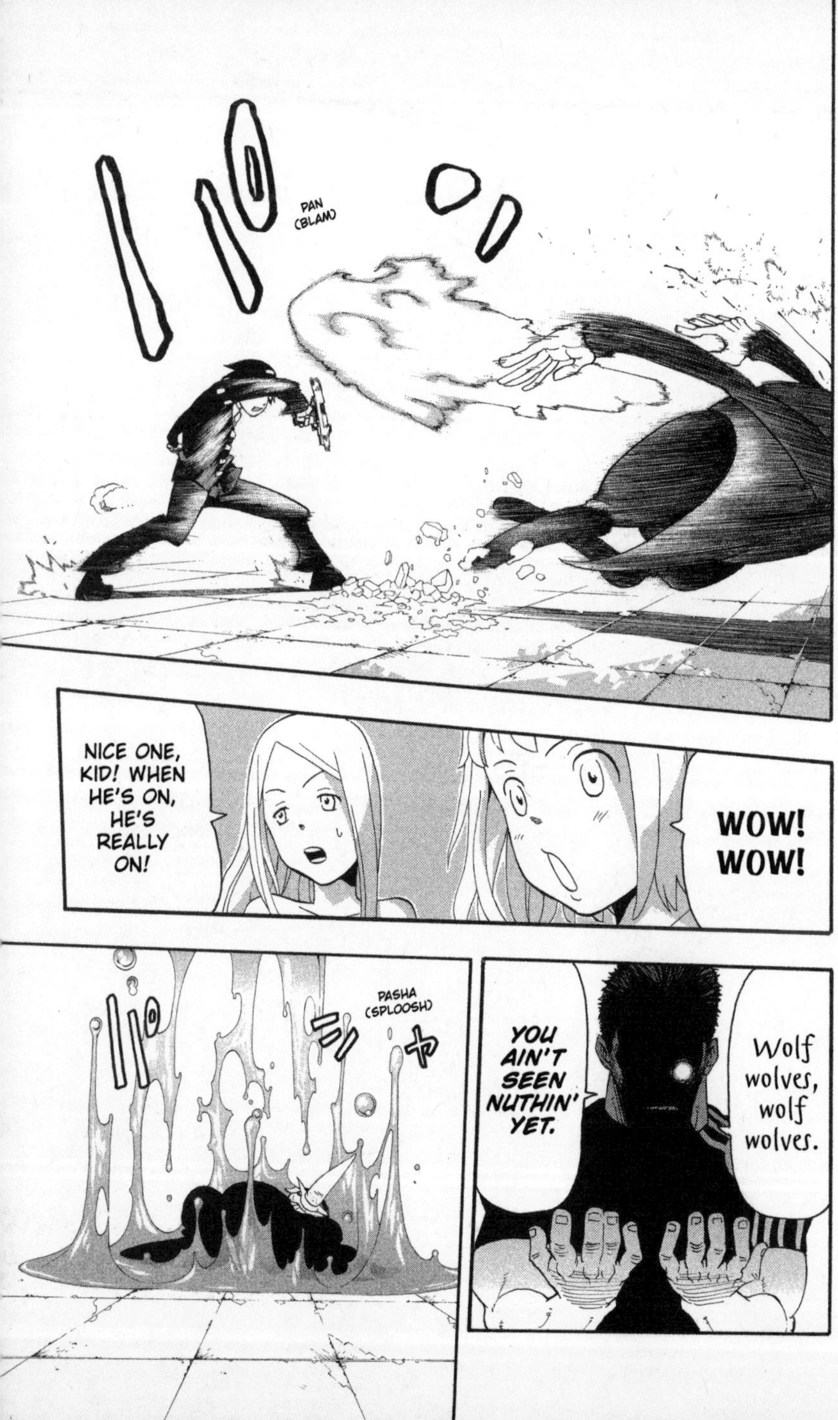
PAN (BLAM)
WOW! WOW!
NICE ONE, KID! WHEN HE'S ON, HE'S REALLY ON!
Wolf wolves, wolf wolves.
YOU AIN'T SEEN NUTHIN' YET.
PASHA (SPLOOSH)

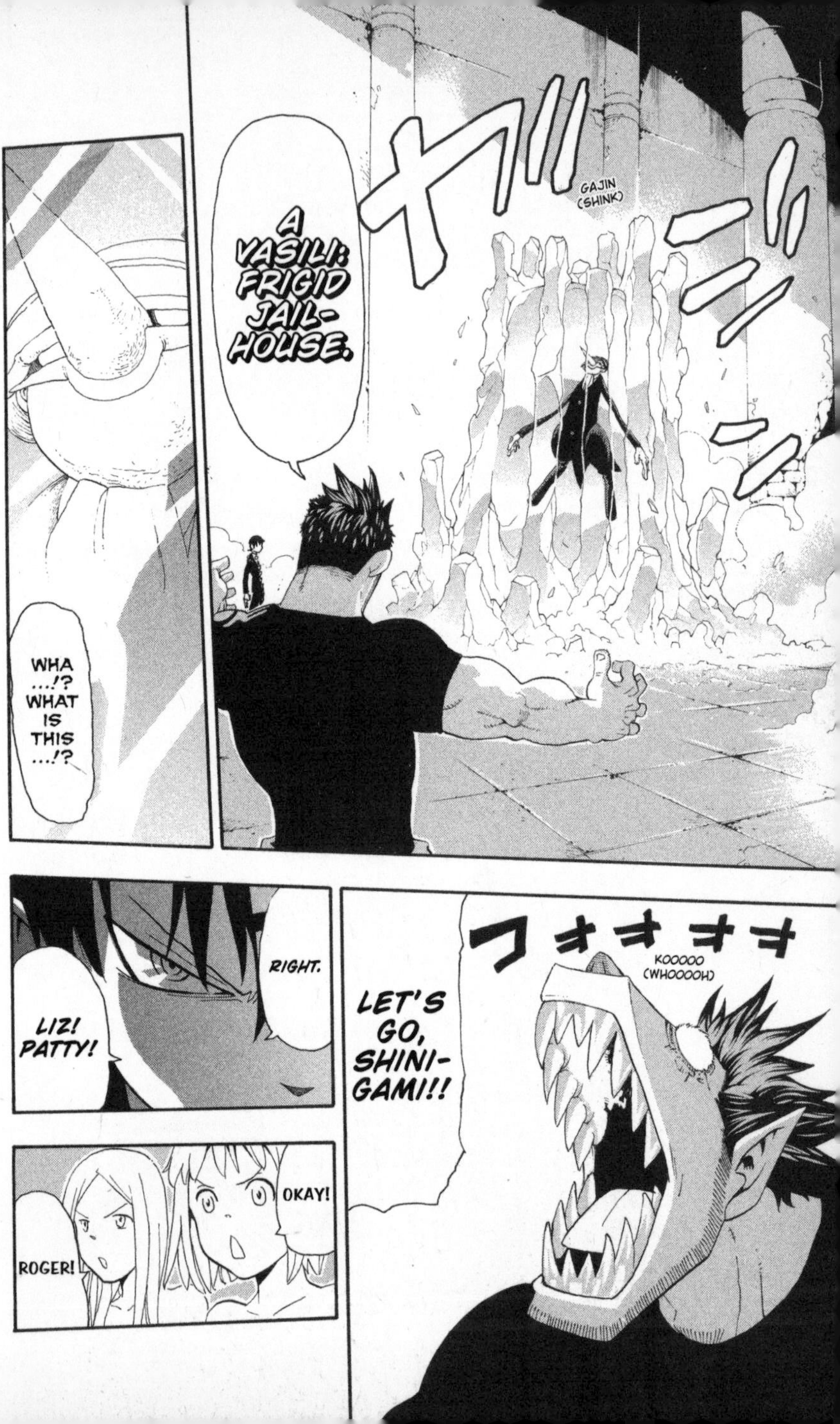
GAJIN (SHINK)
A VASILI: FRIGID JAIL-HOUSE.
WHA ...!? WHAT IS THIS ...!?
KOOOOO (WHOOOOH)
LET'S GO, SHINIGAMI!!
RIGHT.
LIZ! PATTY!
OKAY!
ROGER!

DEATH
CANNON.

DE-
MON
EYE
CAN-
NON.

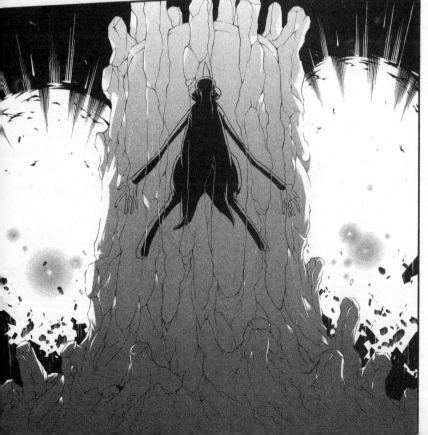

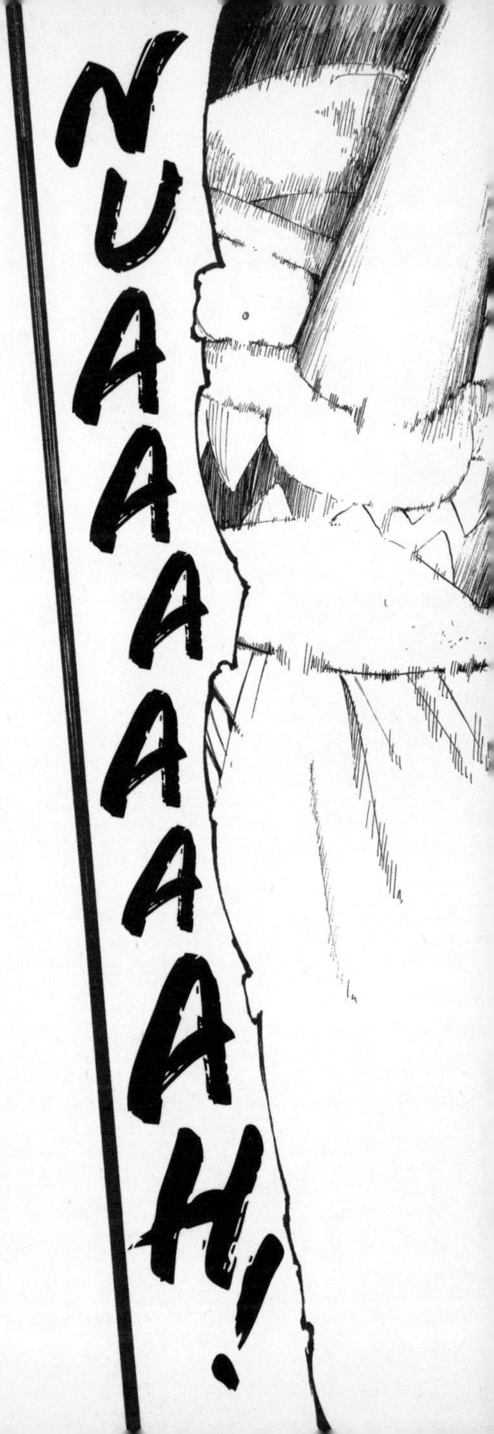
NUAAAAAAAH!

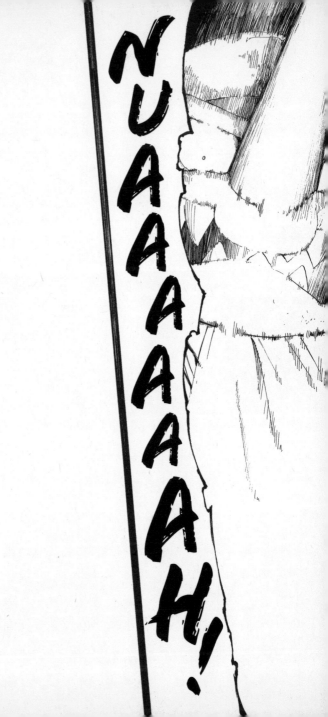

DO
(BOOM)

TOUGH
OLD
BAS-
TARD.

...

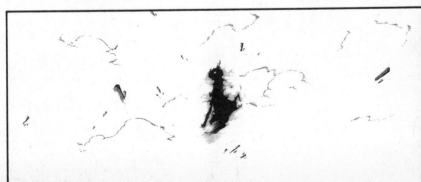

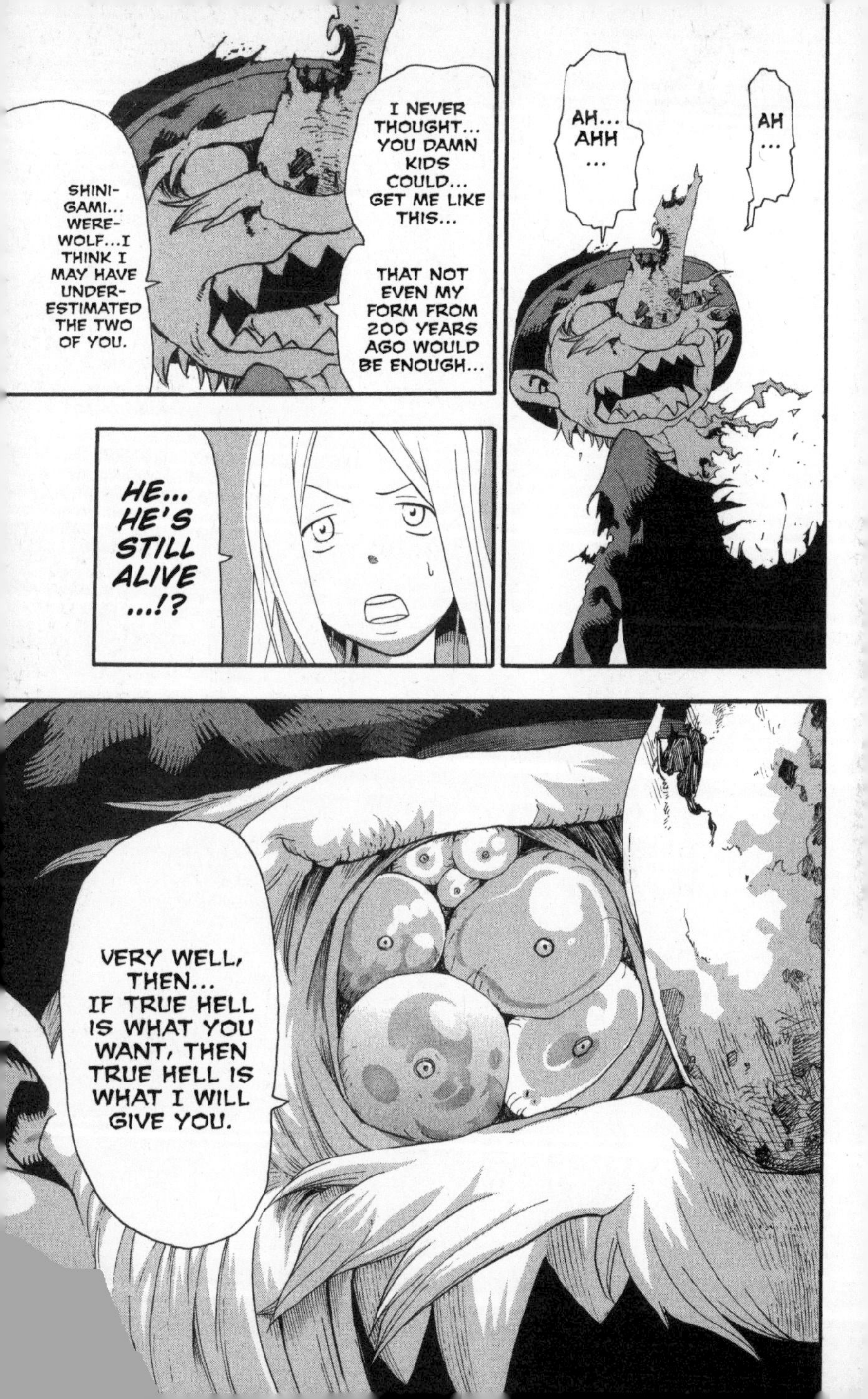
AH ...
AH... AHH ...
I NEVER THOUGHT... YOU DAMN KIDS COULD... GET ME LIKE THIS...
THAT NOT EVEN MY FORM FROM 200 YEARS AGO WOULD BE ENOUGH...
SHINIGAMI... WEREWOLF...I THINK I MAY HAVE UNDERESTIMATED THE TWO OF YOU.
HE... HE'S STILL ALIVE ...!?
VERY WELL, THEN... IF TRUE HELL IS WHAT YOU WANT, THEN TRUE HELL IS WHAT I WILL GIVE YOU.

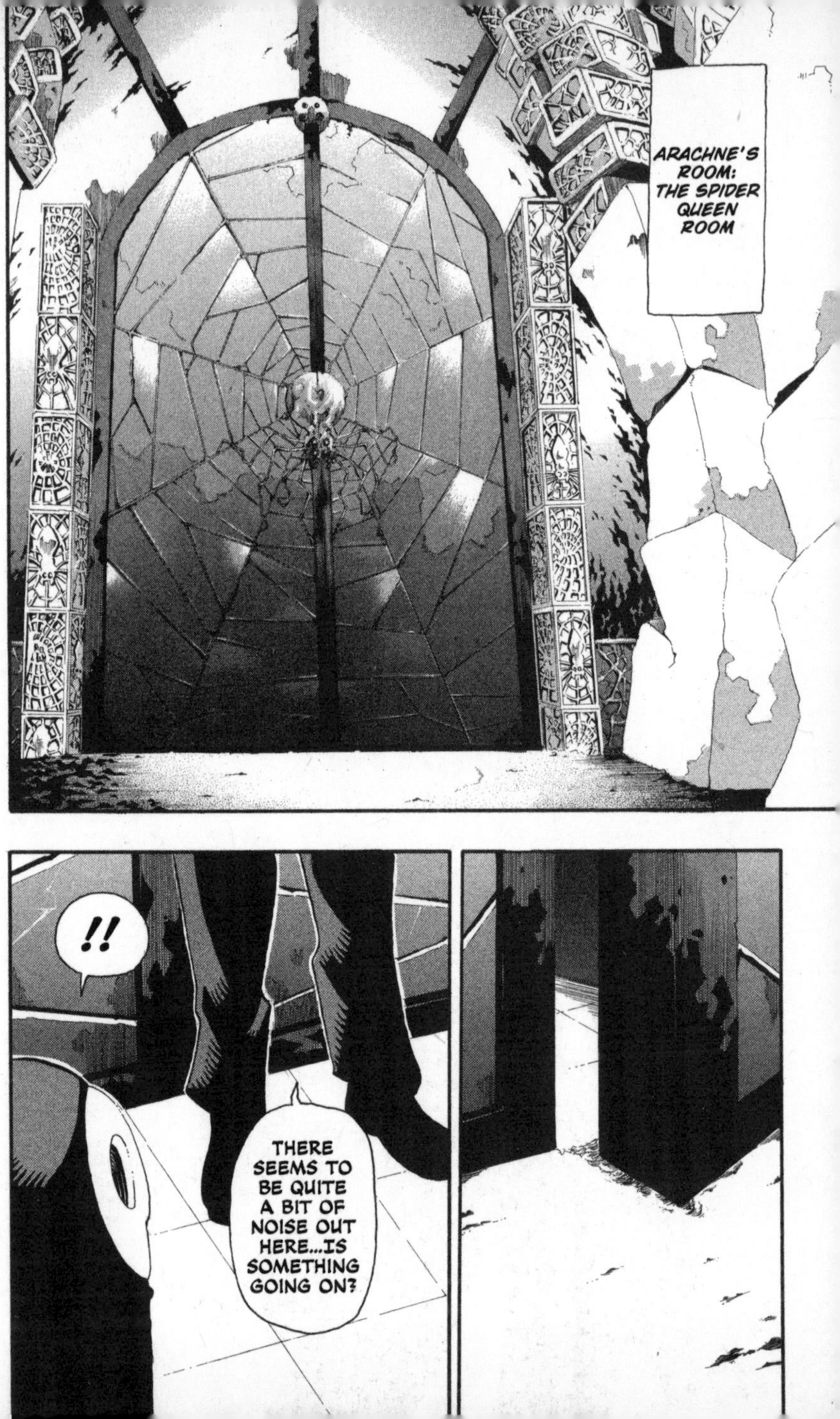
ARACHNE'S ROOM: THE SPIDER QUEEN ROOM
!!
THERE SEEMS TO BE QUITE A BIT OF NOISE OUT HERE...IS SOMETHING GOING ON?

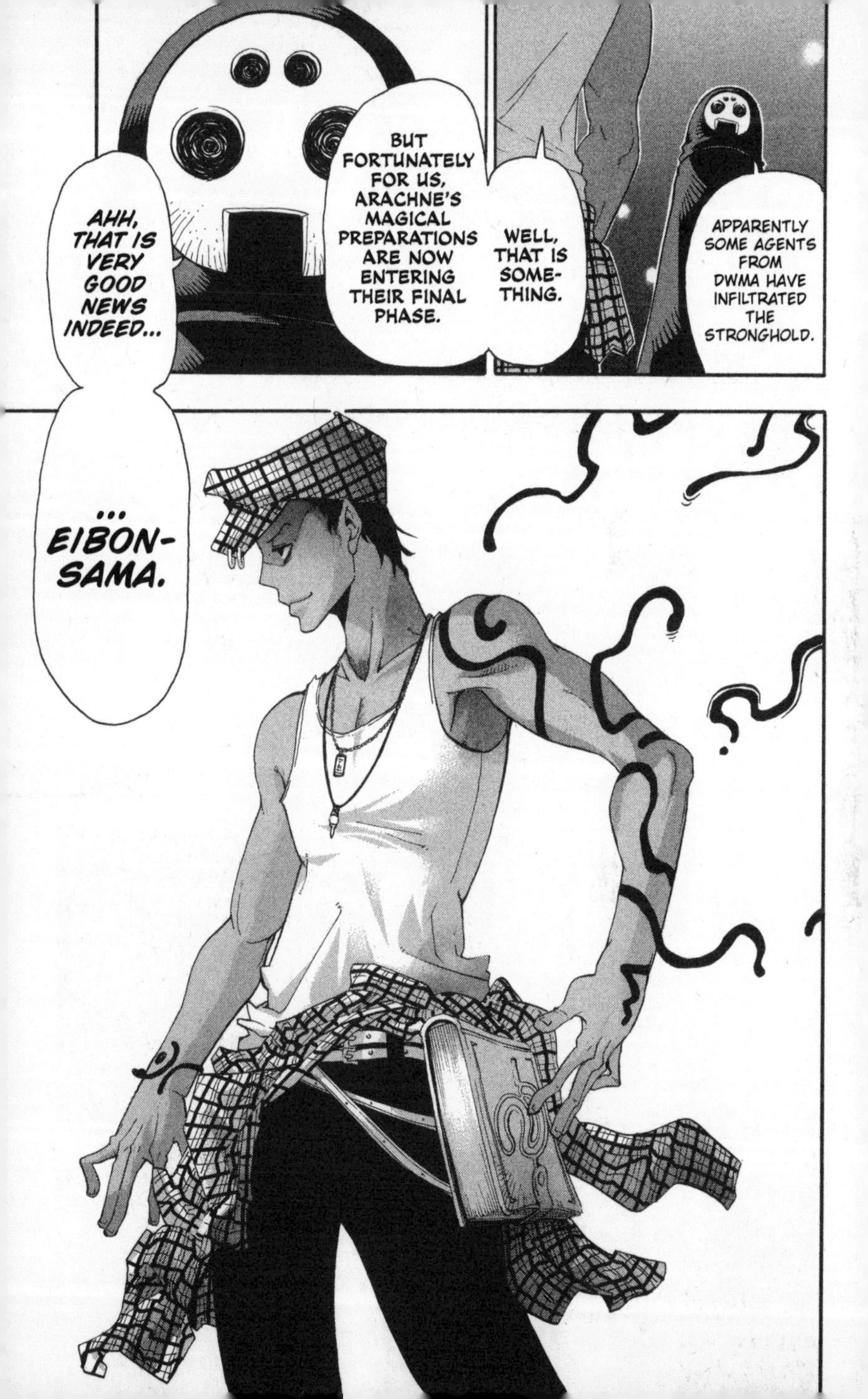
APPARENTLY SOME AGENTS FROM DWMA HAVE INFILTRATED THE STRONGHOLD.
WELL, THAT IS SOME-THING.
BUT FORTUNATELY FOR US, ARACHNE'S MAGICAL PREPARATIONS ARE NOW ENTERING THEIR FINAL PHASE.
AHH, THAT IS VERY GOOD NEWS INDEED...
...EIBON-SAMA.

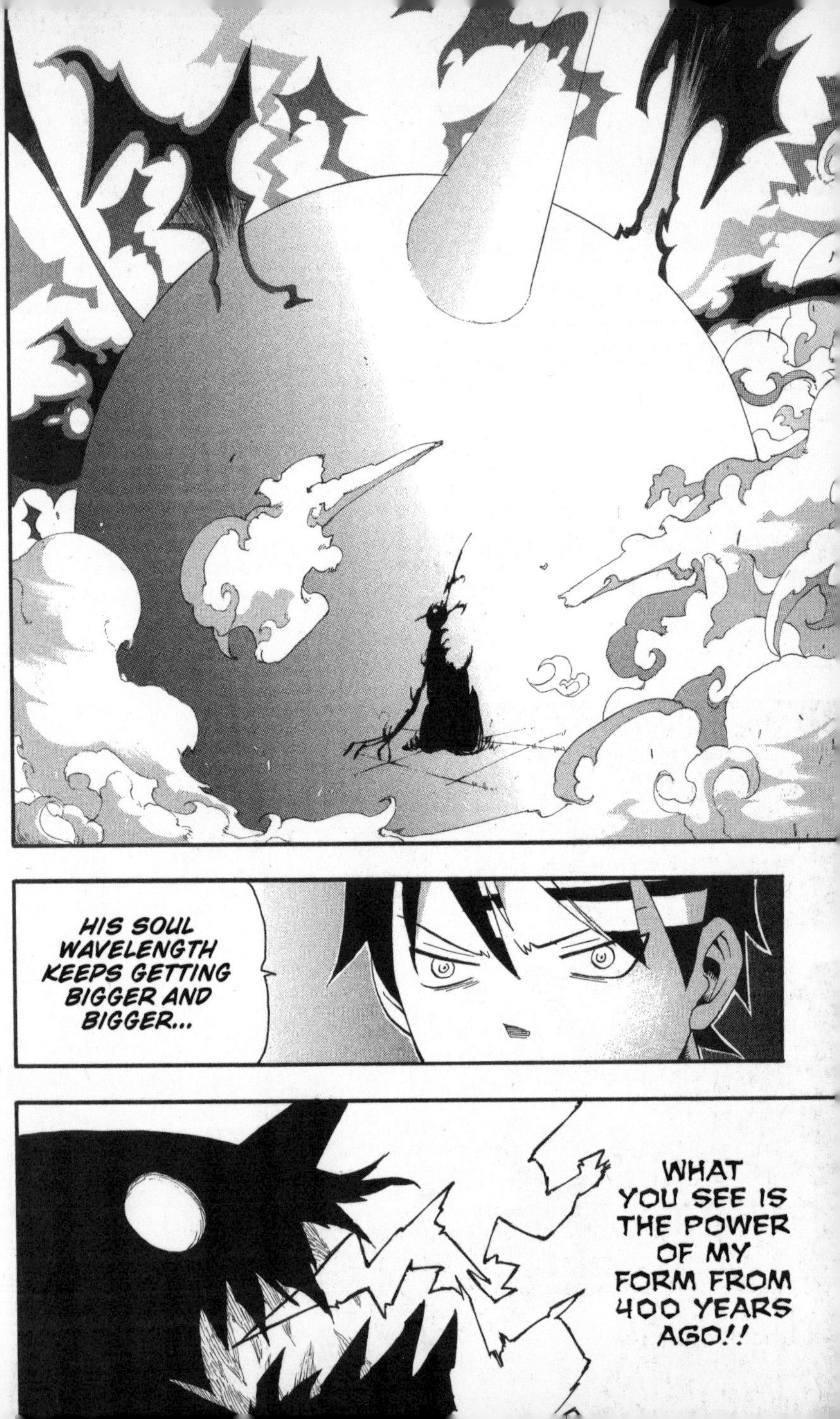
HIS SOUL WAVELENGTH KEEPS GETTING BIGGER AND BIGGER...
WHAT YOU SEE IS THE POWER OF MY FORM FROM 400 YEARS AGO!!

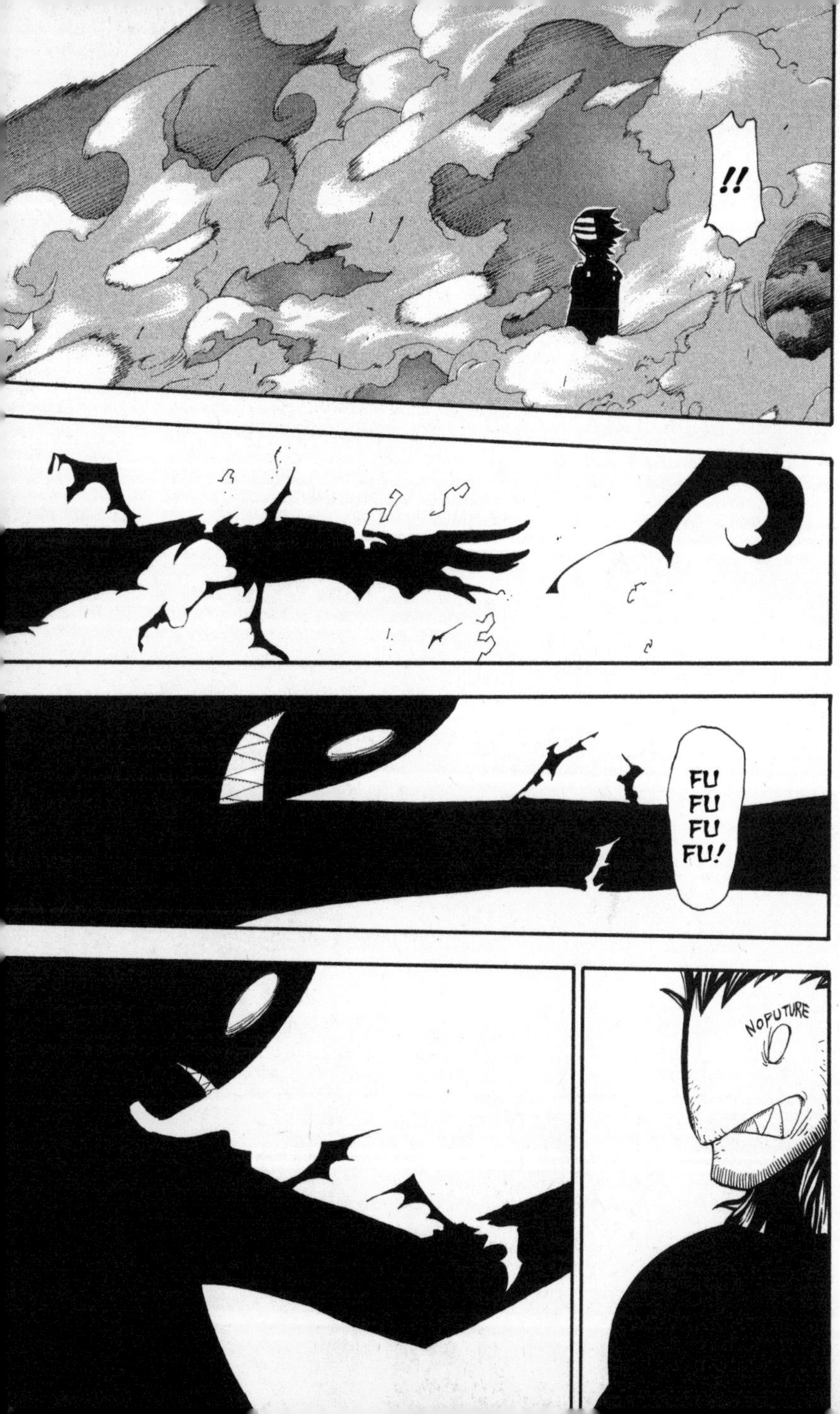
!!
FU FU FU FU!
NOFUTURE

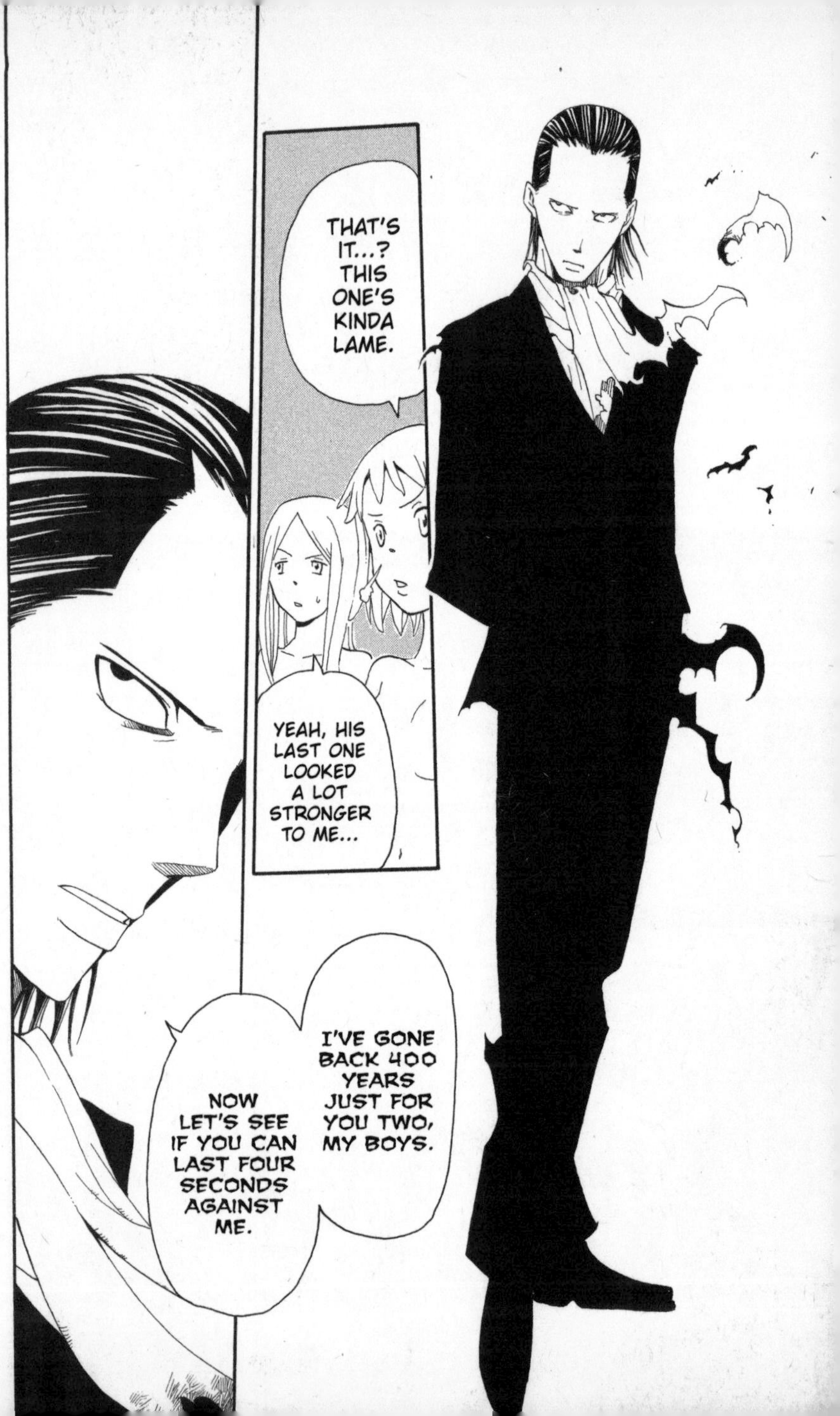
THAT'S IT...? THIS ONE'S KINDA LAME.
YEAH, HIS LAST ONE LOOKED A LOT STRONGER TO ME...
I'VE GONE BACK 400 YEARS JUST FOR YOU TWO, MY BOYS.
NOW LET'S SEE IF YOU CAN LAST FOUR SECONDS AGAINST ME.

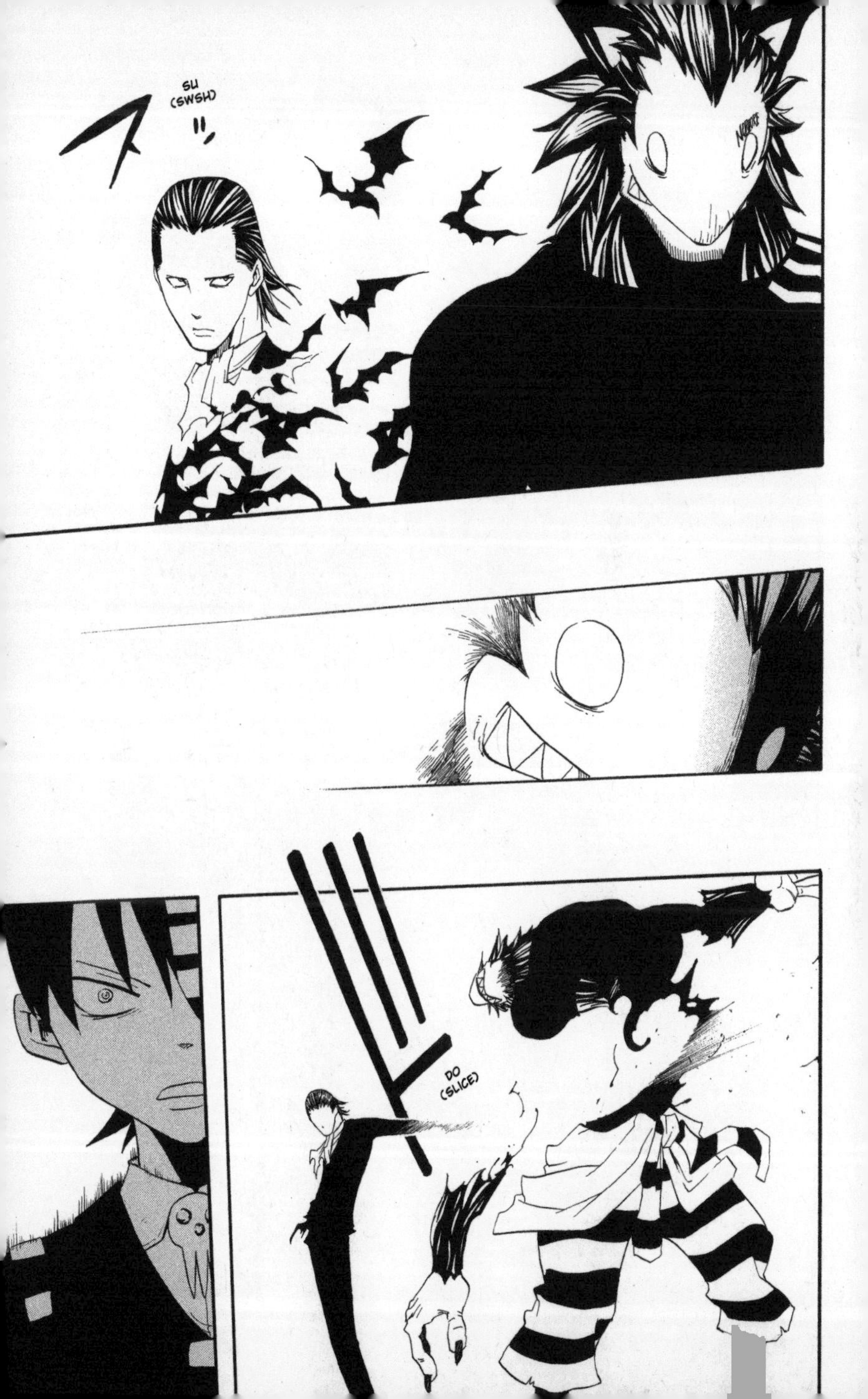
SU (SWSH)
DO (SLICE)

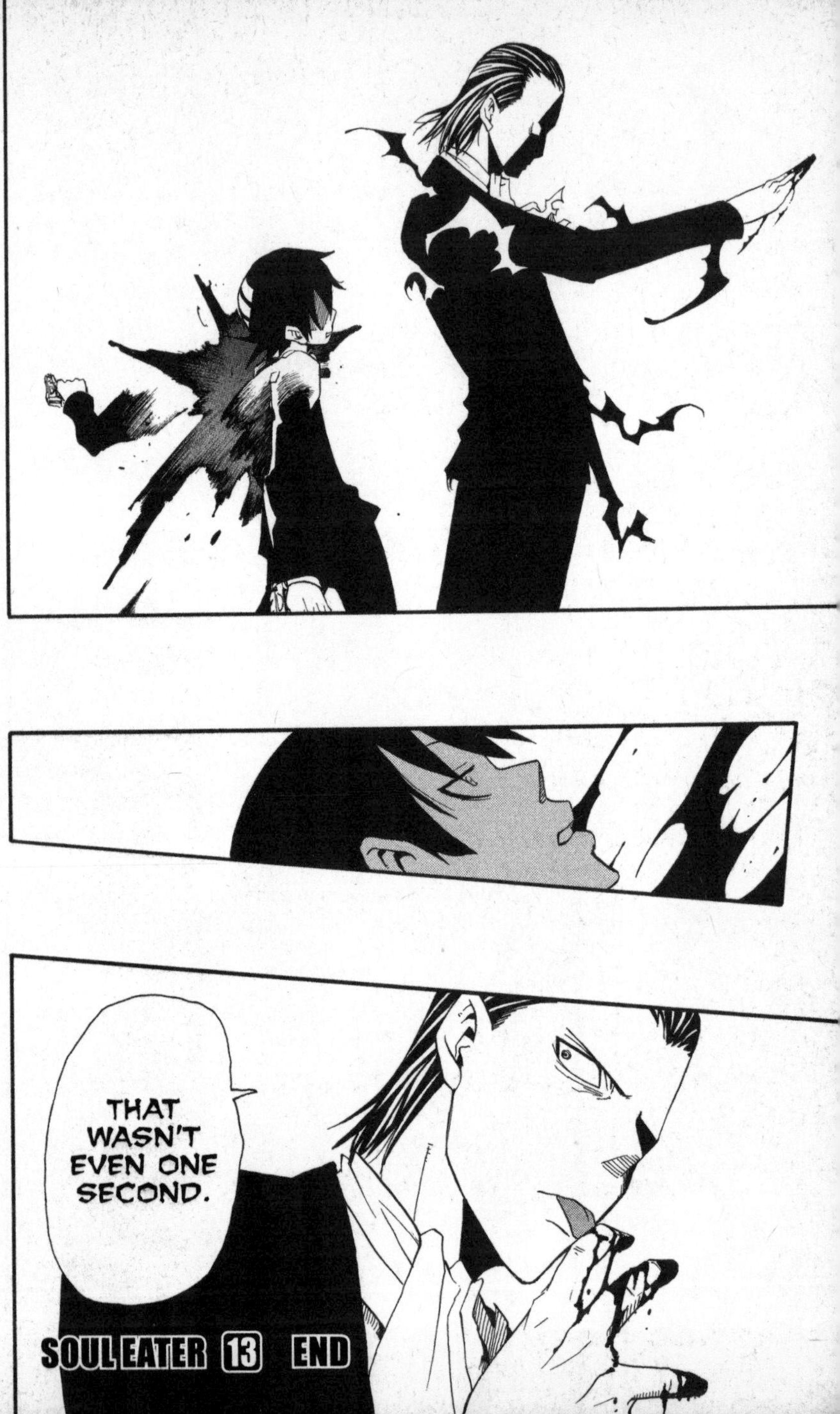
THAT WASN'T EVEN ONE SECOND.
SOUL EATER 13 END

SOUL EATER

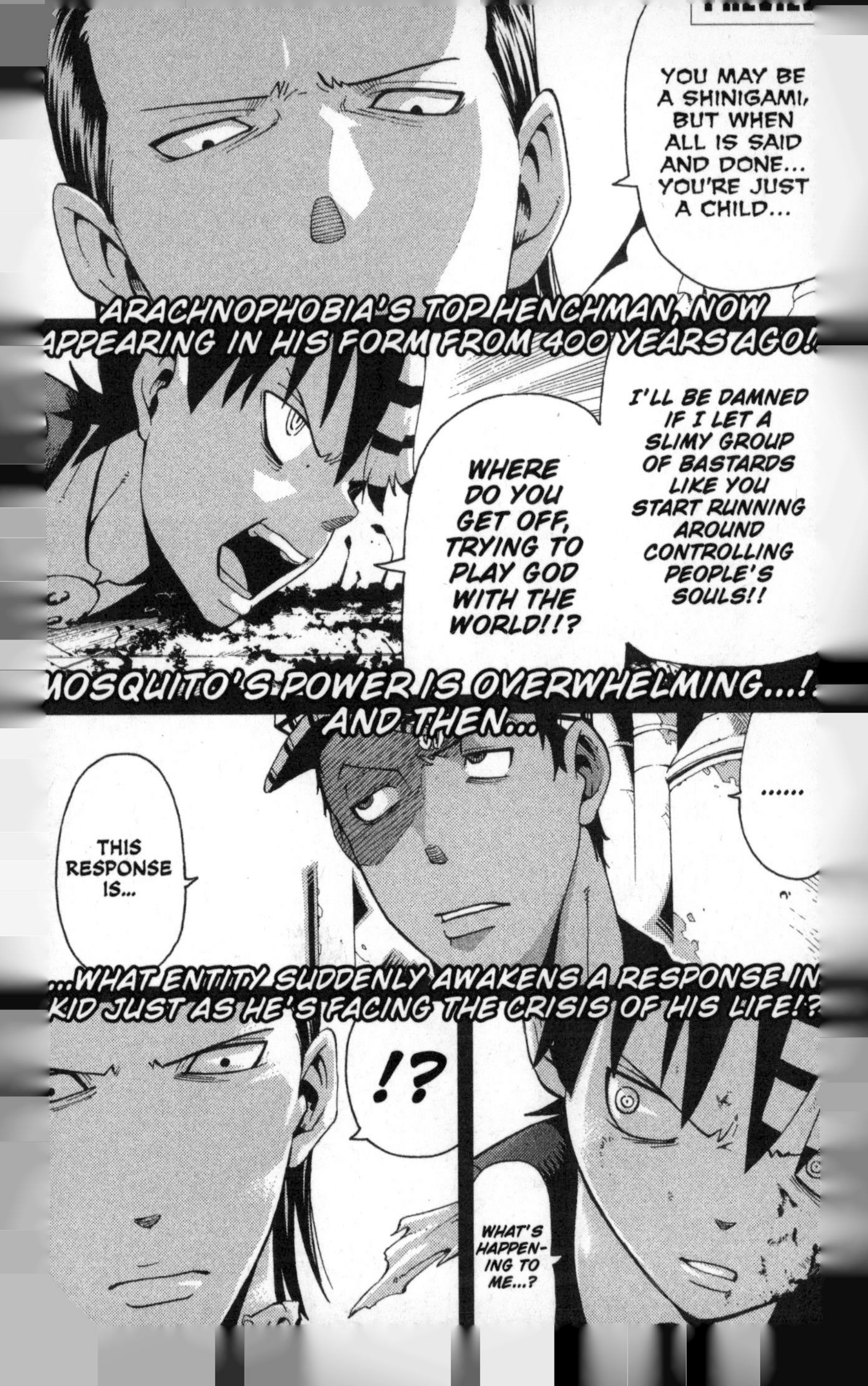
YOU MAY BE A SHINIGAMI, BUT WHEN ALL IS SAID AND DONE... YOU'RE JUST A CHILD...
ARACHNOPHOBIA'S TOP HENCHMAN, NOW APPEARING IN HIS FORM FROM 400 YEARS AGO!!
I'LL BE DAMNED IF I LET A SLIMY GROUP OF BASTARDS LIKE YOU START RUNNING AROUND CONTROLLING PEOPLE'S SOULS!!
WHERE DO YOU GET OFF, TRYING TO PLAY GOD WITH THE WORLD!!?
MOSQUITO'S POWER IS OVERWHELMING...!! AND THEN...
......
THIS RESPONSE IS...
...WHAT ENTITY SUDDENLY AWAKENS A RESPONSE IN KID JUST AS HE'S FACING THE CRISIS OF HIS LIFE!?
WHAT'S HAPPEN-ING TO ME...?
!?

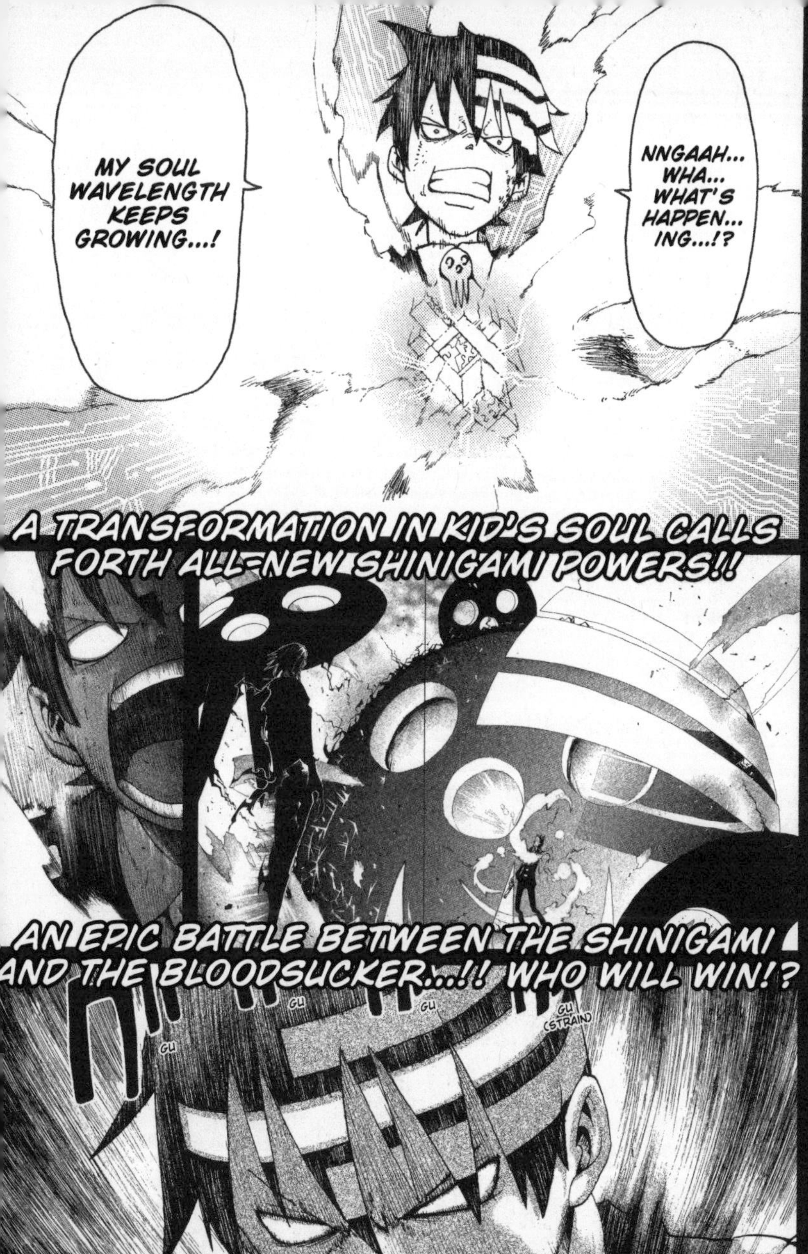
NNGAAH... WHA... WHAT'S HAPPEN... ING...!?
MY SOUL WAVELENGTH KEEPS GROWING...!
A TRANSFORMATION IN KID'S SOUL CALLS FORTH ALL-NEW SHINIGAMI POWERS!!
AN EPIC BATTLE BETWEEN THE SHINIGAMI AND THE BLOODSUCKER...!! WHO WILL WIN!?
GU (STRAIN)
GU
GU
GU

Continued in Soul Eater Volume 14!!

SIGN: KAETTE KITA ATSUSHI-YA

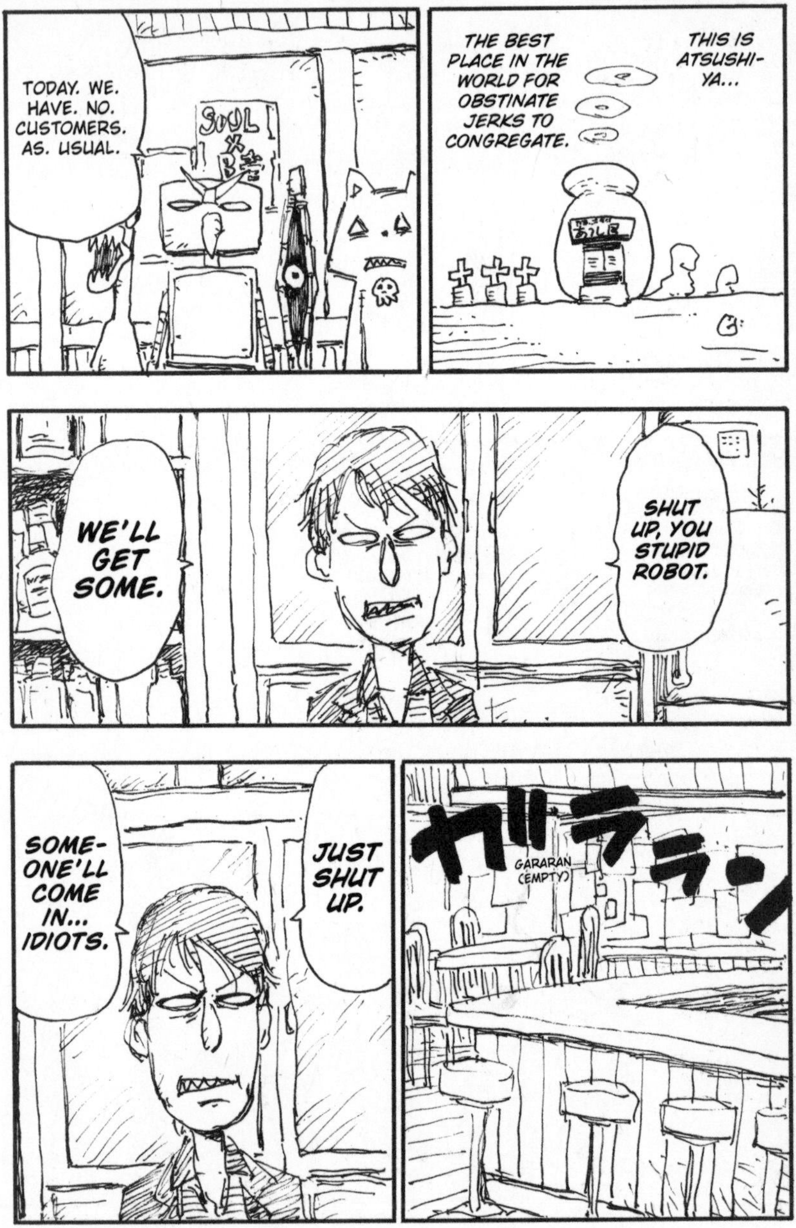
THIS IS ATSUSHI-YA...
THE BEST PLACE IN THE WORLD FOR OBSTINATE JERKS TO CONGREGATE.
TODAY. WE. HAVE. NO. CUSTOMERS. AS. USUAL.
SHUT UP, YOU STUPID ROBOT.
WE'LL GET SOME.
GARARAN (EMPTY)
JUST SHUT UP.
SOME-ONE'LL COME IN... IDIOTS.

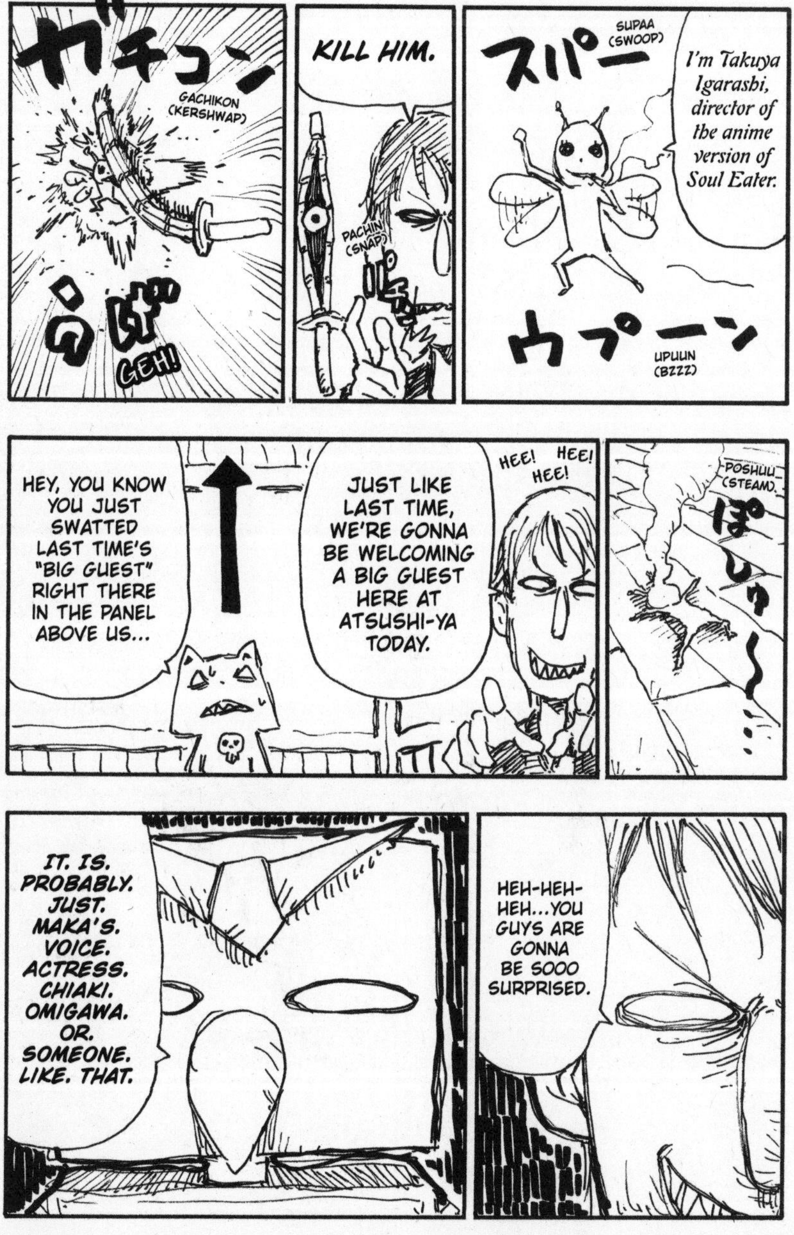
スパー
SUPAA (SWOOP)
I'm Takuya Igarashi, director of the anime version of Soul Eater.
ウプーン
UPUUN (BZZZ)
KILL HIM.
PACHIN (SNAP)
ガチコーン
GACHIKON (KERSHWAP)
GEH!
POSHUU (STEAM)
ぽしゅ～
HEE! HEE! HEE!
JUST LIKE LAST TIME, WE'RE GONNA BE WELCOMING A BIG GUEST HERE AT ATSUSHI-YA TODAY.
HEY, YOU KNOW YOU JUST SWATTED LAST TIME'S "BIG GUEST" RIGHT THERE IN THE PANEL ABOVE US...
HEH-HEH-HEH...YOU GUYS ARE GONNA BE SOOO SURPRISED.
IT. IS. PROBABLY. JUST. MAKA'S. VOICE. ACTRESS. CHIAKI. OMIGAWA. OR. SOMEONE. LIKE. THAT.

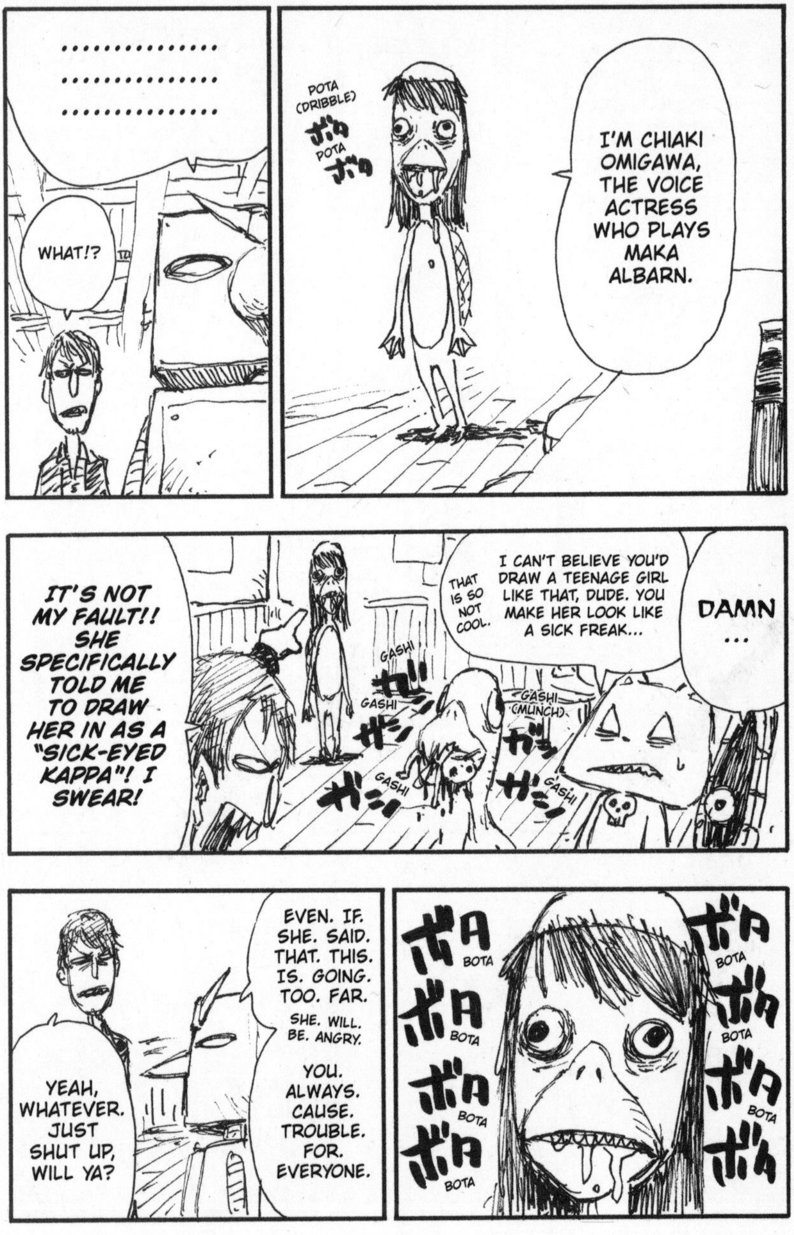

POTA (DRIBBLE)
POTA
I'M CHIAKI OMIGAWA, THE VOICE ACTRESS WHO PLAYS MAKA ALBARN.
....
....
....
WHAT!?
DAMN ...
I CAN'T BELIEVE YOU'D DRAW A TEENAGE GIRL LIKE THAT, DUDE. YOU MAKE HER LOOK LIKE A SICK FREAK...
THAT IS SO NOT COOL.
GASHI (MUNCH)
GASHI
GASHI
GASHI
GASHI
IT'S NOT MY FAULT!! SHE SPECIFICALLY TOLD ME TO DRAW HER IN AS A "SICK-EYED KAPPA"! I SWEAR!
BOTA
BOTA
BOTA
BOTA
BOTA
BOTA
BOTA
BOTA
EVEN. IF. SHE. SAID. THAT. THIS. IS. GOING. TOO. FAR.
SHE. WILL. BE. ANGRY.
YOU. ALWAYS. CAUSE. TROUBLE. FOR. EVERYONE.
YEAH, WHATEVER. JUST SHUT UP, WILL YA?

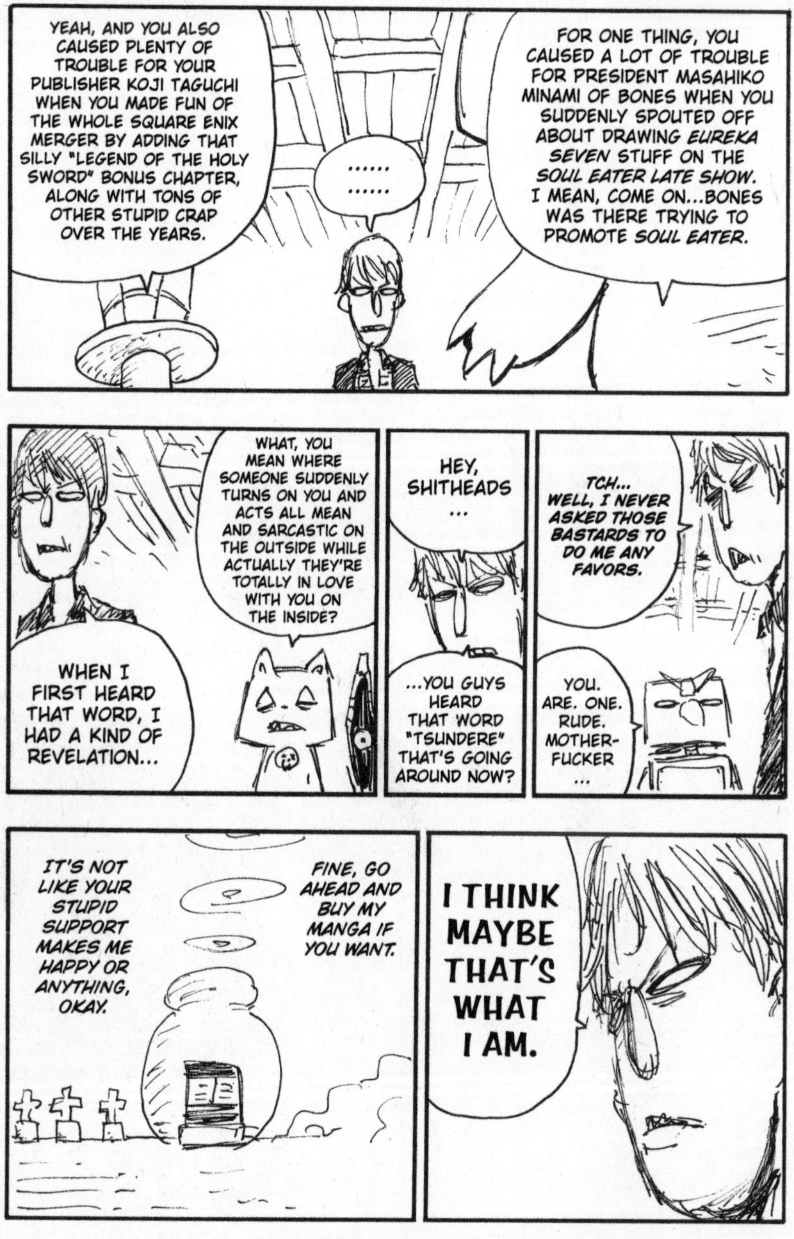
FOR ONE THING, YOU CAUSED A LOT OF TROUBLE FOR PRESIDENT MASAHIKO MINAMI OF BONES WHEN YOU SUDDENLY SPOUTED OFF ABOUT DRAWING *EUREKA SEVEN* STUFF ON THE *SOUL EATER LATE SHOW*. I MEAN, COME ON...BONES WAS THERE TRYING TO PROMOTE *SOUL EATER*.
....
YEAH, AND YOU ALSO CAUSED PLENTY OF TROUBLE FOR YOUR PUBLISHER KOJI TAGUCHI WHEN YOU MADE FUN OF THE WHOLE SQUARE ENIX MERGER BY ADDING THAT SILLY "LEGEND OF THE HOLY SWORD" BONUS CHAPTER, ALONG WITH TONS OF OTHER STUPID CRAP OVER THE YEARS.
TCH... WELL, I NEVER ASKED THOSE BASTARDS TO DO ME ANY FAVORS.
YOU. ARE. ONE. RUDE. MOTHER-FUCKER ...
HEY, SHITHEADS ...
...YOU GUYS HEARD THAT WORD "TSUNDERE" THAT'S GOING AROUND NOW?
WHAT, YOU MEAN WHERE SOMEONE SUDDENLY TURNS ON YOU AND ACTS ALL MEAN AND SARCASTIC ON THE OUTSIDE WHILE ACTUALLY THEY'RE TOTALLY IN LOVE WITH YOU ON THE INSIDE?
WHEN I FIRST HEARD THAT WORD, I HAD A KIND OF REVELATION...
I THINK MAYBE THAT'S WHAT I AM.
FINE, GO AHEAD AND BUY MY MANGA IF YOU WANT.
IT'S NOT LIKE YOUR STUPID SUPPORT MAKES ME HAPPY OR ANYTHING, OKAY.

SOUL EATER

ATSUSHI-YA BACKSTAGE SPECIAL COMMEMORATING THE SOUL EATER ANIME ADAPTATION!!

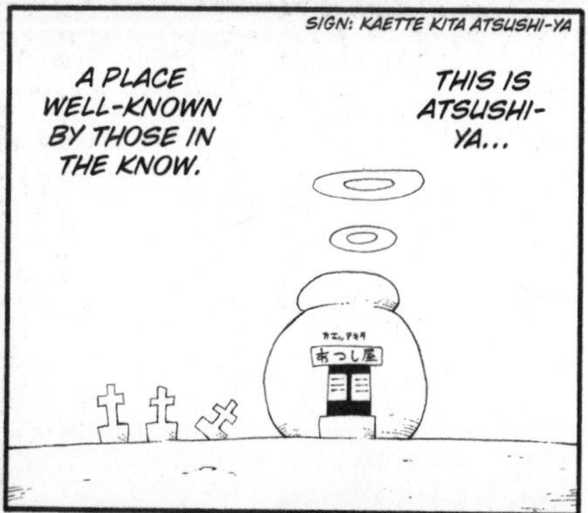
SIGN: KAETTE KITA ATSUSHI-YA
THIS IS ATSUSHI-YA...
A PLACE WELL-KNOWN BY THOSE IN THE KNOW.
あつし屋

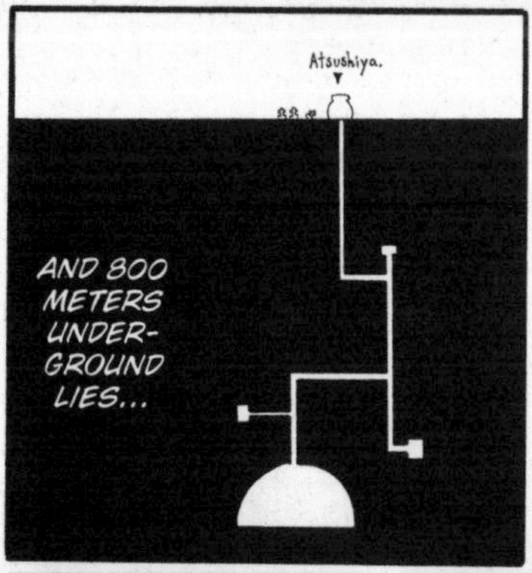
Atsushiya.
AND 800 METERS UNDER-GROUND LIES...

ATSUSHI-YA SIDE STORY

FRESH THE FIRST STAR HEAVY INDUSTRIES ☆

BY THE CATLABOR WELL-KNOWN BY THOSE IN THE KNOW...A.K.A.

TAKUJI KATO

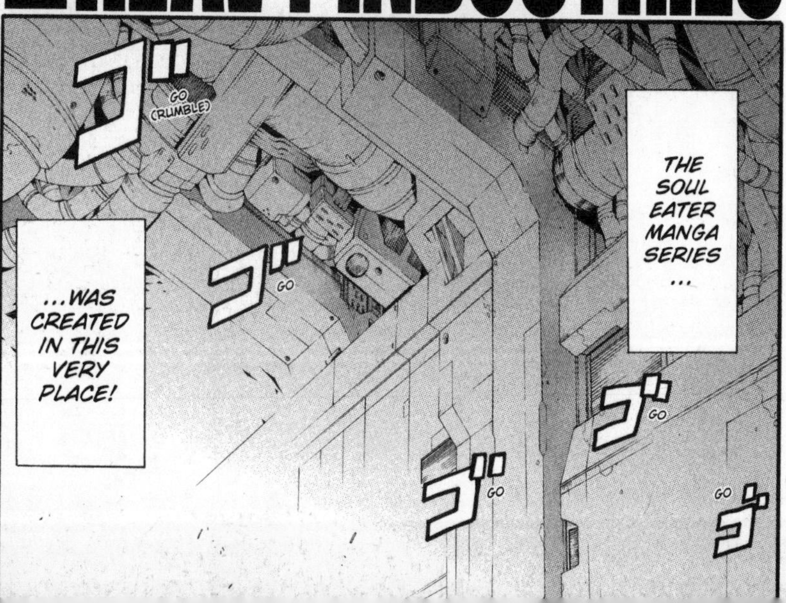
THE SOUL EATER MANGA SERIES ...
GO (RUMBLE)
GO
...WAS CREATED IN THIS VERY PLACE!
GO
GO
GO

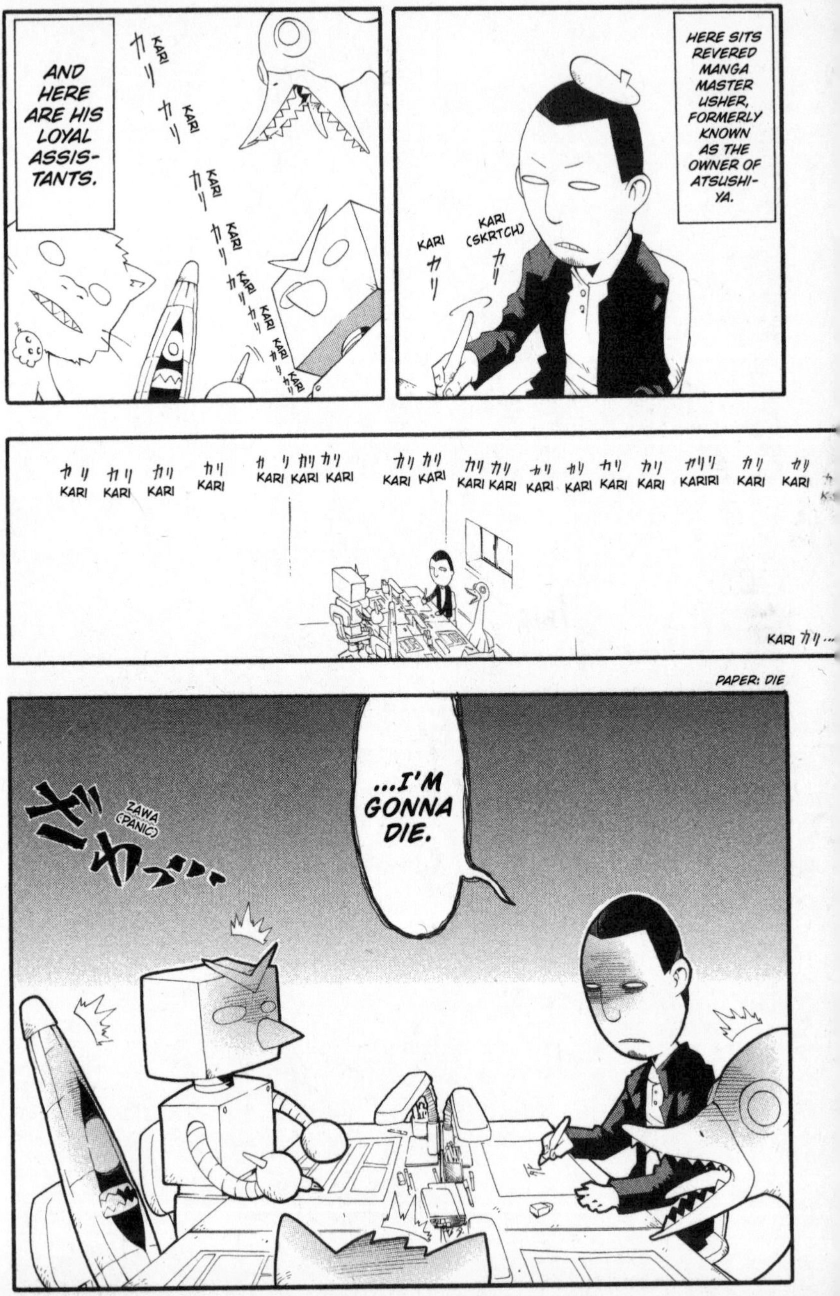
HERE SITS REVERED MANGA MASTER USHER, FORMERLY KNOWN AS THE OWNER OF ATSUSHI-YA.
KARI (SKRTCH) カリ
KARI カリ
AND HERE ARE HIS LOYAL ASSIS-TANTS.
カリ KARI カリ KARI カリ KARI カリ KARI カリカリ KARI KARI カリカリ KARI
カリ KARI カリ KARI カリ KARI カリ KARI カリ KARI カリ KARI カリ KARI カリ KARI カリ KARI カリ KARI カリ KARI カリ KARI カリ KARI カリ KARI カリ KARI カリリ KARIRI カリ KARI カリ KARI
KARI カリ…
PAPER: DIE
…I'M GONNA DIE.
ZAWA (PANIC)
ざわっ…

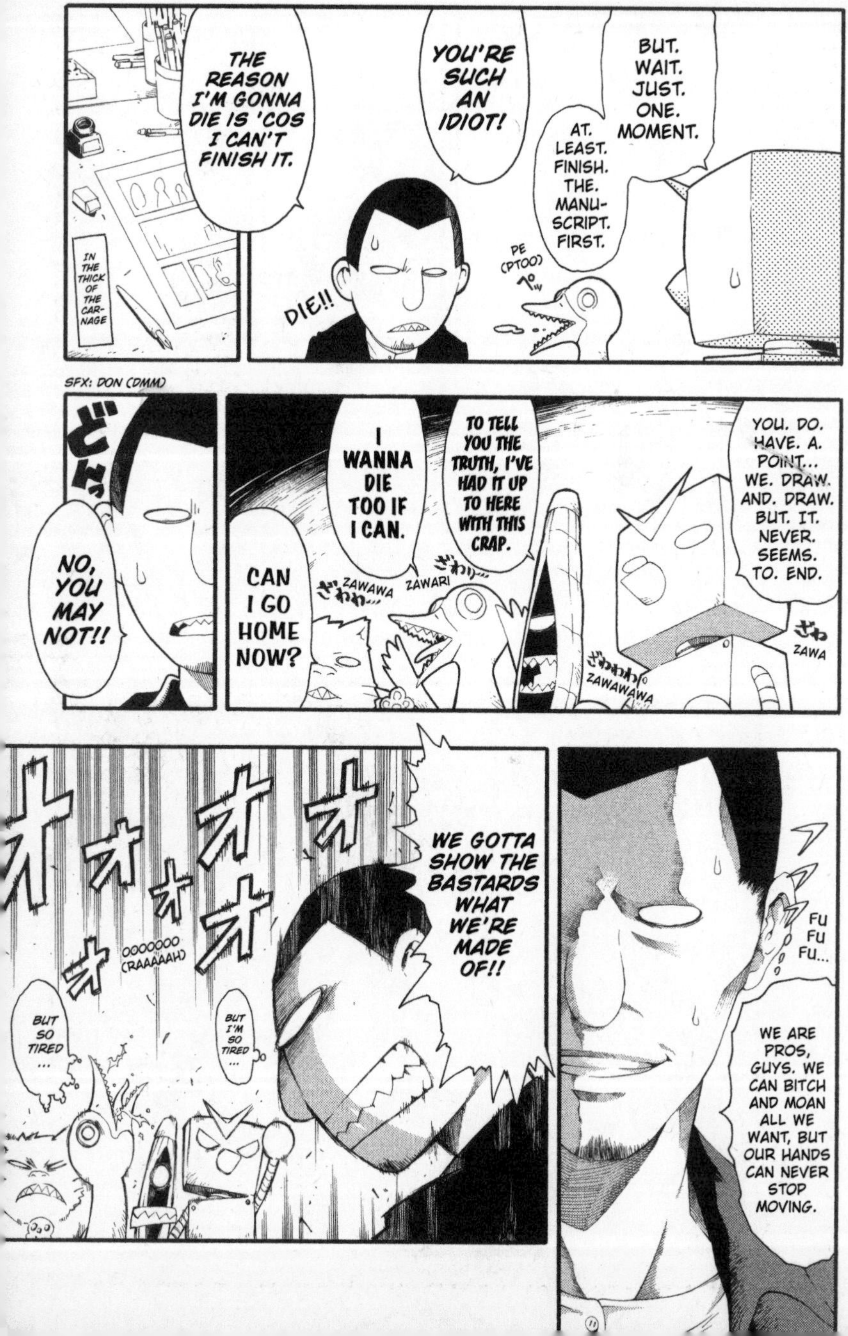
BUT. WAIT. JUST. ONE. MOMENT.
AT. LEAST. FINISH. THE. MANU-SCRIPT. FIRST.
YOU'RE SUCH AN IDIOT!
PE (PTOO)
DIE!!
THE REASON I'M GONNA DIE IS 'COS I CAN'T FINISH IT.
IN THE THICK OF THE CAR-NAGE
SFX: DON (DMM)
YOU. DO. HAVE. A. POINT... WE. DRAW. AND. DRAW. BUT. IT. NEVER. SEEMS. TO. END.
ZAWA
TO TELL YOU THE TRUTH, I'VE HAD IT UP TO HERE WITH THIS CRAP.
I WANNA DIE TOO IF I CAN.
ZAWAWAWA
ZAWARI
ZAWAWA
CAN I GO HOME NOW?
NO, YOU MAY NOT!!
FU FU FU...
WE ARE PROS, GUYS. WE CAN BITCH AND MOAN ALL WE WANT, BUT OUR HANDS CAN NEVER STOP MOVING.
WE GOTTA SHOW THE BASTARDS WHAT WE'RE MADE OF!!
OOOOOOO (RAAAAAH)
BUT I'M SO TIRED ...
BUT SO TIRED ...

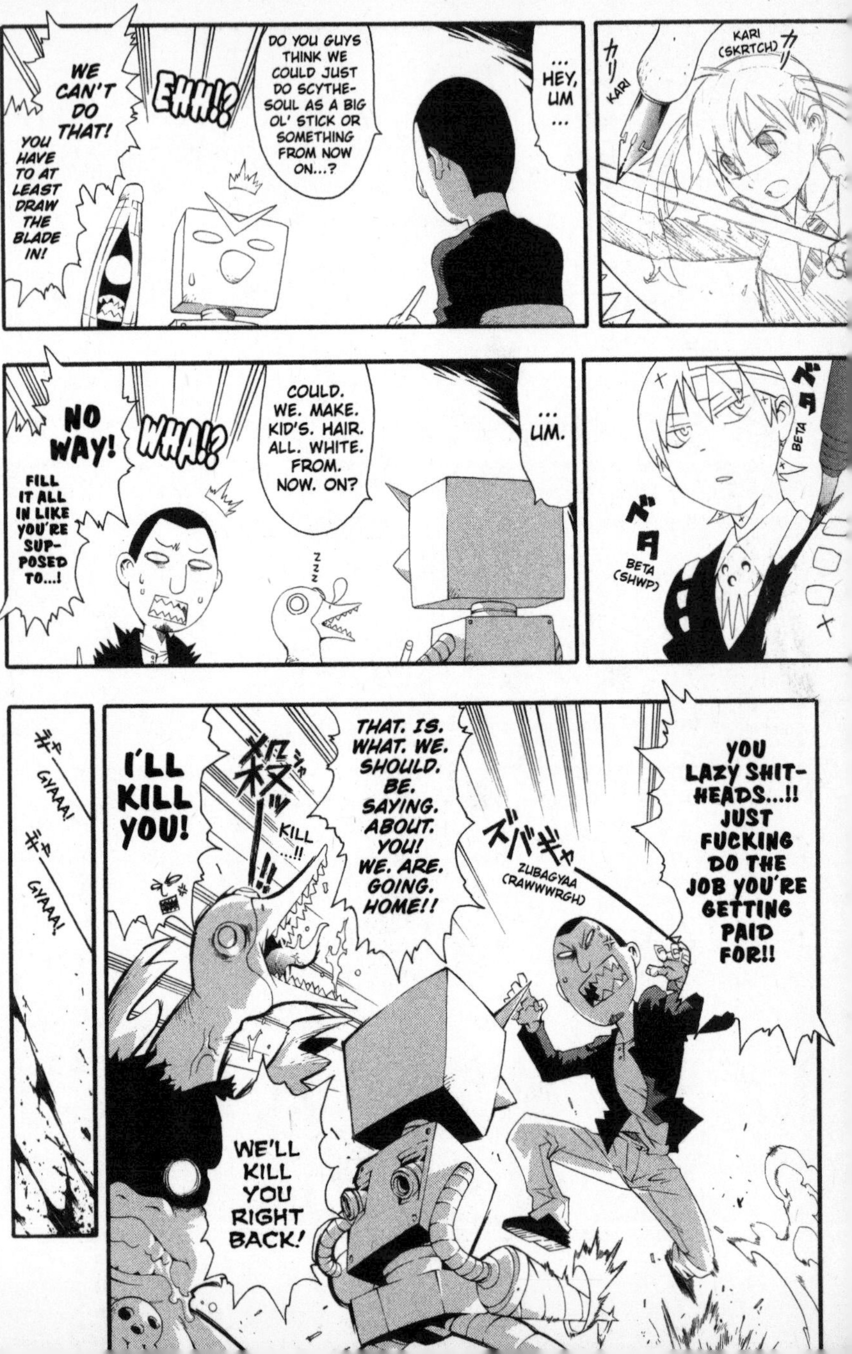

カリ
KARI (SKRTCH)
カリ
KARI
...HEY, UM ...
DO YOU GUYS THINK WE COULD JUST DO SCYTHE-SOUL AS A BIG OL' STICK OR SOMETHING FROM NOW ON...?
EHH!?
WE CAN'T DO THAT!
YOU HAVE TO AT LEAST DRAW THE BLADE IN!
ベタ
BETA
ベタ
BETA (SHWP)
... UM.
COULD. WE. MAKE. KID'S. HAIR. ALL. WHITE. FROM. NOW. ON?
WHA!?
NO WAY!
FILL IT ALL IN LIKE YOU'RE SUP-POSED TO...!
YOU LAZY SHIT-HEADS...!! JUST FUCKING DO THE JOB YOU'RE GETTING PAID FOR!!
ズバギャ
ZUBAGYAA (RAWWWRGH)
THAT. IS. WHAT. WE. SHOULD. BE. SAYING. ABOUT. YOU! WE. ARE. GOING. HOME!!
殺ッ!!
KILL ...!!
I'LL KILL YOU!
WE'LL KILL YOU RIGHT BACK!
ギャ
GYAAA!
ギャ
GYAAA!

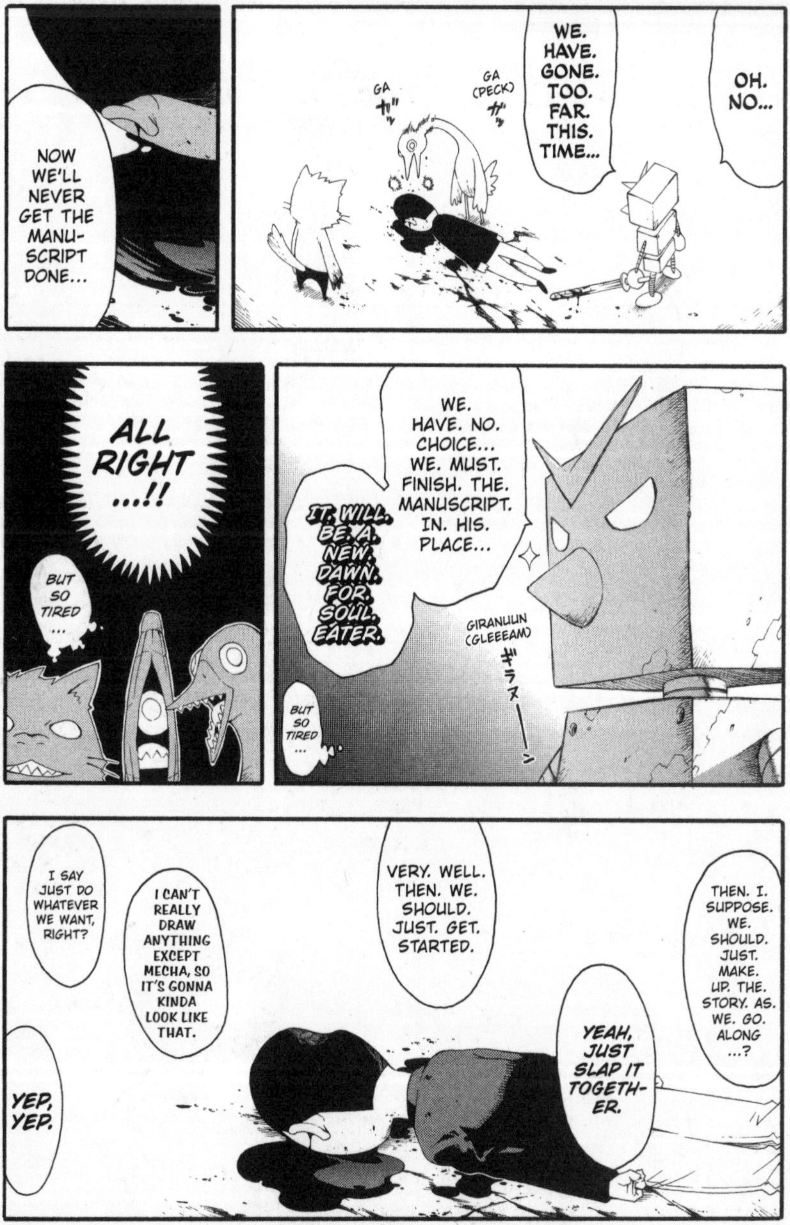
OH. NO...
WE. HAVE. GONE. TOO. FAR. THIS. TIME...
GA (PECK)
GA
NOW WE'LL NEVER GET THE MANU-SCRIPT DONE...
WE. HAVE. NO. CHOICE... WE. MUST. FINISH. THE. MANUSCRIPT. IN. HIS. PLACE...
IT. WILL. BE. A. NEW. DAWN. FOR. SOUL. EATER.
GIRANUUN (GLEEEAM)
ギラヌーン
BUT SO TIRED...
ALL RIGHT ...!!
BUT SO TIRED...
THEN. I. SUPPOSE. WE. SHOULD. JUST. MAKE. UP. THE. STORY. AS. WE. GO. ALONG ...?
VERY. WELL. THEN. WE. SHOULD. JUST. GET. STARTED.
YEAH, JUST SLAP IT TOGETH-ER.
I CAN'T REALLY DRAW ANYTHING EXCEPT MECHA, SO IT'S GONNA KINDA LOOK LIKE THAT.
I SAY JUST DO WHATEVER WE WANT, RIGHT?
YEP, YEP.

A NEW CHAPTER OF SOUL EATER OPENS...!

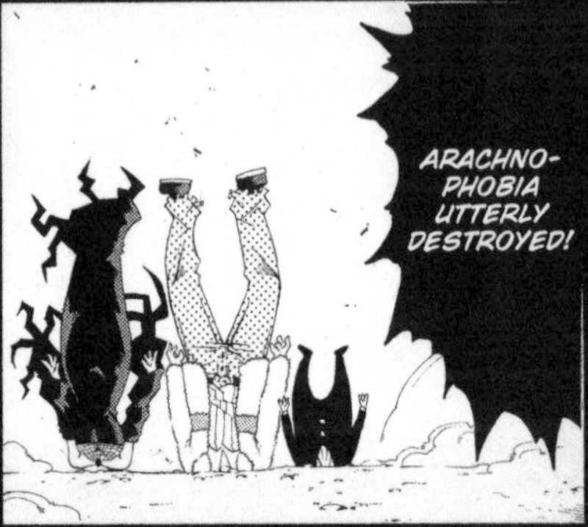
ARACHNO-PHOBIA UTTERLY DESTROYED!

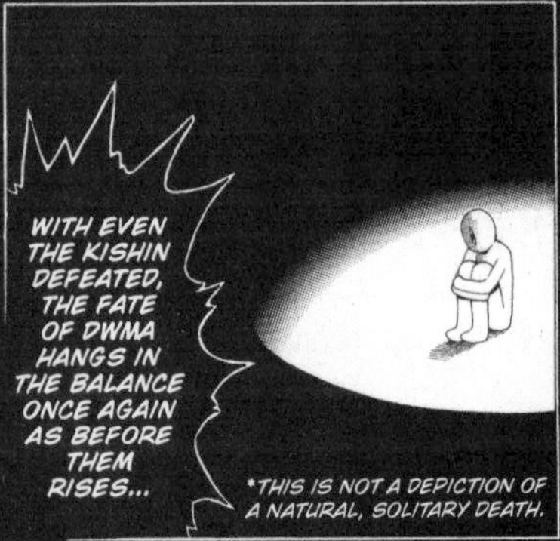
WITH EVEN THE KISHIN DEFEATED, THE FATE OF DWMA HANGS IN THE BALANCE ONCE AGAIN AS BEFORE THEM RISES...
*THIS IS NOT A DEPICTION OF A NATURAL, SOLITARY DEATH.

HERE IT COMES...
A NEW AND TRUE ENEMY...

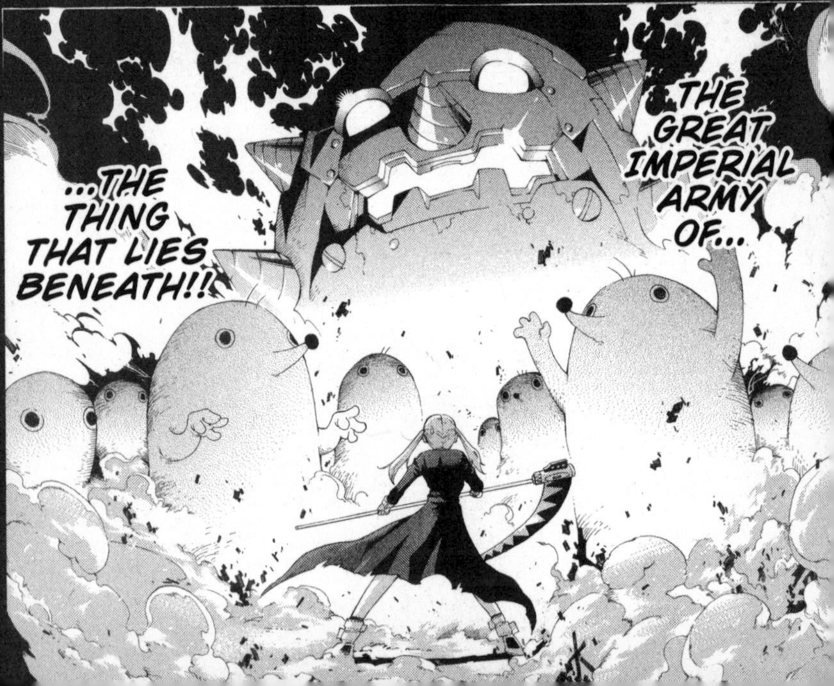
THE GREAT IMPERIAL ARMY OF...
...THE THING THAT LIES BENEATH!!

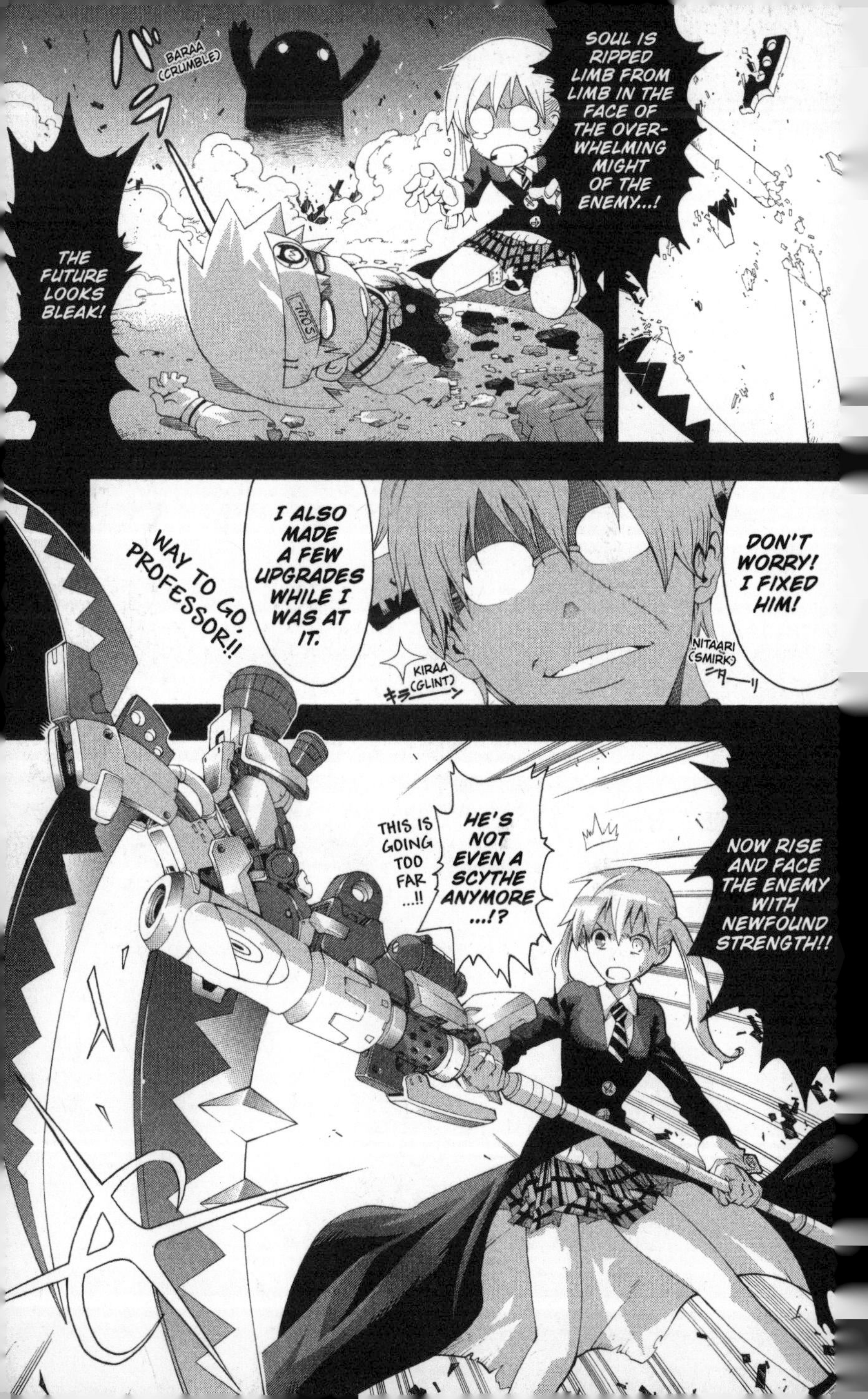
SOUL IS RIPPED LIMB FROM LIMB IN THE FACE OF THE OVER-WHELMING MIGHT OF THE ENEMY...!
BARAA (CRUMBLE)
THE FUTURE LOOKS BLEAK!
DON'T WORRY! I FIXED HIM!
NITAARI (SMIRK)
I ALSO MADE A FEW UPGRADES WHILE I WAS AT IT.
KIRAA (GLINT)
WAY TO GO, PROFESSOR!!
NOW RISE AND FACE THE ENEMY WITH NEWFOUND STRENGTH!!
HE'S NOT EVEN A SCYTHE ANYMORE...!?
THIS IS GOING TOO FAR...!!

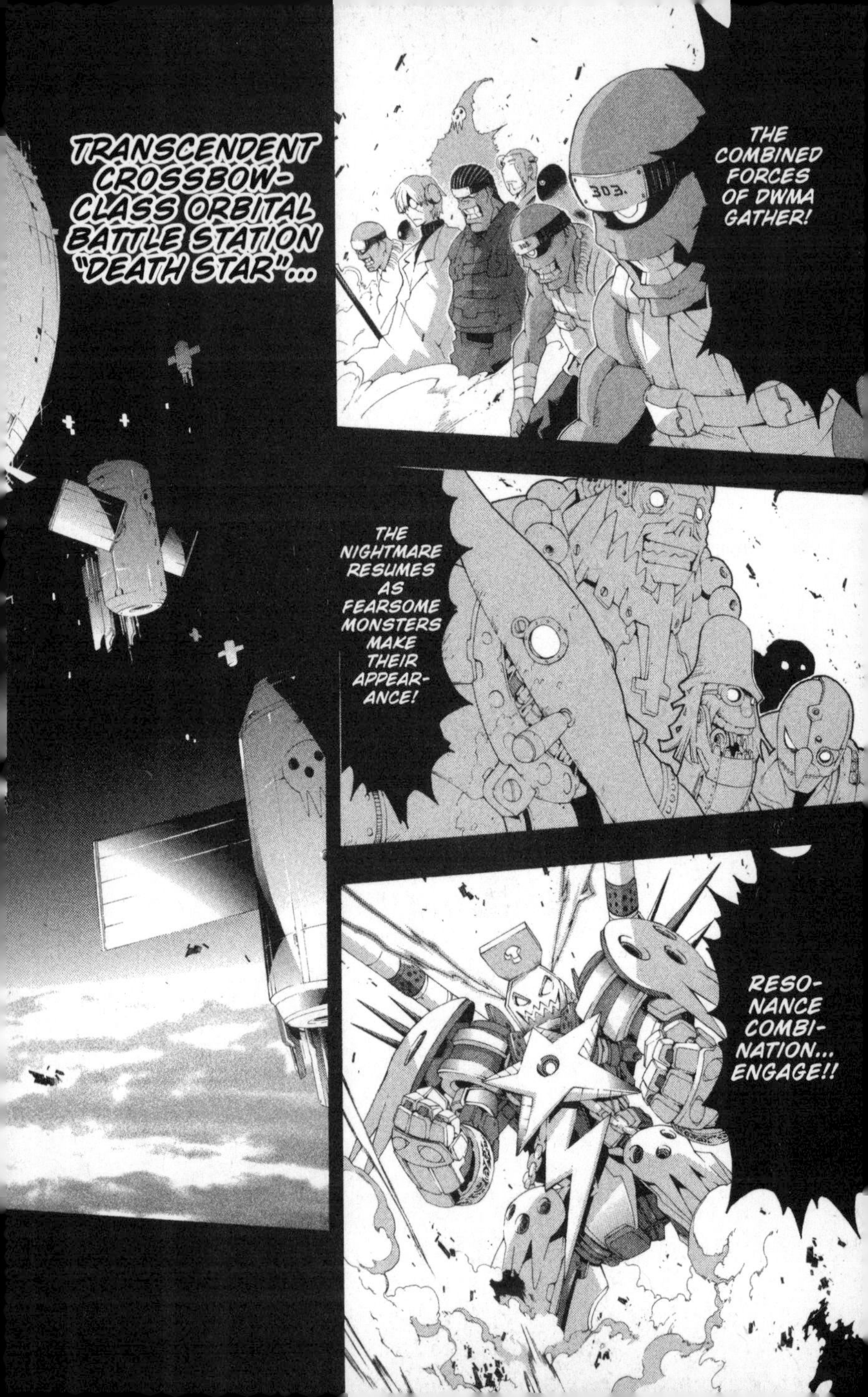
THE COMBINED FORCES OF DWMA GATHER!
303
THE NIGHTMARE RESUMES AS FEARSOME MONSTERS MAKE THEIR APPEARANCE!
RESONANCE COMBINATION... ENGAGE!!
TRANSCENDENT CROSSBOW-CLASS ORBITAL BATTLE STATION "DEATH STAR"...

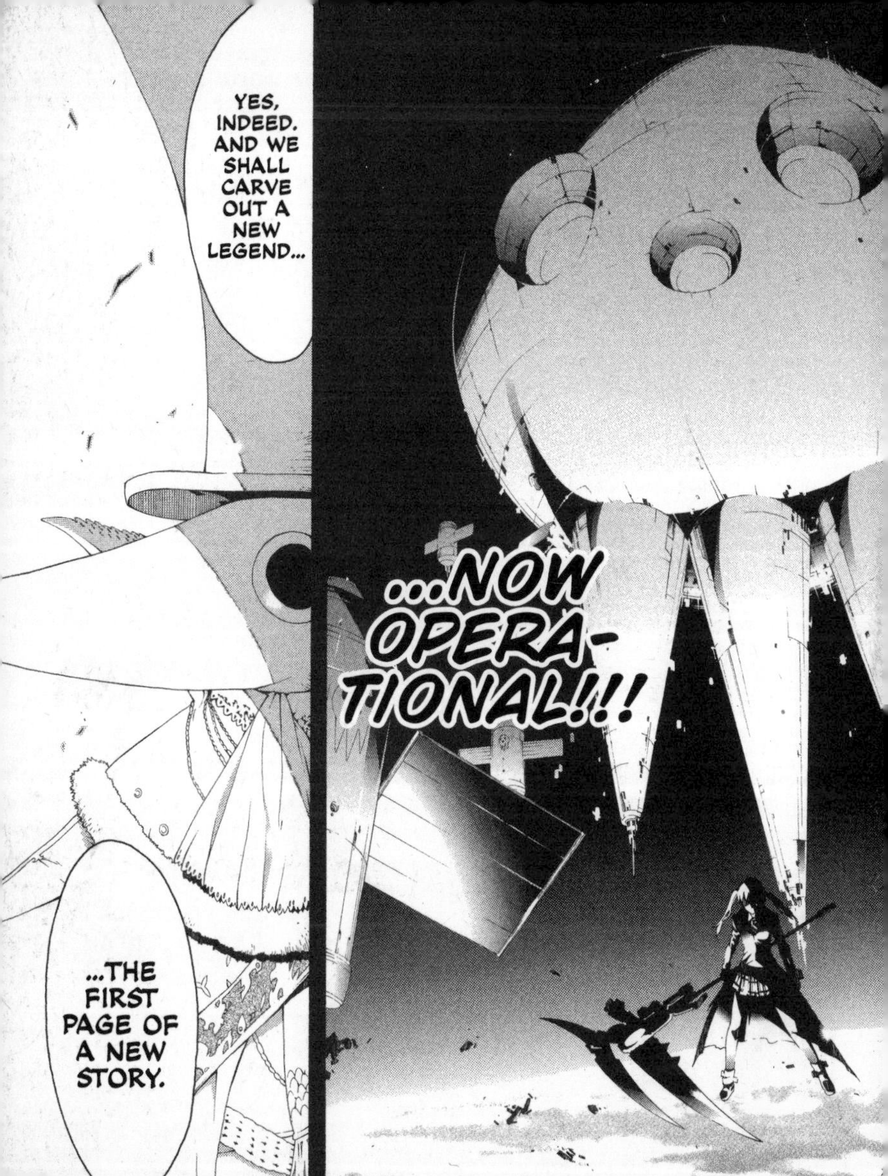
...NOW OPERA-TIONAL!!!
YES, INDEED. AND WE SHALL CARVE OUT A NEW LEGEND...
...THE FIRST PAGE OF A NEW STORY.

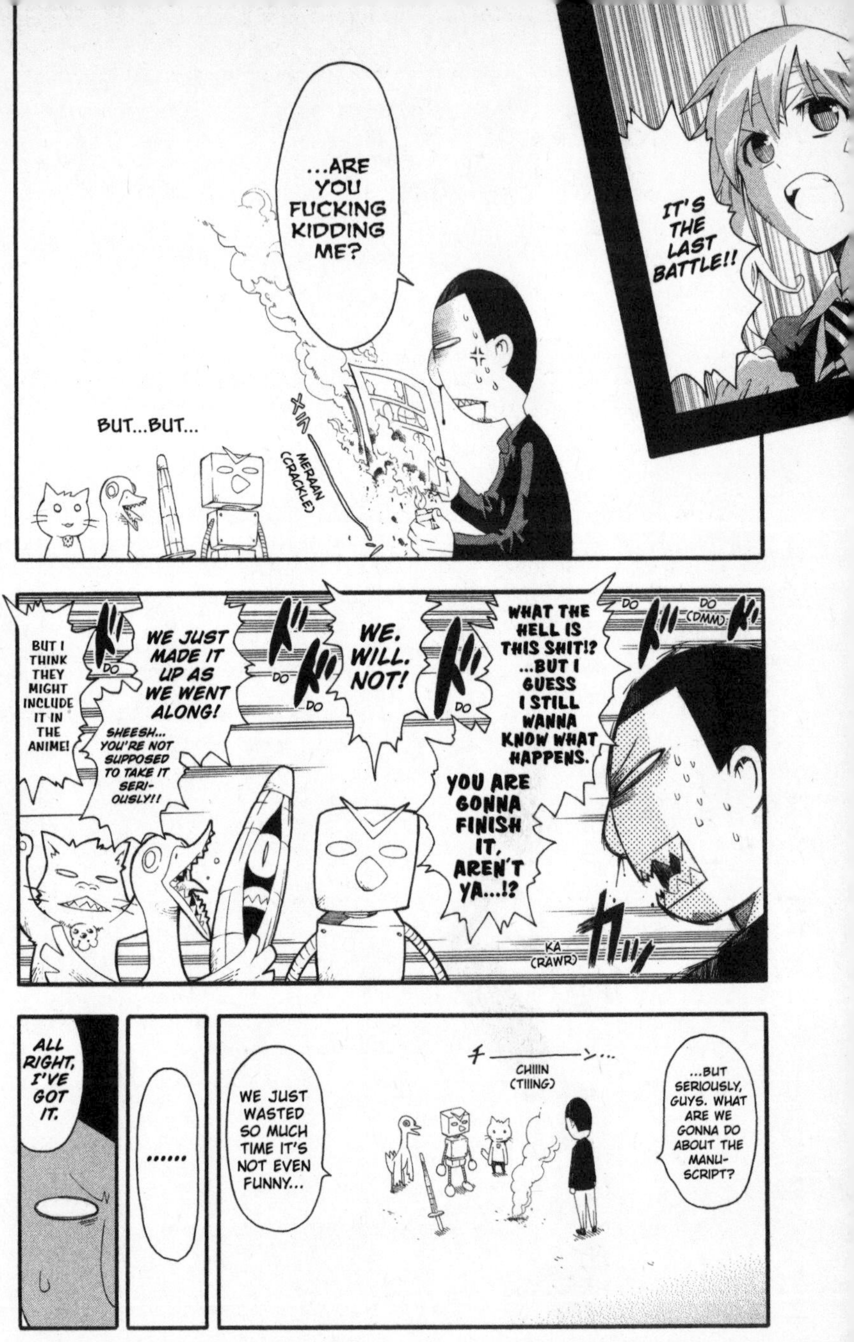
IT'S THE LAST BATTLE!!
...ARE YOU FUCKING KIDDING ME?
MERAAN (CRACKLE)
BUT...BUT...
DO DO (DMM)
WHAT THE HELL IS THIS SHIT!? ...BUT I GUESS I STILL WANNA KNOW WHAT HAPPENS.
YOU ARE GONNA FINISH IT, AREN'T YA...!?
KA (RAWR)
DO
WE. WILL. NOT!
DO
DO
WE JUST MADE IT UP AS WE WENT ALONG!
SHEESH... YOU'RE NOT SUPPOSED TO TAKE IT SERI-OUSLY!!
DO
BUT I THINK THEY MIGHT INCLUDE IT IN THE ANIME!
...BUT SERIOUSLY, GUYS. WHAT ARE WE GONNA DO ABOUT THE MANU-SCRIPT?
CHIIIN (TIIING)
WE JUST WASTED SO MUCH TIME IT'S NOT EVEN FUNNY...
......
ALL RIGHT, I'VE GOT IT.

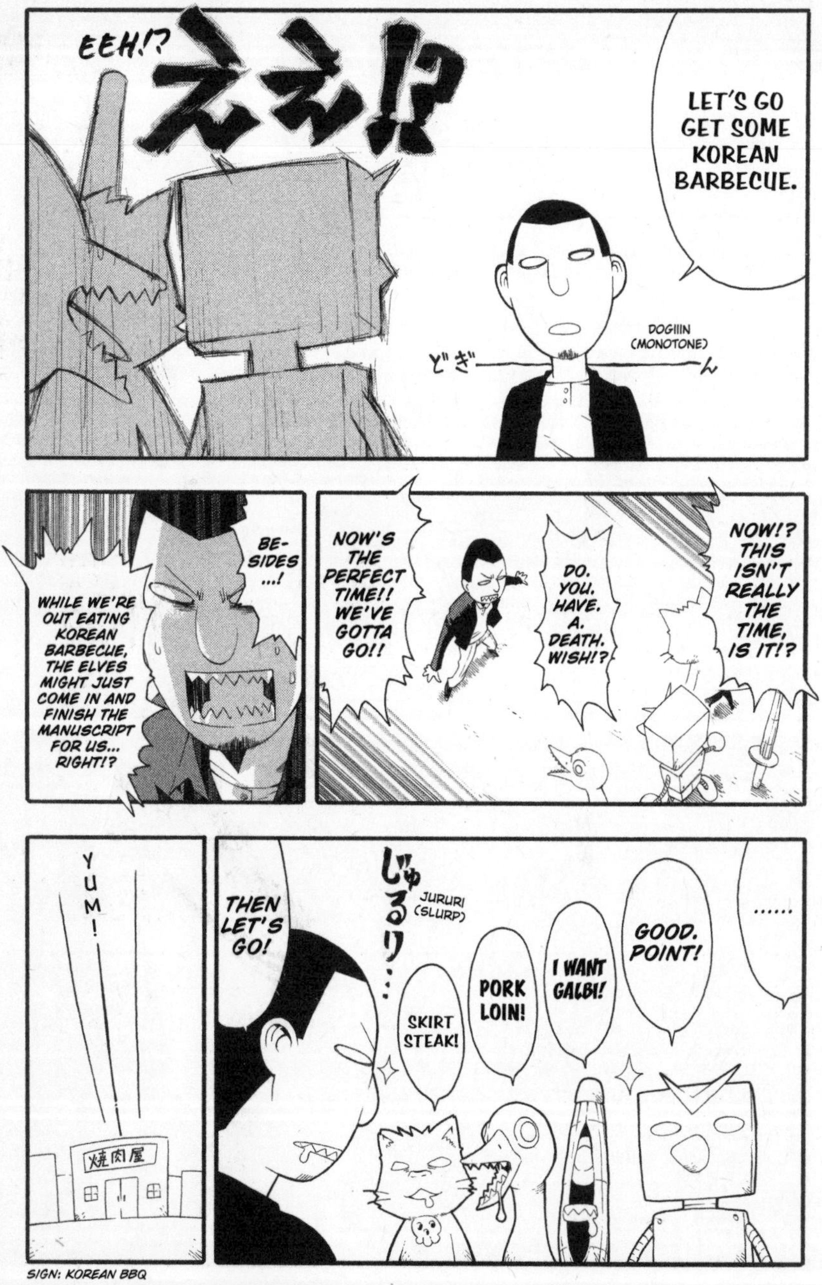
LET'S GO GET SOME KOREAN BARBECUE.
どぎーーーん
DOGIIN (MONOTONE)
ええ!?
EEH!?
NOW!? THIS ISN'T REALLY THE TIME, IS IT!?
DO. YOU. HAVE. A. DEATH. WISH!?
NOW'S THE PERFECT TIME!! WE'VE GOTTA GO!!
BE-SIDES ...!
WHILE WE'RE OUT EATING KOREAN BARBECUE, THE ELVES MIGHT JUST COME IN AND FINISH THE MANUSCRIPT FOR US... RIGHT!?
......
GOOD. POINT!
I WANT GALBI!
PORK LOIN!
SKIRT STEAK!
じゅるり…
JURURI (SLURP)
THEN LET'S GO!
YUM!
焼肉屋
SIGN: KOREAN BBQ

AFTERWARD...

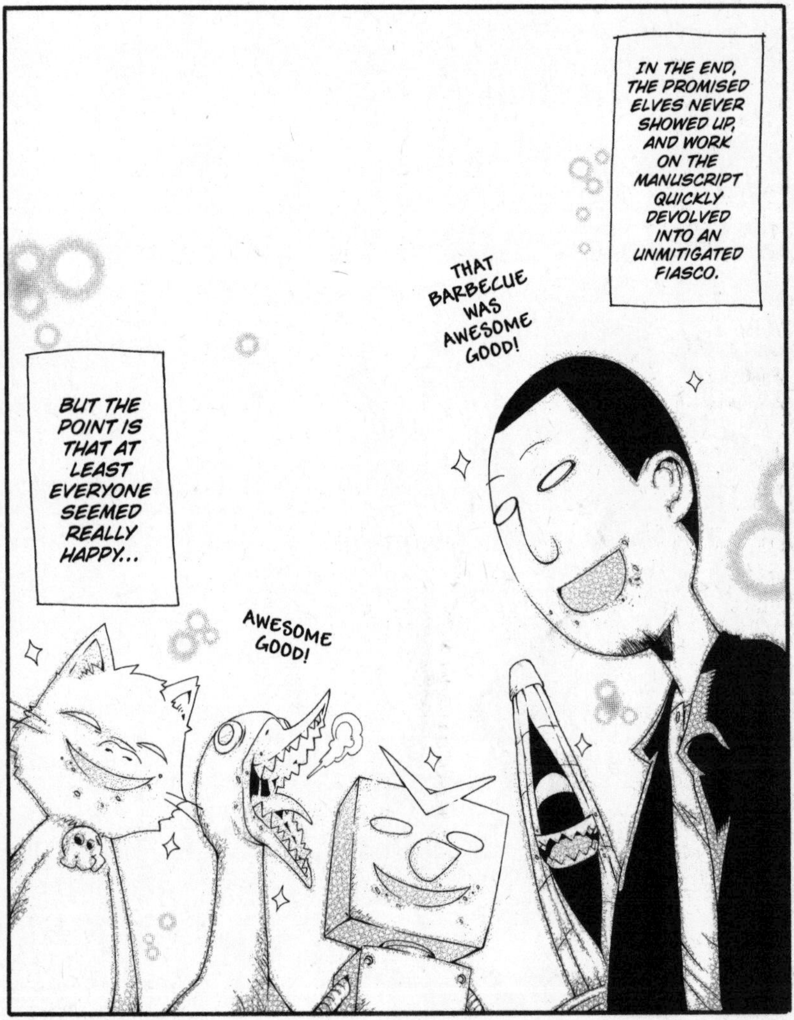
IN THE END, THE PROMISED ELVES NEVER SHOWED UP, AND WORK ON THE MANUSCRIPT QUICKLY DEVOLVED INTO AN UNMITIGATED FIASCO.
THAT BARBECUE WAS AWESOME GOOD!
BUT THE POINT IS THAT AT LEAST EVERYONE SEEMED REALLY HAPPY...
AWESOME GOOD!

NOTE: THIS STORY IS PROBABLY FICTIONAL.

SOUL EATER

Translation Notes

Common Honorifics

no honorific: Indicates familiarity or closeness; if used without permission or reason, addressing someone in this manner would constitute an insult.

-san: The Japanese equivalent of Mr./Mrs./Miss. If a situation calls for politeness, this is the fail-safe honorific.

-sama: Conveys great respect; may also indicate that the social status of the speaker is lower than that of the addressee.

-kun: Used most often when referring to boys, this indicates affection or familiarity. Occasionally used by older men among their peers, but it may also be used by anyone referring to a person of lower standing.

-chan: An affectionate honorific indicating familiarity used mostly in reference to girls; also used in reference to cute persons or animals of either gender.

-senpai: A suffix used to address upperclassmen or more experienced coworkers.

-sensei: A respectful term for teachers, artists, or high-level professionals.

Page 12
The various **signs and banners** seen in the first panel are mainly random (clichéd) references to Japanese names and products associated with samurai or yakuza. For example, one of the signs is *tabi* (traditional Japanese split-toe socks) and another is *chozetsu tabi* (transcendental journey), which is amusing because the homophone between *tabi* (socks) and *tabi* (journey) makes the latter sign sound a little like "transcendental socks" instead.

Page 13
The name **Sanjuro** is a reference to Toshiro Mifune (also the source of Mifune's name)and to the titular character he played Akira Kurosawa's film, *Sanjuro*. The film is a sequel to the better-known *Yojimbo*, with Mifune reprising the role of a crafty and irreverent *ronin* who plays all sides against each other.

Page 21
Here, Black☆Star's name is written in characters that read *ankoku no sekai* (world of darkness) and glossed with kana indicating that it should be pronounced "Black Star" when read aloud. The strangeness (for English speakers) of the posed equivalence between "star" and "world" is explained by the fact that the Japanese word for "star" (*hoshi*) actually refers not only to visible stars but also to planets and comets—generally all visible (and relatively fixed) lights in the sky except for the sun and moon.

Page 40
The name of the **Chain of Blackness** attack (a hybrid of Black☆Star's "Shadow☆Star" attack with Tsubaki's "Chain Scythe" form) is called *rengoku* (chained blackness) in Japanese, which is a homophone with another word meaning "hell of forging" or "Purgatory" (in the Catholic sense). It suggests that Black☆Star has emerged from his psychological crucible and can now control and direct his soul.

Page 102
The **tanuki** (often called "raccoon dogs" in English) is a rare species of canid indigenous only to Japan. It resembles a raccoon in appearance, but is in fact much more closely related to dogs and foxes than raccoons. Being a tanuki witch means that Kim has healing powers as well as the ability of transformation (shown in her Change "Pixie" move), as these are the traditional magic traits of the tanuki in Japan. It also explains why she's so fond of money, as the tanuki is frequently associated with luck in money matters.

Page 108
The name of the **Volantern** attack is a portmanteau of "vol" ("flight" in Latin) and "lantern."

Page 175
The **bonus chapter** spoken of here refers to the "Legend of the Holy Sword" chapter in Volume 9. The title of the bonus chapter is a direct comedic jab at the Square Enix-produced Mana game series, titled *Seiken Densetsu* (Legend of the Holy Sword) in Japan.

This word *tsundere* is relatively recent game/anime/manga slang coinage in Japan, born as a combination of the phrases *tsuntsun* (bitingly critical) and *deredere* (gushingly adoring). It describes a character who runs hot and cold with his or her romantic interest, alternating between giving off the impression of annoyance (or even outright hatred) and sending out signals of being sexually attracted (or even utterly lovestruck).

SOUL EATER ⑬

Atsushi Ohkubo

Translation: Jack Wiedrick

Lettering: Alexis Eckerman

SOUL EATER Vol. 13 ©2008 Atsushi Ohkubo/SQUARE ENIX CO., LTD. First published in Japan in 2008 by SQUARE ENIX CO., LTD. English translation rights arranged with SQUARE ENIX CO., LTD. and Yen Press, LLC through Tuttle-Mori Agency, Inc.

English translation ©2013 by SQUARE ENIX CO., LTD.

Yen Press
1290 Avenue of the Americas
New York, NY 10104

Visit us at yenpress.com
facebook.com/yenpress
twitter.com/yenpress
yenpress.tumblr.com
instagram.com/yenpress

First Yen Press Edition: June 2010

Yen Press is an imprint of Yen Press, LLC.
The Yen Press name and logo are trademarks of Yen Press, LLC.

ISBN: 978-0-316-23057-5

10 9 8 7 6

BVG

Printed in the United States of America